DR. ARTHUR SPOHN

*To Kathryn — a dear,
precious friend —
With love,
Fran*

Jane Clements Monday

Frances B. Vick

Charles W. Monday, Jr., M.D.

Number Thirty-two
Gulf Coast Books, sponsored by Texas A&M–Corpus Christi

John W. Tunnell Jr., General Editor

DR. ARTHUR SPOHN

Surgeon, Inventor, and Texas Medical Pioneer

Jane Clements Monday & Frances Brannen Vick
with Charles W. Monday Jr., MD

Introduction by Kenneth L. Mattox, MD

TEXAS A&M UNIVERSITY PRESS
COLLEGE STATION

This paper meets the requirements of ANSI/NISO Z39.48–1992
(Permanence of Paper).
Binding materials have been chosen for durability.
Manufactured in the United States of America

Library of Congress Cataloging-in-Publication Data

Names: Monday, Jane Clements, 1941- author. | Vick, Frances Brannen, 1935-
    author. | Monday, Charles Woodrow, Jr., author.
Title: Dr. Arthur Spohn: surgeon, inventor, and Texas medical pioneer / Jane
    Clements Monday and Frances Brannen Vick; with Charles Woodrow Monday Jr.;
    introduction by Kenneth L. Mattox.
Other titles: Gulf Coast books; no. 23.
Description: First edition. | College Station: Texas A&M University Press,
    [2018] | Series: Gulf Coast books; no. 23 | Includes bibliographical
    references and index.
Identifiers: LCCN 2018017408 | ISBN 9781623496906 (cloth: alk. paper)
Subjects: LCSH: Spohn, Arthur Ed. | Surgeons—Texas—Corpus
    Christ—Biography. | Spohn Sanitarium (Corpus Christi, Tex.)—History. |
    Spohn family.
Classification: LCC R154.S66 M66 2018 | DDC 617.092 [B] —dc23 LC record
available at https://lccn.loc.gov/2018017408

A list of titles in this series is available at the end of the book.

No night was too dark, no way was too long, no poor so lowly that when a call for help came Doctor Spohn did not answer, "I come."

—from an anonymous inscription in a family scrapbook

Contents

Preface

Istarted my quest to tell stories of people who have been forgotten by history in 1993, when I published with my coauthor Patricia Smith Prather the life story of Joshua Houston, manservant to Sam Houston. I had found his name in Marquis James's book *The Raven*, in a single line stating that Joshua drove Margaret and Sam Houston to Pres. Andrew Jackson's funeral. I began to wonder who Joshua was, where he was from, and how he became so important to Margaret and Sam. I had met Frances Vick, director of the University of North Texas Press, when we both were part of the Leadership Women Texas class of 1990, and our friendship began there. It was Fran who published the biography of Joshua: *From Slave to Statesman: The Legacy of Joshua Houston, Servant to Sam Houston.*

My next three books were written with Betty Colley. Each of them started in a similar way. I had read about the vaqueros on the King and Kenedy ranches in South Texas and wondered who they were and where they came from. Betty and I knew that there had been many stories written about the ranch owners, but there was no book devoted to these talented men and women who were the backbone of the ranches. We took years to record their oral histories, and it gave us great pleasure to see these ranch workers' eyes light up simply because someone wanted to know about them and their experiences. We first published *Voices of the Wild Horse Desert* in 1997, then a children's book, *Tales of the Wild Horse Desert*, in 2001, and then *The Master Showmen of King Ranch* in 2009, all with the University of Texas Press.

Frances Vick and I share the passion for finding stories of important people that have been overlooked in history. Fran writes that her interest in these stories began in the following way: "My father, C. A. Brannen, moved in with my family his last two years. He was a wonderful historian and folklorist, and my interest in those fields was reignited in our time together. Both my parents taught history and were full of family folklore. The folklore interest led me to publishing Texas Folklore Society projects with F. E. Abernethy, the secretary/editor of the society. He was my mentor in publishing, opening that world to me, particularly the stories that remained to be told. Through Jim Lee, folklorist, writer, and chair of the English department at the University of North Texas and a great friend and supporter, I became director of the University of North Texas Press. After my retirement, Jane introduced me to South Texas and I promptly fell in love. Born an East Texan, I developed a passion for exploring the people in this fascinating part of Texas. I remain committed to finding those untold stories of Texas, particularly of Texas women. Jane got me into writing, and in my retirement, in addition to writing the books with Jane, I collected and edited *Literary Dallas* for TCU Press and *Tales of Texas Cooking*, a Texas Folklore Society book published by UNT Press. I have written chapters for anthologies, including *Collective Heart: Texans in World War II*, from Eakin Press, *Texas Women Writers* and *Texas Women on the Cattle Trails*, both published by Texas A&M University Press, *Notes from Texas: On Writing in the Lone Star State*, published by TCU Press, and *Her Texas*, published by Wings Press. Without Jane's urgings, it is doubtful I would have written anything other than folklore papers delivered at the Texas Folklore Society meetings. She, too, has been a great friend and supporter."

Fran and I first wrote about Petra Vela Kenedy and the Kenedy ranching dynasty in *Petra's Legacy: The South Texas Ranching Empire of Petra Vela and Mifflin Kenedy*, published in 2007, and it won the Coral Horton Tullis Memorial Prize from the Texas State Historical Association for Best Book on Texas History. Then we edited and annotated the love letters of Robert Justice Kleberg to Alice Gertrudis King in *Letters to Alice: Birth of the Kleberg-King Ranch Dynasty*, published by Texas A&M University Press in 2012. That project was born when Thomas H. Kreneck, head of Special Collections and Archives at Bell Library, Texas A&M University–Corpus Christi, called us about editing a cache of love letters from Robert Kleberg to Alice King. We immediately said yes. It was a great follow-up to *Petra's Legacy*.

Arthur Spohn can be found in both of those books, as he was important to both the Kenedy and King families, who were a prominent part of the history of South Texas during the late 1800s and early 1900s (and still are today). Spohn played a significant role in their lives, as both their physician and friend. In addition, he married Sarah Josephine Kenedy, the only daughter of Petra and Mifflin Kenedy. Throughout the thirty-seven years the two were married, Spohn took care of Sarah and was intricately involved with her family's tragedies and triumphs.

During our trips to conduct research in Corpus Christi, Kingsville, Sarita, Raymondville, and the surrounding areas, Fran and I saw Arthur Spohn's name everywhere. According to the company website, the CHRISTUS Spohn Health System includes six hospital campuses, a network of nationally accredited cancer centers (six locations), family health clinics (six locations), and the region's leading trauma center. This system serves more than a half million patients throughout South Texas. One hundred twelve years after Dr. Spohn first established his hospital in Corpus Christi with help from many of his family and friends, his dream of providing quality health care to the region is alive and well.

We wanted to learn more about this man and found that remarkably little was known about him. There were a few articles written about his practice in Corpus Christi. Some of them were about his still holding the Guinness World Record for the largest tumor (328 pounds) ever removed from a patient who survived. He was also famous for saving ranching matriarch Henrietta King's half-brother, William Chamberlain, by taking him on a perilous trip to Paris, France, in 1888 to be treated for rabies at Dr. Louis Pasteur's institute. Beyond those few articles we could find little written about him. There were many unanswered questions, such as where he was born, where he grew up, where he was educated, why he came to Texas, and what accomplishments marked his forty-five years of medical practice. So our journey began. My husband, Dr. Charles W. Monday Jr., who is a board-certified surgeon, wanted to come along on the journey and serve as our medical consultant.

We did find one article that mentioned the Spohn family farm in Canada. Located in the community of Ancaster, Ontario (now part of Hamilton, Ontario), the farm was described as having the largest cash value in that township. With our curiosity piqued, we began our journey quite literally by traveling to Canada in 2010. Charles and I were totally unprepared for what we learned about Dr. Arthur Spohn's family. The Spohns were a founding family of Canada West, or what is now the province of Ontario. Dr. Spohn's mother, Elizabeth Bowman Spohn, had written words that were chosen to go on the United Empire Loyalist monument celebrating the British loyalists who settled the Canadian wilderness north of the US border. The Bowman family suffered incredible hardships and cruelty during the American Revolution because of their loyalty to the king of England. Still, the family became highly successful and respected citizens of Canada who above all cherished the importance of education. Dr. Spohn grew up in a household dedicated to discipline, education, and devotion to God. While visiting his hometown of Ancaster, we met Christopher Redford, the archivist at the Fieldcote Memorial Park and Museum. He shared some of the Spohn family history and took us to see Dr. Spohn's birthplace and to meet Keith and Mary Edwards, who gave us a tour of the home. We then met Raymond Wilson, whose family has long farmed the land that belonged to Arthur's brother, Philip Spohn. Raymond still maintains a barn that Philip built in the 1800s. Raymond showed us the famous "sliding church" (see chapter 1)— officially the Bowman Church, named for Arthur's mother's family. He gave us a tour of the church and graveyard, where many of Arthur's family are buried. We left Ancaster with a strong sense of the religious convictions of the family and their strong dedication to duty.

We were told that one member of this outstanding family had a medical practice in Waterloo, Ontario, so we took a chance and called Dr. James Douglas Spohn in Waterloo. His son Peter answered the phone and told us his father had recently died, but he invited us to come for a visit, which we did. While we were there he showed us Dr. Pasteur's personal card on which he had written a note giving Arthur admittance to the Pasteur Institute during his Paris trip. Peter also put us in touch with Beth Dubeau, his cousin and a dedicated Spohn family historian. Beth has a bachelor's degree in history and political science from the University of Waterloo, taught special education, and has worked in guidance and counseling. She has served in many volunteer positions in her hometown of Penetanguishene, Ontario, and has done research in Texas. She is the great-granddaughter of Philip Howard Spohn, Arthur's brother, and the granddaughter of Dr. Philip Douglas Spohn who practiced medicine in Corpus Christi, Texas. She provided pictures and a wealth of family history. She has been a great help in our efforts to research the family.

We later had the good fortune to make contact with another family historian, Barbara Chipman. She earned a bachelor's degree with honors from Glendon College, now York University. Later she was an executive assistant to an industrial psychologist. She studied art in Siena and Amalfi, Italy, and in San Miguel de Allende, Mexico. Her family is a good example of how intertwined Canadian and US history have been. Her husband was a descendant of John Howland and Elizabeth Tilley, who arrived in North America on the *Mayflower* in 1620. She is the great-granddaughter of Arthur Spohn's older brother, Wesley Case, making Arthur Spohn her great-granduncle. Barbara has been an amazing asset to us in telling Dr. Spohn's story. Over the last seven years she has sent hundreds of emails containing the results of her research on family members and events. She is a treasure of information, a relentless researcher, and an excellent historian.

We then traveled to Toronto and met with John Marshall, archivist for the York Pioneer and Historical Society, incorporated in 1869 to "preserve the past for the future." He explained to us that Arthur's brother-in-law was the son of Alexander Hamilton, one of the founding members of the historical society and also one of the early leaders in the establishment of the city of York, now Toronto. We were fortunate to meet these hardworking historians, and they have continued to assist us through our years of research. We also had the good fortune to have the help of Harry Spohn and Paul Harris, who are other Spohn family members. All of these individuals have been cheering us on and are eagerly waiting for Dr. Spohn's story to be told.

Charles and I left Canada with a great appreciation for the Spohn family members and their importance in Canadian history. Arthur's mother stated it well when she wrote the words that were later inscribed on the United Empire Loyalist monument: "Forsaking every possession excepting their honour, [they] set their faces toward the wilderness of British North America to begin, amid untold hardships, life anew under the flag they revered. They drew lots for their lands and with their axes cleared the forest and with their hoes planted the seed of Canada's future greatness." This family instilled its values into Arthur and his siblings and laid the foundation for the exceptional man and surgeon he would become.

We need to add a detail here about our terminology and the compilation of our research. We have used "Spohn" to designate Dr. Arthur Edward Spohn throughout the book except when the context was personal, like with his family, and then we used "Arthur." There are also several other Spohns in the book, and we use their given names, for example, Henry Spohn or Henry.

Acknowledgments

I along with Fran and Charles, want to thank all the people who have helped us along the way, and they are many. We want to acknowledge you because we know that you are truly keepers of the vaults of history , and work hard every day to see to it that our precious written records are preserved so that these untold stories can be told. It is humbling when you find records that are accessible and that you had no idea even existed. Special thanks go to Mary Lee Berner Harris at the Old Ursuline Convent Museum archives in New Orleans, Louisiana, for providing excellent pictures and information about Sarah Kenedy Spohn's exceptional education.

We found very helpful university archivists in Canada, Michigan, New York, and Texas. At McGill University in Montreal they were able to produce an admittance card in Spohn's handwriting written 150 years ago. They also had records of courses he took and awards he won. Thank you to the archivists at McGill University, University of Toronto, City of Toronto, Simcoe County Archives (Ontario), the University of Michigan, and New York University. They helped us piece together the excellent educational opportunities Spohn had at many of these institutions.

One of the biggest challenges we faced was to find any medical articles Spohn had published. He was always determined to stay up to date with the latest medical achievements and to share his knowledge with fellow physicians. We started from zero and had excellent help along our journey from many individuals who went the extra mile to help us. We need to start with Betsy Tyson at the Texas Medical Association Knowledge Center in Austin. She helped us research his articles in their journals and, with the help of Barbara Nolles Tims, to find articles he published in other journals. Our good friend Sammy Phelps at the Newton Gresham Library at Sam Houston State University was an excellent sleuth and contributed greatly to our efforts. Denise Tilson at the Huntsville Public Library put us in touch with David McLellan and Bill Maina at the University of Texas Southwestern Medical Center Library and Archives, and they helped identify a number of Dr. Spohn's printed articles. Some of these articles are included in the first appendix, and we hope you take the opportunity to read them. There is a great deal to learn from Dr. Spohn's own words as he describes many of his breakthrough procedures and practices.

We have been fortunate to have excellent support from many historians across the state of Texas. They have answered our calls, allowed us to interview them, and shared their knowledge. We appreciate our dear friend, the late Fr. Francis Kelly Nemeck, OMI, and the information he provided through the years on the Kenedy family. Rev. Michael A. Howell has been a constant support and provided his research, as well as that of Geraldine McGloin, documenting much of Corpus Christi's early history. Dr. Jerry Thompson, Dr. Paul Carlson, Dr. Tom Kreneck, and Dr. George Diaz shared their expertise on South Texas history. Mary Margaret McAllen shared her knowledge of the family, and Cecilia Venable was remarkable in her support. Murphy Givens, who is Corpus Christi's premier historian, has been most helpful, and our very good friends Homero and Leticia Vera have lent valuable insight into South Texas history.

It is hard for us to express adequately our appreciation for the people who care so much about Corpus history and work every day to preserve it. They opened their archives to us and worked endlessly to support our efforts. As Murphy Givens said to us when we told him about the book, "It is about time." Thanks to Richard Leshin and Karen Bonner, who aided our research at CHRISTUS Spohn Health System, and especially to Michele Mora-Trevino, who helped with pictures and provided information on CHRISTUS Spohn and CHRISTUS Health. Jillian Becquet at the Corpus Christi Museum of Science and History graciously helped to arrange a special photography opportunity with Michael Carlisle, an excellent professional who photographed several of Dr. Arthur Spohn's artifacts from the museum collection. Allison Ehrlich at the *Corpus Christi Caller-Times* and Veronica Martinez, Norma Gonzales, and Pat Garcia from the La Retama Central Library shared their photographs and newspaper articles. The Texas A&M–Corpus Christi Special Collections and Archives at the Mary and Jeff Bell Library shared their material, and in Raymondville, Cruz M. Tijerina and the Willacy County Historical Museum graciously shared excellent family photographs.

It was such a pleasure to do research in the South Texas Archives at the James C. Jernigan Library at Texas A&M University–Kingsville. Lori K. Atkins and her staff were excellent to work with, and it was exciting to see material from the Kenedy Family Collections that has been inaccessible for years now be opened to researchers. We also are glad for the help from the Brownsville Historical Association, the Webb County Heritage Foundation, and the Taft Blackland Museum. Our heartfelt thanks to the Corpus Christi "dynamic duo" Anita Eisenhauer and Andi Estes. Anita is an integral part of the Nueces County Historical Society efforts to preserve their heritage. She is a never-stopping force, from arranging meetings to researching markers and conducting research. Andi is also active in preserving the area history, but she also reached out to me and opened doors, arranged appointments, and acted as my travel guide and host.

We have been blessed to have descendants of Petra Vela and Dr. Henry Hamilton help us with the book. Petra Vela's descendants Michael Hamilton, Susan Seeds, Jesse (Sam) Thornham, and Patrick Thornham provided priceless family pictures. Henry Hamilton's descendant Randolph Slaughter Jr. provided pictures, information, and descriptions of the Spohn Ranch, located outside Laredo and still in the family today.

Throughout our journey we have developed a deep appreciation for the Catholic Church, the Sisters of the Incarnate Word and Blessed Sacrament, and especially the Sisters of Charity of the Incarnate Word, San Antonio. During Dr. Spohn's early years in Corpus Christi the Sisters of the Incarnate Word and Blessed Sacrament would sometimes take in his patients and nurse them, especially if they were from area ranches. Later, when Dr. Spohn asked them to manage the new hospital he had established, they could not do so because their mission was education. However, the Sisters of Charity of the Incarnate Word, San Antonio, took over the hospital and managed it beautifully. We were able to tell the story of the beginning of the hospital and the challenges they faced. Special thanks to Donna Morales Guerra at the Sisters of Charity of the Incarnate Word, San Antonio. The hospital has grown and prospered under their caring administration.

Many of our friends and family members stepped up to help us along the way. Jay Clements helped with research, as did Sierra Repa, Sarah Ondrasky, and William Walsh, and Laura Olsen helped with our graphics. Many thanks to our dear Lauren Marangell for editing our first draft, and Maurizio Turri and Maureen McIntyre.

Sometimes the greatest gifts come at the end of a journey. Fran, Charles, and I came to deeply appreciate Dr. Spohn's many accomplishments through our seven-year quest to write his story. We wanted to have our manuscript reviewed by medical experts. Two of the most prominent surgeons of our day happen to live in Texas. Our daughter Dr. Kimberly Monday, MD, contacted Dr. Kenneth L. Mattox, who generously agreed to write the introduction to the book. Kenneth L. Mattox, MD, is distinguished service professor at Baylor College of Medicine, Department of Surgery, Surgery-Cardio/Thoracic Surgery, and chief of staff and surgeon-in-chief at Ben Taub Hospital. He has a reputation as an innovator in trauma care that is known worldwide. In addition, he is one of the authors of *Sabiston Textbook of Surgery: The Biological Basis of Modern Surgical Practice*, regarded as the preeminent source for definitive guidance in all areas of general surgery.

Our coauthor Fran Vick met Dr. Courtney Townsend, and in the course of their conversation she told him about this book. He expressed interest in reading the manuscript, which Fran sent. She was delighted when it was returned with his comment that he had edited as he read; he "couldn't help himself." Of course he couldn't help himself. He is the editor in chief of the *Sabiston Textbook of Surgery: The Biological Basis of Modern Surgical Practice* (20th ed.), and he is joined in the authorship of the book by none other than Dr. Kenneth Mattox! Both have extensive medical history knowledge and writing skills, and both of them have responded beyond expectations to our judgment of the considerable contributions of this forgotten surgeon.

Texas A&M University Press has been there for us, and our journey started with the previous editor in chief for the Press, Mary Lenn Dixon. She believed in this book and issued the first contract. Then Shannon Davies, Jay Dew, and Emily Seyl helped us complete our journey, and we are very appreciative of their excellent expertise. And always our thanks go to the excellent work of Gayla Christiansen and her staff. Our special thanks to Maureen Creamer Bemko, who once again has come to our rescue with her great copyediting. This is a much better book because of her keen eye and thoughtful suggestions.

I, Fran Vick, must thank Jane for once again coming to my rescue when I needed her most. She and Charles are the kind of friends I would wish for everyone. And I literally could not have come onboard with this project without the extraordinary support and help from my family. Karen and Sam, Ross III and Julie, Pat and Nelda have stood in for me so many times I cannot count them. I have not heard one complaint from them about adding work to their busy lives. They have done whatever was needed without question or complaint. They are wonderful, giving people, and I love them to the depths of my being and have no idea what I would do without them. They are treasures. Thank you, children of my heart, for your help and for keeping me laughing.   .

—Frances Brannen Vick

Charles and I are incredibly grateful that our very good friend Fran Vick joined our quest to tell Dr. Spohn's story. There is no other as good as she is with words and editing. We love being a team with her. We are all pleased Dr. Spohn's story has now been told. This remarkable man will now take his rightful place in medical and South Texas history. We are blessed to have an outstanding and talented family who have always been there with advice, support, suggestions, and most of all love. To Kimberly, Lauren, Julie, Buddie, Jennifer, Adam, and our grandchildren Jack, Ellie, Sarah, Ben, Sam, Annie, Caroline, and Charlie we say thank you.

—Jane Clements Monday

Introduction

As a Texan, historian, surgeon, explorer, inventor, sometimes medical politician, and investigator based on the concept that "there always is a better way—ALWAYS," I have the distinct honor and unique privilege to share with you, the reader, my response to the writings of these remarkable writers. Created here is one of the most unique books I have ever read, not only because of the remarkable individuals, times, and progress of the subjects but also because it is a nonfiction book about a remarkable era in a unique environment in which strong and adventurous people lived. It reflects the creation of a culture, the evolution of which was relatively unknown until now. This book could be housed in all sections of a book store—biography, history, biology, infectious disease, economics, Texas development, business, politics, and personal interests. Although it was written to detail the life of a little-known Texas surgeon, Arthur E. Spohn, MD (1845–1913), readers will find recurrent themes of interest throughout this book. Dr. Spohn lived in Texas after the battles for independence and immediately after the Civil War in the United States. Texas was a state, and the citizens of Texas and the military and government agencies of the United States were responsible for establishing a secure border and settling this untamed land. Both the American Medical Association and the Texas Medical Association were in place during his lifetime, but the American College of Surgeons and the Texas Surgical Association were not established until the last two years of Dr. Spohn's life. The surgical histories written by these two major societies are devoid of any meaningful historical notes about this surgical visionary of his time. This book fills that void and does so with great detail and personal interest. It was ostensibly written about the life of Dr. Arthur E. Spohn, but that life story creates a backdrop for stories about a very unique time in Texas history and society, in general. It will, therefore, be of great interest to a broad variety of readers, regardless of their geographic location or profession.

History of Canada, Michigan, New York City, Texas, and Northern Mexico, 1845–1913

The United States and its individual territories were developed as agrarian states, with support from protective military posts. During the life of Dr. Arthur Spohn, the United States was increasingly being populated in cities, with formation of state, county, and city governments. With the advance west, the settlers faced the untamed wildernesses of Texas with its natural hazards, as well as personal safety hazards—the Native Americans inhabiting Texas and the Mexican bandits in northern Mexico.

The History of Texas during the life of Dr. Spohn Revolves around the Rio Grande

This book could have incorporated either the Rio Grande or the Port of Corpus Christi in its title. The Rio Grande formed the volatile Texas-Mexico border, 1850–1900, during Dr. Spohn's life. Military posts were strategically placed along this river from El Paso to Brownsville, the entire length of the Texas portion of this river. Dr. Spohn served as a military physician as well as a public health officer in many of these military posts. Much of the local color in this book comes from activities on either side or in the river itself.

The Spohn Family

The focus of this book is Dr. Arthur E. Spohn, but his entire family and those close to his family are also explored. Dr. Arthur Spohn was already settled in South Texas by 1873, opening a private practice office in Corpus Christi by the age of twenty-eight. His wife was from among the most influential families of South Texas. He built his practice, established his reputation, served as a mentor to his nephews, and advanced his specialty while in Corpus Christi and its surrounds. This book chronicles the expanded Spohn family.

Development of South Texas Ranching, Particularly among the Kenedy and King Ranches

With the discovery of oil in Spindletop, Texas, in 1901, the twentieth century was to be the "century of oil" for Texas. In 1921, the first oil well was completed in the Permian Basin of West Texas. The nineteenth century saw Texas evolving from being a part of another country (Mexico), to becoming an independent country, and, finally, becoming a state. Texas was in a war for independence and fought multiple skirmishes with Native Americans and raiding Mexican bandits. The settlers were both farmers and ranchers. The ranches west and south from Corpus Christi developed during the nineteenth century, and Dr. Arthur Spohn was a major part of this development. It is against this tumultuous backdrop that his life is revealed in the pages of this book.

Infectious Diseases, Viral and Bacterial, and an Understanding of the Value of Quarantining Patients (Isolation)

In 1868, when a twenty-three-year-old Dr. A. E. Spohn became a public health officer in Corpus Christi, there were no hospitals as we know them, no antibiotics, no laboratory tests to assist in diagnosis, no X-rays, and a poor understanding of bacteriology or virology. Immunology and vaccinations were not yet developed. Perhaps more than the scourges of war, fights, raids, and interpersonal violence, infectious diseases were the most common causes of death. Particularly deadly were yellow fever, scarlet fever, diphtheria, smallpox, cholera, rabies, and tuberculosis. Although some symptomatic treatments were often tried, quarantining was the general approach. Throughout this book, continuing development in combating infectious diseases is traced. Another malady faced by the Texans was the venomous snakebite, particularly that of the western rattlesnake. Again, this book follows new approaches added by Dr. Spohn to treatment of snakebites. Although his skills, interest, and aptitude eventually made Dr. Spohn an administrator and surgeon, this book is an important documentation of the pre-antibiotic and early vaccine era of the treatment of infectious disease.

The Uniqueness of a Semi-Isolated City—Corpus Christi

During the life of Dr. Spohn, the large port cities of the East and West Coasts were well known around the world. The midwestern cities of Chicago and Milwaukee were population centers. In Texas, by 1900 the port city of Galveston was the largest Gulf Coast city in the South, a statistic changed by the unnamed hurricane to hit the city that year. Land routes to the west went through San Antonio and El Paso, or farther north, to routes through the Rocky Mountains. Corpus Christi had fewer than twenty-five hundred citizens when Dr. Spohn settled there. Citizens during his lifetime were often killed by epidemics of infectious disease. Corpus Christi was not the easy port that New Orleans, Mobile, and Galveston were. Corpus Christi was literally a bit off the beaten path. This book becomes a social registry as well as a history of the governmental and cultural development of Corpus Christi and will, in the future, serve as a foundation for the history of this unique city of Texas for the time that Dr. Spohn was one of its principal citizens.

How the Energies of a Few Dedicated and Focused Individuals Can Alter the Course of a City, Country, Culture, and Discipline

This is a book about organization, leadership, planning, and management. Although the skills of physicians, soldiers, ranchers, farmers, and sailors are repeatedly emphasized throughout, one of the most fascinating aspects of this writing is the integration of the planning and management efforts of a relatively few persons in taming and developing this land and its people. It is a lesson in successful leadership and strategic planning. As has often been the case in changing the course of a society, a relatively few strong and intuitive individuals are part of that effort, and their collective focus and energy are in harmony with each other. This book very clearly demonstrates how a relatively few persons in and around Corpus Christi shaped the course of Texas and even the continuing development of the United States.

Progressive Evolution of Medical Education Immediately Pre-Flexner

Dr. Arthur Spohn received his medical and surgical education prior to the Flexner report. Medical school education was nonstandardized. Curriculum was variable from school to school, and the curriculum and technical training to be a surgeon were nonexistent in the United States. Yet, a focused and driven Dr. Spohn received some of the finest medical and surgical training from medical educators in Canada, Michigan, New York, and even Europe. He was an apprentice under some of the most famous names of his time and in some of the best hospitals in the Western Hemisphere. He read extensively and did research, as well as developed surgical instruments. By the end of his career, the American College of Surgeons, Texas Surgical

Society, and even the standardization of undergraduate medical education, as well as the beginnings of specialty boards, were developing. Dr. Spohn had the genome of a surgeon but could have received certification in any one of several specialties of medicine, including public health, infectious disease, general surgery, emergency medicine, military medicine, trauma, family practice, toxicology, and obstetrics and gynecology. He pursued both basic education and technical skill sets in each of these areas. This book shows the movement from untamed rural crude medicine in the United States to a structured and progressively evidence-based environment.

Adaption, Invention, and Innovation in Medical Surgery

Dr. Spohn was an innovator and created adaptations to aid his surgical practice. Throughout this book, those inventions and ideas are recorded. He developed a concept of "staged" operations to make the ultimate outcome better and safer. He devised treatments that must be classified as providing immunotherapy for various conditions. He created a tourniquet to be used in the operating room to reduce blood loss. He defended his invention when others tried to claim it as their own, and he progressively made improvements to this invention and faithfully reported it at meetings and in the literature. Dr. Spohn was a Renaissance man of his time.

The authors have painstakingly researched many resources, from newspapers to personal letters and telegrams, to community, church, and school records. The referencing of these resource documents is presented in detail. Although written to memorialize the life of Dr. Arthur E. Spohn, this is a book of great interest to many whose interest in history involves many previously described areas.

Kenneth L. Mattox, MD
Distinguished Service Professor
Division of Cardiothoracic Surgery
Baylor College of Medicine

Chief of Staff and Surgeon-in-Chief
Ben Taub Hospital Emergency Center and Trauma Center

DR. ARTHUR SPOHN

Chapter 1

The Spohn Family, from Canada to the United States

1776–1865

rthur Edward Spohn, MD, was an accomplished physician in South Texas who founded a hospital that became the basis for a large healthcare system. His life story features many medical firsts and outstanding achievements. For example, he holds the Guinness World Record for removing the largest tumor ever—all 328 pounds of it—from a patient who survived the procedure. He performed the first successful caesarean hysterectomy in the United States, on a patient suffering from malacosteon. He invented the rubber ring tourniquet used by the military around the world. His snakebite remedy was requested from as far away as India. He took a patient with rabies from rural South Texas to Paris, France, to receive inoculations at Dr. Louis Pasteur's institute, saving the patient's life and returning to the United States with the life-saving serum. The US government sent him to Europe twice to study methods of controlling epidemics of diseases such as yellow fever and cholera and to exchange ideas on best practices. He then implemented the ideas through his work in the US Marine Hospital Service, the first line of defense against epidemics in this country. He was a brilliant innovative physician and surgeon whose first thought was how to save his patient's life and who took decisive action to achieve that. His driving quest for knowledge led him to stay on top of new techniques and research in spite of his life as a "country doctor" in remote nineteenth-century Corpus Christi, Texas, and environs.

Spohn's life is also the story of the challenges of being a physician during the late nineteenth and early twentieth centuries. An educated, accomplished physician and surgeon, he brought the best possible treatments of the day with him from Canada and the northern United States to frontier Texas. His story illustrates the training of that day in university centers, the experience and influence of battlefield surgeons during the American Civil War, and his personal involvement as a US Army surgeon on the Texas frontier. Wartime often produces medical breakthroughs. The cause of yellow fever was discovered during the Spanish-American War in 1898, and penicillin was first produced during World War II. The Civil War also saw medical advancements, and Spohn studied with some of the professors who were responsible for them. Dr. Spohn's life coincided with that amazing period of discovery and innovation that startled the scientific and medical world around the turn of the twentieth century. His responsibility, as was the responsibility of all his contemporaries, was to bring the new discoveries into an area that was still a frontier. He was the man for the job.

Born in 1845, Spohn lived in a period when medicine was undergoing dynamic changes, almost in parallel with the Industrial Revolution. In the laboratories of Europe germs were being identified and linked to infection and death. Antiseptic practices were being implemented, and human inoculations were being tested. In Georgia in 1842, Dr. Crawford Long discovered ether to be a general anesthetic for use during surgery.[1] New methods of medical care and instruments were being developed, often encountering resistance from the old guard, who continued to practice and defend the ways of the past. Dr. Arthur Spohn was not one of these. From the early days of his practice he invented new ways of improving the delivery of medical care, published his findings in medical journals, and gave speeches to inform his fellow physicians of his findings, his research, and his inventions.

Spohn was born and raised in Canada by a founding family of a new country launched in the chaos of the American Revolution. His maternal grandfather and his family had survived brutal treatment at the hands of the American patriots during the American Revolution because of their loyalty to the king of England. They were able to relocate to what is now the province of Ontario after great difficulty and suffering. Young Arthur Spohn was the product of a determined, accomplished, and successful family whose experiences of enduring hardships to survive and thrive led to high expectations for their children and grandchildren.

Spohn's family was one of the Canadian colonizing families referred to as the United Empire Loyalists in Canada.[2] The organization devoted to their memory, also known as the United Empire Loyalists (UEL), chose the words of Elizabeth Bowman, Spohn's mother, to represent their struggles, and those words were inscribed on the monument that stands today in the center of Hamilton, Ontario.

FOR THE UNITY OF EMPIRE

The United Empire Loyalists, believing that a Monarchy was better than a Republic, and shrinking with abhorrence from a dismemberment of the Empire, were willing rather than lose the one and endure the other, to bear with temporary injustice. Taking up arms for the King, they passed through all the horrors of civil war and bore what was worse than death, the hatred of their fellow-countrymen, and when the battle went against them, sought no compromise, but, forsaking every possession, excepting their honour, set their faces toward the wilderness of British North America to begin, amid untold hardships, life anew under the flag they revered. They drew lots for their lands and with their axes cleared the forest and with their hoes planted the seeds of Canada's future greatness.[3]

The United Empire Loyalists in Canada chose words written by Dr. Arthur Spohn's mother to represent their struggles. Those words were placed on monuments, memorial plates, and stamps. Photo by Charles W. Monday Jr., MD. Courtesy of Peter Spohn.

Dr. Egerton Ryerson, a Canadian educationist and important figure in Methodism in nineteenth-century Canada, requested information about the Loyalists' early struggles, and Elizabeth Bowman Spohn responded.[4] She wrote how her grandfather, Jacob Bowman, Spohn's great-grandfather, had emigrated from Germany during Queen Anne's reign and settled in New York. He joined the British army in the Seven Years' War (1754–63).[5] The American colonists called it the French and Indian War, and George Washington fought with the British. Bowman received for his service fifteen hundred acres in Pennsylvania, on the Susquehanna River. He, unlike many of his fellow loyalists, did not leave when the Revolutionary War started, because his wife, Elizabeth, was expecting a child at any time. Then the worst happened. According to Elizabeth Spohn, "He was surprised at night, while his wife was sick, by a party of rebels and with his eldest son, a lad of sixteen years of age, was taken prisoner; his house pillaged of every article except the bed on which his sick wife lay; and that they stripped of all but one blanket. Half an hour after my grandfather was marched off, his youngest child was born."[6]

This was only the beginning of the nightmare that Spohn's family faced on that cold November night. His great-grandmother, with an infant and six other children, was left without provisions. Their cattle and grain had been taken away, and they had one blanket among them. Elizabeth's father, Peter Bowman, was just eleven years old but now the man of the house. They had to somehow survive in the dead of winter, and he was the one to whom the task fell. In spite of his heroic efforts, all of them would have died if others had not stepped up to care for them.

With other Loyalist families, Spohn's great-grandmother and her family walked to the banks of the Mohawk River to plant corn and potatoes to survive. Hearing of their plight, the British sent friendly First Nations people to lead the struggling families of five women and thirty-one children to Fort George in what is now upstate New York on November 3, 1776.[7] The people of the First Nations gave the family a blanket, coat, and moccasins and nursed Spohn's great-grandmother back to health. The Loyalists were protected and sent to Montreal and then Quebec, to seek shelter in cold barracks during the Canadian winter.[8] This experience developed the determination and fearlessness that ran in the family. Spohn's grandfather, Peter, joined Butler's Rangers at the age of twelve to fight the Americans as soon as he could. His nine-year-old brother, Abraham, joined as a fifer because he was too young to fight. They were determined to avenge their family's losses, but they too had hardships and often were without provisions. Peter Bowman talked about how he would have given a hat full of gold for a piece of bread or for the opportunity to eat from his father's hog trough.[9]

When a failing Jacob Bowman was finally released after three and a half years of captivity in irons and reunited with his family, they began to build a new life. Peter returned from the army to help his ailing father and married Magdalena "Lena" Lampman, the daughter of a Loyalist, Frederick Lampman, from New York.[10] The family settled near Fort Niagara to start anew. It was a tenuous existence. They cleared land, foraged for nuts, ate tree leaves, and fished. Peter worked all day in the fields and fished at night to provide food as they began to carve a home out of the Canadian wilderness.[11]

The Revolutionary War was drawing to a close, and after the peace treaty was signed in 1783, neither the Loyalists nor First Nations people who had fought with the British could return to their expropriated homes. The British then bought (not confiscated) more land from the First Nations people to give to the refugees.[12]

The Niagara Peninsula and the land between Lakes Erie, Huron, and Ontario, covering nearly three million acres, were purchased for settlement. Refugees and disbanded soldiers rushed to settle the land. The survey was slow and finally completed in 1788. By then most of the choice lands had been settled, causing refugees to move farther west. In 1789, twenty-two or more families settled on lands near the Barton Township line.[13] Peter and Lena Bowman were among the twenty-two families who moved west of Niagara to settle at Wilson's Mills, later named Ancaster.

Spohn's grandparents were founding members of Ancaster. Peter was known as a man of strong mind. He was considered energetic and industrious, devoted to God, and inflexible in his attachment to Methodism. Lena was described as having a very superior intellect and being deeply pious. Peter had four hundred acres awarded because of his service in Butler's Rangers. His brother Abraham had two hundred acres and his brother-in-law, Matthew Lampman, had two hundred acres. Matthew had married Eve, the baby born that November morning in the colonies when her father and brother were carried off by the rebels.[14]

In Ancaster the Bowmans again went to work to establish their family roots, as they had in the American colonies. Ancaster grew, and to Wilson's Mills they added a hotel, blacksmith shop, and general store. Loyalists who had fled the colonies had been able to bring only what they could carry.

Leaving a culture of theater, art, music, and a flourishing book and magazine trade, they were left with no reading rooms, lectures, social gatherings,
libraries, or cultural performances, but they moved quickly to reestablish
what they had left behind.[15]

Peter and Lena had two children: John Wesley Bowman and Spohn's
mother, Elizabeth.[16] However, John Wesley died in 1811 at the age of nine,
leaving Elizabeth an only child.[17] The family values of education, determination to build a new life, and devotion to religion led to a no-nonsense
upbringing for Elizabeth. Peter and Lena saw to it that Elizabeth received
a good education. The Reverend Egerton Ryerson later described Elizabeth
as "a woman of much intelligence, strong convictions, vigorous intellect and
in every way worthy of her parentage."[18]

Peter was a good provider and made good investments. He farmed and
bred and raised horses for the cavalry. He also continued his military career.
Peter lived to be eighty-seven years old and Lena, eighty-one years.[19] Both
of them lived long enough to see their grandson, Arthur Edward Spohn,
born in 1845.

In 1823, Elizabeth Bowman, age eighteen, married Philip Spohn.[20]
Philip was born in Stamford (located on the Niagara Peninsula) with the
name Spaun, and at some point he changed it to Spohn. His parents, Polly
Springstead/steen and Peter Spaun, had left Albany, New York, after the
American Revolution and had become very successful in Canada. Philip's
brother, Jacob Spohn, was the contractor for the Burlington Canal, and his
sister Edith's husband, Henry Van Wagner, built mills in Waterdown and
Saltfleet.[21]

Philip and Elizabeth lived on the Springbank Farm in Ancaster, where
they too bred and raised horses for the cavalry. They also produced eight
sons and three daughters and later financed their children's university educations by selling land.[22] Philip first served as an appointed magistrate and
was later elected a member of Upper Canada's first municipal government.
Magistrates were very important in the early government of Upper Canada.
They were appointed by the government in Toronto, and their decisions in
district administrative matters were final. They appointed constables and
made all the decisions, while the elected officials carried out their orders.[23]

Philip and Elizabeth valued education, religious belief, hard work, innovation, fearlessness, caring for others, loyalty, and dedication to duty.
They maintained a stern and disciplined household. The farm was productive and everyone had a job to do.[24] Their children learned well and led

successful and productive lives. Philip's farm was worth $24,000 (equal to approximately $444,480 today), the highest cash value in the township.[25] He owned 340 acres, of which 275 were cultivated. The 1861 census showed he produced spring and fall wheat, barley, peas, oats, buckwheat, root crops, maple sugar, and cider. In addition to the farm Elizabeth and Philip owned, there were the properties she inherited from her parents. She received property in Southwold, Ancaster, and Hamilton, including the corner of King and James Streets, where her son Jacob later practiced law. She also owned land that became known as the Ainslie Woods, between the townships of Hamilton and Dundas.[26]

One thing Philip and Elizabeth could not control was disease. Nevertheless, of their eleven children, all grew to adulthood except the youngest, William. In 1849, when Spohn was four years old, scarlet fever and diphtheria were serious illnesses, and even smallpox and cholera briefly made an appearance.[27] Diphtheria was particularly dangerous for young children like Spohn. It was a scary disease that was highly contagious and caused a thick gray membrane to develop in a patient's throat, making it difficult to breathe. Even more serious for children was scarlet fever, which is caused by the streptococcus bacteria and can bring on fever, vomiting, rash, chills, and headaches. Serious cases could lead to rheumatic fever, ear infection, pneumonia, and liver and kidney damage.[28] Fortunately, Spohn and his siblings lived on the farm, limiting their exposure to some of the diseases. Spohn's relatives, the Griffin family, were not so fortunate. Eliza, four, and Henry, three, were orphaned during the cholera epidemic in 1847.[29]

Between 1848 and 1849, 150,000 Americans also perished in the first of four deadly cholera epidemics to hit the continent.[30] Cholera was brought to Canada by immigrant ships. Cholera is an intestinal infection that prevents the absorption of water and salt from the lower digestive tract, resulting in severe dehydration brought on by diarrhea. The patients became cold and turned a bluish color, the eyes sank into their sockets, and death took place within a day. Throughout the continent, cholera and typhoid were spread by fecal contamination of water in the camps of soldiers, in slave quarters, and among native populations.[31]

Surrounded by death and political unrest in Canada between the provinces of Lower and Upper Canada, with the Lower being dominated by the French-speaking population, as it is today, and the ongoing fight between religious groups, the Spohns remained a family of faith. At first the Church of England was the only group allowed to perform burial services or marriage ceremonies. Presbyterian and Methodist ministers served the majority of the population but could not call their places of worship "churches." Peter Bowman came under the influence of a Methodist minister and member of Butler's Rangers named Christian Warner and joined the Methodist Church.[32]

There was a split, with the settlers from Britain preferring Wesleyan Methodist preachers and the former colonists siding with the American Methodist Episcopal preachers. This divide caused Henry Hagle and his followers to break away and establish the Canadian Wesleyans or Ryanites.[33] This split led to a humorous and hard-to-believe incident involving Arthur Spohn's family in 1830. The incident is still referred to today as the "sliding church."

On the boundary between Peter Bowman's land and Henry Hagle's, a chapel was constructed, both men having donated land for the church. The two groups shared the chapel for services, but each represented a different faction of the Methodist Church. Peter's group was so disturbed by the Ryanites that it became impossible to continue the status quo. So early one morning in 1830, Peter and his group of loyal followers, using pike poles, crowbars, levers, and rollers, moved the log chapel onto Peter's side of the property line. Squire Hagle promptly sued for £500 damages, but the jury awarded only five pounds to the squire and thus the Bowmanites appeared to have won. All was quiet for a time, but one morning Peter Bowman awoke to find that the chapel had been moved during the night to Henry Hagle's side of the property line. Peter immediately summoned his friends and slid the chapel back, but wisely, he slid it only to the original location on the property line. That eased tensions, and for many years the chapel was known as the "sliding church" or "Old Slide."[34] Today in Ancaster, if you mention Bowman Church, people immediately say, "Oh, the sliding church."

Spohn's grandparents' educational and religious activities at their church affected Methodism throughout Canada. The Bowman Church in Ancaster was chosen as the site of the first Canadian Conference of the Methodist Episcopal Church, held August 29, 1829. Thirty leaders met and decided to create a book room (later Ryerson Press), to establish the Upper Canada Academy (later Victoria College), and to publish a church newspaper (the *Christian Guardian*). They also organized Canada's first Total Abstinence Society. Egerton Ryerson was ordained at that conference. He published the first issue of the *Christian Guardian*, inspired the founding of Victoria

College, and started the Wesleyan Female Institute and Boys Institute of Dundas. Upper Canada developed an unrivaled educational system.[35]

Locally, Peter Bowman helped establish and supported the first children's school in Ancaster. Peter saw to it that Spohn's mother, Elizabeth, received an education well beyond that of most women of that time. Spohn's father, Philip, continued to support the community school that his father-in-law had established.[36]

After their basic education the Spohn children went on to private schools. On his military records Arthur wrote that he had attended Ancaster High School. It was probably referred to as a grammar school as well. One description of Ancaster Grammar School from 1855, when Spohn was ten years old and likely in attendance, indicates that James Regan, MA, "taught English, Commercial Higher Maths, Greek, Latin, French and Italian. He charged forty pounds a year without extras. He was a distinguished scholar, and a graduate of the University of Durham England."[37]

As the tenth child among eleven, Spohn didn't have time to get to know his older siblings very well before they were grown and gone from home. Several of his siblings and their families moved to Texas. The others remained in Canada, but they all stayed close through correspondence and visits. The Texas/Canada connection was a vital part of Spohn's life.

Spohn was not the only accomplished and successful member of his family. It is worth enumerating the Spohn siblings and their accomplishments.

Peter (1824–62) was a barrister who practiced in nearby Hamilton. He graduated from Victoria College, where he won a prize for American literature and writing.[38] Spohn displayed some of his older brother's literary flair later in life in his poems and prose. Peter married Ann Stinson, and their son, Angus Peter Spohn, later moved to Texas, where he became known as the "King of Zapata" in South Texas politics.[39]

Asbury (1826–82) married Mary Ann Terryberry, whose family owned Terryberry Inn, a popular stop between Niagara and Ancaster.[40] Asbury became a prosperous farmer in Hume Township, Michigan. Two of his sons, William E. Spohn and Ulysses G. Spohn, became physicians.[41]

Henry (1828–1909) spent most of his life in Texas with Spohn. Like Arthur Spohn, he was a very popular physician, and the two owned and operated a ranch together along with their sister Catherine.[42] Henry was one of the physicians Spohn called to help him with the world-record-setting tumor operation.

Jacob Von Wagner Spohn (1830–93) graduated from Victoria College and became a barrister, practicing in Hamilton. He married Mary Van Wagner, and together they moved to Texas in 1886.[43]

Mary Margaret (1831–56) married Rev. W. S. Griffin and died after giving birth to her second son. Their older son, Herbert, became an accomplished physician, and Spohn sent family members to him in Canada for treatment and in later years turned to him for help with his wife, Sarah.[44]

Magdalena (or Lena) Jane (1834–1911) married John Huntley of Southwold. She was provided for in their mother's will.[45]

Catherine (1837–1928) married Dr. Alexander Hamilton of Barrie, Ontario, who served as a preceptor for Spohn.[46] Their family moved to Texas, and Alexander practiced medicine with Spohn. They also owned and operated a ranch with Spohn and Henry. Their son Arthur Claud Hamilton became an important lawyer in Laredo, Texas. Their son Henry Hamilton was a physician and trained under Spohn. He was also there to help Spohn operate on the patient with the giant tumor. Catherine later spelled her name Katherine, but we spell it with a C because it is that way in the family Bible.

Wesley Case Spohn (1839–1919) studied for the ministry but dropped out due to a form of palsy. He married Eliza Augusta Griffin from Brantford, Ontario.[47]

Philip Howard Spohn (1842–1918) was another physician. He graduated from the Toronto School of Medicine and practiced in Penetanguishene, Ontario. He was elected the first Reeve of Penetanguishene and in 1891 was elected a Liberal member in the Dominion Parliament for the riding of East Simcoe (an electoral district in Canada). He was a surgeon for twenty-five years in the old reformatory for boys and was the first superintendent of the Hospital for the Insane in Penetanguishene.[48] He sent his son, Douglas Spohn, another physician, to Texas to practice with Arthur Spohn in Corpus Christi.[49]

Spohn was fourteen when his sister Catherine married Dr. Alexander Hamilton, who was from a pioneer family in Toronto, on October 21, 1859.[50] Dr. Hamilton had attended medical school at the University of Toronto. He and Catherine settled in Barrie, Ontario, in 1859, where he practiced medicine. Later in his career, in 1870, he served on the faculty of Trinity University.

Young Arthur Spohn moved from Ancaster to Barrie to live with his sister Catherine and brother-in-law and to attend the Barrie Grammar

School, established in 1856. Rev. W. F. Checkley was appointed headmaster in 1861, when Spohn was sixteen, and would have been one of Spohn's teachers. It was under Checkley that the school achieved an international reputation, attracting students from all parts of Canada and the United States. The curriculum was difficult but provided a strong educational foundation. The school gave exams in 1861 on Greek, Latin, antiquities (ancient history), French, English, grammar, history, geography, arithmetic, algebra, Euclid (geometry), trigonometry, chemistry, and natural history.[51]

Spohn enjoyed Barrie's beauty and intellectual atmosphere. The town had the Barrie Debating Club, the Mechanics' Institute, and the institute's chess club, the forerunner of the library.[52] Spohn enjoyed the waterfront and the fishing, swimming, and boating it offered. He became familiar with boats and maritime skills, which came in handy later, when he spent many of his adult years managing the Marine Service Hospital located on an island in Corpus Christi Bay, Texas. After finishing Barrie Grammar School, Spohn did a preceptorship (i.e., an internship) with his brother-in-law Dr. Alexander Hamilton, thus following the usual path for a student intent on applying to medical school.

Spohn left Barrie after completing his preceptorship and entered McGill University in Montreal, Canada, in 1865. His student card showed he was in the Medicine Section and would be attending both sessions. The first session was from 1865 to 1866 and the second from 1866 to 1867. The card was inscribed with the date of his birth and his birthplace, and his parent or guardian was listed as Dr. Hamilton. His religion was noted as "Wesleyan."[53] When Spohn arrived, the school was using what was known as the Edinburgh curriculum. This involved two six-month courses of basic science lectures and two years of "walking the ward."[54] Spohn received the senior prize (Practical Anatomy Award) at McGill in 1865. He also passed the first examination and had honors in natural history. According to Michael Bliss, author of a biography of William Osler, a Canadian physician and co-founder of Johns Hopkins Hospital, "Medical education at McGill was the best Canada had to offer. . . . McGill's Faculty of Medicine had high admission standards; the faculty had longer teaching sessions than most schools, required students to take its courses in sequence rather than in helter skelter order and required four years of training before graduation rather than the normal two or three."[55]

Bliss writes that the McGill medical graduates were probably as well educated as the graduates of the bachelor of arts program offered there. He also thought Harvard's medical school was probably the best in the United States, but it had been judged at that time to have not been much more than a diploma mill whose many graduates were "of doubtful literacy." Bliss quoted what Harvard president Charles William Eliot wrote in 1870: "The ignorance and general incompetency of the average graduate of American Medical Schools, at the time when he receives the degree which turns him loose upon the community, is something horrible to contemplate."[56]

For some reason Spohn chose to leave McGill after the first year and enroll in the University of Michigan Medical School in Ann Arbor, Michigan. This decision was hard for his parents, especially his mother. He was, after all, going into "enemy" territory. A family story is that Spohn was later asked to come back and accept the position of head of the McGill University School of Medicine, but he refused it despite his mother's desire for him to return to Canada. Dr. William Osler accepted the position instead.

He may have left home due to the Canadian political turmoil over the possible dissolution of the commonwealth into an eastern and western division. It could also have been for financial reasons. Most likely he left because he had discovered his lifelong passion for anatomy. He may have chosen not to "walk the wards" but instead to avail himself of a program in which he could develop his talents academically and as a surgeon. For whatever reason, Spohn left his Canadian homeland and journeyed to the United States of America.

Chapter 2

From the University of Michigan to Postwar New York City

1866–1867

As a young physician, Spohn faced the dilemma of whether to follow the established procedures of surgery and medicine or to seek new innovations. He always chose the latest technology and in many cases invented new techniques himself. Although the young man apparently had an innate talent for surgery and would likely have been successful even without this drive for better methods, it was this quest for the best that made him exceptional. His deep caring for patients and his passion for improved treatments that could save their lives were together a strong force. The University of Michigan was a pivotal point in his medical journey toward excellence.

Spohn was twenty-one years old when he left McGill University in 1866 to attend the University of Michigan in Ann Arbor. During his preceptorship with his brother-in-law and his year in the medical and science departments at McGill he had discovered his talent for anatomical dissection, winning the senior prize for practical anatomy. He also was in the Honor Class.[1]

The rules of the University of Michigan, adopted by the regents, reflected the quality and preparation they expected of their entering medical students. The rules stated that students in medicine and surgery must have studied with a respectable practitioner of medicine for three years. Admission required that students should show evidence of good moral character along with a good English education, knowledge of natural philosophy and elementary mathematical sciences, and acquaintance with Latin and Greek to enable them to appreciate the technical language of medicine and to read and write prescriptions.[2]

When Spohn arrived at Ann Arbor, he was surrounded by strong sentiments and feelings of pride in Union accomplishments in the Civil War. Canadian newspapers had followed the war closely, so Spohn was well aware that the United States was still in turmoil even after the battlefield actions had ceased. The president of the United States had been assassinated, and killed along with Lincoln was his intention to use kindness in bringing the South back into the Union. The South was in a state of collapse, with no government, no courts, no post offices, no sheriffs, and no police but with guerrilla bands looting at will. The South had lost a generation of men and the countryside was devastated. In the North, families also grieved over their lost soldiers, but the elements for recovery and growth were strong. The war had spurred the development of factories and new markets for products that had been needed by the Union army. Successful factories meant jobs and money. Banks and financial institutions were growing at a rapid pace. The North was on the verge of a booming economy.[3]

Ann Arbor and the University of Michigan were no exception. In 1836, Ann Arbor had lost a bid to establish the state capital there, but the town instead offered the land for use by the university. In 1837, the state accepted and moved the University of Michigan from Detroit to Ann Arbor. The community was also able to acquire a rail line linking it to Detroit and markets to the west, in Chicago or Milwaukee, to help secure a positive economic future.[4]

Spohn's decision to go to Ann Arbor was a good one for him. In 1866, when Spohn entered the Medical Department, it had the highest enrollment of any medical school in the United States. Spohn's class had 525 students, with only 130 students from Michigan (23 percent of the class).[5] Students from Canada made up about 13 percent of the class.[6] There were several reasons for the popularity of the university. A student who took one year in medicine training could practice that profession without having a medical diploma. The fee for one year was only five dollars; it was ten dollars for the two-year course. In other medical colleges, many being proprietary, the fees ranged from sixty-five dollars to $125 per term. Perhaps the biggest incentive for Spohn was that there was no difference in fees between Michigan residents and nonresidents.[7] The Medical Department had been established in 1837 and included six professorships: anatomy, surgery, physiology and pathology, practice of physic, obstetrics and the diseases of women and children, and materia medica and medical jurisprudence. Through the years the university had financed appropriate buildings and faculty to help expand the programs it could offer. One of Spohn's professors, Dr. Corydon L. Ford, changed his life.[8]

Dr. Ford came to the university in 1854 as a professor of anatomy and held the position for forty years. He was described as "a sensitive and earnest teacher who had a way of making dry bones and anatomical tissues of absorbing interest."[9] It was said of him that in his day he probably taught more students than any other teacher of anatomy anywhere. Ford's lectures continued to occupy a large part of his teaching curriculum. He utilized work on the microscopes so that his students would be familiar with the minute structures of the body. According to a historical memoir of the university, he spent time developing "investigative methods for creating charts, models, mannikins, and teaching specimens of all kinds. Most of the teaching aids could not be obtained in the markets of the world during Ford's career, and those few that were obtainable were prohibitive in price."[10]

Spohn was fortunate the school had solved the problem of obtaining cadavers before he arrived. Through the years the school had had difficulty acquiring cadavers for dissection. People in the community had even been curious about where the school got bodies to cut up. There was no legal way to obtain bodies for medical research, so people became suspicious that graves were being robbed in the dark of night. It seemed that their suspicion was confirmed when a grave was discovered nearby with fragments of a broken coffin left behind. A mob gathered one evening and wanted to burn down the medical building, calling it a "butcher shop of human flesh." They were soon confronted with a guard of one hundred armed medics patrolling the campus to protect their building; the mob dispersed.[11] The university was able to overcome the problem by the 1861–62 session when the demonstrator of anatomy reported, "To expense of procuring 45 anatomical subjects—$1,367.46."[12] The purchase of cadavers thus came at a considerable price. Today that amount would be approximately $35,500.

The school term commenced the first Wednesday in October and continued until the first Wednesday in April. A student who completed the first year of work in March could enroll in some other college and even receive a medical degree a few months later.[13] Spohn passed his final exam in 1867 and was recommended for a degree but never applied for it. Instead he changed his medical pathway under Dr. Ford's influence. Dr. Ford could teach anatomy in various medical colleges as long as he was present for the six-month medical course offered at the University of Michigan. He could thus teach in other medical schools during the spring and summer and fulfill his passion for teaching anatomy.[14]

During the time of Spohn's attendance, Dr. Ford worked with the surgery and anatomy students for the term, observing them in his anatomy lab. He must have immediately observed Spohn's ability, because from all of his 525 students he chose Spohn for a unique honor. He offered him the opportunity to accompany him to the Long Island College Hospital in New York early in March 1867 to accept the position of intern and assistant professor of surgical anatomy. Spohn chose to accept the position and go to New York with the famed professor.

Spohn was twenty-two years old when he followed Dr. Ford to New York in the spring of 1867. He had years of education for someone so young. He had done his preceptorship, been recognized for unusual ability in anatomy at both McGill and Michigan, and had finished his MD requirements except for the paperwork. Now he was an assistant professor of anatomy and intern at one of the leading hospitals in the United States.

New York City also offered Spohn varied learning experiences outside the field of surgery and anatomy. The city was the most modern in the nation and had a large population of nine hundred thousand people. The northern part of Manhattan was still largely open land and was occupied by scattered shanties, country houses, and small inns. After the Civil War, New York had grown quickly. Most of the roads in the city were dusty and filled with mud holes, and the burgeoning population had overwhelmed the residential buildings and was living in close quarters.[15] The year before Spohn arrived, bad living conditions had come to a head. The action taken by the New York physicians and the Council of Hygiene and Public Health set an example for the entire United States on how to react to an epidemic crisis, and Spohn saw the results firsthand. He later devoted much of his life to fighting disease and preventing epidemics in South Texas.

News had reached New York in 1866 that Europe was experiencing a bad cholera epidemic. A group of New York City physicians suggested through the New York Academy of Medicine, led by Dr. Stephen Smith, that it would not be long before the epidemic reached American shores.[16]

These physicians formed a voluntary group of wealthy New Yorkers to become a part of the Council of Hygiene and Public Health. In 1864, they began a survey of the sanitary conditions of the city, conducting a ward-by-ward sweep and producing a report of more than three hundred pages. The survey cataloged the problems in detail, and seven thousand orders were issued. Workers removed piles of horse manure, mountains of refuse, and rotting animal carcasses from the streets.[17]

The group had to fight merchants and political leaders. Boss Tweed's ward bosses received money from the city for street cleanup but often did not spend it for public health. The legendary Tweed himself embezzled funds, lived in a Fifth Avenue mansion, and had an enormous appetite for food, drink, and mistresses.[18] However, Dr. Stephen Smith and the group, with the help of local police and a newspaper editor, William Cullen Bryant of the *Evening Post*, were able to force many citizens to clean up the city. They also established a quarantine station out in the harbor to assure ship inspections. Quarantine work was difficult. Captains often bribed enforcement personnel, and sometimes the officers on board trading vessels who had no desire to be delayed would ferry cholera sufferers to the shore and dump them on the beaches before entering port. Late in April the first ships full of cholera-infected passengers began to arrive at the wharves despite the efforts of the hygiene council. The first case was reported in May. The Metropolitan Board of Health "dispatched sanitary crews with barrels of chloride and lime to each of the locales where the first victims took ill, boarded up their homes, and relocated the other residents to hospital tents for observation."[19] These labors delayed the spread of the disease, with the next case not being reported until June. However, despite these efforts, more than one thousand New Yorkers died from the cholera.[20]

The Metropolitan Board of Health was the first modern municipal public health authority formed in the United States. The board also led the effort to clean up piers and vacant lots, clear obstructed sewers, repair badly ventilated houses, and connect privies to sewers. It promoted cleaning up stables and yards that were filled with stagnant water, and it tried to keep people from driving cattle through the streets at all hours.[21] These efforts had reaped benefits by the time Spohn arrived in the spring of 1867. The sanitation code in New York laid a foundation for his future work in disease control efforts across Texas and, later, internationally.[22]

Bellevue Hospital was an important feature in the history of US public hospitals. In 1799 it had the first maternity ward, and in 1808 and 1818 doctors there performed the first ligation of the femoral and innominate artery. In 1854 Bellevue physicians promoted the "Bone Bill," which helped legalize dissection of cadavers. In 1856 the physicians popularized the use of the hypodermic syringe.[23] Bellevue had originally been established to cope with the threat of yellow fever and other epidemics, and it served the penal population, the poor, and the mentally ill. That mission had changed by the 1850s, when the hospital began focusing on medical education.

Bellevue Hospital paved the way for the founding physicians of Long Island College Hospital, who wanted to establish a medical college like those in Europe that were associated with universities and hospitals. That thrust allowed Long Island College to establish the first medical school in America associated with a hospital; it came into being on February 13, 1858.[24] In the beginning the school had struggled financially, but by the time Spohn arrived the debt had been paid and it had a first-rate faculty.

First Henry, Spohn's older brother, and then Spohn himself had a chance to study at Bellevue, thereby learning how to treat the poor and diseased. After finishing his postgraduate education, Henry Spohn had practiced medicine in New York until April 18, 1864, when he volunteered with the 17th Vermont Infantry Regiment and was commissioned as an assistant surgeon with the Vermont Volunteer Regiments.[25] These surgeons were not members of the regular army but served the soldiers on the battlefield, so Henry was continuously at the front. He and his fellow army surgeons faced a number of challenges—amputated stumps, shattered limbs, and putrid flesh wounds that had not been dressed for four or five days. Infection and disease were so bad that soldiers had little confidence in doctors. Many did not want a limb amputated. One corporal held a doctor at gunpoint, telling him that if anyone put a hand on him he would kill him. In the doctor's defense, amputation was the wounded soldiers' best chance to survive because of the threat of disease and gangrene. Three-fourths of the surgeon's time was spent doing amputations and about three-fourths of the amputees recovered.[26] However, two-thirds of the soldiers died from disease, not wounds. Causes were poor hygiene, garbage in camps, filth from latrines, overcrowding, exposure to all types of weather, improper diet, spoiled food, disease-carrying insects, and impure water. Illnesses that were pervasive included dysentery, typhoid fever, ague, yellow fever, malaria, scurvy, pneumonia, tuberculosis, smallpox, chickenpox, scarlet fever, measles, mumps, and whooping cough.[27] Walt Whitman described the Civil War as "about nine hundred and ninety-nine parts diarrhea to one part glory."[28]

As a paid intern at the Long Island College Hospital, Spohn had the chance to work in all the disciplines and broaden his medical experiences. It was one of the premier medical education centers in the United States, and some of the physicians he would study under had served in the war and learned battlefield surgery techniques. Spohn's superiors at Long Island College stimulated his lifelong quest for knowledge and his desire to be on the frontiers of learning and medical research.

The Civil War pushed those frontiers of medicine, and Spohn studied with some of the professors who were responsible for them. In 1861, Dr. Frank H. Hamilton, fearing the approach of the Civil War, had started a preliminary one-month course on military surgery. He was an expert on fractures, and his publication *Treatise on Fractures and Dislocations* went through seven editions and was translated into French and German. He also volunteered as a regimental surgeon and published his *Treatise on Military Surgery and Hygiene*.[29] He was one of the first to advocate skin grafting.[30] Spohn later published articles on both fractures and skin grafting.

Another of the medical advances arising from the Civil War was the development of the hospital ambulance service, first used at Antietam and later recognized as an important lifesaving tool. Spohn was able to witness this service firsthand. In 1864, a Bellevue surgeon, Dr. Edward B. Dalton, was appointed to be the inspector for the Army of the Potomac. He rose rapidly through the ranks and was placed in charge of the transportation and care of wounded Union soldiers. He organized corps hospitals that treated thousands of soldiers. He then created the Depot Field Hospital of the Army of the Potomac and was the chief medical officer. By October 1864, that facility had treated 68,540 sick and wounded. It was during this time Dalton developed the horse-drawn ambulance service that coordinated with the mobile hospitals and the front.[31]

Prior to Dr. Dalton's innovations, in New York City any injured persons in the street would hope that a passerby would take them to the nearest druggist or convey them on a cart or by other means either to their home or to the hospital. After the war Dr. Dalton was made the sanitary superintendent for the region that included Manhattan, Brooklyn, and nearby counties. He designed ambulances for the service at Bellevue and the surrounding area. Each ambulance had a foot pedal sounding a bell to warn pedestrians, plus stretchers, a box that contained a quart flask of brandy, two tourniquets, bandages, sponges, splint material, pieces of old blankets, strips of cloth with buckles, and a two-ounce vial of persulfate of iron. By 1869 these ambulances were being used extensively in New York.[32]

Spohn also had the opportunity to study with four nationally known physicians who were giants in their fields. One of the most famous of the faculty members was Dr. Austin Flint—a significant influence in New York medicine in the second half of the nineteenth century. He had acquired an international reputation because of his contributions to the physical diagnosis and study of diseases of the heart and lungs. He was known for his outstanding work with the newly discovered dinaural (two-eared) stethoscope and analysis of the sounds produced by tapping the chest, as well as the sounds of breathing heard through the stethoscope. He discovered and described a murmur in valvular heart disease that is still known today as the "Austin Flint murmur." He also furthered the study of tuberculosis by listening for the symptomatic wheezes of lung disease.[33] Later Spohn was recognized as a tuberculosis expert.

Another outstanding educator at the school was Dr. James Trask, a professor of obstetrics and diseases of women and children. He was a founder of the American Gynecological Society and was widely known for his clinical skill.[34] Spohn also became very interested in women's medicine and later, in Corpus Christi, Texas, opened a facility to do extensive women's surgery.

Dr. John Dalton was the most renowned physiologist in the United States at the time. He had few equals as a demonstrator and teacher. He used anesthesia in his own animal experiments and was the first in the nation to teach physiology by conducting experiments on animals in front of his students. His textbook of physiology, published in 1859, was a standard in American medical schools for two decades.[35]

Dr. Ogden Doremus was professor of chemistry and toxicology and was probably the foremost toxicologist in the country in the nineteenth century. He often gave expert testimony in murder trials that were making headlines in many newspapers.[36]

Spohn was living in an exciting time for physicians. Dr. Joseph Lister, a British surgeon, was making medical history and publishing his results in *The Lancet*, a prominent English medical journal. Dr. Lister was working at the Glasgow Royal Infirmary and wanted to do something about the high surgical-mortality rate. Gangrene and other festering infections left the recovery wards with a horrific smell. He read Louis Pasteur's 1865 report that living microorganisms caused matter to ferment and rot. He reasoned that if microbes caused matter to putrefy and wounds smelled of putrefaction, then keeping microbes off the wounds might cut the infection. He had also read how authorities in Carlisle, England, had used carbolic acid (phenol) to treat smelly sewage and thus reduced disease. Lister reasoned, Why not treat wounds with dilute phenol, clean the surgical instruments, and spray phenol aerosol in the operating theater?[37] In 1867, just as Spohn was starting his training period in anatomy and surgery, Lister performed the first full surgical procedure using these disinfection methods. He was able to report that, by using these procedures, nine months passed without a single case of sepsis among his surgical patients, a statistic that was remarkable at the time.

Spohn valued his time at Long Island College Hospital and returned to New York City ten years later to advance his medical education as a matured physician.

Chapter 3

The Spohns to Lawless Texas

1867–1868

While Spohn was finishing his training in New York, his brother Henry made the decision in 1867 to go to Texas as a citizen physician with the US Army. Henry was thirty-nine years old and a bachelor. He had obtained his medical degree in Canada, completed his advanced training at Bellevue Hospital in New York City, and briefly practiced privately before serving in the Union army as a volunteer surgeon. Henry may have decided to move to Texas because it offered opportunity for further government employment despite the postwar military downsizing or because of private opportunities on the Texas frontier. He later demonstrated his business acumen by successfully investing in businesses, mining, land, and ranching in Texas throughout his career there.

Texas had suffered less hardship than other heavily occupied Confederate states. Still, the economy was in distress and lawlessness was everywhere. This need for soldiers to police the border, and therefore physicians to serve them, created an opportunity for Henry to continue his army career, and it gave Arthur Spohn the same opportunity a year later. By the time Henry and Arthur had arrived in Texas, the state had been deeply scarred. The forts along the Rio Grande where they were stationed played an important part in protecting area residents. Fort Brown in Brownsville had been built during the US-Mexican War and anchored the southernmost end of a line of forts built for defense against Native Americans and raiders. Ringgold Barracks was built near Rio Grande City, which had grown from the original Davis Landing site that had been established as Rancho Davis by Henry Clay Davis.[1] Fort McIntosh at Laredo and Fort Duncan at Eagle Pass were also part of the chain of forts along the Rio Grande.

At the beginning of and during the Civil War the US Army abandoned all the forts in Texas. In the summer and fall of 1865 the army reoccupied posts on the lower Rio Grande, including Fort Brown, Fort McIntosh, and Ringgold Barracks. The troops offered some protection against threats from Native Americans, bandits from Mexico, and the forces of Emperor Maximilian in Mexico, but the people on the frontier located away from these forts received little protection. During the late summer of 1866 the violence in Texas escalated, and more federal troops were requested. Military authorities led by Gen. Philip Sheridan began to send troops to aid in the protection of the citizens.[2] The year Henry Spohn arrived in Texas, the Reconstruction Acts of 1867 organized Texas and Louisiana as the Fifth Military District under the command of General Sheridan.[3]

Henry was headed into a troubled and hostile land in the summer of 1867. He arrived in Texas when significant violence was occurring against both the US troops stationed there and the civilians. He came through Brownsville and Fort Brown and then was sent to Fort McIntosh in Laredo. Henry's army record listed him as part of the 117th Infantry Colored Troops, which was stationed at Fort McIntosh. The year before, in Brownsville, Texas, an unknown assailant had murdered a surgeon, Joel Morse, serving with the very same 117th Regiment. Post tensions were running high, and the assaults by bandits and Native Americans exacerbated the situation. The black soldiers of the 117th Infantry had to overcome prejudice from within the army and from the frontier communities. They were often divided into small companies and performed garrison chores, built roads, escorted mail parties, and helped to patrol the frontier. They were also often engaged in combat against the Native Americans and widely recognized for their bravery.[4]

Henry was first listed as an acting assistant surgeon and then as post surgeon at Fort McIntosh. This designation continued through 1867. By the time Arthur Spohn arrived in 1868, Henry was listed as being in charge of the post hospital. In September 1868 Henry was a witness in a court-martial in Brownsville, and in November he was called away for detached service while he accompanied some of the cavalry on an assignment. He had returned by December and continued to be in charge of the post hospital. During his service his salary was listed as $125 a month.[5]

The army faced many challenges while establishing the forts along the Rio Grande. The effort involved restoring discipline and often interacting with former Confederate soldiers and sympathizers. The year after Spohn arrived in Texas the army was still trying to achieve political stability in the civilian population, with strong opposition from former Confederates. In the spring of 1869 Brevet Lieutenant Colonel Prime took over Fort McIntosh in Laredo. The army posts along the border were understaffed and poorly equipped and were not able to handle the demands of the area. Few officers spoke Spanish, and many times the officers were called upon to handle the chaotic political situations in the towns where the forts were located.[6]

Lieutenant Colonel Prime was a take-charge man and quickly found that most of the Webb County officers elected in 1866 were ineligible to hold office under the Reconstruction government rules, so he promptly dismissed them and appointed other men to take their positions. Prime soon realized that they were only front men for the men he had dismissed, so he let them go, too. He admitted it was very difficult to find men to serve, as not many could speak and write both English and Spanish intelligently. He did finally appoint men over whom he could exert authority and control, and he was finally able to begin restoring order.[7]

The lawlessness in Texas required unusual measures. Many of the men who had supported the Confederacy felt disenfranchised and cheated and consequently were outraged with the so-called "Radical Republican" rule. John McAllen, a prominent landowner, expressed the feelings shared by many former Confederates. He wrote on November 24, 1870, about Gov. Edmund Davis and his government: "Davis is not popular with the people, he is keeping a brache open and flooding us with carpetbaggers for the cause. I don't care for what principle he may have in this but let him take hold of good men, let them belong to any party in place of the men he has selected. If you were here you would not associate with any of the crowd in Brownsville. They are all Dutch and a Dutch jackass was put in place of Col. Nelson Plato who was the quartermaster of this place."[8]

The Radical Republicans who implemented Reconstruction were equally unhappy with the entrenched landowners who had been Confederate supporters. An incident had occurred a year before, on October 12, 1869. Nestor Maxan, a lawyer in Brownsville, had written to another local lawyer, Stephen Powers, that "day before yesterday, Captain R. King and J. J. Richardson and five other persons came into town and were immediately arrested by order of General Clitz for murder. . . . I attended to their cases and succeeded in persuading the Commanding officer to place them under bond, to appear before the next District Court, in the sum of ten thousand dollars each. We created quite an excitement."[9]

Maxan managed to keep the well-known riverboat captain Richard King and his associates out of jail, but tensions ran high. The government officials were not pleased that strong Confederate men like Captain King and his fellow entrepreneur Mifflin Kenedy were now conducting business as usual.

The roads were not safe for military or civilian travel. Spohn and his company faced hazards every time they left camp. Captain King traveled with armed vaqueros, his group usually numbering between eight and ten men. These vaqueros carried rifles and sidearms and rode the finest horses in the country. They wore bandoliers with spare cartridges across their chests and sported large knives and wide-brimmed sombreros. King paid them well, and some of that pay was dedicated to the purchase of whiskey. King set up stage camps at twenty-mile intervals, each camp being provided with guards and fresh horses and mules. He knew his safety depended on traveling fast. He had to carry large sums of money to pay his people, so he had a safe built into the bottom of his coach, and only his wife and ranch manager Reuben Holbein knew of the existence of that mobile vault. He was never successfully robbed.[10]

The law was generally enforced by the Texas Rangers, and because of their close connection to King they became known as the *rinches de la Kineña,* or rangers of the King Ranch. Tejano settlers faced the same threats the Anglos did, plus the fear of being dispossessed of their land. Roberto Villarreal, a descendant of some of the first vaqueros who worked for Mifflin Kenedy, related the story of Doña Eulalia Tijerina's land in the middle of Kenedy's La Parra rancho. Kenedy fenced in Doña Eulalia's property so that the only access was through Kenedy land. She later won the right to stay on the land until her natural death.[11] The original landowners sometimes lost their land in the courts or through intimidation by Anglo immigrants.

The army in the next few years also actively tried to control the Native American threat. Gen. William R. "Pecos Bill" Shafter took charge of the 24th Infantry Regiment of African American troops along the Rio Grande from 1867 to 1868. He later became a field commander. As history records,

> Shafter's most renowned feat in West Texas was the Llano Estacado campaign of 1875. Combining two companies of the Twenty-fourth Infantry with parts of the Twenty-fifth United States Infantry and Tenth United States Cavalry and a company of Seminole Indian scouts, Shafter drove his men more than two thousand five hundred miles from June to December. Often exhausted and short of water, the troops made three crossings of the Llano Estacado (plains between Texas and Mexico border) and swept the plains clear of Native Americans. Shafter's campaign also proved the plains habitable and paved the way for white settlement of the region.[12]

The actions by the Americans were often cruel and unjust. Largely due to infectious diseases, Native American populations in the United States fell from about 600,000 in 1800 to 237,000 in 1900. The destruction of the bison herds led to widespread malnutrition and susceptibility to diseases like smallpox and tuberculosis. Almost all the indigenous groups were forced to migrate to reservations, where they could no longer maintain their traditional diets.[13] Previous generations had had plenty of meat, so the older men had larger physical stature than the younger generation, who looked weak and sickly. As one historian notes, "When Sioux prisoners were taken to a reservation in 1881, one observer noticed tuberculous youths with 'fleshless limbs' who were looking on wistfully at the dances of the warriors in the summer twilight whose magnificent physiques and a boundless vitality . . . contrasted cruelly with their own feeble sickliness."[14]

Even though Henry was a close friend of General Shafter, he found good reason to put his roots down in Laredo and leave the army several years later. One of several reasons for Henry's actions may have been his family's relationship with the Canadian First Nations. His family had great respect and appreciation for the First Nations members who had helped save his great-grandfather's and grandmother's lives. Also, in Canada the government worked at making the First Nations their allies, and they bought the land rather than taking it.

Henry found himself the only American doctor in Laredo during his military service time, and the citizens of Laredo frequently came to him for treatment. He started the first drugstore in Laredo and also invested in ranch lands and city property. According to Henry's obituary, "By the time he was ordered away with Colonel Shafter to his regiment he had become so attached to Laredo by friendly ties professionally and in business that he resigned from the army rather than leave. At the time of his resignation he was an assistant surgeon with the rank of Captain in the regular army of the United States."[15]

Henry paved the way for his brother Arthur Spohn and influenced him to come to Texas. Spohn's experiences in Texas were vastly different from his brother Henry's because of his intimate association with the powerful Kenedy and King families. Those connections had a dramatic impact on his opportunities. Mifflin Kenedy, Richard King, and their friend Charles Stillman controlled the development of South Texas from the 1850s through the 1870s. In 1876, eight years after arriving in Texas, Spohn married Sarah Kenedy, daughter of Mifflin Kenedy. Becoming a member

Mifflin Kenedy was Arthur Spohn's father-in-law. He owned one of the largest cattle ranches in the United States and became an economic czar along the Rio Grande and in the Texas-Mexico borderlands.

Capt. Mifflin Kenedy fell in love with Petra Vela, whose family had been in northern Mexico for six generations. Among the children of their marriage was Sarah Kenedy, who married Dr. Arthur E. Spohn. Courtesy of Jesse (Sam) Thornham and Patrick Thornham.

of one of the most powerful families in Texas had a significant effect on the medical advancements that Spohn accomplished during his forty-plus years as a physician.

Spohn's future father-in-law was a Quaker from Pennsylvania. He had previously worked as a substitute captain and clerk on the steamboat *Champion*, which plied the Apalachicola and Chattahoochee Rivers in the southeastern United States. He came to Texas in August 1846 at the age of twenty-two to work as a pilot on the steamship *Corvette*, transporting men and supplies for the US Army during the US-Mexican War.[16]

Kenedy wrote to his friend Richard King and encouraged him to join him in Texas, and King did so a year later, in May 1847. When the US-Mexican War ended, both remained in Texas to seek their fortunes. Although opposite in personality, they became lifelong friends and business partners. They met Charles Stillman, who had already established multiple industrial enterprises, cotton firms, and silver mines that in the 1850s produced more than $4 million in silver and lead.[17] Stillman became a business partner as well.

Spohn's future in-law family had the strong heritage and religious conviction of Sarah's mother, Petra Vela Kenedy. Petra's family had been in Mier, Mexico, for six generations, and they had established ranchos along the Rio Grande for raising horses and cattle and also renting out breeding

Capt. Richard King relied on Arthur Spohn for his medical care. Arthur treated King's entire family and became their close friend. Courtesy Brownsville Historical Association.

Henrietta Chamberlain King was Capt. Richard King's wife and a close friend of Arthur and Sarah Spohn. She helped raise the money to build Spohn's hospital. Courtesy of CHRISTUS Spohn Health System, Corpus Christi, Tex.

stock. Petra came from a prosperous family, as seen from her grandmother's will, which listed many fine possessions, including silver plates and serving pieces, crosses, portraits, linen, and statues.[18]

As a young girl, Petra fell in love with a Mexican army lieutenant named Luis Vidal and moved with him to Matamoros, Mexico, in January 1837. Petra and Luis had eight children. Luis had a successful military career, became a lieutenant colonel, and was serving under Gen. Adrián Woll when he attacked San Antonio, Texas, in 1842. Luis was promoted to brevet colonel for his valor in that battle and nominated to receive the Cross of Honor.[19] However, Luis had two families, as was the custom of many of the officers. He married Manuela Andrade y Castellanos in southern Mexico on October 9, 1842, but no marriage license for Petra and Luis has ever been found. Luis maintained the two families separately.[20] Luis retired in 1845, and in 1849 Petra received news of his death from *vomito*, caused by the wave of cholera that swept through Mexico that year.[21]

Petra had inherited her share of the estate of her father, Gregorio Vela, and in 1850 moved her children to Brownsville, Texas, for their education

Photograph believed to be of Frederick Edward Starck. He was an officer in the Union army and married Maria Vicenta Vidal on April 2, 1864, in Brownsville, Texas. Sarah and her family did not attend the wedding because they had gone across the river to Matamoros, Mexico, for safety since they were Confederate supporters. Courtesy of Michael W. Hamilton.

and to have access to greater opportunities for them. She had means, because the 1850 census shows her as twenty-six years old and the head of an independent household. At some point Petra lost her oldest three children, probably to either the yellow fever or cholera that plagued the river towns. Petra's son, Adrián, also died before Spohn had a chance to meet him. The remaining children were Luisa (b. 1840), Rosa (b. 1841), Maria Vicenta (b. 1846), and Concepción (b. 1849).[22] Spohn would become familiar with all of them because of Sarah's closeness to her half-sisters.

One history of South Texas records that "Petra, a wealthy widow, married Mifflin Kenedy in 1852 at her family home in Mier, Mexico."[23] On May 10, 1854, Petra and Mifflin had their marriage blessed by Father Verdet at her church in Brownsville, Texas.[24] Through the next decade Mifflin and Petra had six children of their own: Tom (b. April 15, 1853), James (b. February 22, 1855), John (b. April 1856), Sarah (b. October 1857), William (b. April 22, 1859), and Phebe Ann (b. August 7, 1860). Phebe Ann lived only eight months, until April 29, 1861.[25]

Mifflin and Petra made their home in Brownsville, Texas, which had developed into a cosmopolitan city after the US-Mexican War. Many Anglos and other newcomers began to control the major institutions, but Mexican culture continued to pervade the border area. Many of the Anglo and European ranchers and merchants became "Hispanicized" white men. The Tejanos also had to change to become a part of the new society that was in place. Many became active in the development of the Anglo culture and had to adapt and socialize to function.

Brownsville had access to an international port and the products of Mexico through the neighboring city of Matamoros, Mexico. Local residents thus had access to goods from around the world. One could buy cigars from Cuba, fine wines from France, silks from New York, and fabrics from Spain. Within the Kenedy home, the language was Spanish and religion was diligently practiced. Spohn's future wife thus grew up in a multicultural world of wealth, privilege, and devotion.[26]

Mifflin Kenedy introduced his business partner Captain King to Henrietta Chamberlain, the daughter of Rev. Hiram Chamberlain, a Presbyterian minister. The two of them had come to the border region to preach and teach. After Captain King met Henrietta, he worked four years to win Henrietta's hand in marriage, and on December 10, 1854, they were finally wed.[27] For their honeymoon trip from Brownsville to his rancho on Santa Gertrudis Creek, he bought a large closed carriage for $400. The journey took four days, and armed outriders accompanied them. They also had guards who watched over their safety by night and a ranch cook who prepared their meals over coals on the Texas prairie. They slept under the stars until he proudly brought her to his modest rancho, with earth-brown huts and a blockhouse and stockade with a brass cannon brought from his steamboat.[28] Through the years this modest rancho developed into the largest ranch in the United States, and the Kenedy and King families remained close. Spohn, through his marriage to Sarah Kenedy, also became a close friend of the King family, attending to all their medical needs and even saving one family member's life in dramatic fashion.

Sarah Kenedy had been just a young girl when the clouds of civil war gathered over the United States. Mifflin and King formed King and Company and also became ranching partners in King's rancho in the Wild Horse Desert, as well as in riverbank real estate. M. Kenedy and Company was preparing to run Confederate cotton caravans to the Rio Grande and across to Matamoros, Mexico, then on to the notorious coastal town of Bagdad under the Mexican flag. This was one of the few outlets for Confederate cotton due to the Union blockade of southern ports. King ran the business from his isolated rancho along the "cotton road," and Kenedy arranged for the shipments to Brownsville and Matamoros. They were wildly successful, with Stillman reporting in a letter to King that Kenedy had $100,000 in his vaults.[29] Stillman left Texas in 1866, became one of the richest men in the United States, and invested heavily in the National City Bank of New York. Despite leaving Texas, he remained a financial resource for King and Kenedy in their many endeavors.[30]

Complete chaos had raged along the Rio Grande from 1863 to the close of the war in 1865. The North-South conflict was fierce, but the imperial French effort to take Mexico from the Juaristas was equally intense. The French government had enthroned an Austrian archduke, Maximilian, as emperor of Mexico in 1864, but the elected president of Mexico, Benito Juárez, was hiding in the mountains near Durango, Mexico, hoping to mount a counterrevolution.[31] Both Mexico and the United States were involved in civil wars, and the Kenedy family was caught up in the turmoil. Petra's daughter Maria Vicenta had married a Union officer, Fred Starck, stationed at Fort Brown, before the troops evacuated the fort. Petra's son Adrián was initially fighting for the Confederacy, as was a son-in-law, Joseph Putegnat, and Mifflin was helping to run the Confederate cotton caravans.[32]

Adrián, at age seventeen, joined the Confederate army as a private in the fall of 1862. He brought with him a skilled group of mostly Tejano companions who knew the Rio Grande and the lands along it, and they were invaluable as scouts.[33] Mifflin and Petra sent their three oldest sons to Pennsylvania to live with his relatives, while Petra, Mifflin, and the other children moved to Matamoros for their safety. Adrián received praise for his bravery in the capture of a Federal gunboat in July 1863.[34] By October, however, he had deserted the Confederate army and planned an attack on Brownsville. Confederate general Hamilton Bee had lost most of his men to deployment elsewhere and thus had only nineteen men left to defend Brownsville, where millions of dollars' worth of Confederate cotton and supplies were left undefended. Bee sent two privates to order Adrián and his men back to Fort Brown to defend it. Adrián killed one and wounded the other, who escaped and warned Fort Brown about the betrayal.[35]

Adrián and his men then rode to the Ramireño rancho, where he knew the owner, a Mr. Barthelow. He shook hands with him and then tied him up, beat him, and hanged him. Mrs. Barthelow and her children escaped.[36] Adrián then joined forces with the Union army and crossed the river into Mexico to join the famed militant Juan Cortina, sometimes called the

"Robin Hood of the Rio Grande."[37] He and his men acted as scouts to help break up the Confederate cotton trade that Adrián's stepfather was running. His actions were difficult for all the Kenedy family.

On May 30, Adrián resigned from the Union army and took most of his men with him. He was now a deserter from two armies. To complicate matters further, French soldiers under General Mejia arrived in Matamoros, and Cortina, ever the opportunist, joined forces with the French Imperialists while sending a message to the Juaristas that he had to do this because it was expedient. Adrián, with few choices, continued to fight with the Juaristas. He was captured by the Imperialists, found guilty of treason, and executed on June 14, 1865, in Camargo, Mexico. Mifflin used "powerful means" to try and save him but did not succeed.[38] His death broke Petra's heart. Adrián was called "wild and reckless," "daring," and "a crazy young man."[39] He was probably all of these but is still considered a hero as

Adrián Vidal was a brother-in-law Arthur Spohn never knew. He was executed by the French Imperial Army for treason on June 14, 1865, in Camargo, Mexico. This photograph is believed to be of a young Adrián Vidal in New Orleans. Courtesy of the Kenedy Family Collection, A1995-045.0171, South Texas Archives, James C. Jernigan Library, Texas A&M University–Kingsville.

a partisan who fought for freedom for Mexico. Adrián's life is but one example of a family's tormented experience caused by civil wars on both sides of the Rio Bravo at the same time.

The Union army had occupied Fort Brown after General Bee's retreat and was determined to shut down the cotton trade. On December 22, 1863, Union soldiers raided Captain King's rancho while he was away. They killed a servant, plundered, rode horses through the rooms on the main floor, smashed furniture, mirrors, china, and windows, and rounded up the livestock. A pregnant Henrietta, along with her father and children, left on Christmas Day for San Antonio and safety. There she delivered her baby and named him Robert E. Lee King after their friend and in defiance.[40]

On March 1, 1864, the editor of the *New York Herald* wrote,

> Eight to ten capitalists in Brownsville and Matamoros and their supplies to the rebels had done more to sustain the southern cause than eight to ten rebel regiments. They provided half the supplies to Lee's men in Virginia and had made millions by treason. They were able to move one hundred sixty-two million dollars worth of cotton through Mexico. If the North had been able to control this international boundary, the war could have ended a year earlier, sparing some of the six hundred thousand who lost their lives.[41]

King, Kenedy, and associates played a major role in the Civil War by keeping the Confederacy alive and making their fortunes by buying the cotton in Confederate scrip and selling it for gold. Ironically, King and Kenedy, who were possibly the biggest supporters of the Confederacy and made fortunes during the war trading cotton, were able to receive special amnesty. The president of the United States pardoned them. Both claimed they did what they did because they had to protect their property. They had figured out how to work the system to their advantage. King set about rebuilding his rancho after the Union raid, and Kenedy meanwhile was busy consolidating their interests along the river.[42]

This is the background of Spohn's introduction to Texas and the history of the families he would be joining as physician, friend, and finally son-in-law and husband.

Chapter 4

Spohn in Texas

1868–1870

S outh Texas was a land filled with Mexican culture, food, and language. It was also steeped in southern culture, had residents with strong Confederate loyalties, and was part of a former slave state. The landscape was demanding and hostile. Rattlesnakes could grow to eleven or twelve feet in length and were extremely dangerous. Rattlesnake bites were just one of the many different injuries Spohn would encounter as a physician in Texas.

On May 19, 1868, Spohn was approved in New York City as an acting assistant surgeon with the US Army and then assigned to Texas, thus following in his brother Henry's footsteps. The surgeons were under the command of the surgeon general and listed as citizen physicians. Spohn's salary was approved at one hundred dollars a month.[1] He went to Texas and was placed in charge of military quarantine for the army along the Gulf coast, including Galveston, Corpus Christi, and Brownsville.[2] Having acquired excellent training and knowledge of quarantine practices in New York, Spohn was well qualified for his new role.

The year before Spohn's arrival, Texas had been hard hit by yellow fever, which first appeared in Galveston. By November the reported deaths from yellow fever stood at 999.[3] This death toll prompted officials to establish quarantines. In 1867, Dr. Greensville Dowell confirmed that poor sanitary conditions in postwar Galveston were aiding the spread of the disease when he said, "Often dead cats, dogs, hogs, and goats lie for days and

Dr. Arthur Edward Spohn
arrived in Texas in 1868 as a
citizen physician in the US
Army with the rank of captain.
Courtesy of the Kenedy Family
Collection, A1995-045-1304,
South Texas Archives, James C.
Jernigan Library, Texas A&M
University–Kingsville.

weeks, with rats, mice and old bones, fish and fowls. The yards of many of
our citizens are as bad as our alleys; and I really do not believe there is a
city in the world that is more neglected than ours in this respect."[4]

On March 13, 1867, the editor of the *Galveston News* concurred, calling
the gutter at Twenty-Third and Market Streets "a disgrace to any civilized
community." A Galveston woman wrote, "The oleanders were sickeningly
sweet and a terrible depression hung over the city. . . . The moaning of the
sick, the weeping for the dead and dying, the haggard faces of those well
enough to nurse, are living memories of that awful town."[5]

Many towns tried quarantines, but often the merchants would write
letters denying the disease was in their town, afraid that it would hurt
their businesses. Also, ships would take on passengers regardless of the
danger they could represent to others.[6] These were some of the challenges
Spohn faced when he arrived in Texas and took charge of quarantining.

Spohn received help from the Howard Associations. These benevolent
groups were organized nationally and, in Texas, did a great deal to help the
victims of the epidemics. The earliest confirmed such group, named after
the British philanthropist John Howard, was present in Boston in 1812.

These groups sprang up in most major cities in the United States and were autonomous. They had goals such as crime reduction, prison reform, and public health. They operated hospitals and "pest houses" and provided sanitary burial for deceased patients. They also hired physicians and provided for nursing.[7]

Corpus Christi, Texas, was also hit hard in the 1867 yellow fever epidemic. The town tried to stave off the epidemic by sealing entry points, changing mail carriers thirty miles out, and treating the mail with smoke for an hour before it could be delivered. However, when a traveler on horseback from the infected town of Indianola arrived in town and died two days later, the fever spread quickly. Shops closed and the streets were deserted. Three of the town's doctors died from yellow fever.

The Howard Association in Corpus Christi had been organized in December 1865. Some of the organizers were Rev. Hiram Chamberlain, Col. John J. Dix Sr., and Capt. Richard King, along with other community leaders. They helped to build and pay for a pest house on the bluff. People without anyone to care for them were taken there to either get well or die. The association hired undertakers to bury the dead and also had coffins made.[8]

A chemist in town named William DeRyee developed a treatment he believed could cure the victims. His treatment included keeping the victims' extremities warm with hot ashes and reducing the fever with cold towels. He also used doses of potassium salicylate or salicin and morphine to help control convulsions. After the epidemic he was known as Dr. DeRyee, and he opened a successful drugstore.[9]

It was estimated that three hundred out of the one thousand residents of Corpus Christi died in the 1867 epidemic. Every household was affected, and, in some, all the family members died. One positive result that came out of the 1867 epidemic was that the army established a quarantine station on Padre Island near Corpus Christi. Ships from infected ports were held for twenty-one days under a bright yellow flag. A year later, in 1868, a twenty-three-year-old Dr. Arthur E. Spohn was put in charge of the quarantine station.

Spohn made a very important contact while he was in Corpus Christi. He requested permission to treat patients at the Santa Gertrudis rancho. Capt. Richard King and his wife Henrietta were rebuilding the rancho after the chaos of the Civil War. They were delighted at the opportunity to utilize the services of this highly trained young surgeon.[10] The captain

Early Texas, 1800s

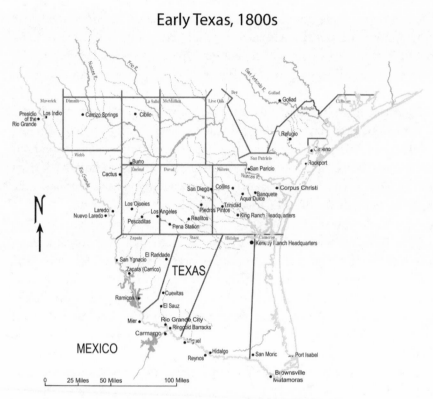

Early Texas and Mexico settlements. Cartography by Nancy Tiller.

and Henrietta developed both fondness of and trust for this young man and became his lifelong friends. He would take care of them and, later, their children. Captain King was also a powerful ally to have in Texas. Neither Spohn nor King imagined that in fewer than ten years this young surgeon would marry Sarah Kenedy, daughter of King's best friend, Mifflin Kenedy.

Spohn was stationed at Rancho San Ygnacio deep in South Texas in August 1868 and would remain there until November, when he reported to Ringgold Barracks on the Rio Grande. He then was at Carrizo from January to April 1869, when he was relieved and sent back to Ringgold Barracks. These military posts were established after the Civil War to protect the border of the United States all the way from the mouth of the Rio Grande to Fort Bliss, near El Paso.[11]

Both Arthur and Henry Spohn worked in the forts located along the river from Brownsville to Laredo. At the mouth of the Rio Grande, Fort

Brown had the responsibility from 1866 to 1886 for a number of outposts along the river and some points in the interior. In 1872, a post at Santa Maria Ranch, thirty miles upriver from Fort Brown, was established. These posts were located at ranches because they had water and pastures where the horses could graze. The ranches welcomed the troops because they provided them and the surrounding region with protection.[12]

Roma, Texas, located farther upriver and west of Fort Brown, was under the authority of Ringgold Barracks. In 1870, a detachment from Ringgold Barracks was sent to protect the customs house at Roma. In 1871, troops had to again protect Roma from attack by forty armed Mexican bandits.[13] In 1872, another outpost was created at Penitas Ranch, eighty-five miles up the Rio Grande from Brownsville. It was common practice to have a civilian physician attached to the units stationed there.[14] Fort Brown and Ringgold Barracks also had shared control over an interior post at Edinburg. These posts helped provide scouting parties to monitor the Rio Grande and prevent raids from across the border by bandits and Native Americans.

Spohn was on the Rio Grande border when these posts endured numerous Native American and bandit raids during the Reconstruction period. Renegade bands of Comanche, Kiowa, Lipan, Apache, and especially Kickapoo had been displaced from their homelands. They had lost their hunting grounds, and their primary food source, the buffalo, was gone. They crossed over to Mexico, and from there they raided cattle and horses on the American side with little resistance. The raids became more violent, with the taking of hostages and killing of many citizens. Juan Cortina seized on this opportunity and formed a large smuggling ring utilizing both the Native Americans and the Mexican bandits. He obtained lucrative contracts with the Cuban government to supply beef. He shipped the stolen cattle to Cuba from the Mexican ports of Bagdad and Tampico.[15]

Ringgold Barracks oversaw a number of sub-posts and camps between 1866 and 1886. The most important ones were Edinburg, Roma, and San Ygnacio. The units from Ringgold Barracks also used San Ygnacio, also known as Rancho Ygnacio, where H Company was stationed. In October 1868, Lt. Daniel F. Stiles was the commander of a twenty-eight-man detachment at this sub-post. Listed among those men was A. E. Spohn, a civilian physician serving as a medical officer.[16]

For three months Spohn served at the sub-post of San Ygnacio, which is the oldest town in Zapata County. The town is named for Ignatius of

Loyola, founder of the Jesuit order of Catholic priests in Spain in the mid-1500s.[17] San Ygnacio is on the Rio Grande about thirty miles south of Laredo and fourteen miles northwest of Zapata. In Spohn's time, however, the town was known as Carrizo. Citizens of Revilla (now Guerrero), Tamaulipas, in Mexico, settled the town in 1830. The leader of that group of settlers was José Treviño, who built a sandstone home known as Fort Treviño in 1830.[18]

San Ygnacio is an example of how important these river towns were to the US Army and the early settlers of Texas. According to Roberto Uribe,

> Don Blas Maria was the only rancher to have open passage thru "La Kineña," the King's Ranch. Captain King and Don Blas had a mutual agreement. Don Blas Maria's herds could pass thru King's land and Captain King's herds and wagon trains could go thru Uribe land. At the time the river was very wide and navigable with flat boats. Captain King kept a riverboat tied to the banks of the river just across from the fort, with permission from Don Blas Maria. The riverboat was used to transport cattle and dry goods or cotton to Brownsville or even to New Orleans. During a very heavy storm the boat was destroyed. Parts from the boat were around the fort for a long time. The part that is on the wall is the crank that used to turn the paddlewheel.[19]

To his advantage, Spohn was fluent in French and English and had had Latin in school. He was from a German family and his grandmother spoke mainly German, so he was probably fluent in the German as well, as were many Texan Anglos who were members of first- and second-generation German immigrant families. The German and Latin had been helpful in his medical studies. San Ygnacio provided him an opportunity to perfect another language, Spanish, which probably was not difficult for Spohn. The advantage he had was that he learned it from native speakers, not from textbooks. His mastery of languages would be critical to his practice, which served patients who spoke Spanish, and to his marital life, as he later married into a Spanish-speaking family. Nevertheless, although Spohn had lived in Canada, Michigan, and New York before coming to Texas, he still had a lot to learn about the people and culture of the Rio Grande frontier.

Things had not changed much from the end of the Civil War for the US troops when Spohn arrived. Food was plentiful but limited in variety. The rations consisted of flour, pickled pork, a particularly nasty version of bacon cured in the dust of ground charcoal, and fresh meat from game they hunted. With no available fresh vegetables, the men made their own *pulque* to solve their nutritional problems. This drink was made from the fermented leaves of the maguey, a type of agave. The men were given a cup every morning. General Sheridan remembered, "It was worse in odor than sulphureted hydrogen."[20]

The regional foods Spohn encountered were very different from what he had been accustomed to eating. The poorer Mexican families ate primarily tortillas and dried beef, supplemented by any fruits and vegetables they could obtain. The mealtime drink was coffee or chocolate. In the more affluent homes, cooks prepared fresh beef, lamb with raisins, fresh fruits, and varieties of bread, including tortillas. On feast days they had a special treat of tamales, which were cornhusks spread with masa and wrapped around a mixture of chopped meats, vegetables, spices, and dried fruits. Chile peppers were widely used. The residents held feasts, often for a religious celebration at a church property, if one was available, or when the priest came to visit.

A French missionary in mid-nineteenth-century Texas, Father Domenech, also known as Abbé Domenech, was shocked by the casual attitude the people had toward religion. On the other hand, General Sheridan was impressed by the devotion of the people. The sacraments of baptism and matrimony were important, and people especially wanted the sacrament of confession at the hour of their death. For entertainment the people held fandangos and *bailes*, or dances, and social gatherings. Gambling and cockfighting were prevalent as entertainment for the men.[21]

Spohn learned to appreciate the people's particular religious practices, which included aspects of the supernatural, as seen in the work of shamans, or healers. The priest often had to work with this element in bringing Christianity to the region. Even though they might consider themselves Christians, the people often turned to the shaman to handle their personal issues and illnesses. Home remedies were passed from generation to generation, developed from observation and trial and error until people had confidence in the cure.[22] Many Anglos, including Spohn's future brother in-law, Joseph Putegnat, refined these remedies and sold them as patented cures. Joe Putegnat is still recognized in the *United States Dispensatory* reference for his knowledge of native herbs. He used one herb, chaparro amargosa, to treat dysentery and fevers. An example of the native's observation and the development of an herbal medicine was treatment for the bite of venomous creatures. A Native American was watching a battle between a *paisano*—a roadrunner—and a rattlesnake. The snake struck the bird, which then ate a nearby plant and returned to kill the snake. After observing this phenomenon, the Native Americans used this plant to treat the bites of venomous snakes and insects. Joe Putegnat made an extract from the plant and sold it to the public.[23]

Fortunately, most striking venomous rattlesnakes, especially the older and wiser ones, do not waste venom on a human. They may simply bite without injecting the venom so as to scare off the aggressor and preserve their valuable supply of toxic fluid for use on smaller animals that can be consumed. This phenomenon might allow a snakebite cure to work on one or two out of three victims. Worthless medications may improve symptoms due to the placebo effect. Many a medicine man thrived on this susceptibility.

Perhaps, as things turned out, Spohn entered the army at the ideal time. After the Civil War the army was scattered in small stations throughout the South and West. With the large expansion in the number of forts, the army was forced to employ 264 acting assistant (contract) surgeons in 1866, and by 1868 it had hired another 282. In March 1869 a directive stipulated no new appointments were to be made in the Medical Department.[24] By December 1868, Spohn had been pulled back to Ringgold Barracks. The next month, in January 1869, he was at Carrizo, Texas.

Spohn was deposed on February 10, 1870, in Brownsville, Texas, concerning a court-martial involving him personally. The testimony gives insight into both the personalities of the individuals Spohn had to deal with as well as his style and manner of dealing with aggression. It also provides a unique glimpse of the daily life of an army physician on the Texas frontier following the Civil War.

The accused, Lt. Hamilton Peterson, was a classically educated and alcoholic western gunslinger. Spohn's statements described Peterson's doggedly persistent unethical conduct that doctors and nurses, as well as any other variety of health-care provider, come to expect from patients in pain and/or receiving mind-altering drugs (alcohol being the most common example). Such a patient may, when recovered, exhibit a totally different personality. Even permission to treat is questioned when the patient is under the influence, and bad outcomes may prompt accusations against the provider. An ill but intimidating patient often suppresses the willingness of a provider to do what is best for the patient, especially when confronted with death threats. Also, the contract surgeons were not greatly respected by military officers. Many of the regular army soldiers had served in the Civil War and had developed poor opinions of doctors from that experience.

Pain medications, especially narcotics like opium and its derivatives, are habituating. Thus, over time a patient may need double or quadruple the original dosage to alleviate pain. The same drug taken by mouth will require several times the necessary dosage given by injection. The active drug discussed in the court-martial case, given in grains, is difficult to quantify without knowing the concentration. In addition, alcohol and narcotics taken together are especially toxic.

The court-martial case against Lt. Hamilton C. Peterson related a story of violence and false accusations that Lieutenant Peterson lodged against Dr. Arthur Spohn. When questioned by the judge advocate, Spohn testified that he was in Carrizo, Texas, in the latter part of 1868 and the early part of 1869 and serving as acting assistant surgeon. Major Steinburger had sent an orderly to him saying that Lieutenant Peterson had shot himself at Rancho La Peña.[25]

N. A. Jennings, a Texas Ranger, related a story about Peterson in 1875, saying that Peterson was a good lawyer and expert civil engineer:

> He was the best revolver shot he had ever seen and was always ready to bet anything from a drink of whiskey to a basket of champagne on his marksmanship. Physically, Peterson was a fine looking man. His face was handsome, and his big, fierce, black moustache gave the impression that he was a daredevil of the most pronounced type, shading, as it did, a resolute, well-modeled chin. His appearance did not belie his character.... He was a hard drinker, and very quarrelsome when drinking. Every time he had a dispute with a man he would challenge him to fight a duel.[26]

Peterson's principal occupation at the time Jennings made his acquaintance was challenging men to fight duels. Jennings said sometimes Peterson would get him to write a challenge for him. His challenges were rarely accepted because of his skill and fame as a marksman.[27]

In a summary of the testimonies given during the trial, Spohn said he treated Peterson at Carrizo until the end of January 1869. He played cards with Peterson and decided the late-night card games were hazardous to Peterson's health. He asked for a second opinion and sent for the post surgeon at Laredo, who happened to be his brother, Dr. Henry Spohn. Henry agreed that the late-night activities were injurious to Peterson's health.

Spohn still played cards with him, but one evening at about ten o'clock Spohn proposed that the game end. Spohn and Lieutenant Pope retired, but Peterson and friends continued to play.

In an effort to help Lieutenant Peterson, Spohn told Lieutenant Pope that it was injurious for Lieutenant Peterson to stay up so late and asked him as commanding officer to make them to stop. Lieutenant Pope wanted nothing to do with it and told Spohn he was leaving the post soon and did not want trouble, that Spohn should do it himself. Spohn went into the tent and asked them to stop. Lieutenant Peterson told Spohn he had no right to interfere with him and said, "I want you to remember that I am an officer and have rank. What rank have you, you goddamned puke of an Acting Assistant Surgeon? Were you an officer or an assistant surgeon I might put myself under your treatment and take your advice. You can go to Hell."[28]

Later, when Spohn dressed Peterson's hand, Peterson told him if he interfered with him or what he did, "he would shoot the goddamned shit out of him."[29] Peterson continued the abuse until the whole company and the citizens were talking about it. At the end of January Spohn went to Guerrero, Mexico, to purchase wine, nuts, and raisins. When Lieutenant Peterson found the wine to be Mexican wine, he was furious because it was not strong enough for him. Peterson said he "would as soon drink piss."[30] He said if Spohn left camp without his permission he would blow Spohn's brains out, and he also threatened Spohn with his derringer. Spohn had had enough and told Lieutenant Stiles he demanded protection, that if Peterson was not arrested Spohn wanted a guard when he attended Peterson.

About the first of February, because of smallpox, the camp was forced to move from Carrizo. The move left Spohn with no place to put his trunk in the new camp, so with Peterson's permission he foolishly put the trunk in Peterson's tent. Spohn had $400 in an envelope in the trunk. He had previously asked Mr. Lovell if he could place the money in Mr. Redmond's safe but found out that Redmond was not there. Spohn was suspicious of Lovell and decided not to put the money in the safe with Redmond out of town. The next morning Spohn was gone from the tent about two to three hours, and when he returned his money was gone. Lieutenant Peterson's nurse was suspected because a guard had been on the tent, but even under punishment the nurse denied he took the money. Nothing more was done about it. Peterson continued to verbally abuse Spohn.

On February 2, Spohn and Lieutenant Peterson went to a feast at Guerrero, Mexico. They stayed with Dr. Winslow and visited the monte bank games with Winslow and his family. Spohn, Lieutenant Peterson, and Dr. Winslow all played monte.[31] Spohn, in good faith, lent Peterson money that evening and was never fully paid back.

On February 8, 1869, Lieutenant Peterson was to leave for Ringgold Barracks and Spohn was ordered to accompany him. The morning of their departure, Spohn went to see a man in camp with smallpox before going to Peterson's tent to dress his hand. When Spohn got to Peterson's tent, the patient again abused Spohn, and Spohn announced he would no longer treat him. He put that request in writing to Lieutenant Stiles, and it was granted. Lieutenant Peterson's abuse of Spohn was just one instance of his bad conduct, however.

During the court-martial, Lieutenant Peterson acted in his own defense and cross-examined Spohn. He questioned Spohn about the large quantities of opium and morphine Spohn gave him. Spohn responded that Peterson told him he was in the habit of using morphia, so he gave him a medium dose rather than a small one. Spohn said he usually gave him between three and five grains at night. He told Peterson that was one of the reasons for urging him to go to bed earlier, so that he might go to sleep before the drugs made him wakeful and irritable. Peterson also accused Spohn of losing money and getting angry, as well as frequently gambling at the monte banks. Spohn denied all of the accusations.

Spohn's testimony was straightforward, but some aspects should be clarified, such as his distrust of Lovell. Dr. David D. Lovell was an Englishman who had come to Carrizo in 1864 and was soon known as "Red" because of his red hair. He was well educated, so the local judge, Henry Redmond, made him county clerk and turned over the management of his mercantile business to him. Spohn had heard complaints about Lovell altering the books.

Judge Redmond, born in England, had come to the United States in 1834, landing in Galveston. In 1842, Pres. Sam Houston appointed Henry collector of the port at Port Aransas. Redmond had already settled in Corpus Christi and by 1844 had partnered with William Mann in a wholesale merchandise and brokerage business. He and Mann made trading trips into northern Mexico. By 1859 he had moved to Carrizo, becoming the first Anglo in that erstwhile Native American village. In 1858, with the creation of Zapata County, Henry Redman became the first chief justice of the county, so the rest of his life he was known as Judge Redmond. Judge Redmond first named the county seat Bellville, after the governor (Peter Hansbrough Bell) who had appointed him, but later it was again called Carrizo before being renamed Zapata.[32]

Judge Redmond's son, Henry Redmond Jr., later practiced medicine with Spohn in Corpus Christi. He was a close friend of Spohn and Sarah. This young man, his sister Sarah, and his brother John had been educated in Corpus Christi and lived with the Frederick Belden family. Spohn, after only a short time in Texas, was continuing to make powerful friends along the Rio Grande.[33]

Dr. Charles Winslow, with whom Spohn played monte in Guerrero, was born in Madras, India, in 1839 and educated in England and at Yale and Williams College. He studied medicine at the University of Pennsylvania and was a surgeon in the Civil War. After the war he settled in Guerrero, Mexico.[34]

Lieutenant Peterson was not pleased with the trial being conducted in February 1870, and on February 4 he asked for a delay because he had not been notified until January 22, 1870, of the trial date and thus did not have time to get his witnesses there to testify in his defense. Lieutenant Peterson was accused of a number of violations besides those against Spohn. The charges included conduct unbecoming an officer due to his actions in a billiard game in Brownsville on November 18, 1868, during which he used foul language to Lieutenant Bradford. Peterson was accused of grabbing Bradford by the mustache when Bradford attempted to persuade him to not insult citizens in the room and of then threatening to shoot him. Eight charges were made against him for his conduct against Spohn. In addition, other charges for disobedience of orders, conduct prejudicial to good order and military discipline, and conduct unbecoming an officer and a gentleman were made. These charges related to an incident in Laredo on July 20, 1869, when Peterson was wearing a pistol in the streets of Laredo. He confronted the chief of police, who took Peterson's pistol away, and then Peterson falsely represented to the city marshal of Laredo that an enlisted man of the US Army Cavalry was his servant. Peterson was accused of using abusive language to the chief of police, recorded as "You God damn stinking son of a bitch, what in Hell do you mean by taking a pistol away from my servant[?]"[35]

Peterson was given an additional four days to have his witnesses present. The court reconvened on February 8 and Peterson again asked for a delay.

It was denied. Lieutenant Peterson was convicted on eleven of the twelve charges brought against him, and the sentence was that he be dismissed from the service of the United States. Peterson then appealed to the judge advocate, J. Holt, and on April 4, 1870, Judge Holt agreed that Peterson should have been allowed to call his witnesses, so he dismissed the case. On April 11, 1870, Gen. W. T. Sherman disagreed with the judge advocate and recommended to the secretary of war that Peterson be discharged. Lt. Hamilton C. Peterson was dismissed from the army at Fort McIntosh on April 16, 1870, where he had been held in confinement.[36] Spohn had proven his case.

Chapter 5

Mier, Mexico

1870–1872

S pohn lived in Mier, Mexico, from 1870 to 1872. The town was built on the right bank of the Río del Álamo, three kilometers from where it flows into the Bravo del Norte (Rio Grande). The townsite was eighty meters above sea level on high, rocky terrain. Two rivulets crossed the town and emptied into the Álamo. The climate was semiarid, very hot in the summer, and prone to violent changes in the winter. Formally known as the Villa de Mier, it was settled in 1757, with some of the original settlers being Petra Vela Kenedy's ancestors—Don Lazaro Vela and his wife, María García.[1] Lazaro was granted *porción* number 57 along the Rio Grande, which lies in what is now in Starr County, Texas, and was then under the jurisdiction of Mier. Don Lazaro was Petra's great-grandfather, and Mier is where Petra grew up.[2]

On April 6, 1870, Spohn received a report from the Property Division of the Surgeon General's Office addressed to him at Point Isabel, Texas. His title is listed as acting assistant surgeon. The communication stated that his report and vouchers from the period of June 14, 1869, to December 31, 1869, had been examined and found to be correct.[3] Spohn was stationed there and attending to his quarantine duties.

The next official record of Spohn is another Property Division/Surgeon General's Office report addressed from Mier, Mexico, on December 30, 1871. In this report Spohn states under oath that "Arthur E. Spohn, A. A.

Surgeon U. S. Army[,] being duly sworn and deposed and say, that I have never received formally or informally, any money or property whatever belonging to the Medical Department of the Army of the United States for which I have not, to the best of my ability rendered complete and correct Returns, and that I have not now in my possession any such money or property."[4] Spohn was still in the army at the end of 1871 and in Mier, performing his official quarantine duties for the army. This report may have been paperwork required before leaving the army, because in March 1872 he was nominated for a vice commercial agent position in Mier by Charles Mayer, the US commercial agent in Mier. The nomination letter referred to Spohn as a resident of "this city."[5] Spohn may well have been engaged in private practice while simultaneously serving in the army and decided to resign from the army to continue his private practice. Later he advised a nephew, Henry J. Hamilton, to go to Mexico and make his money as he had.[6]

Mier had been important in the Confederate cotton trade. Because of the Union blockades, the cotton had been transported to Mier and then moved by land or water to Matamoros and on to Europe. Thus, Mier was a way station on King and Kenedy's Confederate "cotton road," so the two men and certainly Petra had many contacts, friends, and relatives in Mier. Judge Henry Redmond also had trade contacts in Mier, so it may have been that these individuals opened doors for Spohn's medical practice during his time there.

Spohn's private practice while he was in Mier is also evidenced by an article he wrote for the *Richmond and Louisville Medical Journal* in November 1876. Spohn described how he first used the concept of a new "bloodless operation." He reported that he was residing in a city of Mexico and was attempting to remove a needle from the thumb of a young lady in April 1870. Spohn wrote, "Having made several unsuccessful attempts, on account of hemorrhage, I wound an ordinary elastic band around the end of the thumb, and rolled it back beyond the site of the needle, noticing that the thumb was completely bloodless, presenting a waxy appearance, which enabled me to remove the needle without difficulty or loss of blood."[7] This successful experience prompted Spohn to perfect this method and eventually led to his invention of the "New Elastic Rubber-Ring Tourniquet."[8]

During Spohn's stay in Mier, the town was at a historic peak of economic health. When the Civil War ended, the so-called Free Zone was established at the frontiers. That status favored local towns with increased economic activity, but the designation also brought in contraband on a large scale.[9] Spohn did not escape experiencing the revolutionary and smuggling activities taking place there because of his service as vice commercial agent, thanks to his nomination to the post in 1872 by Charles Mayer.[10] Spohn later represented the United States two more times in an official capacity.

John Dunlevie had been appointed commercial agent at Mier in December 1869, and the position remained designated "commercial agent" until March 19, 1880, when it became a consular agency under the jurisdiction of the consulate at Matamoros.[11] It was usual for smaller towns to have the commercial agent until they became large enough to support a consulate. The officials reported on the fees received and on trade. Commercial Agent Mayer reported on March 31, 1872, that his report contained the oath of allegiance for A. E. Spohn.[12]

In a dispatch from Nuevo Laredo in April 1872, the local US commercial agent, Thomas Gilgan, described the difficulties he and his fellow agents faced. The revolutionists were in possession of the customs house and other offices controlled by the treasury department of the Republic of Mexico. Duties were being collected under the Mexican tariff of January 31, 1836. With the ports controlled by the revolutionists, flour, coffee, sugar, rice, lard, and all classes of grain for seed were being imported at a duty of 5 percent on the value of these articles at the port of introduction. Trade had increased considerably due to the low rate of duties collected.[13] Gilgan noted that the local merchants controlled very little capital and acted as commission merchants. The United States owned much of the capital, and very few dollars were in circulation.[14]

Revolutionary forces were active along the entire border. In January 1871, Porfirio Díaz formally accepted a nomination to be a candidate for president of Mexico against the incumbent president, Benito Juárez. Díaz promised to respect the constitution, guarantee free elections, and support the sovereignty of the Mexican states. The election results showed no candidate received a majority of the votes: Juárez received 5,838, Díaz earned 3,555, and Sebastián Lerdo de Tejada got 2,874 votes. The National Congress decided the race in October, and Juárez was reelected. Díaz immediately announced his Plan of La Noria, declaring himself to be in rebellion against Juárez. Díaz was unable to gather enough support to overthrow Juárez, so the fighting continued through the spring of 1872.[15]

Six weeks after Spohn became vice commercial agent, Mayer wrote on May 13, 1872, that the revolutionists had entered Mier. Commercial Agent Mayer was writing to the acting secretary of state in Washington and reported that the revolutionary forces had entered the city and were extracting forced loans from the inhabitants in order to pay the rebels and buy supplies. He reported that he had been taken from his office and imprisoned in the guardhouse for several hours and offered release on the condition that he would pay the forced loan. Mayer then indicated that he had little confidence that the Mexican government would be able to help much.[16] A little more than two weeks later, on May 31, 1872, Agent Mayer wrote to inform the Honorable William Hunter, under secretary of state in Washington, that he would be absent from his post of duties for some time and in the meantime A. E. Spohn Esq. would discharge all official duties.[17]

Thus, just two months after taking the oath of office, Spohn, while waiting for his official confirmation as vice commercial agent in Mier, was actually serving in the position of commercial agent. He served in that position until late August, when Charles Mayer returned to duty. On June 22, 1872, Spohn wrote to William Hunter that he acknowledged his receipt of certificate of appointment as vice commercial agent and his official passport. He also stated that he had commenced his official duties. Through the summer, until August 23, Spohn wrote to confirm the receipt of circular reports and submitted quarterly treasury fees collected for services rendered. At the end of the year Mayer filed a report of the fees collected by Spohn. During the period from March 31 to December 31, Spohn collected $227 in fees.[18]

During Spohn's service as commercial agent at Mier, President Juárez died suddenly in office, on July 18. The next day Lerdo de Tejada, president of the Supreme Court of Mexico, was nominated as interim president. He then called for a presidential election in October and offered presidential amnesty to Porfirista rebels. Most of Díaz's supporters accepted the offer, and Díaz finally accepted the defeat of his rebellion in October.[19]

Spohn's obituary states that he was the personal physician to Pres. Porfirio Díaz. There were two times this could have reasonably occurred, but neither could be documented. During Spohn's time in Mier the rebellion was going on. Earlier, Díaz had suffered wounds during a battle in Ixtapa in August 1857. These wounds subsequently led to acute peritonitis and may have led to the need for extended care during his lifetime.[20] Possibly

Spohn treated him in Mier or perhaps it was in 1876, when Díaz was in Brownsville seeking support for another rebellion against the government in his pursuit of the presidency in Mexico.[21]

On February 9, 1873, Agent Mayer wrote to William Hunter in Washington, DC, "Spohn has left this place." Mayer wrote that Spohn was visiting the United States and would be absent for some time. He then requested that the department forward to him all the necessary forms for the oath and official bond so he could nominate another vice commercial agent to serve during his absence.[22]

The entire border remained in a state of conflict, with many violent incidents. Finally, Pres. Ulysses S. Grant authorized the expenditure of $6,000 to send a commission to Texas to investigate the bandit raids and loss of property. The commissioners were Thomas Robb, Richard Savage, and J. J. Mead, known collectively as the Robb Commission. They reached the Rio Grande in July 1872 and took approximately eleven hundred depositions from people living between the Nueces River and the Rio Grande. These residents claimed losses totaling $48,496,235.25. Both Richard King and Mifflin Kenedy were among those deposed. Captain King related how he had been forced to travel with an escort for protection. Despite the escort, he had been ambushed on a trip from Corpus Christi to Brownsville in July 1872 by eight to ten Mexicans. They had fired from twenty-five to thirty shots at his ambulance (coach) and killed a passenger, Franz Specht, who was riding with him. Mifflin Kenedy in his deposition told how Juan Cortina had raided his San Salvador de Tule rancho, located about forty miles from Brownsville. Most of the raids were blamed on Cortina and bandits.[23]

The Mexican government was not about to let these claims go unanswered. In September 1872, the Mexican government created a special commission to investigate the charges levied against it. The Comisión Pesquisidora de la Frontera del Norte received the US Commission's report but came to very different conclusions. They found some of the raids were conducted by Native Americans, former Confederate soldiers, and Mexicans working with Texas ranchers, as well as Mexicans living in Mexico. They thought Texas served as a refuge for Mexican outlaws and that newly arrived Texans wanted wealth and would break the law to get it. They had an opposing view on Cortina's role in the raids. They noted that the Mexican government had reprimanded him but that in some cases he was trying to punish smugglers. Cortina felt he was simply sending raiders into Texas to steal what he termed *ganado de Nanita*, or "Grandmother's cattle."[24] More importantly, the Mexican commissioners asserted that the US government was using Cortina as a scapegoat in order to provide a reason for the United States to invade Mexico and thus increase American ownership of Mexican territory all the way to the Sierra Madre.[25]

Spohn had come to a border region caught up in conflict both in Texas and Mexico in 1868, and it was the same when he left it in 1873. Many problems remained to be worked out between Mexico and the United States. The journey toward peace was not an easy one.

Chapter 6

Corpus Christi, the City by the Sea

1873–1875

W hen Spohn left Mier and the Rio Grande border region, he must have been happy to be away from the continuing conflict there. No doubt he took time to see his brother Henry, at Fort McIntosh in Laredo, to discuss his future plans.

Arthur Spohn had already established himself with an excellent reputation. Only twenty-eight years old, he had experienced the cultures on both sides of the Rio Grande and used his medical skills both in the army and in civilian practice. His Spanish had been perfected, as well as his knowledge of border weather, geography, and transportation. He had made powerful friends along the border and was ready to launch his career. Those powerful connections guided him back to Corpus Christi to establish his practice and his home there.

On February 1, 1873, the *Nueces Valley* newspaper in Corpus Christi printed this notice: "Dr. Spohn of Laredo (Henry) and his brother (Arthur) both prominent Physicians and Surgeons are in town. The latter came recently from Mier, Mexico, where he made an enviable reputation in his practice. We learn he intends locating here, which, if true, we congratulate the people upon the acquisition. Of the former gentleman we simply say that Laredo can't spare him or we should hope to have him locate here also."[1] It did not take Spohn long to make his decision and inform the public. Fourteen days later, on February 15, Spohn inserted his card and the newspaper editorialized, "The experience and excellent reputation of the gentleman in the profession commend him sufficiently to the community."[2]

It was fortunate Spohn was back in Corpus Christi. Only three weeks after his return on February 22, the newspaper reported, "We regret to state that Capt. R. King lies severely ill at his Santa Gertrudis residence."[3] Whatever his illness was, Spohn was there to help him through it. During her husband's illness Henrietta King had her hands full. Mifflin Kenedy had notified her that the Robb Commission was coming to inspect the ranch. This appointed group planned to take testimony about Kenedy's and King's cattle losses to raiders. Mifflin was informed by letter on February 28 of the situation. He knew Henrietta would take care of it.[4]

Meanwhile, Spohn was extremely busy himself. On March 22 the *Nueces Valley* reported that smallpox was epidemic in the area surrounding Corpus Christi. The city had been quarantined, and the mayor received a lot of praise for taking the necessary precautions to prevent the epidemic from spreading. It was reported that doctors were seeing concerned patients by the score and that one doctor had vaccinated more than three hundred persons in three days.[5]

Smallpox had been a dreaded disease for centuries. England had mandated vaccinations in 1835. Symptoms began with a fever and lethargy about two weeks after exposure. Often headache, sore throat, and vomiting were symptoms as well. Then a raised rash appeared and sores often formed inside the mouth, throat, and nose. The fluid-filled pustules appeared and expanded, sometimes joining together and then forming scabs that separated from the skin. About 30 percent of patients died, and many of those who survived were scarred for life. The disease spread by contact with the sores or droplets of fluid from the infected person. Bed linens and clothing could be contaminated, so close living conditions were particularly favorable for the spread of the disease.[6] Edward Jenner had developed the first successful vaccine in 1798. He observed that milkmaids who had previously had cowpox did not later catch smallpox. He inoculated individuals with cowpox to protect them against smallpox.[7] In Spohn's day securing pus from infected patients may have been the method of making the vaccine. The physician would then scratch the surface of the skin of the person being inoculated and rub the infected matter into the scratch. As soon as an outbreak of the disease occurred in an area, everyone wanted to protect themselves and their families. One chance of survival was quarantine. With

Spohn's recognized expertise in this practice, he was no doubt advising the mayor and city officials as well as his patients.

Typical practice of medicine in Spohn's early days was fraught with theories of what makes a person sick and what to do about it. Some American physicians believed in an updated version of the "fourth-century Hippocratic system" in which illness erupted when something upset the flow of the body's "four humors": yellow bile, black bile, phlegm, and blood. Nineteenth-century American physicians had added additional fluids to the ancient quartet. Any "juice" or fluid of the body might lead to sickness. Running noses, sweating, diarrhea, and vomiting were seen as the body's means of restoring balance by getting rid of excess corrupted liquids. Medical practitioners should aid that process, they believed, by regulating and hastening the excretion of the fluids through bleeding, blistering, and purging, and they believed it should be done aggressively.[8] Sir William Osler, arguably the most influential teacher and writer in American medicine during the late 1800s and early 1900s, promoted bleeding for pneumonia in his textbook published in 1892 and retained that advice up to the 1921 edition.[9]

A rival faction of physicians believed sickness was due to abnormalities of the solid parts of the body and that disease involved blood vessels or nerve fibers becoming irritated and inflamed as a result of pathological stimulation. Swelling in the body impeded the flow of liquids, which compromised the body's functions. Cold or noxious air weakened the heart, which led to dangerous accumulation of blood in the vena cava and the liver. Also popular was the miasma theory, which held that diseases were caused by noxious air.[10]

These theories shared some basic beliefs about treating disease. Medicine nearly always involved regulating the patient's intakes and outputs in order to restore bodily harmony: bleeding, diuretics to promote urination, cathartics to accelerate defecation, emetics to induce vomiting, and various dietary regimens. In the early 1800s, most physicians favored these so-called "heroic" measures. Patients ingested substantial quantities of harsh depletives, such as the element antimony, known as tartar emetic, and the element mercury in the form of mercurous oxide, popularly known as calomel. Physicians understood that quinine sulfate alleviated the symptoms of malaria, but they tended to believe that the malarial patient should first undergo a thorough vomit or bloodletting to ready the body for the quinine.[11]

As with most wars, the Civil War was a turning point in medicine, with heroic medicine fading. Surgeon General William Hammond banned calomel and other violent purgatives from the army, a move that proved disquieting to older physicians.[12] Anesthesia was a boon to surgery, but in the aftermath infections were uncontrolled and dangerous vapors, or miasmas, were still thought to be the cause of infections and most diseases.[13] Part of Spohn's genius was always choosing the right medical path to follow as new discoveries were made.

The germ theory that Spohn so completely embraced was not accepted by many American physicians. They perhaps found it hard to recognize that they had been wrong in their diagnoses and practices. Others simply could not concede that they had unknowingly spread infections from their hands, clothes, and instruments. For others, the importance of laboratory research or how something as tiny as a germ could kill a human being was unfathomable.[14] In many ways the germ theory of disease had only a limited impact on American medicine prior to the twentieth century. A painful example is Frank Hamilton, "one of America's finest military surgeons[,] who was brought down to Washington to help treat President James A. Garfield following the assassination attempt in 1881 that eventually took Garfield's life."[15] Hamilton and other attending physicians did not believe in antiseptic methods, so Garfield died of infection caused by the physicians' unwashed fingers and probes, not from the gunshot wound he sustained.

For diagnostic purposes most doctors had modern stethoscopes, and others "gradually adopted thermometers, the sphygmomanometer for measuring blood pressure, the sphy[g]mograph for gauging the pulse, the spirometer for measuring the lungs' vital capacity, chemical urine analyses to detect Bright's disease or gout and the X-ray machine."[16] They could cast and splint fractures and suture wounds, although many still used unsterile methods. They practiced obstetrics, but, again, many used unsterile methods. Physicians in Texas received their training in one of three ways: some in northern US medical schools prior to coming to Texas; some simply under a preceptor or mentor until "sufficiently trained," without formal medical institutional training; and some in Europe, then coming to Texas already highly trained in their fields of medicine.[17]

Common medicines they used were calomel, quinine, blue mass pills, belladonna, ipecac, whiskey, various herbal mixtures, pokeweed, hog's foot oil, castor oil, columbo, asafetida, boneset, squill, and digitalis. Many

In 1873, Spohn opened his practice in Corpus Christi in the Meuly Building on Chaparral Street. The front was distinctively decorated with iron grillwork from New Orleans. In 1866, according to *Corpus Christi Caller-Times* columnist Murphy Givens, Mrs. Meuly kept a lynch mob from hanging a bandit on the grillwork. From the collection of the Corpus Christi Museum of Science and History.

doctors, like Spohn, made up their own remedies based on their experience, and many sold them. Patients expected medicine to have a foul taste or smell, and powders were thought to be superior to tablets. Colored tablets were better than white, and ointments (again, foul-smelling) were often used. For pain, doctors used opium as a tincture, morphine (laudanum), and paregoric. Alcohol was used frequently, and many patients suffered addiction, as Spohn experienced later in his own family.[18]

Potions were developed for treatment, such as the amargosa that Spohn's future brother-in-law, the pharmacist J. L. Putegnat, developed. The *Nueces Valley* on July 26, 1873, stated that amargosa, a new Texas remedy (diarrhea specific) was warranted free of narcotics and minerals and a certain cure for diarrhea, dysentery, cholera, summer complaint, colic, and looseness of the bowels. The ad also said the remedy was sold in Corpus Christi, Galveston, and New Orleans.[19]

In 1873 Spohn opened his medical practice in Corpus Christi in the Meuly Building on Chaparral Street.[20] Corpus Christi was a community of twelve hundred in 1850 and then was decimated by yellow fever in 1854 and again in 1867, reducing the population to seven hundred. When

Spohn began his practice there, the community was still rebuilding, from a medical perspective. The town had lost two doctors early in the epidemics. A Dr. Thomas Kearney and a German doctor from Indianola were the only physicians left to help the remaining residents.[21] In 1871, Dr. T. J. Turpin came to Corpus Christi to practice. He had just graduated from Jefferson College in 1870 and was the grandson of Mary Jefferson Turpin, the sister of Thomas Jefferson. His brother, Dr. P. Butler Turpin, joined him in 1874. That year they ran an ad advertising "Turpin & Turpin, Physicians & Surgeons." The doctors had a third brother, Phillip, who operated a perfumerie and sold oils, paints, and pharmaceuticals.[22] Turpin & Turpin did not last long, and by the end of 1874 Butler Turpin was practicing alone "and giving special attention to diseases of the eye and all chronic diseases."[23]

Spohn settled in Corpus Christi at an ideal time. Despite the fevers and the economic panic of 1873, the town was rapidly growing. Businesses were recovering, and there were seventy-five "places of trade." The amount of goods sold was up to $2.5 million, and exports were about $5 million for the year. Rather than trading through New Orleans, local business operators established direct trade through the regular call of vessels from New York, Boston, Philadelphia, and Louisville, to mention a few. The dredging of the harbor channel to eight feet allowed larger ships to pass, with great benefit to the community. The population had been recorded at four thousand, but it was expected to top five thousand by the end of 1874.[24]

Although Spohn's medical practice kept him busy, he found time to adjust to a social environment new to him. He had not had time or opportunity to cultivate social skills in academic settings at McGill and the University of Michigan, at the hospital on Long Island, or in army life at frontier camps. Corpus Christi, similar to Brownsville, was an international community of diverse ethnic groups. Many individuals were wealthy and had brought their traditions with them. They observed societal rules; for example, formal affairs required the presentation of a card before being admitted. Formal balls with quadrilles, minuets, polkas, waltzes, and schottisches were entered into with vigor. The women in attendance wore elegant and costly gowns.

Music heard around town might have had roots in Ireland, Germany, or Mexico. The African Americans sang spirituals and work songs and played on improvised instruments, from harmonicas to washboards.

Diversions for locals included hunting trips to neighboring ranches, and buggy rides were popular. On Sunday afternoons ladies and gentlemen would promenade together on the Central Wharf. The game of billiards was also popular, for both men and women. Sometimes the large rancho owners would hold multiday gatherings for their friends, offering such amusements as bullfights, horse racing, cockfighting, and target shooting.[25]

In the Meuly-Daimwood Family Papers collection at Texas A&M University–Corpus Christi is a letter from Spohn to "Miss Amelia," believed to be Amelia Meuly, daughter of Conrad Meuly, who had moved to Corpus Christi in 1836 and operated a general store and bakery in the Meuly house. In the letter Arthur requested the pleasure of her company at a picnic that day. He said he would like to leave by twelve o'clock so they could be with the party for dinner. He signed it "Best Wishes, Arthur Spohn."[26] Miss Amelia was about seventeen at the time, and it is not known if she accepted. She never married and lived in the family home until 1941, when she died at the age of eighty-four.[27]

Despite the development of Corpus Christi, violence was never far outside of town. In July 1873, Dr. J. C. Crockett was murdered fifteen miles from Santa Gertrudis. He was stationed with the Ninth Cavalry of the United States near Captain King's rancho to offer protection for the area against bandits and cattle rustlers. After Dr. Crockett had camped for the night, a group of Mexicans passed by on the road. Later they returned, shooting him in the head, side, and arm. Lt. D. H. Floyd, a graduate of West Point, was sent out to investigate.[28]

Captain King and Mifflin Kenedy knew the dangers on the remote ranchlands. Their children were sent out of Texas for their safety as well as to enhance their educational and religious training. The Kings sent their daughters to Henderson Female Institute in Kentucky and their boys to Presbyterian Centre College, also in Kentucky. Petra Kenedy sent her daughter Sarah to Ursuline Academy in New Orleans and her sons to Spring Hill College in Alabama. Both were excellent Catholic schools.[29]

On June 22, 1873, the *Corpus Christi Caller* reported extensively on Mifflin and Petra's ranch, Los Laureles, located about twenty miles out of town. The ranch contained 131,000 acres of grazing land. Kenedy had fenced the pastures with thirty-six miles of heart-pine boards, sawed to uniform length, along with cypress posts and six miles of wire and board. The fence had galvanized wire passing through holes in the posts with winches attached one-fourth mile apart. Mifflin had invented winches that were attached to tighten the wire. The ranch had thirty thousand cattle, five thousand horses (and colts and mules), and two thousand hogs. Each year the ranch branded from ten thousand to twelve thousand calves. The tank had a capacity of twenty-five hundred gallons.[30]

The *Nueces Valley* reported that Captain Kenedy was one of the largest stock owners in the West, and he had enclosed the largest stock pasture in the state. Wealth and power, however, could not protect Petra from a life-threatening condition. By September 1873, Petra Kenedy had developed a large growth in her throat and was dangerously ill. The word spread and by September 18 Capt. William Kelly in Brownsville, who managed their business affairs, wrote Mifflin that he was "exceedingly sorry to hear your almost gloomy anticipation of Mrs. Kenedy's health. I trust her strong constitution will carry her through."[31]

In 1875, Spohn wrote an article about neck tumors and had it published in the *Richmond and Louisville Medical Journal.* He stated that these "deep-seated tumors of the neck are comparatively rare and the source of as much anxiety to the patient as to the surgeon." He described three cases he had seen in 1870. He said that in one of these patients he was forced to remove an advanced tumor that was causing suffocation. He had done so in less than ideal conditions. Scarring from previous surgery had obscured the anatomy, and Spohn had to use assistants without medical training; one of them fainted when Spohn cut an artery, which led to hemorrhaging. The patient was left with partial facial paralysis. He used needle aspiration to treat another patient's neck mass; that patient eventually died without an attempted surgery. Spohn's plea was for early removal of such tumors, when they are small and complications less likely.[32]

Even today this operation would be difficult, but in 1873, with the facilities available then, the outcome Spohn achieved was commendable. Spohn described the third case in detail. Names were never used in these articles, but the location, age, and timing of treatment for the third patient fit Petra's illness perfectly. He wrote, "On the 3rd of September, 1873, I was called to see a lady of about forty-seven living near Corpus Christi, Texas, who had been suffering for many years with a tumor of the neck."[33] Although Spohn had been living in Corpus Christi for less than a year, the Kenedys would have known about him from Richard and Henrietta King.

Spohn noted that when the patient first noticed the tumor, it was giving her little trouble and he prescribed some palliative. However, it increased in size and produced a great deal of irritation near the larynx, causing a dry cough, husky voice, difficulty breathing, and a sense of suffocation. He

Petra Vela Kenedy was Arthur Spohn's mother-in-law. She was a devout Catholic and depended on Arthur's advice and health care. Arthur was called to see her because she had been suffering for many years with a tumor in the neck and her condition had worsened. The tumor is possibly visible in this image.

recommended keeping her under observation for a few weeks, and after visiting her on September 7 he found her condition worse and she was depressed and suffering. Undoubtedly, he was reluctant to attempt removal because of the great risk for uncontrollable hemorrhage (blood transfusions were not an option at this time) and nerve injuries causing paralysis of the lower face. She could also face loss of voice and have difficulty breathing, not to mention disfigurement of a beautiful woman. Nevertheless he advised an operation. Fine suturing was available to the surgeon, but he had to operate with only an oil lamp or sunlight to illuminate the area.

On October 1, 1873, at two in the afternoon, Spohn performed Petra's operation in an hour, assisted by Drs. Combe and Reamey. Dr. Combe was an army physician stationed in Brownsville, and Dr. Reamey may also have been in the army.[34] When the patient was asleep and prepared for surgery, likely in the semi-sitting position typical with use of the surgical chair that was common during this period, Spohn had to extend his original incision from the back of the jawbone, beneath the earlobe, to the collarbone. He also had to partially divide the muscles beside the larynx as well as a portion of the large muscle that attaches just outside the larynx, to have room to bluntly, likely with fingers, dissect the tumor. Initially he had attempted to drain the thick, gelatinous contents with a syringe just prior to the surgery, but that was not successful. However, during manipulation the tumor ruptured, leaking several ounces of this fluid and thus allowing him to see around it. He was better able to see surrounding structures, such as the carotid artery, the jugular veins, small nerves, and the thyroid gland itself next to the larynx. He placed a tie about the thyroid gland and tumor junction. This maneuver separated the structures without causing bleeding. The tumor was fortunately not tethered by vital structures and could be separated, leaving a dry bed of tissue with minimal bleeding. He treated the tissue with a dilute cauterizing and sterilizing solution of phenol (carbolic acid). His description suggests he closed the skin superficially with sterilized horsehair. After surgery the patient suffered infection and pus drainage for "a few weeks," with residual scarring that softened after time. The patient had no residual functional problems. The exact source of the cystic (fluid containing) tumor can only be guessed, but the patient lived another thirteen years and photographed well.[35]

Cystic tumors of the type described are very uncommon and in modern times, where medical care is available, are removed at a much earlier stage and smaller size, as Spohn advised, with fewer blood vessels supplying the offending tissue; no exceptional surgical technique is needed to extirpate such tumors. In Spohn's time only skillful, quick, and accurate clamping and tying of fleetingly visible bleeding tissues, as well as avoiding vital nerves hidden deep in a wound constantly filling with opaque blood— all under poorly lit conditions—would result in the successful removal of such a tumor and a good outcome for the patient. No suction or blood

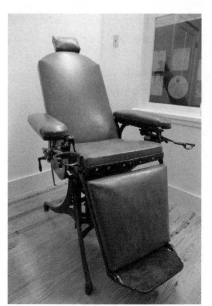

This operating chair is on display in the Corpus Christi Museum of Science and History in the Dr. Arthur Spohn exhibit. It is the type of chair Dr. Spohn would have used to operate on Petra Vela Kenedy's neck tumor in 1873. From the collection of the Corpus Christi Museum of Science and History. Photograph by Michael Carlisle MCC Media.

replacement was available; there was only absorbent cloth to stop the flow of blood if a talented assistant were there to wield it. Fortuitously, Petra Kenedy benefited greatly from Spohn's desperate prior attempts, which had resulted in one death and one facial paralysis.

By September 28, ten days after Petra's operation, Kelly wrote Mifflin, saying, "I trust that by this time, Mrs. Kenedy had passed through the ordeal of the operation and is now enjoying her usual good health." There were more details revealed about Petra's operation in Kelly's letter of October 13 to Joseph Cooper: "Mrs. Kenedy has been dangerously sick. She has had an operation performed on her throat but she is fast recovering."[36]

Petra had loving support from family in Brownsville. Her daughter Luisa, married to Capt. Robert Dalzell, and their party had been to Los Laureles to visit Petra and were returning shortly after October 8.[37] Spohn undoubtedly grew closer to the entire family during Petra's illness, and soon Sarah Kenedy would be returning to Corpus Christi after she completed her education at Ursuline Academy. Only three years later, Spohn had become a member of this close family.

During this time, Mifflin and Petra's children were grown, and after completing their educations they were coming back home and settling down. Thomas was twenty-one and James nineteen. Both were at Los Laureles helping Mifflin run the ranch. John was eighteen and had graduated from Spring Hill and met a young lady. His classmate William Turcotte had introduced him to his sister, Marie Stella, who was in New Orleans, where the family lived. John had decided to go to New Orleans and work for Perkins, Swenson & Co., bankers and cotton commissioners.[38] Sarah was attending Ursuline Academy there and also knew Marie Stella, probably talking to her about her brother John.

Sarah was seventeen when it seems she had become involved with a young man. She was persuaded to end the relationship, and Petra deemed it necessary to bring her daughter home from Ursuline Academy. Evidently Petra's health was good enough for her to make the trip. On July 12, 1874, Captain King wrote to Mifflin Kenedy, saying, "I am now satisfied that your Daughter [Sarah] has come to her sinces [sic] at last—I am very glad of it—for you. She handed me the letter to read and in my opinion it is a good letter and all to the point—she cares nothing for him now. She is cheerful and Mrs. Kenedy stood the trip well."[39]

Also that year, Drs. Arthur Spohn, P. Butler Turpin, and Thomas J. Turpin were appointed to the Board of Medical Examiners of Nueces County by

Sarah Kenedy went through a troubling time in 1874. Petra went to New Orleans to bring Sarah back from school, and on their way from New Orleans they stopped at the King rancho, where Captain King wrote a reassuring letter to Mifflin that his daughter was doing well. Courtesy of CHRISTUS Spohn Health System.

the Nueces County Commissioners Court, on January 31, 1874. Texas had early on begun to regulate medical care. The Texas Medical Board had been established the year after the Battle of the Alamo and the Texas Declaration of Independence. In 1837, Dr. Anson Jones, who was a surgeon in the Texas army during the revolution, wrote the Medical Practice Act, the first such law in Texas. He was one of the few formally trained physicians in Texas at that time. The Congress of the Republic of Texas created the Board of Medical Censors for the purpose of administering examinations and granting medical licenses to physicians in the state. The president of the Republic of Texas, Sam Houston, signed the bill. Unfortunately, shortly after Texas joined the United States in 1845 the board was discontinued. For the next twenty-five years, during the US-Mexico War, the Civil War, and some of the Reconstruction period, medical practitioners were not regulated. In 1873, state legislators passed a law creating a board of examiners in each county and requiring physicians to have a degree from a medical school or a certificate from one of the county boards of medical examiners.[40] Nueces County officials in 1874 were complying with the new state law. Spohn now had an opportunity to help monitor the quality of medical practice in Corpus Christi and the surrounding area.

Spohn received additional support with the arrival of Mother Angelique, who replaced Mother Ignatius as superior for the Sisters of the Incarnate Word in Corpus Christi. The sisters had arrived in 1871 to start a school. By 1874 the successful school was advertising in the *Corpus Christi Weekly Gazette* with the following offerings: "English, French, Spanish and German languages; Mathematics; Drawing and Painting; Plain and Ornamental needlework; Embroidery in gold, Chenille, Silk; Artificial Flowers in Wax and Muslin."[41] With the arrival of Mother Angelique, the sisters sometimes allowed Spohn to perform surgery at the convent and then in turn, they would nurse the patients. They offered this service particularly to patients who lived on the outlying ranches. Even though their primary function was education, the sisters would thus sometimes offer what help they could to provide medical care.[42]

On October 7, 1874, Spohn again had the chance to test his idea of a bloodless operation. He had a young man come to him with a thorn in his knee. Spohn had heard favorable reports on an instrument devised by Professor Friedrich von Esmarch. He had developed a rubber bandage that would both control bleeding and exsanguinate the limb. His invention became known as Esmarch's bandage or tourniquet, still routinely used today.[43] However, in 1872 Richard von Volkmann showed that paralysis could occur from the prolonged use of the tourniquet.[44] Spohn used Esmarch's instrument in the removal of the thorn, but he thought a simpler method might be more successful: using solid and hollow rubber rings that would be sized to fit and roll up to drain limbs of differing sizes. He had not given up on this idea he had first had in 1870, and in 1875 he pursued further development of it. In January 1875, at the meeting of the Southwestern Texas Medical Association, he described his tourniquet before the professional members and continued to vigorously explore the expansion of his idea.

He contacted the well-known firm of Tiemann & Co. of New York to bring his idea into production. George Tiemann had immigrated to New York from Germany in 1826 and opened a cutlery shop in an area with highly skilled craft workers located near New York medical facilities. By 1841 he was manufacturing mainly surgical instruments. When Spohn turned to this company, it was the leading producer of medical instruments in the United States.[45]

A new medical provider, Dr. T. Somerville Burke, arrived in Corpus Christi, and he was "respectfully offering" his professional services to the local residents, as he noted in an advertisement he ran in the *Corpus Christi Gazette* on January 30, 1875. Dr. Burke was born in Mississippi, graduated from the University of Louisiana in 1861, and was elected to membership in the Texas State Medical Association in 1867. By April 1875, only a few months after placing his ad in the local newspaper, Dr. Burke and Dr. A. E.

Spohn had merged their practices, with their office located in Dr. Spohn's residence.[46]

The month after Dr. Burke joined him in practice, Spohn had an unusual medical request. A lynching mob was again having trouble finding anything tall enough from which to hang a bandit. On May 26, 1875, a group of bandits from Mexico had ridden into Nuecestown, twelve miles from Corpus Christi. Along the road, they captured several people and forced them to march on foot to Nuecestown. In town they killed a man, plundered a Mr. Noakes's store, and burned it. A posse from Corpus heard about the bandits and rode hard to catch them. The bandits escaped, but not before they killed a sheepman and left a wounded bandit behind. The posse had the wounded bandit tied up in a cart. On the way to town, they sent for Dr. Spohn. He met the posse and treated the bandit's wound as they continued toward Corpus Christi. Evidently Spohn's medical care was for nothing. As soon as they reached town the posse was joined by other townspeople and again they started looking for a place to hang the bandit. They finally went back to a field and found a gate with the crosspole barely high enough. They put the noose around the bandit's neck and the cart was driven off. The next morning a priest from St. Patrick's Church came out and cut the bandit down.[47]

On June 17, 1875, George Tiemann & Co. wrote to Spohn: "Regarding your new idea of rolling-rubber rings for Esmarch's operation, we think the idea is capital. It must be a remarkably quick process and so simple." They wrote to him again on June 29, 1875: "We just now finished a number of your new tourniquet rings. The idea strikes us as really excellent." On October 15, 1875, they wrote to say, "You must publish them—the sooner the better—before others may catch the idea."[48]

Spohn went on the road to promote his new invention. In August 1875 Spohn traveled home to Ancaster and exhibited his rings at Hamilton, Ontario. It is interesting that he took them first to Canada for display. He may also have gone to take care of family business.

Spohn's mother, Elizabeth, had died on January 24, 1875, at the family residence, Springbank Farm. Her obituary was later printed in the *Christian Guardian*. Rev. Egerton Ryerson wrote the following:

> Mrs. Spaun was the only child of the late Peter and Elizabeth Bowman. For half a century and more devoted and honored members of the Methodist Church and who a few years since, finished, as they had long pur-

sued their course in the joys of God's Salvation. In a letter addressed to
me thirteen years since which I will now give to the public, Mrs. Spaun
recorded the loyalty, patriotism, sufferings, energy and industry of her
parents and grandparents and other founders of our Country. . . . Mrs.
Elizabeth Bowman Spaun was born near the village of Ancaster, the 17th
of March, 1805 and died at the place of her birth the 24th of January,
1875. She received a good public school education, was truly converted
and became a member of the Methodist Church in the fiftieth year of her
age, was married to Mr. Phillip Spaun who survives her, was an affection-
ate wife and mother, a blameless, faithful, active member of the Church
for fifty-seven years—a lover of its institutions, and hospitality itself to its
ministers. She enjoyed the high esteem of her neighbours having "a good
report of those that were without."[49]

A short time before her death she requested the friends present to sing
the hymn "Glory to the Lamb," and when they sang "My sins are washed
away by the blood of the Lamb," she said, "It is enough, my sins are washed
away." Her funeral, as might be expected, was attended by many and held in
the "old Bowman Church."[50]

Elizabeth appears to have been an astute businesswoman. Her will
clearly delineated how she wanted her estate divided, with provisions for
each child. Spohn was no longer an executor nor was Henry, since they had
left Canada. Their brothers Wesley Case and Philip Howard acted as executors along with their brother-in-law Alexander Hamilton. She provided
for her husband and then detailed how the estate would be distributed
upon his death. Spohn had his portion of land changed, but he still inherited under the will.[51]

It must have been good to see his brothers and sisters and to have a visit
with them and his father but also difficult since his mother was no longer
there. He, Catherine, and Alexander engaged in serious conversations about
Texas and the opportunities there for Alexander. In 1875 Alexander was
thirty-nine, Catherine was thirty-eight, and they had three boys. Alexander
had been practicing in Barrie, where he had served as Spohn's preceptor and
mentor. Spohn finally convinced Alexander and Catherine to leave Canada
and join him in Corpus Christi. They became very close, supported each
other, and invested in ranches in Texas. One of these ranches, outside of
Laredo, is still in the family today.

On the way home to Texas in September, Spohn stopped in Danville,
Kentucky, at the Boyle County Medical Society and exhibited his rubber-

ring tourniquets to the society.[52] A couple of weeks later he exhibited his new invention at Charity Hospital in New Orleans, in October 1875. Among those present for the demonstration were Drs. Choppin, Schuppert, and Smythe. These three doctors were accomplished and memorable each in his own way. Dr. A. W. Smythe was the house surgeon at Charity Hospital in New Orleans, which had opened its doors in 1736. It was the second-oldest continuously operating public hospital in the United States, the oldest being Bellevue in New York by one and half months. Dr. Smythe became well known for being the first surgeon to cure a subclavian aneurysm by surgically tying off the innominate, the vertebral, and other arteries, with survival by collateral circulation.[53]

Dr. Moritz Schuppert was a breath of fresh air to all who knew him. He had graduated from the University of Marburg and settled in New Orleans in the 1850s. He kept in touch with German medical literature and had heard of Joseph Lister's astounding method of preventing infection. Lister, in Scotland, using Dr. Pasteur's advances in microbiology, had developed the use of carbolic acid to clean surgical instruments and wounds, thus greatly reducing the incidence of infection. Schuppert was so impressed that he traveled back to Germany to see the technique. When Spohn arrived in New Orleans to demonstrate his tourniquet, Schuppert had returned from Germany brimming with so much enthusiasm that he promptly wrote, "Lister's method was one of the most important improvements in modern surgery." In the face of skepticism and hostilities from colleagues he declared, "I stand today fully committed to it."[54] His endorsement of the method had an effect on Spohn and provided him with eyewitness knowledge of this major surgical innovation.

Dr. Samuel Choppin was a well-respected surgeon and was serving as president of the Louisiana State Board of Health when Spohn arrived. Choppin and Schuppert had established orthopedic institutions taking care of patients with deformities. He was also a colorful character. He and Dr. John Foster became known as the "dueling doctors." Dr. Choppin was called to take care of one of his medical students who had been shot by a law student in a melee at a carnival ball. Dr. Foster was the house surgeon at the time and was assigned to treat the young man. However, Dr. Choppin insisted on treating the student. Foster ordered the nurse to disregard Choppin's prescription for the student. While making rounds, Foster encountered Choppin with the gravely ill student and an argument ensued. It soon became a fistfight by the bedside of the dying student, and it was settled by dueling with shotguns in the yard of the hospital. Thankfully, they both missed and the dispute was over.[55]

Spohn returned home to disturbing news about Mifflin and Petra's son James, who had joined McNelly's Texas Rangers on November 3, 1875. McNelly's men were described as being able to "ride like a Mexican, trail like an Indian, shoot like a Tennessean, and fight like a devil."[56] The legendary Captain McNelly had arrived in the border area after the Nuecestown raid. Sheriff John McClane of Nueces County sent a telegram: "Is Capt. McNelly Coming. We Are In Trouble. Five Ranches Burned By Disguised Men Near La Parra Last Week."[57] The whole area was in turmoil, with violence being produced on both sides. Captain McNelly came with fifty men and immediately dissolved the vigilante committees that were unleashing violence on the Tejanos in the wake of depredations by bandits out of Mexico.

McNelly decided that the only way to stop the violence and the theft of Texas cattle was to strike the camps in Mexico. On November 18, 1875, he rode into the army encampment on the border near Ringgold Barracks and announced he intended to go into Mexico after cattle that had been reported stolen. McNelly arranged with the army that they would aid him if needed. When the news reached Washington, permission was refused for the US Army to enter Mexico. McNelly would not back down and crossed the Rio Grande to attack the strongholds of the Mexican bandits. McNelly refused to return when ordered to do so and told them to "give my compliments to the Secretary of War and tell him the United States troops may go to hell."[58]

Mifflin and Petra received a telegram from Captain King on November 22 through his manager, Reuben Holbein, who was worried about the "unfortunate condition of Captain McNelly. . . . Do not know the problem but they think he could have been betrayed and prepare for the worse." Petra and Mifflin waited, fearing that their son had been killed in the conflict.[59] However, McNelly was successful and managed, with the help of the army firing from the Texas side of the river, to get seventy-five cattle back. James, Spohn's future brother-in-law, was safe.

Spohn had returned home to the chaos that still existed in his world on the South Texas coast. After his recent experiences in Canada and at medical facilities in the United States, he faced the challenge of incorporating his new knowledge into his practice and bringing better medical care to the community.

Chapter 7

A Pivotal Year

1876

I n 1875, when Spohn was thirty years old, his sister Catherine and her husband, Dr. Alexander Hamilton, arrived from Canada to make their home in Texas. Spohn had convinced them to move to Texas and for Alexander to practice with him and help run the Marine Service Hospital. Two of the couple's three boys—Alexander and Henry—remained in Canada to continue schooling until January 1878. Arthur Claud came with his parents, as he was but four years old.[1]

Alexander and Catherine may have been motivated to move by the general financial collapse and economic depression of 1873–79. It affected both the United States and Europe, as well as Canada, since their economies have historically been closely linked. The prospects in Texas at this time must have seemed very good to entice them to leave their roots and transplant themselves to a place with a foreign culture and climate. Their son Henry, known as Harry to the family, related in a letter how he had spent summers at his grandfather's house in Toronto after his family left for Texas. His father, Alexander, had been born in the Teraulay Cottage on Trinity Square in Toronto. Across the street lived Bishop Scudder, and his grandchildren came to visit in the summer, too. One of the bishop's granddaughters, Adelaide, was Harry's sweetheart at the time he finally left for Texas in 1878. He said he came to Texas against his will. She had given him a long lock of her hair as a keepsake, which he kept for years.[2]

Catherine Spohn Hamilton was Arthur Spohn's sister. She came to Texas with her husband, Dr. Alexander Hamilton, in 1875. They had three sons and lived in Corpus Christi, where Alexander practiced medicine with Arthur. After Alexander's death, she moved to Laredo, Texas, where she and her two sons, Henry J. and Arthur Claud, were prominent members of the community. Courtesy of Randolph Slaughter Jr.

The *Corpus Christi Daily Gazette* reported on January 4, 1876, that Dr. Hamilton was in town and that it was certainly hoped he would stay.[3] On January 13 the newspaper reported that Dr. Hamilton and Dr. Spohn had returned from a hunt of several days in which they "met with abundant success."[4] It did not take long for Alexander to run an ad announcing the opening of his practice:

> Dr. Hamilton, recently of Canada, has taken the office of P. B. Turpin, upstairs over E. D. Sidbury & Co., and is now ready to answer all professional calls that may be made upon him. Dr. Hamilton is an old practitioner and has the honor of being the preceptor of our distinguished fellow towns-man, Dr. A. E. Spohn—a fact that is of itself sufficient to establish his reputation as a gentlemen [sic] and a physician. We welcome the Doctor to our City, and trust he may always be pleased with the change of residence he has made.[5]

Dr. Hamilton came to Texas to work at the Aransas Pass Quarantine Station, where he would share duties with Spohn and Dr. Burke, the officer in charge. Alexander also had the added advantage of assuming the patients of Dr. P. B. Turpin. On February 10 Dr. Hamilton announced the opening of his practice in Dr. Turpin's former office, and the next day Dr. Turpin ran an ad announcing he was leaving and recommending Dr. Hamilton to his patients. His ad in the *Daily Gazette* on February 11 said, "Having determined to leave Corpus Christi, I would take this occasion to thank all of my old friends for their patronage, and also to recommend to them Dr. Hamilton, who may be found at my old office. I can also be found there for the next month or so for the purpose of settling up my old accounts."[6] Spohn had arranged an easy transition for his brother-in-law.

An article from the *Daily Gazette* in June explained the physician oversight requirements for a quarantine station: "Officer Burke, from the quarantine station at Aransas Pass, arrived by the steamship on a visit to his family. Dr. Hamilton will leave on the steamship to take his place, in turn he will again be relieved by Dr. Spohn." While this arrangement might not have been in exact accordance with the letter of the law, it nevertheless complied with the spirit thereof, that a "competent physician" be at all times in charge of the station. The condition on which Dr. Burke accepted the appointment stipulated that he should have the privilege of leaving his station if the same was left in charge of a thorough physician, and on no other grounds would he accept the position. He had written to the attorney general for instructions regarding quarantine, and it was his intention to "comply with the law in every particular and conciliate all concerned."[7]

The work of a quarantine officer came with considerable responsibility and tension. The captain of the steamer *Aransas* recorded in his diary in 1878 that his steamer was put in quarantine on August 2, so he hired lighters, which were flat-bottom boats used to load and unload cargo from ships anchored offshore, to begin offloading cargo to Corpus Christi. Dr. Burke was the quarantine officer on duty on this occasion, and he refused to allow the lighters out of quarantine, so they remained anchored near St. Joseph's Island. The steamer moved on to other ports that were not under quarantine. At first the time under quarantine passed quickly for the seamen on board, as each lighter had crew members who could play a musical instrument and thus entertain their fellow detainees. Dr. Burke left the crews and told them to hoist a flag if any crew member had chills and fever. When one of the crew developed symptoms, they were afraid to report it and also afraid not to. Dr. Burke checked and said the sickness was malaria. After twenty-one days the doctor fumigated the hold of each lighter and the boats spent the rest of the time at Shell Bank. When the lighters got to Corpus Christi, they were met by a mob of shotgun-toting men who were not going to let them disembark. After dark the crew slipped away in small boats and were in Corpus Christi for two hours drinking "milkshakes" before the mob found them and forced them back to the boats. Quarantine was a very serious business and meant life or death to the residents.[8]

Alexander and Catherine had been in Corpus Christi only a short time when Alexander's younger brother, William Kent Hamilton, who had been wasting away with consumption (tuberculosis) in Canada, was advised to seek a warmer climate in the southern states as a last resort. The family decided William should join Alexander in Texas. However, William died only a short time after arriving in Corpus Christi, and it must have been difficult for Alexander and Spohn not to be able to help this young man. William's body was shipped back to Toronto. His funeral there was attended by members of the York Pioneers and Odd Fellows, of which he had been a prominent member. William and Alexander's father was one of the most honored members of the York Pioneers and had played a prominent part in establishing the Covenant Lodge of the Independent Order of Odd Fellows.

Alexander Hamilton's father, Alexander Hamilton I, was a member of the York Pioneers in York (now Toronto), Canada. Alexander I, shown here with the York Pioneers, restored the oldest cabin in Toronto in 1890. Courtesy City of Toronto Archives.

Upon his own arrival in Texas, Dr. Alexander Hamilton had been quickly introduced to the perils facing lawmen, and quarantine officers were considered to be law enforcement personnel. Returning from the quarantine station at one point, he heard a sheriff's deputy named Walker had been injured. Walker had left his home a week before to serve an arrest writ. He made the arrest near San Diego and tied the prisoner on a horse. He hired a Mexican to help him bring the prisoner into town. The new guard fell back, however, shot Walker and the prisoner, and rode away. Walker, knowing he was seriously wounded, was able to reach a rancho. A messenger was immediately sent to get a doctor, and Dr. Hamilton was able to reach him by three o'clock in the morning. Walker asked Dr. Hamilton if he was going to die, and Hamilton confirmed that opinion. Walker talked privately with his wife and his relatives and friends. He said several fervent prayers and asked Dr. Hamilton to read him a chapter from St. Paul's letter to the Hebrews. Doctors were often called upon to deliver comfort to both the patients and family, and someone of Alexander's experience was probably of great comfort.[9]

On February 12, 1876, having returned to Corpus from his trip to Canada, Kentucky, and New Orleans, Spohn seized the initiative of organizing medical care locally. He placed an advertisement in the *Daily Gazette* announcing the agreement of a number of physicians in Corpus Christi and other neighboring towns to hold a meeting on March 1 for the purpose of organizing the Medical Association for Western Texas. It invited full participation for every practicing physician holding a diploma from a known college of medicine. This was another attempt to both unify and solidify qualified physicians in the area. Earlier they had formed the Nueces County Board of Health, and now Spohn moved to form the medical society. They reached out to surrounding areas because of the need to combat the threat of yellow fever and other epidemics.[10]

At the organizational meeting they elected their first slate of officers: Dr. Rufus A. Nott from Rockport as president; Dr. A. E. Spohn, vice president; Dr. T. H. Nott from Goliad, corresponding secretary; Dr. T. S. Burke, recording secretary; and Dr. Hamilton, treasurer.[11] Dr. Rufus A. Nott was practicing medicine and also in the drug business with his pharmacist son-in-law, Willie Williamson. His son, Dr. T. H. Nott, was married to Julia Robertson, daughter of J. B. Robertson, who had been a general in the Confederate army. On March 15 there was a published notice for a meeting, called for March 23 at the direction of R. A. Nott and T. S. Burke.

At that meeting they established the by-laws, adopted a constitution, and appointed six delegates to attend the Texas Medical Association meeting in Marshall, Texas, in April 1877.[12]

Spohn was not only busy with the medical society; he was also attracting attention in the social circles of Corpus Christi. One of Spohn's cousins from Canada said she thought he was the handsomest man in Texas.[13] He was on the social scene in a big way. The women of the Catholic congregations produced a comedy show at Market Hall called *Rough Diamond*. The popular comedy was the story of a beautiful, simple-minded young lady, captivated by a city man, and she moves in, pretending to be his wife. A cousin with Yankee wit comes to visit and the fun begins. It is quite possible that Spohn fit the cousin's role perfectly with his "Yankee" background. After the play everyone pitched in and cleared the benches, and the crowd danced until 3:00 a.m. Spohn's many friends gathered to celebrate his thirty-first birthday on April 29, coming to his residence on Mesquite Street and bringing him bouquets of flowers and rich cakes. Later they went to a Mrs. Merriman's home for dancing that lasted several hours. The newspaper reported Spohn "was highly esteemed by his friends, particularly his lady friends."[14]

On May 24, Spohn invited a representative of the *Corpus Christi Caller* to watch a bloodless operation using his rubber rings on a patient bitten by a snake. Dr. Spohn used chloroform for the procedure, which took about fifteen minutes. The newspaper reported, "There were only five drips of blood and loss scarcely perceptible."[15]

He continued to promote his rubber-ring tourniquet invention. Later that year, in August, he read an article in the American edition of the British medical journal *The Lancet* that a surgeon in West Broomwich was reporting as an original idea his "Improved Appliance for Bloodless Operations." Spohn immediately wrote a reply, sending it to the *Richmond and Louisville Medical Journal*, which published it on November 18, to clarify his position of having worked on his invention for six years. Spohn wrote,

> As the subject of elastic-ring tourniquets has been attracting my attention for the past six years, during which time I have made many experiments with the same, I can not, in justice to myself, allow said article to pass unnoticed, as it seems to me impossible that the use of said tourniquet, which has been on exhibition in many of the principal cities of America, been shown and explained in several prominent hospitals and before several medical societies, should not have reached Mr. H. L. Browne; however,

should the use of the elastic rings have been conceived by Mr. Browne independently and without knowledge of their use in America, I can not, of course, take any exception to said article.[16]

Spohn then describes where he has demonstrated his rings and quotes an article he had submitted to the *New York Medical Record* in February that had not been published. He had described in the unpublished article how the larger solid rings were difficult to roll well, especially in situations of considerable obesity. On the advice of his partner, Dr. T. Somerville Burke, he had the larger rings made hollow, which he thought was a decided advantage. Also, this innovation prevented the patient's hairs from rolling around the ring, thus avoiding additional pain. He explained the medical advantages of the rings and said he had applied the instrument many times to his own arm, rendering it perfectly bloodless, and never suffered any injury from it. He recommended it particularly for the treatment of dissecting wounds, animal bites (including snakebites), and contact with any poisonous matter. He took exception to the way the rings were constructed in the *Lancet* article and ended by again referring the reader to his instruments being manufactured by Tiemann & Co. in New York. Spohn was tenacious and determined to defend his work.[17]

Meanwhile, Sarah Kenedy had arrived home from school in July 1875. If Spohn was one of the most eligible and attractive bachelors in Corpus Christi in 1876, Sarah Kenedy was his equal on the ladies' side. She was described as "charming in manner, engaging in conversation, a gifted pianist, and mistress of French, Spanish and English." She was also the only Kenedy daughter and one of the heirs of Mifflin Kenedy's vast fortune.[18] Sarah was now a part of the elite and privileged society of Corpus Christi, with her family's strong social ties and experiences also molding her. It is not known when Sarah and Spohn first started their courtship, but they would have been together in the Corpus Christi social set.

Sarah had been born in Brownsville, Texas, on October 23, 1857, a day both joyous and frightening for her parents. A destructive fire broke out that day near the waterfront. The rumor was that a group of men, sitting on powder kegs and drinking Irish whiskey, had put a candle on one of the kegs, igniting it. The blast was so strong that one man, Henry Miller, was blown through the brick wall of Charles Stillman's counting house but survived. When additional kegs blew up, the fire swept onto Elizabeth Street, where Petra and Mifflin lived. Petra had a house full of children. Her older girls, Luisa, Rosa, Concepción, and Maria Vicenta, helped with Thomas (five), James (three), and Gregorio (eighteen months). Adrián, who was thirteen, probably joined Mifflin and other men who were pumping water from river steamers to fight the fire. The town was filled with screams, bells ringing, and smoke and heat. Businesses were being destroyed and people killed. Petra had to make the difficult decision on what to do to protect her family. Even in her condition she had to remain calm and strong. A midwife probably helped her deliver Sarah. She was able to remain safely in her home and, with her strong faith, calm her family in the face of a crisis.[19]

In 1869 Mifflin and Petra decided to leave Brownsville and settle at their new ranch, Los Laureles, in the Wild Horse Desert. It was located about twenty-two miles south of Corpus Christi and more than one hundred miles from Brownsville. Mifflin had decided to invest his money in cattle and move away from the Rio Grande. The move was very difficult for Petra because her older daughters had married and were living in Brownsville with her grandchildren. The trip back to Brownsville was over nearly impassable roads and thus a hard and arduous journey. The other loss was her church community, such an important part of her life.[20]

However, Petra was important to the running of the ranch. She supervised the domestic staff and saw to food preparation, gardens, slaughtering, repairs, medical problems, and the general welfare of the ranch employees. Eventually she would have five servants to help with the household chores and to prepare food. There was a boatman who hauled materials to the Laguna Madre, which connected to the Gulf of Mexico, where supplies were delivered from Corpus Christi. The ranch employed many vaqueros, called *Kenedeños*, to take care of the cattle and livestock. Many of them were related and very loyal to the ranch. Petra was an unusual and caring woman. She employed a schoolmaster, who worked at the ranch to teach the children of the employees.[21] She also had to make a decision about her younger children's education. She wanted them to continue their Catholic education, so she chose Spring Hill College in Mobile, Alabama, for the boys.[22] As noted earlier, for Sarah she had selected Ursuline Academy in New Orleans.[23]

Sarah was eleven when she traveled to New Orleans to enter Ursuline. The term went from October 1 to July 31. She attended six years, from 1868 to 1874. The students were not only Creole ladies of high standing but also the elite of American society.[24] The school provided a list of references who would vouch for the school when requested by families in-

Sarah Kenedy attended Ursuline Academy in New Orleans because her parents wanted to provide her with the best Catholic education in the South. She went there at the age of eleven. Courtesy of Willacy County Historical Museum, Raymondville, Texas.

terested in sending their daughters to the school. In New Orleans the list included the Catholic archbishop, a US senator, a future chief justice of the Supreme Court of the United States, consuls of the Netherlands and Mexico, and several bank presidents. From Texas it listed Capt. M. Kenedy and Mr. F. Yturria of Brownsville. Mifflin also sent Adrián's daughter, Ana Adrianne, to the school. John Kenedy's future wife, Marie Stella Turcotte, was a graduate of Ursuline.[25]

The school emphasized amiable manners, industry, order, and neatness. Each girl's room was private and supplied with both hot and cold water. They were always under the supervision of the sisters, with twelve vigilant religious women sleeping in the boarders' dormitory at night. The school was open to all religious denominations and the program did not include attempting to change the students' religion, but they were required to attend the exercises of divine worship.[26]

The courses studied were Christian doctrine, French, English grammar, rhetoric, literature, logic, ancient and modern history, geography, astronomy, arithmetic and higher mathematics, bookkeeping, botany, geology, physiology, and chemistry. Daily lessons were given in penmanship, reading, and elocution. Interestingly, Spanish was not listed, but by request of the parents the student could be instructed in Spanish and Latin. Sarah

could have helped teach that class. In order to assure the students' fluency
in the languages, the girls were exposed each day to speaking the language.
French and English both received equal attention, not only in theory but
in practice. During their recreation period the pupils were required to con-
verse in the language of the sister who presided.[27]

The school had a library of more than four thousand volumes, along
with chemical apparatus, telescopes, a large assortment of globes and maps,
and a fine collection of minerals. The musical department was excellent,
with concerts being given from time to time. All students were required to
perform. Certainly Sarah performed, since she graduated as a gifted pianist. The drawing and painting department had a large studio and offered
a wide variety of media in which to work.[28] Sarah also excelled in this

Ursuline Academy
students included
young women of high
standing and the elite
of American society.
The course of study
was superior. Ursuline
Convent Archives
and Museum, New
Orleans.

area. In 1876 she painted a special picture for her "Papa." This painting still hangs in one of the homes at the La Parra ranch in Sarita, Texas.[29] Mifflin and Petra paid for a superior education and training for their daughter. The price for a one-year term with extras added came to approximately $200, equivalent to about $4,500 today. In addition, there were expenses for travel, spending money, and extras provided for Sarah.[30] They wanted her to have the best Catholic education possible.

On the Fourth of July in 1876, the city of Corpus Christi fired a one-hundred-gun salute from the bluff in celebration of the national centennial. Later on there was a parade, as well as a meal for more than one thousand people attending and a toast and grand ball at city hall. The celebration was dampened by a serious accident on the firing of the twelfth round of

The school had a library of more than 4,000 volumes, along with chemical apparatus, telescopes, a large assortment of globes and maps, and a fine collection of minerals. Ursuline Convent Archives and Museum, New Orleans.

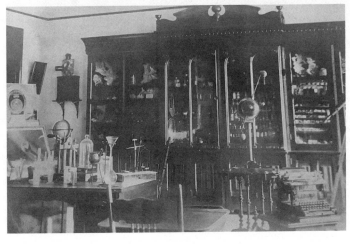

the gun. It misfired, and Stanley Welch, a former district judge, suffered terrible mutilation of his right arm. Drs. Spohn, Burke, and Ansell were called upon to amputate the arm. Dr. Ansell was a military surgeon probably present for the celebration. Spohn described the accident:

> On the 4th of July, while firing the midday centennial salute, Mr. Stanley Welch, Deputy Collector U.S. Customs, District of Corpus Christ, had his right hand and part of the forearm blown away by a discharge of a cannon. He lost considerable blood, which was difficult to control until I placed one of my rings over the arm near the shoulder, when the hemorrhage immediately ceased. The forearm was amputated near the elbow, and although the instrument was not rolled up, but applied as an ordinary tourniquet, there was no hemorrhage during the operation. He made a quick recovery.[31]

This is believed to be a photograph of John William (Willie) Kenedy taken at Louis De Planque's studio in Matamoros about 1867, when William was eight years old. Courtesy Helen Carol Femat Fisher (Egly-Lerma).

Three days later a loss struck Sarah's family from which they would never recover. Petra and Mifflin's son Willie, "the apple of his father's eye," died at the age of seventeen. He had been away at Spring Hill College in Alabama and had developed consumption. He had been sent to New Orleans for treatment before his death, and he was buried there on July 8, 1876, in a vault for which Mifflin paid $100. In 1890 Mifflin moved Willie's body to the Brownsville cemetery, where it was interred next to that of his sister Phebe Ann and his half-brother Adrián.[32]

Amid the bad times, there were good times. Corpus Christi had an active social scene for a small town with a surrounding county population of about five thousand. Sarah Kenedy was nineteen years old and returning from one of the best schools in the South. She was beautiful, with dark, curly hair and her mother's dark eyes. She was also the only daughter of one of the richest men in Texas. She had grown up in Brownsville and been away from home since the age of eleven. Her time in Corpus Christi had been limited to her summer breaks, but she knew many of the young people her age because the social circles were small. At school she had been exposed to daughters of the most prominent families in New Orleans and leading families in the South.[33] She was at home in a world filled with new ideas and had a broad view of the world. To Spohn she must have looked like the perfect choice for a wife, one who would appreciate his desire to travel, learn, and experience life to the fullest.

Spohn and Sarah had quietly decided to join their lives together in marriage. There was no advance publicity or elaborate party to celebrate the engagement. She had lost her brother four months earlier and the family was still in mourning. It was ironic that the "Belle of Corpus Christi" and one of the most eligible bachelors in town were marrying without an elaborate wedding. They married on November 22, 1876, at the Los Laureles ranch. It was a small, intimate gathering. Sarah's brothers James and Tom were probably there, since they had returned home to help Mifflin run the ranch.

The wedding was held at the ranch because Spohn was Episcopalian and Sarah was Catholic. Spohn, like Mifflin, had kept the religion of his youth rather than convert to Catholicism. Petra and Mifflin were already supporting St. Patrick's Catholic Church in Corpus Christi, so Father P. de St. Jean officiated at Spohn and Sarah's ceremony and then listed the marriage in the church's records.[34]

For attendants they chose Sarah's brother John and Rachel Doddridge. John Kenedy was the third son of Petra and Mifflin. He had been born on

April 21, 1856, and was twenty years old. He had graduated from Spring Hill College as a good student, with his main interest being business. He had returned home to work for George F. Evans Wholesale Grocery, Hides and Wool.[35] John was only one year older than Sarah, so they had grown up as close and trusted friends. Through the years Spohn and John would be involved in many business deals, and together they helped manage Sarah's affairs.

Rachel Doddridge was the wife of Perry Doddridge, and they were two of the most prominent members of Corpus Christi society.[36] The Doddridge home on the bluff was one of the social centers of town and a frequent informal gathering place on Thursday evenings, where the young amused themselves and had a feast provided for them. They played games, danced, conversed, and passed happy times. This is where Sarah and Spohn probably advanced their courtship. Since Sarah's parents were living out at Los Laureles, she spent her time at the Doddridge home when she was in town for her visits. Rachel was a good friend and confidant. Since Mifflin had such a strong relationship with Perry, Spohn and Sarah's personal business would have been kept quiet.

Spohn and Sarah made an interesting match. He was twelve years her senior, so Mifflin and Petra considered him mature and accomplished enough to take good care of their only daughter. Spohn had earned their trust by saving Petra in a life-threatening operation. Their good friend Captain King had spotted Spohn's talents immediately and had retained him as his family's physician. At thirty-one Spohn was ready to settle down but would continue to study the latest medical techniques and be in the company of the best physicians in the nation.

After the wedding Sarah and Spohn headed for Europe on their honeymoon.[37] Spohn had obviously been planning not only for the wedding but also for a yearlong sabbatical away from his practice. In October his brother-in-law Dr. Alexander Hamilton had joined the practice along with Dr. Burke. This arrangement allowed Spohn to be gone for a year in New York to do postgraduate work after the honeymoon. All the arrangements were made well in advance, but Spohn and Sarah had kept their plans secret. Spohn was financially successful in his own right, and the marriage into the Kenedy family gave him additional resources to help fund his further medical education. Now he had his bride with him as they ventured off to the excitement of Europe and a year in New York City.

Chapter 8

In New York

1877

Returning from their honeymoon, Spohn and Sarah stopped in New York, where he was to do postgraduate work in 1877. They arrived there soon after Dr. Lewis Stimson, on November 19, 1876, at Presbyterian Hospital, performed the first operation in the United States using the full Listerian antiseptic technique. Dr. Joseph Lister had visited the United States in September 1876 and presented his paper on antiseptic practice before the International Medical Congress in Philadelphia.[1] Spohn quickly adopted Lister's practices and refined them through the years. Unfortunately, "as late as 1882 at the annual meeting of the American Surgical Association, America's most prestigious academic surgical society (then and now), the majority of its members were still anti-Listerism."[2]

When Spohn and Sarah went on their honeymoon in late 1876, the world they saw was very unlike that of Corpus Christi, Texas, and the Wild Horse Desert. Sarah had spent the first eleven years of her life in Brownsville, in a cosmopolitan society but with limited exposure and travel. The next six years of life were spent in school at Ursuline Academy in New Orleans. She was well educated, an artist, and a musician and spoke three languages, but her environmental and cultural exposures were still somewhat limited. Spohn, educated in Canada and the northeastern United States, spoke four languages and had lived and worked in New York City. However, the previous seven years of his life had been spent with the US Army on the dangerous frontier along the Rio Grande and in Corpus Christi.

Sarah Josephine Kenedy and Arthur Edward Spohn were married on November 22, 1876, and went abroad for a honeymoon. They are pictured here in Egypt on one stop of their journey. From the collection of the Corpus Christi Museum of Science and History.

Sarah Josephine Kenedy, one of the heirs to the Mifflin Kenedy cattle kingdom, was known as the belle of Corpus Christi when Arthur Spohn married her. Sarah was described as charming, was a gifted pianist, and could speak French and Spanish as well as English. Courtesy of South Texas Archives, James C. Jernigan Library, Texas A&M University–Kingsville.

Arthur Spohn was one of the most eligible bachelors in Corpus Christi. A cousin described him as "the handsomest man in Texas." Kenedy Family Collection, A1995-045-0008, South Texas Archives, James C. Jernigan Library, Texas A&M University–Kingsville.

Spohn had taken Sarah to southern France and Europe, enriching both their lives. They found Europe in the process of nation-building and revolution. The British queen, Victoria, was proclaimed empress of India; storms were flooding the Dutch coastal area; Britain annexed the Transvaal region in South Africa; and Russia declared war on the Ottoman Empire while Romania declared independence from it.[3] Spohn had decided to take time off from his medical practice in South Texas to further his education in New York City. The newlyweds were back in the United States in early 1877 to allow time for establishing societal connections and finding a place to stay during his postgraduate work. The spring term at the University of the City of New York began March 1.

The University of the City of New York records show that Dr. Spohn graduated from both Bellevue Hospital Medical College and the City of New York School of Medicine in 1877. They also show that he had already received a medical degree from Long Island College Hospital in 1867–68. The acting archivist at the New York University archives interpreted his records to indicate that Spohn took postgraduate courses separately at both Bellevue and UCNY during 1877. That would have been easily accomplished, since both institutions were located at or near Bellevue Hospital, which was a public hospital and hosted students from several medical schools in New York City.[4]

The 1877–78 UCNY *Bulletin* contained a description of the postgraduate course:

> This Course is to consist of Clinical Lectures delivered during the Winter and Spring Sessions by the several professors of the Post-Graduate Faculty, in Bellevue and Charity Hospitals, and in the college. After an attendance of one regular session on these lectures any candidate who is already a graduate of a recognized Medical College can obtain a Diploma Certificate, countersigned by the Chancellor of the University and the Dean of the Faculty of the medical Department, and by four or more professors of the Post-Graduate Course, to the effect that the candidate has passed an examination by them in their respective branches of special medical instruction. The fee for the Diploma Certificate of the Course is thirty dollars.[5]

The Bellevue Hospital Medical College annual catalog for 1876–77 states that the school offers assistance in finding lodging by maintaining a list of boardinghouses near the hospital, easily accessed by streetcars. Rooms could be had for a cost of five to seven dollars a week.[6]

However, it is unlikely that Spohn and Sarah stayed at a boardinghouse. More likely they stayed at the Grand Central Hotel, which opened in 1870 with much fanfare. It was eight stories tall and one of the largest hotels in the United States. The brick-and-marble palace set new standards for comfort and opulence. The hotel had both nightly and resident guests and was located near New York University. Sarah was probably there when, in April 1877, a disgruntled waiter who had been discharged the day before arrived near noon and fired three shots at the headwaiter, wounding him three times. The headwaiter, Mr. Larney, survived and Mr. Peters was arraigned for attempted murder. Certainly it was the talk of the guests for several days. The Spohns had already gone back to Texas by August 4, 1877, when a chambermaid found a guest, Mr. James Grover, dead in his room from an overdose of chloral hydrate.[7]

In 1877 New York City was complex and changing rapidly, as was the United States as a whole. In the West, the Lakota warrior Crazy Horse fought his last battle with the US Cavalry and the Lakota chief Sitting Bull led his band into Canada for safety. Henry Flipper became the first African American to graduate from the US Military Academy at West Point, and the first Easter Egg Roll was held on the White House lawn. In politics, Samuel J. Tilden won the popular vote for president of the United States but fell one vote short of winning the Electoral College vote, so Rutherford B. Hayes was sworn in as president on March 5, 1877. President Hayes appointed the famous abolitionist Frederick Douglass as marshal of Washington, DC. In the South, Reconstruction was ending. On April 24 the last federal occupying troops withdrew from New Orleans and the South.[8]

Spohn and Sarah witnessed firsthand the burgeoning growth of diverse cultural activity in New York, with the founding of such institutions as the Metropolitan Museum of Art, the Metropolitan Opera, and the American Museum of Natural History. In 1877, the first Westminster Kennel Club Dog Show was held at the Westminster Hotel, hence the name it carries to this day. The hotel was a popular spot for a cigar and scotch for New York gentlemen.[9]

Also, the nineteenth century saw people moving into American cities, particularly New York, looking for better lives. They were joined by immigrants leaving behind desperate lives of famine or the financial panic of

1873 that had triggered a depression in both Europe and North America. With the arrival of immigrants, single-family dwellings were increasingly divided into multiple living spaces to accommodate the population. These spaces were cramped, poorly lit, and lacked indoor plumbing. Interior rooms had no ventilation, and perhaps as many as twelve adults slept in a room thirteen feet across.[10] It was a situation begging for epidemics and other calamities.

The financial crisis of 1873 had affected both Spohn's and Sarah's families as it had so many others. They were still feeling the effects upon their return to the United States in 1877. Discontent among New Yorkers and railroad workers across the nation caused great turmoil. The panic had started when the firm of Jay Cooke, heavily invested in railroads, went out of business in 1873. Many other banking firms also closed their doors, and 89 of the 360 railroads in the country went into bankruptcy. Three years later unemployment had risen to 14 percent. By 1877, when Sarah and Spohn arrived in New York City, the depression had led to railroad strikes. Railroad workers were suffering wage cuts and bad working conditions, and their strikes stopped railroad traffic.[11] The average American worker put the blame on government, corporations, and banks. The move to an industrial society had left many workers at the mercy of their employers. This was the political and economic situation when Spohn and Sarah settled into their quarters in New York City.[12]

The Great Railroad Strike began in July 1877. Before it was over, the strike involved more than one hundred thousand railroad workers in fourteen states. More than one hundred were dead, many more injured, thousands jailed, and more than $5 million worth of property destroyed. This strike became a wake-up call across the nation about how workers were treated and the consequences of such treatment.[13] The strike reached Texas, and Mifflin and his friends were watching carefully and probably worried about Spohn and Sarah, as well as about their own investments.

Spohn had come to New York to learn, and he was in exactly the right place. The Bellevue Hospital Medical College had a convenient link to the large Bellevue Hospital facility, thus providing ready access to everything the medical students needed. The hospital received between ten thousand and twelve thousand patients a year. It provided an "Out Door Poor" facility that provided a large amount of material for the clinics it operated, including the Charitable Hospital on Blackwell Island, the Fever Hospital, the Hospital for Epileptics and Paralytics, the Nursery Hospital, and the Insane Asylum. The Anatomical Room in the college was probably the finest in the world, providing every convenience and comfort for the student. This was exactly what Spohn had sought in his advanced studies. The school also provided fresh specimens daily, and students had access to the Autopsy Room, where a large number of coroner's cases were referred for postmortem examinations.[14]

The school provided instruction from some of the top professors in the United States, and many were also well known internationally in their fields. In 1876 William Thompson Lusk, chair of the Department of Obstetrics and Diseases of Women and Children, wrote one of the first papers to come out in support of the germ theory. His paper discussed the cause and prevention of puerperal fever. In 1880 he published "The Prognosis of Cesarean Operations." In 1882 he published *The Science and Art of Midwifery*, and it was translated into many languages, including French, Italian, Spanish, and Arabic. He later served as president of Bellevue Hospital Medical College.[15]

Edward Keyes established the first genitourinary ward in the United States in 1875 at Bellevue, two years before Spohn arrived. Keyes's textbook was the premier urology text in North America. One of his primary interests was the study of treating syphilis by administering small doses of mercury, which became the standard treatment for more than twenty years. He was the primary force in founding the American Association of Genitourinary Surgeons. He was also a pioneer in American dermatology.[16]

Austin Flint, a gifted teacher, was still there. Spohn had studied with him at Long Island College Hospital earlier in his career and had a chance now to be under his tutelage again. Dr. Flint had founded two medical schools, was a professor at six, was well known as a prolific writer, and was an outstanding clinician. Dr. Samuel Gross described Dr. Flint: "He was tall, handsome and of manly form with well-modulated voice of great compass. He is as a lecturer at once clear, distinct, and inspiring. . . . As a diagnostician in diseases of the chest he has few equals."[17] Another description of him from *The Lancet* shows his influence on Arthur Spohn in the characteristics mentioned: "America may well be proud of having produced a man whose indefatigable industry and gift of genius have done so much to advance medicine. One of his characteristics of his mind was its openness to new thoughts and impressions."[18] Spohn was always open to "new thoughts and impressions."

Not only did the college have exceptional physicians, but some of them, like Robert Ogden Doremus, had many diverse talents that they utilized for the public good. Dr. Doremus was a professor of chemistry and physics as well as a medical physician. He led a colorful and productive life. At the New York Medical College in 1850 he equipped the first laboratory in the United States for instructing medical students in analytical chemistry. In 1861 he went to Paris and spent two years developing the use of compressed granulated gunpowder in firearms, and his system was demonstrated before Napoleon III and adopted by the French government. While at Bellevue, Doremus instructed coroners and district attorneys to examine poison cases, and he established a special toxicological laboratory. He probably aided Spohn later in his role with the Marine Hospital Service and with state quarantines. For disinfecting a ship on which passengers had been afflicted with cholera, he used enormous quantities of chlorine gas between decks and in hatches to destroy the germs.[19]

Another young doctor Spohn would have encountered in New York was William Stewart Halsted. Halsted began his internship at Bellevue on October 1, 1876, only one month after Dr. Lister had addressed the International Medical Congress in Philadelphia on the importance of sterile practices in surgery. Most physicians declined to embrace Lister's protocols for antiseptic surgery, but many "were opened-minded enough to allow interns to adopt the new method." Results showed reductions in postoperative infection, but that did not change the minds of many established physicians. In 1880, after Halsted returned from study in Europe, he raised $10,000 for Bellevue to build a special tentlike structure so that he could perform surgery using his antiseptic technique.[20] He also developed the modern hospital bedside chart that traces pulse, temperature, and respiration to track patient vital signs.[21]

Spohn was particularly fortunate to be studying with Halsted, as he later became a famous surgeon. One assessment of Halsted's life reported that "every individual in America who undergoes successful surgery owes William Stewart Halsted a nod and a debt of gratitude. . . . Every well-trained surgeon in the world is trained in the Halsted principles of surgery. Aseptic technique, gentle handling of tissue, scrupulous hemostasis, and tension-free, crush-free, and anatomically proper surgery are the rules." Halsted also used scrub suits and sterile gloves.[22] Spohn shared Halsted's passion for Lister's antiseptic surgery, taking it back to Texas, and he copied as well as he could the sterile outerwear he had used during surgery. They were in the minority of doctors following these protocols during this time in medical history.

In contrast, Dr. Frank Hamilton, who had been one of Spohn's instructors ten years before, had his book on fractures translated into French and German and was recognized throughout the metropolis as one of the most skillful surgeons. He was an expert on military surgery and gunshot wounds. He was also an expert on skin grafts. Despite his accomplishments, "Hamilton examined patients and operated bare-handed without washing or decontaminating his hands after his horseback ride to work."[23]

Spohn had an exceptional opportunity to study with the newfangled "magic lantern" device. Professor Edward Janeway, in pathological anatomy and histology, offered illustrations with the magic lantern, which was an important and attractive feature of his course. Dr. Janeway also was forward-thinking in that he brought pathology specimens to class as well as specimens from postmortem examinations.[24] Dr. Janeway's utilization of medical specimens provided Spohn a unique opportunity for study in the medical field. The combination of facilities, patients, technological inventions, and professors produced a challenging and enriching experience for Spohn as he advanced his own knowledge and skills.

With Spohn engrossed in his studies, Sarah had an opportunity to enjoy New York society and culture. Her father had had a close friendship with Charles Stillman until his death in 1875 and then with his son James, who had acquired his father's business interests in 1872. No doubt James Stillman and his good friend and business partner William Rockefeller Jr. entertained Sarah and Spohn during their stay in New York City. James Stillman's two daughters married William Rockefeller Jr.'s two sons, who were Stillman's friends as well as business partners.[25]

Sarah's education allowed her to fit gracefully into the social scene. She had friends from prominent families throughout the South. Her dress was formal for most occasions and varied for every event. Fashionable ladies wore under their frocks various combinations of underwear, corset, bustle, and petticoats. The material for the dresses was often silk in colors of pearl gray, blue, or pink. The dresses had skirts trimmed with ruffles, lace, and folds of damask. Often they had a low neck, elbow-length sleeves, and embellishments such as silk flowers enhancing the shoulder or neckline.[26]

Sarah and Spohn may have traveled out to the Stillman home at Cornwall-on-Hudson. When Charles Stillman left the Rio Grande region, he moved to this home. His wife, Elizabeth Stillman, had brought their young family there in 1861, before the Civil War, while Charles was making his fortune in Texas. In 1870 Charles and Elizabeth formally bought the house they had been renting and purchased forty-seven adjoining acres. This is the home that Spohn and Sarah would have visited. Later James Stillman built a mansion next to his mother's home. He entertained lavishly. James liked to bring his guests up from New York aboard his yacht and have them arrive at sunset for the charm of a twilight arrival.[27]

Sarah and Spohn had experienced New York during the Gilded Age. By the end of summer of 1877 they were back in Texas, where they spent some time in San Antonio before returning to Corpus Christi, family, and friends. Spohn, now reinforced with the latest and current practices, resumed his special brand of medicine.

Chapter 9

The Wild West

1878–1881

Befefore Spohn left Corpus Christi in 1876, he made a large invest-
ment. He had either prospered enough to purchase land with cash
or he had access to loans. Whatever his source of funds, on April
30, 1876, he purchased a one-third interest in his brother Henry's
Laredo ranch, which was stocked with a large number of sheep.[1] Catherine
Spohn Hamilton and her husband, Dr. Alexander Hamilton, had purchased
a one-third interest in the ranch when they arrived in Texas, and now the
three Canadian siblings were in the sheep business together. They had grown
up on a Canadian farm with cattle and horses, but none of them had been
involved with sheep previously. Spohn purchased his third of the ranch for
$4,755, an amount equal to approximately $105,666 today.[2]

Henry Spohn had left the army in 1875 and practiced medicine in Laredo until 1877, when he moved to the ranch.[3] He chose to raise sheep
and persuaded his brother and sister to join him in the endeavor. Sheep
raising in Texas had begun with the Spanish as early as 1691. Most of the
Spanish colonial–era sheep were *chaurros*, a gaunt breed that was more important for mutton than wool. The sheepherders who cared for them often
had as many as fifteen thousand animals to watch. These herders generally
worked on a contract basis with livestock owners, who would share the
profits. Some owners, however, operated a hierarchical system in which a
mayordomo working for the owner was in charge of the entire operation,
including workers known as *caporales*, *vaqueros*, and *pastores*. In the 1830s

Henry Spohn, Arthur's brother, shown here (*upper right*) in his pith helmet at his Mowry Ranch, was a gracious host and enjoyed socializing with the ranching community. Patients often visited Dr. Henry at dinnertime. Mary Cook Collection, Webb County Heritage Foundation, Laredo, Texas.

and 1840s Anglo settlers came in and introduced the Merino and Rambouillet breeds to Texas. These breeds produced more wool, and after the Civil War there was a boom in sheep ranching, which expanded rapidly in the 1870s and peaked in the 1880s. The Spohn siblings were riding the crest of profitability.[4]

The sheep business had peak labor seasons. The sheep were bred in the fall, and after a 150-day gestation period the lambs would arrive between February and May. During the spring the ranch workers would also shear the sheep, castrate some of the rams, and dock the tails for sanitary and reproductive reasons. Often they would mark the animals for identification purposes.[5]

Another of Spohn's Canadian relatives joined the siblings in Texas in the 1870s. Angus Peter Spohn was the son of Peter Bowman Spohn, the oldest of Henry and Arthur's brothers. Peter, a barrister, had married Ann Stinson, who came from a family of merchants, landowners, and bankers. Peter had died in 1862 at the age of thirty-eight, when Angus was about eight years old. Records show that he had finished school as a barrister, and prior to his immigration to Texas in 1872 Angus was a clerk in a dry goods store, perhaps the one his family owned in downtown Hamilton, Ontario.[6] After moving to Texas to join his relatives, he acquired the nickname "Dump" or "Dumpy."

Shortly after his arrival, Angus went to work for his Uncle Henry at the rancho outside of Laredo. On February 14, 1877, he wrote to his uncle-in-law, Dr. Alexander Hamilton, in Corpus Christi and described life on a sheep rancho in the late 1870s. The letter said that Dr. Henry had gone to Eagle Pass to look at some grazing land they wanted to rent from the railroad. He was to meet the surveyors there. Angus was heading out to go get the sheep and wanted Dr. Hamilton to confirm that the money orders he had written had been executed so he could keep the books straight. He cast doubt on the plans for the Eagle Pass land, saying he didn't think it was going to work. They would have to find some land themselves because they must have more. He ended by asking Hamilton to send his letters to Fort Ewell in care of Captain Jones.[7] Fort Ewell was located on the south bank of the Nueces River at the crossing of the road from San Antonio to Laredo, and it was closer to the rancho than Laredo. The fort had been deserted since 1854, but the post office for Fort Ewell continued to serve the area until 1886.[8]

On March 12, 1877, Angus again wrote from Henry's Buena Vista rancho to Dr. Hamilton to report on the progress of the sheep. Dr. Henry had not taken the land he first looked at in Eagle Pass, having found better land closer to the rancho. He had 997 pregnant ewes, and about 400 of them launched fine lambs. He also reported that Paucho, one of the ranch workers, had left for Corpus Christi, but his horse was completely broken down and he doubted if he would be able to reach Corpus. Paucho received $4.75 from his account and the Doctor (Henry) gave him another $3.00 for the road.[9]

At the end of the agricultural season Angus wrote from the Buena Vista rancho to report to the siblings on their finances. He argued that they would do better to raise fewer, higher-quality sheep rather than more of the lesser-quality breed. The difference in the price was $5 versus $1.50 each. He reported $156.55 in expenses. They sold 1,547 pounds of wool at $0.18, 150 lambs at $1.50, and 80 kids at $0.50 for a profit of $386.91. Their profit was equivalent to approximately $8,000 today.[10]

Arthur Spohn had returned from New York in the latter part of 1877 and resumed his practice with Drs. Hamilton and Burke. On December

5, 1877, Dr. Henry Spohn wrote to Dr. Alexander Hamilton asking him to settle a bill for him. He would send the money to Hamilton by a Mr. Paschal, who would be coming soon.[11] Mr. Paschal was probably Ridge Paschal, a Union man who in 1874 was appointed customs collector for the district of Corpus Christi, which encompassed the Gulf region and 150 miles of the Rio Grande frontier.[12] In the same letter Henry asks if Spohn had "success in operating on Mr. Borden and had he left for San Antonio."[13] Mr. Borden is probably Sidney Gail Borden, a successful businessman who had established the community of Sharpsburg twenty miles from Corpus Christi. In the mercantile business, Borden shipped wool, hides, cotton, and wine out of the port. He also operated a ferry, the main link for travelers heading north. He was elected justice of the peace and, later, county judge.[14]

In January 1878 Dr. Henry wrote to Dr. Hamilton that his nephew Dumpy was a lonely and lovesick young man: "Dumpy leaves here in the morning for your city. He has stuck well at the rancho since he has come up. And I suppose he could not remain any longer without seeing his girl. I suppose a small pause will do him some good for the rancho is a lonely place. Dumpy says he will be here again by the last of this month so you see that he does not spoon around Miss M. Spohn too long." Henry also asked for fifty pounds of rice and one dozen shears. He assured Alexander that every person who had seen his sheep said they looked better than any other sheep in the section. His postscript is revealing, as it indicates the unpaid status of the young relatives' work at the ranch: "Dumpy has not received any money since he has come up."[15]

Dr. Hamilton and Catherine were pleased in January when their younger two sons joined them in Texas after finishing their schooling in Canada. Young Henry Hamilton and his brother Alexander Hamilton Jr. started their journey to Texas in December 1877 and arrived in January 1878. In a letter that Henry Hamilton wrote many years later, in 1942, he stated that he came to Texas against his will but that his mother was glad to have all of her children with her again.[16]

Spohn was very fortunate that his brother Henry was not killed when a band of raiders crossed the Rio Grande at Apache Hill, north of Laredo, and began a wave of attacks that started on April 14, 1878. The raiders, who included Kickapoos, Lipans, Seminoles, Mexicans, and one white man, were in Texas for six days and left eighteen known dead and five wounded.[17] They were after horses and other things, including, oddly enough, socks. Their first victim was Jorge Garcia. They stole his horse, saddle, goatskin leggings, and a drove of his saddle horses. Their second stop was Henry Spohn's ranch, where they stole thirty horses and were thus able to mount all their party.[18] Henry later testified before Commissioner Joseph Fitzsimmons on May 25, 1878, about his experiences during the raid. On April 16 he was superintending the sheep shearers at the ranch when at about three o'clock in the afternoon Felipe Villereal [sic] reported that raiders were in the area and stealing horses. Henry said his horses were about twelve miles away, and he sent two men to drive the horses and dispatched a party of six armed men to find the raiders. A man then came from an adjoining rancho and said that a man was lying at his house badly wounded by the raiders. Henry left for the house and found the man with two pistol balls through his body and an arrow wound through his abdomen. He extracted the pistol ball from his breast and dressed his wounds. The man told Henry the raiders were Mexicans who spoke good Spanish, as well as Native Americans. The man who had shot him demanded the victim's socks, and when he refused to give them up they ordered him to run to his rancho and shot him as he ran. He said he fainted, and when he awoke he found an arrow shaft protruding from his abdomen, and he broke it off and extracted the head.[19]

Henry returned to the rancho to find that his party of six men had returned. He then raised another party, this one of twelve to fifteen men, and sent them out, but they lost the trail in the dark. In the morning he sent out another party, and they trailed the raiders to Fort Ewell and found they had turned down country from there. From the information he gathered, Henry figured there were about thirty or forty of them.[20]

Not only did these men kill ultimately eighteen people, but they did so in a terrible manner. At a sheep ranch owned by William Steele the raiders scalped and mutilated Steele's two stepsons and his brother. The boys were eight and twelve. Jane Steele climbed onto the roof and watched helplessly as her brother-in-law and her two sons were murdered. She gathered her other three children, the youngest only nine months, and crawled through the grass to the river. She then put them on a branch and pushed them across the river and hid herself in the brush until the raiders left. At another ranch the raiders killed a shepherd and his wife, tying their bodies over a horse; their bodies were never found. At Richard Jordan's sheep ranch they killed the oldest son. Searchers found him with three bullet holes and an arrow in him, his boots cut open and his socks taken. Frank Gravis, a sheep rancher, gathered a posse, including the sheriff of Nueces County, and trailed the raiders to the Rio Grande south of Laredo. The raiders had made rafts of dry wood to float their stolen goods across the river and also drove about two hundred horses with them as they escaped.[21]

Perhaps tiring of the intermittent loneliness and terror, Angus Spohn at some point left the ranch to work at a general merchandising store in Encinal, Texas, a town that began thanks to Henry Spohn's foresight. Henry had originally established a town on his land in La Salle County and named it Ancaster, for his home in Canada.[22] Knowing full well that a railroad would spur the growth of a community, he donated some land and persuaded a railroad company to lay tracks near his town. In the early 1880s tracks were placed about a mile and a half from Ancaster, and the new community became known as Encinal. The railroad officials reportedly named the town after the Spanish word for oak grove.[23] Angus was working at the store in Encinal when he married his wife, Juana Estrada.[24]

By 1887, Angus had been appointed a mounted inspector in the US Customs Service and assigned to Carrizo, which became Zapata, in Zapata

Angus Peter Spohn (bottom right), shown here when he was an official of Zapata County. He was Arthur Spohn's nephew and served as county judge for twenty-four years. He was referred to as the "King of Zapata."

County. He prospered there, and in 1893 he was appointed superintendent of schools. Four years later, following the death of Judge Jose A. Navarro, he was appointed both judge as well as ex-officio county superintendent, holding those positions for twenty-four years, until his death in 1921. He was a strong Republican who wielded considerable political power in the county. There was a saying that one could never forecast how Zapata County would vote; only Judge Spohn and his political associates knew. He was referred to as the "King of Zapata[,] and as County Judge he ruled supreme."[25]

In 1899 there was a challenge to Angus's imperial position when Dr. A. D. McCabe arrived in town. At first Angus was glad to have the doctor in town; he appointed him county physician. The friendship ended when Dr. McCabe disagreed with Judge Spohn on a political matter and denounced his political machine. Since Angus was absolute ruler in the county and allowed no one to challenge his views, he fired Dr. McCabe, who then began to organize a new political operation. In 1902, he signed up to run for county judge against Angus. The race looked close until Angus sent one of his lieutenants, Mercurio Martinez of San Ygnacio, out to round up votes, and he delivered fifty votes for Spohn's ticket on Election Day, thus assuring victory.[26]

Dr. McCabe now had a burning hatred for Angus, and he vowed he would never stop fighting until he landed Angus in the state penitentiary in Huntsville. Dr. McCabe continued to inflame the situation by carrying a .45 six-shooter in defiance of the law. As time went on, McCabe continued to threaten Angus, and Judge Spohn simply listened. Angus had many powerful friends who would do anything to protect him and his regime. The matter came to an end one night in 1903, when Dr. McCabe was mysteriously shot to death. He kept a gun under his pillow and was found dead, kneeling by his bed with his hand on his pistol. It appeared he had been called to the door and shot but had managed to get to the bedroom and his gun but to no avail. The assassin was never found, and Dr. McCabe was buried in an unmarked grave in the Zapata cemetery. Angus continued to be viewed as the Honorable A. P. Spohn and the undisputed champion of the Republican Party throughout southwestern Texas. Zapata County never failed to vote Republican, although the state was firmly in control of the Democratic Party at the time.[27] From his start in an unassuming, unpaid position on his uncle's ranch, he had managed to become one of the most important men in South Texas history.

Another Spohn nephew was destined to spend time at the ranch with Uncle Henry. Henry J. Hamilton, Alexander and Catherine's son, said in a letter written in 1942 that he arrived in Corpus Christi in January 1878, his health having been too delicate for him to attend school. Uncle Arthur, Uncle Henry, and his father thought he was in the first stage of tuberculosis. He was sent to the Spohn ranch with Uncle Henry to rough it. He remained there for six years, until 1884, working on the ranch. Every year he went to Corpus Christi with the wool clip, or harvest. Fortunately, the ranch had an *Encyclopaedia Britannica*, and that is how he obtained his education. He had had only a sixth- or seventh-grade education when he left Canada. In a familiar story, he tended the sheep for his mother and uncles and received no salary. The only things he received were his overalls and board. He, too, made an excellent life for himself, even becoming a Special Texas Ranger while on the ranch and capturing at least one murderer. But

Sarah as a young woman, probably in the summer of 1878 when Sarah and Arthur Spohn went to Canada to attend his brother Philip Howard Spohn's wedding. Courtesy of Barbara Chipman, B.A. Hons.

his more usual activities were working in a store as a bookkeeper and in the post office at Encinal, where Uncle Henry, who was the postmaster, let him keep the fees since he did most of the work. He also received the fees from their agency of the Texas Express Company. With these privileges, he was able to accumulate a little money. He invested in buying and selling horses, of which he was a good judge. He bought both wild and tame horses, shipping them by the carload to sell in San Antonio. He sold them at more than 50 percent profit and soon had $1,500 in hand. Henry Hamilton then decided it was time for him to study medicine. He already had experience helping Uncle Henry attend to neighbors and people on the ranch. He had also read Uncle Henry's medical books and studied his patient cases. In 1883, he went to Corpus Christi to study with Uncle Arthur.[28]

Sometime in the summer of 1878, Spohn and Sarah were off again, this time to Canada. Spohn's brother Philip Howard was getting married, and Spohn wanted to be there and to see his family. Philip Howard married Editha Sarah Thompson on July 24, 1878. The wedding was held in the Parish of All Saints in the village of Penetanguishene. The petite bride was lovely in a white ruffled gown with long sleeves and mid-length veil. The dress had a long train made of the same ruffles. She wore short white gloves with her long-sleeve gown. A garland of flowers was attached to the front of the gown and more flowers adorned her hair.[29]

Dr. Philip Howard Spohn was Arthur's older brother. He served in the Canadian government as a Reeve (elected official) of the town of Penetanguishene. He and Arthur remained close, and his son Douglas was sent to Texas to help out his uncle in his medical practice. Courtesy of Beth Dubeau.

Dr. Philip Spohn had a well-respected position in the community and was serving as the physician and superintendent of a reformatory for boys. Editha's family members were, like the Spohns, United Empire Loyalists. They had settled in New Brunswick following the events of 1776 and had a long history of involvement with the British military. The family was already in the Penetanguishene area by about 1830, and they were operating a trading post, trading with the native people, and involved in politics in the area. They also supplied the local military establishment.[30]

Spohn was back in Texas by August 28, 1878. Dr. Henry Spohn continued to run the sheep ranch, and it was hard work. In a letter Henry wrote on August 28 to Dr. Hamilton he expressed his frustration at his two partners, Alexander and Arthur. He told both of them he had to be in San Antonio on September 5 or 6 and they must come to help him decide what kind of sheep to buy. He could not understand why they didn't have any

Editha Sarah Thompson married Philip Howard Spohn on July 24, 1878, in Penetanguishene. The petite bride was lovely in a white ruffled gown with a garland of flowers attached to the front of her gown and another in her hair. Courtesy of Beth Dubeau.

time to help him. He also said that Kate (Catherine) wanted to come back to Laredo with him.[31]

Spohn now had a number of Canadian relatives in Texas—a brother, a sister, brother-in-law, and four nephews. Along with his family, he also had Sarah's family. Petra's children by Luis Vidal were raised in Mifflin and Petra's household as full sisters and brothers. They were all close and remained so through the years. Petra's older girls (Luisa, Rosa, Maria Vicenta, and Concepción) all married well and lived successful lives in Brownsville and Laredo. Her younger children with Mifflin were different in character. Tom, the oldest, was rather like his brother James, as well as Petra's son Adrián Vidal. Tom liked the good life and did not particularly enjoy working. James, his younger brother, was also good looking and lived on the wild side. John, on the other hand, was studious, business-minded, and serious. He was most like Mifflin. The youngest son, Willie, had been a warm and loving young man before his early death. Sarah was particularly close to her half-sisters Rosa and Maria Vicenta throughout her life.

Although Spohn knew well by now what life was like in South Texas, where violence was common, he must have been taken aback to find the Wild West was also to be found in his in-laws' family. It began simply enough in 1878, with John and James trailing Los Laureles cattle to the

James "Spike" Kenedy killed Dora Hand in Dodge City and was wounded by the posse of Sheriff Bat Masterson, Deputy Sheriff William Tilghman, Marshal Charley Bassett, and Assistant Marshal Wyatt Earp.

Kansas railhead, fattening them there, and then selling the cattle and shipping them east at a big profit. John the businessman had no trouble, but James the "hot head" became involved in an epic western episode.

James stayed in Kansas to winter the cattle and fatten them up for sale. On August 17, 1878, James had an altercation with Jim Kelly, who was the mayor of Dodge City and the owner of the Alhambra saloon, over an accusation that a dealer was manipulating cards. James was thrown out of the saloon and wanted revenge. He went to Kelly's house and fired one shot into it, intending to kill him, but Kelly was not at home. He had lent his home to Dora Hand, a saloon singer and one of the most famous women in the West. The bullet found Dora instead, killing her.

A posse made up of men who became legends of the Wild West— Sheriff Bat Masterson of Ford County, Deputy Sheriff William Tilghman, Marshal Charley Bassett, and Assistant Marshal Wyatt Earp—rode after James and shot him at Wagon Spring on the Cimarron River. He was taken to jail, where surgery on his wound was performed in his cell. Mifflin came to Dodge City with a great deal of money to see about his son. A week later James's case was dismissed for lack of evidence. Wyatt Earp and Bat Masterson had few resources before the incident, but within a year both men appeared to have come into some funds; one can easily assume that those funds came from Mifflin Kenedy paying them to drop the charges against James. Meanwhile, James developed an infection in his shoulder and the doctors decided to operate. They found that his left humerus (upper arm bone) had been badly shattered. They took the humerus out of the socket and cut off five inches. He hovered between life and death for ten hours with Mifflin beside his bed. They saved the arm, but James suffered ill effects the rest of his life.[32] The incident in Dodge City brought great distress to the entire family.

During this time Spohn officially made the decision to become an American citizen. On November 4, 1878, he swore before District County Clerk Patrick McDonough that he renounced all allegiance to Queen Victoria of England of whom he was a subject and became a citizen of the United States of America. Spohn had decided to make Texas his permanent home.[33]

Spohn spent a large part of his life serving the public as a member of the US Marine Hospital Service, the first line of defense against epidemic diseases. Created in 1798 under Pres. John Adams, the service was organized to take care of ill and disabled merchant seamen, Coast Guard members, and other government employees, with merchant seamen paying twenty cents a month to support the service.[34]

Following the Civil War and a public outcry, an investigation showed the hospital funds to be inadequate and the Marine Hospital Service completely unorganized. In 1871, a Union army surgeon, Dr. John N. Woodworth, reorganized the Marine Service and placed it under a "Supervising Surgeon General," the forerunner of the US Surgeon General of today. This led to the development of the Public Health Service.[35] This was the group that Drs. Spohn, Hamilton, and Burke were operating under while supervising the Shell Bank quarantine station.

In an address to the Sixteenth Annual Meeting of the American Public Health Association meeting in 1888, Robert Rutherford, the state health officer, described the history of quarantine in Texas from 1878 to 1888. Texas first had an organized quarantine effort in 1873, but the stations were constantly under assault by storms. In 1875 a terrific cyclone swept Dr. George Peete, from the Galveston Island station, out to sea.[36] The first test of the Texas system was in 1878, when New Orleans had a yellow fever epidemic and implemented a quarantine that worked well but needed expansion. In 1879, Texas governor O. M. Roberts appropriated $12,500 to construct five stations along the border, including one at Aransas Pass, where Dr. T. S. Burke served and Dr. Spohn and Dr. Hamilton provided relief. When the stations opened on May 1, 1879, one concern was the cattle shipments coming from Havana. Those ships were fumigated by spraying sulfurous gas in the cargo holds and chlorine gas in the cabins. The station charged fifteen dollars for the fumigation. The coastal service had one steam tug, one schooner, two sloops, and twelve small sailboats and boarding boats at their disposal.[37]

An annual report written by Sanitary Inspector Jno. H. Pope on August 2, 1879, from Corpus Christi, described the activities of the Shell Bank station, where Spohn was involved in quarantine work. The station was on an island twenty-three miles northeast of Corpus Christi, along the channel that was the only approach to Rockport. The station consisted of one house used by the quarantine officers, as well as a small outbuilding that the boatman used. The nearest neighbors were on Hog Island, two miles away. There was no hospital, and twenty-five miles of the island could be used for quarantine. All vessels from countries south of latitude 25°N were to be quarantined. The diseases quarantined were yellow fever, smallpox, cholera, plague, and typhus fever. Pope forwarded a record from the station in 1878 indicating there were eighteen vessels stopped from June 27 to November 1. All the vessels were inspected and eleven were fumigated and detained from two hours to seventeen days, depending on the condition of the ship. The ships came mainly from Texas and Louisiana ports. They carried general merchandise, lumber, shingles, and fruit. There was one international ship, from Jamaica, and it carried bone dust.[38]

This station had never had an instance of disease spreading from ships it inspected. All cargo had been fumigated on board or on lighters but not landed on shore. If there was sickness on board, the quarantine physician would lend assistance. Bills for these services were sent to the collector of customs, but they were never paid. If the quarantine physician deemed a vessel not properly clean, the vessel was thoroughly washed with salt water, then with carbolized water, and then fumigated with chlorine gas. The expenses of the station were paid by the quarantine physician and then supposedly reimbursed, which in the case of Shell Bank had not occurred. The physicians' salary was ten dollars per day, paid by the state. The physician had to furnish his own boat and pay his boatman fifty dollars a month. The inspector stated that there was no quarantine guard at the station, but there did need to be provisions for sick and well passengers. He stated that tents could be used and they would need accommodations for twelve passengers.[39]

The inspector also went into Corpus Christi and addressed the city council, whose members were responsive to his suggestions and passed an ordinance adopting the quarantine regulations of the National Board of Health. They declared quarantines against New Orleans and Morgan City and indicated a strong desire to place one against Indianola unless quarantines were put in place on the cities where yellow fever had been discovered. Inspector Pope told the council that although he knew they were trying to improve their sanitary conditions, parts of the town were in bad condition. In the lower areas of town, filth of every description was on the streets. Drought and a strong sea breeze had helped, but the areas were likely sources of fevers that could affect people.[40]

Spohn and the other two quarantine doctors had a lonely, hot, and exhausting time during their Shell Bank station rotation. The constant stream of vessels arriving and being detained and fumigated, the sicknesses treated, the fierce weather, and the exposure to disease were exacting a toll. The wind blew constantly, sand was everywhere, and there was little or no vegetation, and no family or friends. The conditions for the crews

The 1880 Census listed Arthur and Sarah Spohn as residing on unsurfaced Mesquite Street. He was thirty-four, while she was twenty-one. They had one domestic servant, Eugenia Hernandez. Photograph courtesy of Barbara Chipman, B.A. Hons.

and passengers were equally difficult. Vessels with crew and cargo could be held up for weeks at a time while cargo rotted or supplies sat undelivered, depending on inspections by the quarantine officers. They were the gatekeepers attempting to keep the coastal cities, and ultimately the entire state of Texas, safe from the fevers.

Meanwhile, Spohn's medical practice in Corpus Christi was growing. The 1880 Census listed Arthur and Sarah living on unsurfaced Mesquite Street. He was thirty-four, and she was twenty-one. They had one domestic servant, named Eugenia Hernandez.[41] Drs. Spohn, Burke, and Hamilton had expanded their practice to include a small hospital. The county and city were paying the rent on the building, entitling them to a certain number of patients free of charge. At the same time, Spohn had been appointed the temporary city physician.

Spohn was busy serving his time at the quarantine station and at the sheep ranch and taking care of his medical practice. On July 25, 1880, a local newspaper reported that Dr. Spohn was at the Shell Bank Quarantine Station and Dr. Hamilton was relieving him.[42] On September 22 he was superintending the flocks at the ranch when a heavy storm hit, one of the heaviest rainstorms ever seen, with both heavy thunder and lightning.[43] On November 21, 1880, the newspaper ran an ad stating that "SPOHN, BURKE & HAMILTON, physicians and surgeons had their offices over the R. H. Berry drug store located on Market Square."[44] On December 5 the newspaper reported that Dr. Spohn had left for New Orleans to attend a convention where he would report on the diseases in his quarantine section.[45] Spohn was a busy man.

Around this time Sarah received the good news that her father had decided to move to Corpus Christi and that for $25,000 he had purchased the homestead of M. S. Culver, located on the bluff. According to a newspaper report, it was one of the few remaining desirable building sites in the city. The newspaper interpreted Mifflin Kenedy's move as an endorsement of the future of Corpus Christi.[46] For Sarah, it meant her parents would be nearby and Arthur could treat Petra when needed.

Meanwhile, the community was caught up in the railroad fever that would define the future of the city. Mifflin and his friends Uriah Lott and Richard King made a railroad from Corpus Christi to Laredo a reality after vigorous negotiations and New York financial backing from their friend James Stillman and associates. They also developed the wharf area and harbor to increase the business they could handle from goods brought in from Mexico by rail.[47]

Other changes in the works were new office locations for the physicians in town. Dr. Turpin decided to move to Laredo. Dr. Turner settled into his new offices on Chaparral Street in Corpus Christi.[48] Spohn and his group moved their offices above Dr. DeRyee and Westervelt's store.[49]

Spohn was very busy in the month of April. On April 20 one of the most prominent citizens in South Texas had been shot by accident. James Downing had fought in the Union army and been captured at Petersburg, and he had then suffered the hardships of prison life. After the war he served in the military as a brevetted major and retired to live in Corpus Christi, where he married Mary Blucher and served as mayor pro tem and city marshal. He had joined the service of the US government as deputy collector of customs at Carrizo when the accident happened. A pistol discharged, and his leg was shattered below the knee. Dr. Spohn was summoned, and he traveled more than 150 miles to reach the patient. When he arrived, he found Downing under the influence of chloroform, and it seemed that amputation was necessary. Spohn immediately proceeded to perform the operation. After the effects of the anesthesia wore off, Downing was overcome by his emotions, which was uncommon for him.[50] He went on to recover and live another ten years.

Back in Corpus Christi four days later, on April 24, Spohn was again involved in an intricate operation. Edward Noessel had been bitten by a rattlesnake and brought to Spohn, who grafted living flesh onto his leg wound. Edward's little brother had submitted willingly to the sacrifice of donating his skin for the operation. The newspaper reported that the operation had proven a perfect success and new flesh was forming rapidly.[51]

Spohn probably missed the biggest party held to date in Corpus Christi on April 20, 1881, because he was taking care of James Downing in Carrizo. That night the citizens of Corpus Christi expressed their gratitude to the donors, associates, stockholders, and directors of the Corpus Christi, San Diego and Rio Grande Railroad.[52] They were able to sell the railroad to Gen. William Palmer, and Kenedy, King, and Lott thus realized a profit of $481,174, an amount equal to about $11 million today.[53] General Palmer hosted a gala and a local newspaper announced that "fried oysters were in abundance and the affair closed amid good cheer and the music of champagne corks."[54]

Spohn did not miss the next big party, celebrating the completion of the railroad, held on September 27, 1881. The event had been postponed from an earlier date because of Pres. James Garfield's death on September 19. There were 150 invitations sent out for the train trip from Corpus Christi to Laredo and the return trip the next day. The invitations were greatly sought after, and the guests included bishops, merchants, bankers, doctors, lawyers, judges, scientists, preachers, deacons, and vestrymen. One of the guests on the train was a young lawyer named Robert Kleberg who had recently moved to Corpus Christi and who would play an important role in both the Kenedy and the King families. During the rail excursion, he wrote a poem about the trip that included some of the following information. The train was loaded with enough supplies to make the trip comfortable. The day was hot, and some of the travelers decided to make a barrelful of cold punch for the trip, to ease the heat. The "Roman Punch" was made from pineapple, lemon, and other fruit juices. When the people making the punch went off to visit guests on some of the other train cars, someone poured three gallons of Rosebud whiskey (bourbon) and twelve quarts of Champagne into the punch and everyone thus had a very happy trip. Also available were two thousand cigars, forty baskets of Champagne, and other types of liquor as well. The Corpus Quartet provided music, with Spohn playing drums.[55] Spohn had a musical heritage going back to his Canadian ancestors, among whom was the fife player Abraham Bowman, and his living cousins included concert pianists and violinists who were described as "world class" by the media of their day.[56]

Chapter 10

Medical and Family Drama

1882–1884

In 1882 a yellow fever epidemic broke out along the Texas-Mexico border, and the State of Texas turned to the Marine Hospital Service for aid. Spohn was chosen to take charge, and he received a telegram from the US Treasury secretary telling him to "spare no expense."[1] This assignment came as Arthur and Sarah were juggling many demands on them during their first years of marriage. He and Sarah had branched out and started their own small ranch, while her father and Captain King provided plenty of activity in which they were to participate on the huge Kenedy and King ranches. Family members demanded their attention as they experienced marriages, gun battles, declining health, the births of new family members, and the deaths of loved ones. The Spohns were also expected to take their place in society.

The summer of 1882 found the Gulf Coast region, from Pensacola, Florida, all the way to Laredo, on the Rio Grande, facing a yellow fever epidemic that threatened to sweep the nation. Dr. Arthur Spohn played a significant role in stopping the spread of the disease. On August 11, 1882, Surgeon General John Hamilton of the US Marine Hospital Service (MHS) ordered all medical officers and assistant surgeons of the MHS to inform themselves of the health laws in place in the state and community where they were assigned and to aid and assist in the enforcement of them. They were also to report outbreaks of any other epidemic diseases, such as cholera, smallpox, and typhus. The acting secretary of the US Treasury communicated a decision that $100,000 would be made available to fight yellow fever in the Gulf Coast area, an effort that would be under the control of the Office of the Surgeon-General of the United States. In order to receive some of these funds, the governor of the state had to request help.[2]

That same day telegrams had been received in Washington, DC, from Brownsville and Galveston, with Brownsville reporting twenty new cases of yellow fever, five of them from the Cortina rancho seven miles up the river. Matamoros, Mexico, had about five hundred cases. Galveston reported that an epidemic seemed imminent.[3] The next communication came a day later, on August 12, with the acting customs collector in Brownsville, a Mr. Goodrich, giving a history of the epidemic in Texas. He said the first case of yellow fever had occurred in Matamoros a month before. It was introduced by railroad vagrants from Tampico who had come through Bagdad, Mexico. For the previous ten days, ten people a day had been dying in Matamoros, and Brownsville had sixty-two cases so far. That same day, Jackson, Mississippi, reported an immediate quarantine of the railroads around the major towns.[4]

In a 1900 address to the thirty-second session of the Texas State Medical Association, Spohn described his involvement with the 1882 yellow fever epidemic. He was pleased to be addressing the physicians as a representative of the Marine Hospital Service because he did not believe the physicians of Texas understood the MHS position.

In 1882, when yellow fever broke out in Brownsville, Spohn had appealed to the State of Texas for aid. The reply had come from Austin that there had been no appropriation for that purpose. The citizens had appealed to the Marine Hospital Service for help, and the MHS had selected Spohn to take charge. He had received the telegram from the US Treasury secretary to spare no expense. The MHS wished to establish an experimental cordon—a line of police, soldiers, or guards who would prevent access to an area. Spohn believed this was the first experimental cordon ever established in the United States to prevent the spread of yellow fever, and he did not believe many of the physicians of Texas had heard of it before.[5]

The Marine Hospital Service established a cordon from the city of Corpus Christi to Laredo, 161 miles; from the city of Laredo down the Rio Grande about 200 miles; and from the Rio Grande to the Gulf, about 40 miles. About 400 miles were thus protected by mounted guards paid three dollars a day, controlled by physicians who were selected by the service to oversee and utilize the guards.[6]

In Matamoros, Mexico, a city of twenty-five thousand inhabitants, there were more than twelve hundred deaths from yellow fever during the 1882 outbreak. Brownsville had more than seven hundred deaths from the disease, and in Reynosa, Mexico, there were three hundred. These cities were located on the Rio Grande outside the MHS cordon. The moment they established these cordons, refugees left Brownsville and Matamoros to come to the interior of Texas. Spohn sent advance guards out on the road because in this region it was almost impossible to travel from Brownsville and Matamoros to the interior unless one used the regularly traveled road, along which one could get water. He placed guards on all the roads that had these water holes, and in under four days some four hundred refugees had gathered in makeshift camps, because they were unable to penetrate the cordon. These camps extended from Brownsville, Texas, to Galveston along Padre Island. One person died at a camp in San Patricio. Not a single person from Brownsville made it past this cordon.[7]

Spohn explained the situation in Mexico. The Mexican government did not believe in quarantining, so the entire valley of the Rio Grande for 250 miles was swept by the yellow fever. Although the US side of the border was quarantined, having the MHS cordon in place, there was nothing to prevent Mexicans from leaving their country and entering the state of Texas.[8]

Spohn went to the Mexican city of Monterrey and had an interview with the governor of the region. Although Mexico was typically opposed to quarantining, the governor in Monterrey recognized the importance of this matter and immediately issued orders quarantining the whole coastal region. Thus, the Marine Hospital Service, thanks to the influence it had in Mexico, had established a quarantine line extending more than five hundred miles.[9]

On August 22, 1882, Spohn communicated with the Office of the Surgeon-General about the local conditions. Corpus Christi had issued quarantines against Brownsville, Laredo, Nuevo Laredo, and all towns along the Texas Mexican Railway. Corpus Christi and Nueces County had sixteen paid guards covering two cordon lines south of the railroad, and one hundred volunteers were guarding the approaches to the city. Spohn reported he had nine quarantine stations in addition to one at Aransas Pass. The Aransas Pass hospital had burned a few days before, so there was no proper shelter for the sick and no boat for service. They needed tents and medicines for the refugees, as well as a hospital for the sick seamen since it was the principal port supplying central Mexico. Spohn did receive a reply that the Office of the Surgeon-General would be sending a hospital tent.[10]

On October 3 the *New York Times* reported great opposition to the Brownsville quarantine by Mexican merchants and ambitious politicians. One surgeon said people had approached his men offering bribes, and they had threats made against them, including threats to their lives. He reported that he would continue to hold the cordon. Quarantines were very difficult for the residents, who were unable to leave or receive family or other visitors. They could not receive mail or have any contact with the outside world, and so they were angry. In Pensacola, Florida, the MHS received strong criticism for not doing enough to prevent the spread of yellow fever. Surgeon-General John Hamilton answered that accusation by explaining that the Marine Hospital Service could do nothing unless requested to do so by the governor of the state. The Florida governor had agreed to MHS help one day and then withdrawn the request the next. The *New York Times* reported that "in Texas the State authorities took action and the Marine Hospital Bureau has gone to the full limit of the law in affording relief, and within that limit has spared neither money nor labor."[11]

An alternative view of the 1882 fight against yellow fever has been presented in Dr. John McKiernan-González's book *Fevered Measures*. The author described the situation:

> Surgeon General Hamilton had wrested control and financing of the yellow fever effort away from National Board of Health. In order to prove the United States Marine Health [sic] Service competence Surgeon General Hamilton chose surgeon Robert Drake Murray to lead the effort. Dr. Murray was a good choice because he had treated yellow fever in Memphis, Vicksburg and the great Mississippi Valley. In Texas, Dr. Murray had to try to organize all the small and larger towns in the affected area into uniform action against significant opposition. He decided to consolidate the different quarantines along the Texas-Mexican Railroad into a Corpus Christi to Laredo Cordon.[12]

McKiernan-González quoted Spohn as saying that he, as Corpus Christi health officer and chief medical officer of the Texas Mexican Railway, was best positioned to supervise the quarantine. Spohn said the railroad company provided telegraph operators and coaling stations at regular intervals between Corpus Christi and Laredo, as well as supplies that might be needed for the guards. McKiernan-González asserted that, with Dr. Spohn coordinating the MHS effort, the interests of the Texas Mexican Railway, the King Ranch, and Corpus Christi became tied to the effort. Dr. Spohn dismissed the railroad workers who volunteered their services as mounted medical police, because he thought it unwise to send men who knew nothing about the area out into the brush, where they would probably get lost. Instead he used the hands from the King Ranch because they knew every path and water hole. The author asserts that by hiring King Ranch cowboys, the MHS turned the medical cordon into another instrument of intimate domination over local Mexican rancheros; he calls it a "shotgun quarantine."[13]

The quarantine effort occurred in the wake of some major real estate projects undertaken by Spohn and his extended family. In January 1881, Arthur Spohn, Henry Spohn, and Alexander Hamilton had purchased two large tracts of land. The first was 51,130 acres out of the Palafox Tract along the Rio Grande; the second was approximately 31,688 acres. In February the three conveyed a half interest to Abraham de la Garza and Thomas O'Connor. The land was located in Webb County, about forty miles from Laredo, and would provide the extra acreage they needed for their growing sheep and livestock business.[14]

Shortly afterward, Mifflin Kenedy decided the time was right to put his Los Laureles ranch up for sale. He needed a place with additional water and wanted to be closer to Corpus Christi, so he sold the 242,000 fenced acres of Los Laureles to a syndicate from Dundee, Scotland, known as the Texas Land & Cattle Company for $1.1 million in cash. For his fifty thousand head of cattle and five thousand horses, mares, and mules Mifflin then purchased a new ranch named La Parra, meaning grapevine. This ranch had frontage on Baffin Bay, which would facilitate travel and delivery of supplies. He intended to fence all 400,000 acres of it.[15]

Mifflin put the land in the name of the Kenedy Pasture Company, with shares valued at $1,000 each. He held ninety-six shares, his three sons had one share each, and his secretary, Edwin Mallory, had one. The value of Mifflin's shares, including the land and livestock, was estimated at $900,000. This arrangement affected Arthur and Sarah at Mifflin's death.[16]

In July 1882, a *Galveston Daily News* headline announced, "The Kenedy Pasture the Largest in the United States." The story declared the pasture to be sixty miles from Corpus Christi and ninety miles from Brownsville. Large dwellings, a storehouse, a stable, and cow houses had been erected, and workers were busy fencing the pastures. Tom Kenedy had driven the reporter around the ranch, where he saw tall grass, fresh and saltwater lakes full of fish, thousands of wild ducks, cranes, and waterfowl, and fat turkeys, large herds of deer, and antelope.[17]

Mifflin was headed for problems in his acquiring of all the land he wanted while managing La Parra. He had his eye on the La Atravesada ranch, owned by Doña Eulalia Tijerina. It consisted of 4,428 acres, had a big lake on the property, and was bordered on the north by Los Olmos Creek. When Doña Eulalia refused to sell to Mifflin, he fenced in her entire property in hopes of forcing her to sell.[18] Her situation was just one example of the difficulty some Tejano ranchers had with land titles. Other problems included lawlessness, changing geographic boundaries, divided heirs, language, and Anglo courts. In desperation some gave up their land or sold at low prices, thus abandoning land belonging to the family for generations. In this case Doña Eulalia stubbornly refused to give up her portion of the ranch, and today it remains outside the Kenedy ranch property after being purchased from her by G. A. Riskin in 1930.[19]

Mifflin micromanaged his ranch from afar. He wanted his sons to work it under his close supervision. The problem was that Sarah's brothers had very different personalities, and fraternal conflict was common. Tom was thirty, James twenty-eight, and John twenty-seven. None was married at the time. Between 1882 and 1884 Mifflin changed management among the sons several times. Tom's interest was in Brownsville, so Mifflin turned to James to run the ranch. James and John did not get along, and James resigned on January 11, 1883.[20] By January 22 Mifflin had changed his mind again. He wrote John that James was back in charge. John then resigned.

On April 7, 1884, James was involved in another shooting incident. The Brownsville newspaper reported that Sheriff Santiago Brito had received a telegram from James at La Parra ranch saying he had accidentally shot and killed a man and was thus asking for advice. The next day the newspaper reported that they were truly glad that Mr. Kenedy had been completely exonerated after a careful examination by Deputy Sheriff Tomas Trevino. James explained that he had ordered a former employee to leave the premises, and when the man did not comply James had struck at him with his right hand (his left being useless). The man hit James in the chest, and when he fell he injured his right hand. James drew his pistol to strike the man and during the struggle it accidentally discharged and killed the man.[21] The blow to the chest accelerated James's deteriorating physical condition. Mifflin wrote to John, who was the acting ranch manager at that time, asking his son to try to get along with James until after the case was decided.[22] Because of James's ill health, John was put back in charge of the ranch, and by August he had moved out to the ranch and was living there.[23]

Meanwhile, Arthur and Sarah were enjoying the Corpus social scene. The women and men enjoyed boating, yachting, skating, and picnics. The *Corpus Christi Caller* reported on August 12, 1883, that Sarah Kenedy Spohn was the chairperson of a boating excursion to Ingleside, Texas. The young people had a grand excursion, even though it was predicted to be 90 degrees. The hardiest of souls departed Corpus Christi at 6:00 a.m. They spent the day fishing, dancing, and flirting. Late in the afternoon there were bottles on the beach with the well-known mark of the Bachelors Club. Few fish were caught, but there were many blistered noses. Overall it was a grand time.[24]

In the fall Arthur and Sarah helped with a pumpkin pie social sponsored by the local Episcopal church as part of Arthur's role as a vestry member. Even though he had married into Sarah's strongly Catholic family, he remained active in his Protestant faith, serving on the vestry of the church in a leadership position. Easter morning the church had been filled with flowers, and an offertory taken at the request of the rector produced $100 toward retiring the church debt. This made a total of $450 they raised for the year, thus clearing the debt. Spohn and the other vestry members were reelected.[25]

By the spring of 1884, Spohn was planting a large number of trees around his property on the bluff. He wrapped them with wire to protect them from stock that still roamed at large. Spohn was also an active member of the local gun club, and at the end of March he placed third in the weekly shoot.[26] Sarah had been busy arranging the details for the Leap Year Ball.[27] Leap year balls were always special because it was the women who extended an invitation to the gentleman of their choice.

Sarah and Arthur welcomed her brother John and his new bride, Stella, to Texas in March. The couple had been married in a ceremony in New Orleans on January 30, 1884, at the St. Louis Cathedral. The headlines in the *Brownsville Reporter* read, "The Son of a Texas Cattle King Leads a New Orleans Belle to the Altar." John married Marie Stella Turcotte, the daughter of a well-known New Orleans merchant. The wedding was an elaborate affair, with a large wedding party. Marie Stella was nineteen years old and loved music and art. John had friends in Brownsville and Corpus Christi, and he would pursue his interest in business in one of those communities. The newspaper expressed hope he would choose Brownsville.[28]

James's and Petra's health determined John's future. He and his new bride returned to Corpus Christi, and by August they had moved to La Parra to manage the ranch. It was a lonely and isolated place for a city girl like Marie Stella. She loved to speak French and bonded with Padre Juanito, a member of the Cavalry of Christ who visited La Parra on his missionary trips.[29]

Petra's health had continued to decline, and she had been hesitant to make the move to Corpus Christi. She was not a social person, and although she had Sarah and Arthur nearby, all her other family was in Brownsville, more than 150 miles away. Mifflin decided that he would build a house for his Petrita, as he called Petra, on the bluff in Corpus Christi, and he proclaimed that it would be the finest house in Texas. In the future, the house would be Arthur and Sarah's home. It was in the order of an Italian villa, and construction began in 1883.[30] Not only was the house to have all the modern conveniences, but Mifflin also wanted it to be furnished elegantly. He and Petra sat down together and decided what to order. Late in 1884 they ordered china consisting of dinner, breakfast, tea, dessert, ice cream, chocolate, and fruit sets, all with Petra's monogram, PVK. Mifflin also ordered European art, which was unusual for a South Texas rancher. He ordered sixty-eight pieces in all.[31] He knew time was running short for Petra, and he pushed the workers to finish the house as quickly as possible.

Between 1882 and 1884 Sarah's and Arthur's families both experienced illnesses and deaths, as well as marriages. Sarah was the only Kenedy child married, as her three brothers were all still single. That all changed in two years' time, first with John's marriage to Marie Stella and his return to La Parra to run the ranch. Tom, her wayward brother, began courting a beautiful and prominent young woman in Brownsville, Miss Yrene Yznaga, daughter of a Brownsville merchant. James, despite his many hardships and troubles, had managed to court and win the hand of another beautiful young lady from a highly respected South Texas family. In April 1883, James, sometimes known as Santiago, became engaged to Corina Ballí Treviño. She was the half-sister of Salomé B. McAllen, wife of John McAllen, an important South Texas cattleman. Corina was living with John and Salomé when James came to ask for her hand in marriage.[32]

Petra wrote Salomé a letter in Spanish saying she was very happy that young people from the same town should marry, and she knew Santiago would fulfill his obligations to maintain Corina. She said she wished all her sons would marry Mexicans, for she had a great fear that she would be presented with a *gringita* who could not speak Castilian. She told Salomé she was anxious to see her and she viewed her as a sister.[33]

James and Corina were married November 3, 1883. She was twenty-four and he was twenty-eight. Their marriage lasted a little more than a year. James became critically ill with typhoid malarial fever and congestion of the left lung. He and Corina had been staying with Mifflin and Petra for three months during the summer, and James and Corina's son was born on August 24, 1884, in Corpus Christi. Mifflin had his first grandchild and new heir. Shortly after that James left for Monterrey and Saltillo to search for a cure, but as it turned out he only had four months left.[34]

Then Stella became ill at La Parra, and John sent for Spohn. Sarah and Arthur left for La Parra by boat to bring her back to Corpus to stay with Mifflin and Petra until Spohn nursed her back to health. She stayed six weeks, and Mifflin said "the old house has been quite a hospital this last year."[35]

Spohn had lost several of his own family members in 1882. He lost his brother-in-law and preceptor, Dr. Alexander Hamilton, on July 16.[36] He had been a close friend and a medical colleague as well as his sister's husband. Alexander's biographical sketch, written by his son Arthur Claud Hamilton, described his father as "one of Canada's great statesmen, a man who endeared the name to all citizens of the Dominion. Dr. Hamilton transferred his allegiance to the United States and came to Texas in 1875, bringing his wife and three sons with him. He took charge of the U.S. Marine Hospital at Corpus Christi in 1875 and remained there until his death in 1882."[37]

Less than two weeks after Alexander's death, on July 29, 1882, Spohn received news that his father, Philip Spaun, had passed away in Ancaster, Canada.[38] The family sustained another blow when later in that same year Alexander and Catherine's son Alexander passed away while at medical school. Catherine had lost her husband and son almost at the same time.[39] These deaths were followed in the next two years by the illnesses and deaths in Sarah's family.

Petra had continued to decline in health. She mentioned to both Salomé and Henrietta King that she thought the move to Corpus Christi had been bad for her health. Henrietta, good friend that she was, wrote Petra in September 1883 inviting her to come to the ranch and stay because she thought

Sarah Spohn's brother-in-law Joseph L. Putegnat died in Mifflin and Petra Kenedy's home in Corpus Christi on November 10, 1882. He and his wife Rosa and the children were visiting. Courtesy of Jesse (Sam) Thornham and Patrick Thornham.

Rosa Putegnat, Sarah Spohn's half-sister, was forty-five years old when her husband, Joseph, died, leaving eight surviving children, the youngest only nine months old. Mifflin helped her get a new start. Courtesy of Jesse (Sam) Thornham and Patrick Thornham.

it might be good for her.[40] This was a very generous offer, considering that she and Captain King had lost their youngest son, Robert Lee King, on March 1. Lee was the one who loved the ranch, the grass, and water. His death broke his father's heart, and Captain King started drinking heavily and developed stomach pains that the alcohol could not cure. Petra had written Henrietta after Lee's death to express her condolences. She had a great deal of empathy for them because she and Mifflin had lost their own young son, Willie.[41]

In August 1883 another death hit Sarah. Her close half-sister, Rosa, and her husband, Joseph Putegnat, had come to visit the family in Corpus Christi that month. On October 17 the Brownsville newspaper reported that Dr. Putegnat was ill. Neither Spohn nor his associates could do anything for him, and he died on November 10 at Mifflin's home.[42] He was forty-five years old and had eight surviving children, the youngest only nine months old. Mifflin was concerned about Rosa's welfare and wrote his lawyer, James Wells, that he wanted to help her get a clean start.[43]

The year 1884 thus ended sadly for Sarah and Arthur. Mifflin had received news that his mother was dying in Pennsylvania, but he could not get away because both James and Petra were in poor health. Petra's condition had deteriorated, and by August Mifflin had written to Rosa, "Your mother says if you can possibly do so she wishes you to come to her. Sarah says if you wish to bring two or three of your children she will take care of them."[44]

Petra was able to rally on October 3 and stand as sponsor at the baptism of George Mifflin Kenedy, James and Corina's son.[45] By Christmas Eve James lay dying. Everyone walked lightly and the house was dark. Santiago could barely talk, but he whispered to Corina how sorry he was that he would not be there to help raise their son.

Mifflin had word that his mother had died in Pennsylvania. The Coatesville, Pennsylvania, newspaper said she was highly respected and ninety-two years of age. The Brownsville newspaper reported that "she faithfully attended the sick and administered with impartial tenderness to the poor as to the rich."[46]

Father Jaillet administered the last rites to Santiago and prepared him for death. He passed away December 29, 1884. The funeral was from the Catholic Church. Father Jaillet gave assurances to the family during the service that Santiago had been forgiven for his sins.[47] Santiago's death led to such overpowering grief in Petra in her weakened condition that she could not throw it off.

Sarah and Arthur had witnessed a great deal of joy and sorrow in their families during the year.

Chapter 11

Tragedy and Triumph

1885–1887

A rthur and Sarah realized in 1885 that they were going to lose Sarah's mother. Petra had been declining, and the loss of James had severely taxed her health. Mifflin was very proud of the house he had built for his "Petrita," and he wanted her to live long enough to take up residence in it. She was looking forward to the house and remarked that she did not want to be the third person to die in the "hut"—her term for the rented house where both her son-in-law J. P. Putegnat and her son James (Santiago) had died.[1]

On the morning of February 26, 1885, Mifflin had Petra's monogrammed coach pull up to the "hut," and she was helped into it for the journey to see the new house for the first time. Nene (Maria Vicenta) was there to help her. Mifflin told the driver to proceed very slowly and carefully. When Petra saw the house, she was overwhelmed. Mifflin proudly opened the beautiful glass-and-wood door with the etched letters MK. The elegant house Petra entered was one of the finest in the South. Mifflin used walnut, oak, mahogany, cherry, pine, and cypress woods brought from all over the world to finish the interior. Two hundred gas burners cast halos of light, creating a setting of warmth and opulence. The library was floored with fine tile and carpet. A beautiful staircase had been carved of mesquite wood and polished till it shone. Each room had etched-glass transoms and luxurious furniture. The dining room had a table set with china they had chosen,

The house built by Mifflin Kenedy for his beloved wife, Petra, whom he called Petrita. It was described as the "finest house in Texas." Later it became Arthur and Sarah's home. Courtesy of Anita Eisenhauer.

On the morning of February 26, 1885, Petra was helped into her monogrammed coach for the journey to see the new house for the first time. Nene (Maria Vicenta) was there to help her. When Petra saw the house, she was overwhelmed. Courtesy of Michael Hamilton.

monogrammed with her initials. Petra was assisted upstairs to her large mahogany bed, while the steam heat surrounded her in comfort. Her bath had hot water from hand-painted ceramic fixtures.[2]

Sarah and Arthur and the family stayed close to see what she might need. Mifflin again brought bad news on March 8. John and Stella had lost their newborn child, Anne, due to a breech delivery. She was buried in the Corpus Christi cemetery, and Petra again had a child to lift in prayer to God, asking him to bless the young soul.[3] Petra's pain worsened, and Mifflin wrote to his sister Jo in Pennsylvania saying she required morphine to try to be comfortable. Mifflin had wanted to take Petra to New Orleans the previous October to see the doctors, but she refused to leave Santiago.[4] Now she was too ill to travel.

Mifflin summoned Dr. Ferdinand Herff, a German-educated physician who had practiced in San Antonio since 1850. He believed, like Spohn, in washing hands and in cleanliness. The Texas Medical Association reported that of the 1,875 surgical cases performed in the state in 1886, Dr. Herff had performed 12 percent of them. He was particularly qualified to attend Petra because he was one of the first surgeons in the United States to perform a hysterectomy.[5]

Dr. Herff examined Petra under anesthesia and consulted with three other doctors. He found that uterine cancer had spread throughout her body. He told Petra personally and explained there was nothing he could do. He said she might get somewhat better, but she would be in constant pain and would need morphine.[6] He advised her to make her final arrangements. Through her pain she instructed Nene and Sarah how she wanted to be dressed. She gave them instructions for her burial and then asked them to call for Mifflin. She said she wanted to be buried on the right side of her son Santiago. Mifflin called Father Jaillet, who administered the last rites, as he had so recently done for Santiago.[7] He did what he could to comfort this grieving family, for Father Jaillet knew Petra would be in the hands of her God. She had a strong faith, and that faith was the legacy she passed on to her children.

Petra Vela Kenedy died March 16, 1885, surrounded by her family. When she died, she had thirty-two grandchildren and only one, James's son George, was Mifflin's. She had been the family's rock and had held these two families together with love and faith. She had blended two cultures, raised successful children, supported Mifflin, and passed on the Catholic faith for generations to come.[8]

Mifflin was stunned at the quickness of her death because Dr. Herff had told him she would have several months to live. Word of her death spread quickly. William Kelly in Brownsville wrote in his minute book that he attended a memorial mass for Mrs. Kenedy at 8:30 for all of her Brownsville friends and family.[9] Her obituary noted "the poor never appealed to her in vain and their wants were often anticipated."[10]

Soon after Petra died the family was also confronted with the death of their closest friend, Capt. Richard King. Fortunately, he had lived to see his heir born before his death. Richard King III was born on December 17, 1884, at the Puerta de Agua Dulce ranch house, to Richard King II and Pearl Lizzie Ashbrook King.[11] By January 13, Captain King was in such pain that he knew he was mortally ill. Even his faithful companion, Rosebud whiskey, could not ease his abdominal pain. Despite that, it took Henrietta and Alice a month to convince him he needed to travel to San Antonio to put himself under Dr. Herff's care. Finally, on February 25, Captain King left his Santa Gertrudis rancho for the last time. He asked his secretary, Reuben Holbein, to write to Jim Wells, "Tell him to keep on buying. And tell him not to let a foot of dear old Santa Gertrudis get away from us."[12] He had built his empire.

The family stayed at the Menger Hotel in San Antonio, and when Dr. Herff told him that his stomach cancer was at a terminal stage, he took it calmly until Dr. Herff suggested that he stop drinking. Henrietta had asked the doctor to tell him that she wanted him to live longer because she needed him. Richard got up, dressed, and stormed into her room demanding to know if she had said she needed him. After their discussion, he did not take another drink.[13] William Kelly wrote that on April 8 Drs. Logan and Sanchon, both surgeons at Charity Hospital in New Orleans, were called to San Antonio for consultation.[14] Dr. Edward Sanchon had written about cancer surgery he had performed at Charity.[15]

Captain King's family and Robert Kleberg, who was courting King's daughter Alice, were there. Mifflin, in grief and mourning over Petra, came to sit by the bedside of his friend. On April 2, Captain King made his will, leaving everything to Henrietta and naming his "trusted friends" Mifflin Kenedy and Perry Doddridge as executors. Twelve days later, on April 14, just short of a month after Petra's death, Mifflin's closest friend took his last breath at dusk.[16]

Mifflin returned home to immediately begin dealing with Petra's estate. She had died intestate because Mifflin wanted it that way. He did

Manuel Rodríguez was an important member of Sarah Kenedy Spohn's family. He was married to her half-sister Concepción and was the mayor of Nuevo Laredo. He and Concepción provided contacts and information on the Mexican side of the border. Courtesy of Jesse (Sam) Thornham and Patrick Thornham.

not want to divide up his holdings. Instead, he worked to settle with her heirs. According to state law he inherited half of her estate and her children inherited half. At the time of her death, Petra had the following nine living children or heirs: Tom, James's son George, John, Sarah, Luisa, Rosa, Adrián's daughter Anita, Concepción, and Maria Vicenta. Petra's estate was estimated at about $700,000, so from the children's half—$350,000—they would receive about $40,000 each, worth just under $1 million today. However, Mifflin was short of cash, so he put together an elaborate plan consisting of promissory notes due at various times along with deeds to land and real estate. Being the businessman he was, he also deducted any money the individual heirs owed him from the total they were to receive. The fairness of the settlements was disputed in the courts for the next seventy-five years.[17]

Throughout this difficult time there was a silent courtship going on between Robert Kleberg and Alice King, starting with Robert's initial visit to see Captain King at the Santa Gertrudis rancho in July 1881. When Robert first met Alice, she was nineteen years old, had dark hair, dark eyes, and a sweet face.[18] She was well educated, shy, and heir to a vast fortune. Robert was twenty-eight and an up-and-coming lawyer

Concepción Vidal, Sarah Kenedy Spohn's half-sister, was also one of Petra Vela Kenedy's heirs. She was a beautiful woman with red hair and green eyes, and she liked to entertain lavishly while wearing elegant gowns, fine jewelry, and lacy mantillas. Courtesy of Jesse (Sam) Thornham and Patrick Thornham.

The beautiful Luisa Vidal Dalzell was another half-sister of Sarah Kenedy Spohn and another of Petra Vela Kenedy's heirs. She and her husband, Robert Dalzell, were active in Brownsville social and political life. Courtesy of Susan Seeds.

Yrene Yznaga married Tom Kenedy, Sarah Kenedy Spohn's brother and thus another of Petra Vela Kenedy's heirs, in Brownsville, Texas, on July 29, 1888. He was later assassinated on his thirty-fifth birthday while running for sheriff. Courtesy Willacy County Historical Museum.

from a distinguished German-Texan family. Word began to circulate about their possible relationship. Sarah Spohn, who was always in the middle of Corpus Christi social life, became very interested in their courtship. Her intense interest became a problem for Robert and Alice. They were trying to keep their relationship quiet because Robert had received Henrietta's blessing but not that of Captain King, who never did grant consent to the courtship. Captain King had been reluctant to let his little girl leave Santa Gertrudis. After the loss of his son Lee, he depended on her a great deal. By May 18, 1884, Robert was in Corpus Christi and wrote to Alice at Santa Gertrudis:

> I have a little piece of gossip to tell you. I met our friend Mrs. Dr. S [Spohn] the other evening out in front of the St. James [hotel]. She was in the buggy while the Dr. had gone in. She called me up and congratulated me. When I told her she was too precocious she said that on that day your father had been at her mother's house and she told him that she

understood we were engaged. Our conversation was interrupted about that time. I have not seen her since. I never saw such busy people about other people's affairs. This, however, is nothing new to me. I am getting use to it.[19]

By July, Robert had adopted another tactic to avoid the gossip and had begun playing a little trick on the nosy women. On July 6 he wrote to "My Dear Little Heart," which is what he called Alice. He said that he had accepted an invitation to a nice lunch by Mrs. Spohn and Miss Lovenskiold. He then wrote,

> I thought of the scheme I had mentioned to you. I at once asked Miss Lovenskiold to accompany me to the picnic ground and I think I have pretty well succeeded in starting my interested friend on a new track. I drove through the many streets of the city by Mrs. Doddridge, giving her a full benefit, and during the evening acted the gallant so well that Mrs. S. has become decidedly doubtful as to the true state of affairs. I have heard from them today. Gossip now says that I have taken a new departure, something must have gone wrong elsewhere with me, etc. I think I shall now leave the city while this impression is abroad & perhaps they will let you rest for a little while.[20]

In the same letter Robert mentioned that he had gone by to have tea with Captain Kenedy and found him not well. He said he was suffering from some irritation of the ileus (intestine).[21] Later he wrote and expressed Mifflin's worries about fixing his business with his children and his late wife's children and Robert said he hoped they would behave themselves.[22]

Alice and Robert waited the respectable year of mourning after Captain King's death before marrying. By that time, Henrietta had turned to Robert to help her manage the ranch. Finally, on June 17, 1886, at six o'clock in the morning in the parlor of the house at Santa Gertrudis, Alice Gertrudis King became the wife of Robert Justus Kleberg. Mifflin Kenedy gave her away in place of his friend Captain King. Following the ceremony the couple left for a summer trip up north, accompanied by her mother, Henrietta King.[23] When they returned, their relationship with Arthur and Sarah Spohn became even closer.

Robert Kleberg continued to work in Corpus Christi and travel to the ranch on the weekends. Good news came to them in early 1887 that they

Alice King was a loving daughter who stayed home to take care of her father, Capt. Richard King, until his death. Following his death, Henrietta King turned to local attorney Robert Kleberg to help her manage the ranch. After waiting a respectable year of mourning, Robert and Alice were married June 17, 1886, at six o'clock in the morning at the Santa Gertrudis rancho. Courtesy CHRISTUS Spohn Health System.

Robert Kleberg, a prominent lawyer, quietly courted Alice King after the deaths of Petra Kenedy and Captain King. Among the society members who were unaware of the courtship was Sarah Spohn. Courtesy Corpus Christi Public Libraries, Corpus Christi, Tex.

were expecting their first child. Robert turned to Spohn about the upcoming delivery. He wanted Alice to be in town to be close to Spohn, as her time got close. On July 27 he wrote Alice to tell her that Dr. Spohn said "unless I could get a comfortable and good place for you here you had better remain at home."[24] On August 17 Robert again relayed information from Spohn: "Dr. Spohn called on me today for the gray horse I told him he could use so I sent a note by a man today to Mr. Doughty [ranch manager] to send the horse down by him. Tell mother [Henrietta] about it. I feel it quite important just at this time to keep my promises with the Dr. to keep on the good side of him. I will make the matter all right."[25] Alice was six months pregnant at this time, and Robert wanted to keep Spohn in the best of moods.

Robert found a two-story residence called the Greer House to rent that was a good and comfortable place where Alice could stay. Spohn delivered their firstborn child on November 18, 1887. They named him Richard Mifflin Kleberg after his grandfather, Richard King, and his grandfather's

Carmen Morell was adopted by Mifflin Kenedy as his legal daughter on July 25, 1887. Her new status entitled her to a fourth of Mifflin's fortune upon his death. Kenedy Family Collection, A1995-045-0485, South Texas Archives, James C. Jernigan Library, Texas A&M University–Kingsville.

best friend, Mifflin Kenedy.[26] Sarah, Arthur, and Mifflin must have been honored at their choice of names. The closeness of these two families extended down to the next generation as it had with the two captains. Robert and Alice had four more children, and Spohn delivered all of them: Henrietta Rosa Kleberg (b. July 17, 1889), Alice Gertrudis Kleberg (b. January 9, 1893), Robert J. Kleberg Jr. (b. March 29, 1896), and Sarah Spohn Kleberg (b. April 12, 1898).[27]

On July 25, 1887, a little more than two years after Petra's death and after Mifflin had settled her estate with her children, he legally adopted Maria del Carmen Morell as his daughter. Mifflin was sixty-nine years old and Carmen was thirty-two. Why would Mifflin in his later years adopt a daughter with the rights to inherit an equal share of his estate? He already had a large and supportive family. His children Sarah, Tom, and John were surprised by this adoption. A stranger would become an equal heir to the Kenedy fortune. Sarah, thirty years old, had suddenly acquired a sister two years older.[28]

Mifflin endured great opposition to the adoption from family, friends, and business associates. Mifflin said he was adopting Carmen to pay back obligations he had from the favors that her father, Jose Morell, had done for him. It is true that during the Civil War Jose Morell had served as his trusted accountant.[29] However, Morell had died in 1875 and this adoption occurred twelve years later. The other problem is that Carmen had other sisters and brothers, and none of them was adopted. Her two older sisters, Maria Isabel and Josefa Francisca, stayed with Carmen in Corpus Christi much of the time after the adoption but were never made part of the family. Another theory was that Mifflin adopted Carmen to look after him and the house in his old age. This made no sense, because after Petra's death Sarah and Arthur stayed in the house with Mifflin. Also, Mifflin's stepdaughter, Maria Vicenta, was available to stay there when he needed her. Another speculation was that Mifflin adopted her to be his mistress or lover and that the way to mask this relationship was to adopt her. Again, this is unlikely because Petra had been dead two years and Mifflin could simply have married her.

Mifflin may have adopted Carmen because she was his biological daughter. It is possible that he sired her by an unknown mother in the early 1850s and the Morells took her into their home and raised her as their own child. After her adoption, Carmen called Mifflin "Father" or "Papa" both privately and publicly. Mifflin did not object, and she moved into his home and managed the household for him, and they traveled together as well. She attended balls and was an active part of the Corpus Christi social set. Through the years John Kenedy displayed an extreme dislike for her. Spohn also had major disagreements with her and felt she was a bad influence on Sarah. No records indicate that the family discussed her adoption publicly or what they knew about Carmen prior to her adoption.

These questions about Carmen's background have remained unanswered, but there are two interesting clues to Carmen's relationship with the family. A Corpus Christi newspaper on December 18, 1886, reported that the Misses Morell of Monterrey were visiting the city as guests of Capt. M. Kenedy.[30] By the end of 1886, Carmen and her sisters were on the scene in Corpus Christi and the family was aware they were staying with their father. The other interesting clue comes from an autograph book that Sarah Spohn gave to Carmen. The front of the book has Sarah's calling card printed with "Mrs. Arthur E. Spohn" and, at the bottom, "Corpus Christi, Texas." The inscription reads, "May this simple letter remembrance, my dear Carmen, be a proof of the affection I bear you. Lovingly yours, Sarah," and the date is June 13, 1887.[31] There is a notation that the book was given to Carmen by Sarah when Carmen moved into the cottage on the mansion grounds, where she stayed before her official adoption. At least initially Sarah seemed to have been fond of her new sister.[32]

Despite all of the personal issues that he and Sarah faced, Spohn stayed very busy with his medical practice during these two years. Earlier in 1886, another Corpus Christi physician, Dr. W. W. McGregor, had been feeling unwell and went for a visit to Puerta Lake on the Puerta Agua Dulce rancho belonging to Richard King II. He continued to visit the ranch and by March 7 the paper reported he was greatly improved.[33] His absence certainly increased the workload on Spohn.

By April, Dr. Burke was making preparations for the Marine Service Hospital to open on May 1. A newspaper reported on April 13 that Dr. Burke had received the governor's proclamation stating he would go to the station at Aransas Pass on May 1 and the quarantine would be established.[34] Spohn also took his turn at staffing the station. By June, Arthur and Sarah were anticipating the birth of John's child. He and Marie Stella had lost baby Anne at birth the year before, so they were particularly anxious about this child. The local newspaper paper reported on June 6, 1886 that "John Kenedy of the Kenedy Pasture Company and manager of the model livestock ranch of Texas is in the city. Mr. Kenedy and wife are visiting friends and relatives here."[35] The couple was in town to be near Spohn for the birth of their baby. On June 13, 1886, John Kenedy announced in the newspaper the birth of his son in the early part of the week.[36]

Spohn was also acting as preceptor to Henry J. Hamilton, just as Henry's father had done for Spohn in Barrie, Ontario. Henry had been sent by his Canadian family to the family ranch near Encinal to work because the doctors in the family thought he might have early signs of tuberculosis. While working on the ranch he had become interested in medicine and read his Uncle Henry's medical books. He came to Corpus Christi in 1883 to work under his Uncle Arthur, and by 1887 he felt he was ready to attempt formal medical training. He had been a great help to Spohn during this time and worked primarily with his obstetric patients. In 1887 he entered the Medical Department of the University of Louisville in Kentucky and spent his vacation time up north at the Spaun farm in Canada and also at Penetanguishene with his Uncle Howard, who was also a doctor. He went back to Louisville, and after presenting his credentials he was appointed assistant demonstrator of anatomy and thus did not have to pay any entrance fee. He graduated after three terms and obtained three gold medals, two for surgery and one for general proficiency. Spohn had taught him well. He then returned to Corpus Christi to help Spohn establish the Bay View Infirmary for Women. In the meantime his brother, Arthur Claud, named for his Uncle Arthur, finished up at San Marcos Military Academy in 1887 and entered the University of Texas, where he received his bachelor of science degree in 1892 and a law degree in 1894.[37]

Spohn's practice was geographically large, with calls for emergency care coming from faraway ranches. F. W. Shaeffer, a prominent citizen in Duval County, had a serious accident in mid-October 1886. He was going from his ranch to San Diego when his team was frightened and ran away. Shaeffer and his wife were thrown out of the vehicle. He broke his leg above the knee and his wife was seriously bruised. A local newspaper reported that Dr. Spohn went on a special run to see him. It appeared that he would be all right, but on October 31 it was reported that Shaeffer had been doing well but at about three in the morning he had trouble breathing. He was given a little brandy and a few moments later died without a struggle.[38]

During that year Spohn had one of his most unusual experiences. He worked closely with the Sisters of the Incarnate Word and Blessed Sacrament. They helped him on occasion with patients. In May 1887, Sister Paul, the mother superior, became ill. Spohn was called and he determined he needed to operate. He did surgery, but it was to no avail as she died on May 21. During the operation Sister Paul, under the influence of anesthetic, sang an entire high mass. Spohn remarked to the sisters after the surgery that he had "never heard it sung so beautifully," adding that it was quite different from what he was accustomed to hear on such occasions.[39]

Spohn's time was not spent exclusively on direct patient care and surgeries in varied locations. He was also on a never-ending quest to improve procedures or to invent new methods of doing something. When he developed a new approach, he was eager to share it with his colleagues around the country. He kept up with all the newest information published in the various medical journals and contributed to the medical literature on a regular basis. The year 1887 was productive for him, and he wrote papers on three procedures based on his experience.

Spohn published an article entitled "Country Practice in Texas" that appeared in the *Medical and Surgical Reporter* in August 1887. The article was about a bedside treatment for prostatitis, or inflamed prostate and/or urethra. A soft tubular product made of cocoa butter was often inserted to separate and shrink the swollen membranes, allowing free passage of urine, whereas the stiffer devices typically used would stretch scarred tissue. This treatment was also used on sinus tracts, not to be confused with the nasal sinuses, but instead referring to openings in the skin where chronically infected cavities were drained, to allow the noxious contents to escape the body. Sinus tracts were enlarged as well, to prevent renewed illness should the tract or tunnel close. A stiffened appliance, narrow and smooth, held the tissues apart and sometimes carried medication that needed to be kept in place for an extended period. Spohn knew that a different product was needed because cocoa butter was not available in Texas. Spohn devised an easily constructed substitute product prepared quickly at the bedside from readily available materials. Spohn described his innovative solution:

> At last I thought of the ordinary tallow candle, selected a tube of proper size and strength, pulled a wick through it made of several threads of silk twist. I then melted in a test tube, oil of theobroma, medicated to suit the case, pouring it into the tube, so as to have the medicated portion just where I wanted it. The tube is held a few moments in ice water until the oil hardens. Now rub gently through the fingers and the oil next to the tube softens. When the candle is drawn out, again insert it into ice water and it immediately hardens and you have a medicated bougie, manufactured in less time than I can describe it, at a nominal cost. I always prepare them at the bedside and have used them in all cases of gonorrhea stricture, diseased prostate; in fact, whenever I wish to keep the disease surfaces apart, or introduce remedial agents into cavities, sinuses, etc.[40]

Later in his career Spohn specialized in women's health and opened the Sanitarium for Women in Corpus Christi. During his earlier years, delivering mothers benefited from his reasoning and self-confidence and thus prevented birth injuries. In his day, when the vaginal tract was damaged it was usually ignored and left to heal. This worked most of the time but could result in a deformed vaginal canal, causing problems with sexual intercourse or generating chronic pain, leakage of feces from the rectum into the vagina, or constantly draining sinus tracts.

In February 1888, he published his recommended repair of vaginal injuries in the *Medical and Surgical Reporter*. As part of his report about the primary closure of such wounds, he threw in a few tips on proper vaginal delivery. Spohn emphasized washing and antisepsis (boric acid) and lubrication (warm olive oil or Vaseline) while carefully slowing and directing the baby's head through the birth canal. To repair injuries that occurred despite his best effort, he emphasized immediate closure of the wounds with silk suture, while avoiding deep tissue bites and approximating the outer layer closely and carefully. Spohn stated, "If then any rupture be detected, no matter how small it may be, it should be stitched up immediately; for in them as in any other wound, the sooner the parts are nicely adjusted the better. [This] is the method I am now using, and I am pleased to say with perfect results . . . and the patient is afterward treated as if no rupture had taken place." The sutures were to be removed nine days later.[41]

In December 1887 Spohn published in the *Medical and Surgical Reporter* his treatment for clavicle fracture and included with his article his own drawings of the innovative splint he had invented (see "Fracture of the Clavicle," in appendix 1).

Spohn, like many country doctors, traveled hours to get to patients on barely visible roads, across streams, sometimes in the dark of night, and in inclement weather, always in a horse and buggy. He could carry only the bare necessities with him, and sometimes he had to invent solutions to the problems he faced when he arrived. His creative solutions served him well, and he thus wanted to share them with his fellow physicians.

Chapter 12

A Race to Paris and the Pasteur Institute

1888

I n March 1888, a thirty-seven-year-old rancher, William Chapman Chamberlain, known as Willie, was asleep on the porch of his ranch house near Brownsville, Texas. As Willie slept, a rabid coyote, foaming at the mouth, staggered onto the porch and attacked him, leaving three deep, ragged wounds on the right side of his face and several scratches on the side of his nose. Willie fought off the coyote and killed it. It was not uncommon in South Texas to find rabid animals, especially coyotes, skunks, and dogs. During a drought the problem became more dangerous, because wild animals such as rabbits would come to the ranch houses searching for water and food and rabid predators would follow them.[1] Rabies and the story of Willie Chamberlain soon garnered national attention in the press, but many newspapers mistakenly referred to the animal that attacked him as a wolf rather than a coyote.

Willie was a lucky young man, for he was related to one of the richest women in the United States: his half-sister, Henrietta Chamberlain King, wife of Capt. Richard King. Henrietta was very fond of Willie because he had grown up with Henrietta and Captain King on the ranch. He and his brother Edwin had come to live with them when their father, Hiram Chamberlain, died. Willie was also fortunate because anyone on the ranch needing medical care saw Dr. Arthur Spohn. Spohn had recently read an article about Dr. Louis Pasteur in Paris and his work on inoculating rabies-infected humans. Had Spohn not read that article, Willie's fate would likely have been that of a neighbor rancher's wife, Mollie Durst Armstrong, who was bitten and died on Christmas Day locked in her bedroom and suffering greatly.[2] The custom at the time was to isolate the infected person, sometimes tying them down, perhaps to a tree or fence post, leaving them to suffer madness and die.[3]

This was not to be the case with Willie, who immediately cauterized his own wounds with carbonic acid and then sent one of the cowboys from the ranch to town to contact Henrietta King in Corpus Christi and tell her what had happened. She contacted Spohn and Dr. T. J. Turpin and asked them to set out on the trail to Brownsville, giving them her buggy and her fastest horses. She then instructed the cowboys to load Willie into a wagon and start for Corpus Christi. Hours later Spohn and Dr. Turpin met the wagon. When they examined Willie, they decided to cauterize the wounds again. By one account they decided to cauterize the wounds by using a fence post to start a fire and a branding iron from Willie's wagon to cauterize his face. However, Spohn's account given to the Paris correspondent of the *New York Herald* differed. Spohn said that he first saw Willie on March 12 and found three deep, ragged wounds on his face. He thought that the first cauterization that had been done before he saw Willie was not sufficient because the wounds were so deep. He chose to use carbolic acid to treat the wounds and then cleaned out the dead tissue.

When they reached Corpus Christi, Spohn forbade water, gave bromide freely, and began a bedside watch for the dreaded symptoms of rabies. Four days later, on March 15, Willie Chamberlain had his first seizure. The seizures were so severe that Chamberlain asked to be tied to the bed to keep from hurting himself. After an even worse attack the next day, Dr. Spohn told Henrietta King that the only hope for saving Willie was to take him to the Pasteur Institute in Paris, France. She did not hesitate and said to do whatever was necessary to save his life. Spohn, Willie, and his brother Edwin left for Galveston by boat and continued on to New York, where they barely caught a tugboat that took them out to board the ship named *Alaska*, bound for Paris.[4]

Spohn later described the voyage to a *New York Herald* reporter in Paris on April 2, 1888. This article and others were picked up across the nation. Spohn said one of the first things Willie said to him was a request to not mention water in his presence. One of the symptoms of rabies is an irrational fear of water, or hydrophobia. He also asked that if they saw water to please notify him so he could cover his head. During the trip he experienced other seizures. Spohn said that before the seizure his eyes would become red, his eyelids would tremble, and he would lose consciousness for about two or three hours. When he awoke he complained of being exhausted. Willie said that no one knew how much he suffered during the trip. He tried hard to control himself but could not always do so, and he asked at one point to be restrained.

Spohn gave him bromide, probably potassium bromide, a relatively safe drug used for seizure prevention. It was also used as an epilepsy treatment well into the twentieth century due to sedative and antiemetic effects. Willie suffered from despondency and sometimes would not communicate with Edwin or Spohn. Other times he imagined he was being abused and insisted on his way or he became terribly agitated and abusive. After these attacks he always apologized. He also liked to go off to a part of the vessel and lie down and would not notice anyone.

The New York Herald reporter interviewed some of the passengers on the Alaska to get their impression of Willie's trip. Passengers said they noticed Willie's strange appearance, but the facial scar was explained by saying that he had been shot. The news soon leaked out about the bite, but little was observed about Willie except his moodiness and shyness. There were a few jokes about the danger of a bite from him, but there seemed to be nothing but good wishes for his recovery.[5] Spohn related that when they arrived in Paris, Willie was nervous and despondent.

According to Spohn, when patients entered Pasteur's institution it was with awe and astonishment on their faces, rather than the pain and suffering usually seen in the countenances of those in the late stages of disease. Spohn described Monsieur Pasteur as calm, courteous, and decisive. He spoke extremely slowly and gave the impression that every word was studied and thought out.[6]

A New York Herald reporter was present in Paris on April 1, 1888, when Willie received his double inoculation treatment. He described Willie as bravely stepping forward to bare himself for the stiletto-like instrument that Dr. Émile Roux used to introduce the dose of virus. The reporter described Willie as handsome, with dark coal-black eyes. He compared him to a Spanish priest or matador.[7] Spohn said he reassured Willie and did not excite him. He added that the Pasteur treatment had given him the comfort of preventing the dread disease. Willie underwent a series of inoculations during his stay and hoped to be an example of the effectiveness of the Pasteur method. Dr. Pasteur said the case was a bad one and the fact he had been bitten by a wolf (actually a coyote) meant the bite went much deeper than that of a dog. Also of concern was the length of time since the bite. Dr. Pasteur suggested that Willie be kept quiet and that he amuse himself, eat a good diet with red wine, and avoid spirits. He also suggested an occasional bath. He stated that Dr. Spohn's treatment had been excellent.[8]

Back home in Texas, Henrietta King, like so many others, followed the case in the American newspapers and was distressed when she read in the *New York Herald* that Dr. Pasteur had said, "I never had a more dreadful case." The entire ranch was worried. Henrietta then became despondent over a report that Willie had suffered a severe attack while in Liverpool awaiting passage to Paris. All she could do was wait with the nation to hear if he would live.[9]

Willie's treatment in Paris was the innovative work of Louis Pasteur, who was born in Dole, France, in 1822. He earned his advanced degrees from the École Normale Supérieure, and his passions were chemistry and research. He played a prominent role in researching vaccination and fermentation, and the process of pasteurization bears his name. In that process, his carefully controlled heating of wine and milk killed microorganisms and led to breakthroughs in the dairy and wine industries. He also aided the silkworm industry by determining the cause of a devastating blight. In 1868 he had suffered a stroke that partially paralyzed his left side, but he continued his work with fowl cholera and anthrax.[10]

Pasteur wanted to protect humans from disease, but he had a major hurdle to overcome: he was not a physician. Fortunately, Émile Roux, who had a doctorate in medicine, became Pasteur's assistant. Together the two men, as well as Charles Chamberland, worked on vaccinations to protect livestock from cholera, anthrax, and rabies, with his two physician partners administering all inoculations.[11]

Pasteur had been critical of physicians and their disregard for unsterile conditions, and they in turn did not appreciate criticism from a chemist who didn't treat patients. And it was true that Pasteur had never tested his treatments (which had worked well on animals) on a human. However, the opportunity to do so came on July 6, 1885, three years before Spohn brought Willie Chamberlain to Paris. Joseph Meister, a nine-year-old boy, had been bitten by a dog that was frothing at the mouth. The boy faced almost certain death.[12] He had fourteen wounds, and his doctor

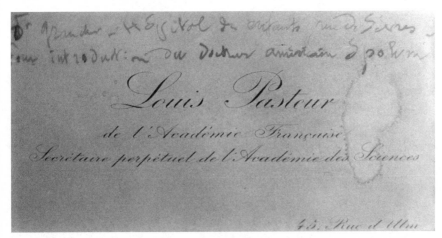

In 1888, Henrietta King's half-brother, Willie Chamberlain, was bitten by a rabid
coyote and Dr. Arthur Spohn took him to the Louis Pasteur Institute in Paris for rabies
inoculation. During Spohn's stay in Paris, Dr. Pasteur gave him this card giving him access
to the institute and hospital. Courtesy of Peter Spohn.

cauterized them and advised the boy's father to take his son to Paris to
see Monsieur Pasteur. The child was inoculated, and Pasteur told Spohn
how distressed he was about the patient, passing sleepless nights worrying
about the boy. Remarkably, the boy survived and was able to return home
in perfect health.[13] Pasteur took a major risk in treating the first human,
but with this success and others to follow, support came in from all over the
world. While Spohn was there with Willie, Pasteur wrote on his personal
card instructions giving Spohn access to the institute and the hospital.
Spohn was able to observe all the procedures and presented a paper about
his experiences at the Pasteur Institute to the Texas Medical Association
in April 1889.

On Friday, May 18, 1888, a headline in the *Fort Worth Daily Gazette*
read, "Pasteur Saved Him." The article quoted William C. Chamberlain
as saying, "I went away a dead man and I returned alive!" Willie arrived
in France aboard the French steamship *La Gascogne* at eight o'clock in the
evening and then went to Paris, where he was placed under the care of Dr.
Pasteur immediately upon his arrival on March 30. The newspaper article
described his condition as pitiable. Although the pain from the injury was
great, it was nothing compared to the mental agony he endured with the
fear of death from rabies. Willie's case was number 5,803 of those who
had been given the protection against hydrophobia by Dr. Pasteur and his

assistants. The article said that Dr. Spohn had brought a quantity of the rabies virus back to the United States as well as the necessary instruments for its application. Spohn hoped that everyone would appreciate the value of Dr. Pasteur's work and that there would someday be a similar institute in the United States. Willie's closing words to the reporter were, "I never felt better in my life. I've had a splendid time coming home—ah, so different from my experience going abroad, when I didn't know from hour to hour when that terrible madness would seize me!"[14]

The *Texas Courier-Record of Medicine* reported in May 1888 that Dr. Spohn proposed to establish at San Antonio a hospital for the cure of rabies based on Dr. Pasteur's methods. He had secured $15,000 in New York and $5,000 at San Antonio, and he had a promise for $10,000 more.[15] The hospital never materialized, but Henrietta King did contribute $10,000 to Dr. Pasteur in appreciation for saving her brother. When Willie was released, he presented Dr. Pasteur with a gold-headed cane in addition to his sister's check. Dr. Pasteur replied, "My dear friends, it is a great joy for me to see the treatment to which I have devoted my life has once again succeeded. Do not speak of gratitude. I only hope Dr. Spohn will just take back two preparations of the rabies vaccine. With that he will start the biggest thing in America. Adieu," said Pasteur, as Chamberlain seized his hand and kissed it. The great scientist added, "And take back with loving embrace my best wishes to a great country I shall never see." Dr. Pasteur had an agreement with Spohn he would never use the vaccine commercially but only for the benefit of patients.[16]

Willie and Henrietta were eternally grateful to Spohn. It is almost certain that if Spohn had not been Henrietta's physician, Willie would have died a difficult and painful death. Spohn displayed uncommon courage in risking a voyage across the ocean to Paris with a patient like Willie. He knew he had a remote chance of getting him there in time to save his life, but he did not hesitate. He exhibited great patience and expertise in nursing his patient through the seizures and keeping his spirits up during the voyage so he would not give up in despair. Even after he arrived in Paris he gave Willie confidence and support through the painful and difficult treatments.[17] The trip also allowed Spohn the chance of a lifetime to study and observe with an outstanding scientist of the century.

After returning home Willie Chamberlain kept three large portraits in his entry hall in San Antonio, Texas. The center one was of Henrietta, and on either side he placed a portrait of Dr. Spohn and one of Dr. Pasteur. He went on to honor the people who had played such an important role in saving his life. After marrying Carmen Pizana, he and his wife had seven sons and one daughter. Some of the sons were named after the most important men in his life: Richard King Chamberlain after Captain King, Hiram Griswold Chamberlain after his father Hiram Chamberlain, Mifflin Kenedy Chamberlain for Sarah's father, Louis Pasteur Chamberlain, and Arthur Spohn Chamberlain.

In 1912, four children were bitten by a rabid dog in Laredo, Texas, and taken to Monterrey, Mexico, for the Pasteur treatment. They were the grandchildren of Willie Chamberlain.[18]

Chapter 13

Medical Passions

1889–1894

W hen Spohn returned from Europe in 1888 he was full of passion for medicine and the potential it had to help humankind. Spohn had evolved through the years to become an unusually knowledgeable and innovative physician by 1889. Many influential physicians of the day, however, were fairly staid in their opinions. Long-established tradition and experience militated against real changes in medical practice. As already noted, as late as 1881, Pres. James Garfield, who had received non-fatal gunshot wounds, was killed by a medical practice of the day—using unwashed fingers, ungloved hands, and nonsterile instruments to probe his wounds. If the physicians attending Garfield had been followers of Joseph Lister, or if they had just made Garfield comfortable, he might have survived. The overwhelming infection that ensued required eighty painful days to kill him. Some attending physicians blamed "dangerous miasmas" in the presidential mansion or "pestilential vapors of the Potomac flats," in accord with older medical beliefs.[1]

Spohn's writings suggest direct candor without apology. He did not hesitate to criticize those who were afraid to act or attempt new techniques to save patients. His journal descriptions were succinct but detailed. He also illustrated his inventions in his articles. His anterior chest splint made of wood and shoe-sole leather, to allow general mobility while recovering from a collarbone dislocation or break, was unique (see "Fracture of the Clavicle," appendix 1).

Arthur Spohn's difficult medical practice took a daily toll on him, yet he continued his pursuit of excellence and continued to share his knowledge. Kenedy Family Collection, A1995-045.0499 South Texas Archives, James C. Jernigan Library, Texas A&M University–Kingsville.

Spohn was forty-four years old and Sarah was thirty-two in 1889. He had an established practice in Corpus Christi, shared a Marine Service Hospital practice, and participated in a family ranching business. By all accounts he was a successful man. It was not enough, though. A fire still burned in him to improve medicine and patient care. He had earned a national reputation and recognition for his treatment of Willie Chamberlain. This was facilitated by his academic knowledge based on the pursuit of the latest medical breakthroughs. One of the things that distinguished Spohn from other leaders in medicine was that he did not practice in a medical center or large metropolitan area. He practiced in a small city in South Texas. Many times he was pushed to develop new techniques out of necessity, as when he did not have access to what he needed at a rural ranch house, along a dusty road, or at a remote railway station. He had to figure out a solution or watch the patient die. He chose to act, and out of his actions came new developments that he eagerly shared with colleagues around the world.

Spohn had a case on June 25, 1889, that demonstrated his willingness to strive for patient survival rather than the easy declaration of hopelessness. Adrian Bocanegra was a healthy twenty-year-old who was playing with his pistol when it discharged next to his abdomen. This incident was particularly bad because the pistol was an old-fashioned .45-caliber Colt six-shooter. Dr. Spohn got to him about two hours later. He found him lying on his back, pallid, with a feeble pulse and suffering from heavy internal hemorrhage. There was air passing occasionally from the abdominal wound, and a crackling emphysematous sound that indicated gas was escaping into the tissues. Spohn gave him a half a grain of morphia hypodermically and arranged to operate immediately. Dr. Jones of Corpus Christi and Dr. Cock of San Marcos assisted.[2]

Spohn described the situation in his usual crisp and succinct fashion, reprinted here in part:

> The ball entered about two inches to the left of and a little above the navel, passed through the abdominal cavity and lodged under the skin about one inch to the left of the spine near the tenth dorsal vertebra. I sterilized about ten gallons of water by boiling and I added ten percent of carbolic acid for the hands and instruments to the remainder five per cent of boric acid, for flooding the abdominal cavity. I washed the surface of the abdomen with a ten per cent solution of carbolic acid, shaved off all his hair, and dusted it with powdered boric acid. It was two o'clock, four hours after the injury occurred, when Dr. Jones commenced administering the chloroform. I made an incision through the linea alba [vertical up-and-down incision between the rectus muscles to minimize bleeding], from the navel to about two inches above the pubis [pubic bone], arresting all hemorrhage with hot water, and ligatures [thread where necessary], the peritoneal cavity contained clots of blood, and ingested matter; gas also escaped from the intestines. The hemorrhage, which had been very profuse, had evidently eased, but recommenced when I began to examine the intestines, one point bleeding very freely . . . where the ball had passed through the transverse mesocolon [blood vessels contained in an apron of tissue supplying blood to the intestine across the upper abdomen] very near the bowel and cut off quite a large vessel, which I ligated. . . . [I] kept the abdomen flooded with boric acid solution at a temperature of from one hundred to one hundred twelve degrees. . . . [There were] eight openings in all [in the bowel]. . . . I now enlarged the opening by two inches above the navel. . . . Upon passing my hand into the cavity of the pelvis, I found it filled with clotted blood, which I removed. . . . I next turned my attention to closing the openings in the intestine, using ordinary sewing needles, and a fine ligature known as West India Islands grass.[3]

Spohn reported that his patient recovered well. He treated him with mucilaginous (gruel) drinks and beef peptonoids (broth). On the third postoperative day he allowed a little coffee and the next day some chicken broth. He went on with a detailed description of what he saw and how he repaired the damage as well as how close to make the stitches and what to use, how to bandage the wound, and how to nurse and feed the patient after the incision was healing and the stitches were removed (see "Gunshot Wound of the Abdomen," in appendix 1 for the full report).

In his article about the surgery, Spohn explained the details he thought were important in operating. Ideally surgery should be done in a well-ventilated room with a temperature of 98 to 100 degrees. There should be plenty of sterilized water, and the operator and assistants should be very clean. He always bathed and changed his clothing before an operation, and he believed that the hands must be thoroughly disinfected using a strong solution of carbolic acid. He also believed in not checking the wound until the fifth day but changing the dressing daily until the ninth or tenth day, when he removed the stitches.[4]

His discussion of drains, abdominal irrigation, and having a bloodless field before closing the wound are very close to current medical management, much of which changes in approximately ten-year cycles as technology advances. His principles of immediate exploration of the injured abdomen did not change until the 1990s and especially in the early twenty-first century in the United States, when imaging technologies and small-scale video equipment became available.

He also described another surgical procedure, done on a man he had found on a walking trail after the train Spohn was on stopped for fuel. In desperation and with only bystanders to help, he placed the man, whose lower extremities had been paralyzed from a .45-caliber bullet that had passed through the abdomen and into the spine, onto a baggage car and performed the surgery at the next train station on the railway. He cleaned out the blood and sutured the bleeding blood vessel, as well as surgically repairing the man's intestines, all as though it was a simple task.

Spohn's comment was that "we may often save lives by acting promptly and fearlessly."

I frequently see notices in our state newspaper saying, "shot through the bowel; died a few hours after"; and I find invariably that no attempt was made to save the unfortunate, or at least to give him a chance for life. I live in a rural district myself, or rather in a little country town [population of Corpus Christi was about forty-three hundred in 1890], so that I know how one feels to stand by and see the life of a fellow-man slowly ebbing away; and if this report will stimulate my fellow practitioners of the rural districts to do their duty under all circumstances, I am more than repaid for my trouble in making it.[5]

Later in the year, on October 19, 1889, Spohn had another article published in the *Medical and Surgical Reporter*. This time he wrote about a "reliable remedy" he used for infections of the throat and lungs. Spohn reported that he used pure oil of turpentine and had better results than those from any other remedy he tried. He used a hand atomizer as a spray and was surprised at how a diphtheric membrane would melt away. He used it for any sore throat and in cases of tuberculosis of the lungs, bronchitis, and later stages of pneumonia. He sometimes had the family hang flannel cloths saturated with oil of turpentine around the room and bed, and his patients expressed much relief.[6]

People in poorer countries and in rural America had for years used kerosene and turpentine for medical purposes. Spohn was relating a successful, inexpensive solution he had utilized in a rural setting with good results. The medical journals in which he published his reports were the key method of spreading the word about good practices and the latest advances. His article on the use of turpentine was reprinted on December 27, 1889, by the *Hickman Courier* in Hickman, Kentucky.[7]

Spohn had another article published in the *Medical and Surgical Reporter* in February 1891, and it discussed his treatment for carbuncles.[8] Several years before, he had been called to see a patient who lived in the remote countryside some fifty miles from Corpus Christi. A house call of that magnitude was not unusual in South Texas. Traveling that distance, with stops to water and rest the horse, would take the better part of a day or night. Many of the pastures comprised some ten to five hundred acres in one enclosure, which he would have to pass through or go around. This case was another illustration of invention through necessity and learning by observation, causing the established "best practice" to be suspect.

During this trip Spohn met a man on the road who was suffering fearfully with carbuncles, which are severe abscesses or multiple boils. The man had three carbuncles, one each on his wrist, on his neck, and on his back. The one on his back was three inches across. Spohn used the only medicine he had with him, a saturated solution of chloral hydrate in water and glycerin, to try to give the man some relief. Spohn had nothing to use for poultices (a soft mass of material), so he used bread. After relieving the patient's pain, he planned to do the usual incisions. He was surprised the

Dr. Arthur Spohn spent hours in this buggy, traveling day and night over difficult roads and in inclement weather to treat his patients throughout South Texas. Photograph by Michael Carlisle MCC Media. Buggy from the collection of the Corpus Christi Museum of Science and History.

Dr. Arthur Spohn's desk and medical bag. Photograph by Michael Carlisle MCC Media. From the collection of the Corpus Christi Museum of Science and History.

next morning to see the carbuncles looking so much better that he decided
not to lance them as planned. Two months later the man came to his office to get a prescription for the treatment of carbuncles, remarking that it
had healed them. After that case, Spohn used the same solution but used
absorbent cotton and added sulfide of calcium, given internally. What is
astounding about this method is that Spohn realized that bread could be
used as a poultice and he did not hesitate to use it. This is another example
of Spohn's ability to use what was at hand in order to deliver relief to a
sufferer. He was always willing to learn, and to benefit from that learning
and experimentation and then pass the information along in the medical
journals.

Spohn continued to follow the latest advances in medicine, and in his
article he mentioned the treatment of carbuncles by Professor Verneuil of
Paris, who used carbolic acid as a spray. Spohn thought that approach had
a lot of merit. His conclusion in the article was that he now would never
make incisions into a carbuncle. He considered lancing a carbuncle to be a
relic of surgical barbarism. The incision was useless, painful, and exposed a
fresh surface to virus. He also cited the benefit of a sixty-thousand-gallon-
a-day artesian well in Corpus Christi that contained principally chloride
of sodium and sulfate of sodium and was impregnated with sulfurated
hydrogen gas. He said it was an excellent laxative and free to everyone in
town.[9]

Later in his career, on October 14, 1891, Spohn wrote a letter on his
Marine Hospital Service stationery to George Fulton, Esq. George Fulton
was a graduate of Harvard Law School who was practicing in Rockport
and taking care of the legal affairs of the Coleman-Fulton Pasture Company. He was also serving in the Texas House of Representatives in 1891,
representing the Eighty-Fifth District.[10] The Coleman-Fulton company
at one point controlled up to 265,000 acres. George Fulton and his wife
Leonora (Caruthers) had three children, and he received Spohn's letter after having contacted the doctor about his daughter. A dog had bitten the
girl, and George, fearing rabies, had contacted Spohn for advice. Spohn
expressed his regret that the little girl had been bitten and said the chances
were that nothing was wrong with the dog, but as a precaution he said
he recommended that the man "destroy" the surface of the girl's wound.
Spohn instructed George to immediately touch the wound surface with
pure carbolic acid and a minute later to wash the surface, removing all
the acid. He then suggested sending the child to him so he could see the

wound; he also recommended keeping an eye on the dog. Spohn also sent him a pamphlet about such wounds. The pamphlet was the result of much study and research on the subject, and it included advice from Paris that had not changed since it was written. Spohn closed the letter by saying he thought the girl would have no problem after the pure acid treatment but that he thought it best for the man to bring his daughter to see him in Corpus Christi.

In October, Spohn had another unfortunate incident to attend. Price Staples, a prominent merchant whose family name is familiar to Corpus Christi residents because of Staples Street, was in a pen trying to rope a steer for branding when he accidentally discharged his weapon. The bullet struck him in the right knee. After he was brought in to the medical office Spohn and Dr. Heaney extracted the ball, but his recovery did not go well and he died two and a half weeks later, at only twenty-nine years of age.[11]

While Spohn was busy with his practice and medical journal articles, he still had to deal with certain domestic issues at home. Mifflin was having eye problems, and the adopted sister, Carmen Morell, was causing difficulties for him. She had been living with Mifflin since her adoption in 1887 and was enjoying being a part of the Corpus Christi social scene. She had become accustomed to wearing the latest fashions and was in a dispute with Wolff & Marx Dry Goods and Clothing in San Antonio over a special hand-made dress she had ordered. The dress had not arrived on time, so she sent a wire canceling the order. However, the dress had already been shipped. The store owner wrote to Mifflin Kenedy on April 19, sending a bill for purchased merchandise of $48.91 (the equivalent of about $1,248 today). The owner explained that there had been some difficulties when the order was placed, but the dress had turned out so nicely that he was sure his daughter would be pleased.[12]

Evidently the matter was still not settled. On May 1 the owner again wrote to Captain Kenedy saying that his daughter had been in the store picking out more items. The owner said his clerks "felt a delicacy to refuse it in order not to hurt your daughter's feelings." He requested that if Captain Kenedy did not approve the purchases he should return them at the store's expense.[13]

As for Mifflin's eye problems, on May 6 he received a letter from Robert Kleberg inquiring if he was still going to New York for an eye treatment and, if so, when he would be leaving. Evidently Mifflin did go to New York and was away from Corpus Christi when Sarah became ill.[14]

Spohn wrote Mifflin a letter on June 1 explaining Sarah's harrowing experience. She had at that point been ill for several months, evidently after giving birth. There had been family stories about Arthur and Sarah having a stillborn baby, but this letter provides the first documentary evidence of it. Spohn became very concerned about her health and consulted Professors Goodell and Thomas in Philadelphia in hopes of conclusively determining and treating the cause of her illness. They said to bring her at once. Spohn wrote that doing so would be very difficult because she had already been sick for more than two months, but they were able to make the trip successfully with the help of Dr. Heaney, Mrs. Doddridge, and Nene (Maria Vicenta). According to Spohn, Sarah came very near dying several times.

They reached Philadelphia on May 27, 1890, and had a consultation with the most prominent surgeons of Philadelphia. Her only chance for survival was an immediate operation—the most dangerous and difficult surgery known to medicine. Spohn was afraid to tell Sarah how difficult it was, as it might make her fearful in her already weakened condition, and she might give up. Spohn told Mifflin she was very brave and went into surgery without a murmur.

Spohn explained the situation to Mifflin. As he had suspected all along, the afterbirth had remained in place, along with membranes and several pints of clotted blood. It was very fortunate the doctors had made a correct diagnosis or she would certainly have died. Spohn assured Mifflin that Dr. Heaney would fully explain the surgery to him in Corpus Christi. It had been thirty hours since the operation and she was resting well. He thought if she passed the next forty-eight hours she would be in little danger.[15]

Sarah's family had been very concerned about her and followed her progress closely. On May 25 Robert Dalzell, Mifflin's stepson-in-law, wrote Mifflin, telling him how anxious they all were about Sarah, because they knew her condition was very critical. They had learned the previous day that she had been taken to Philadelphia, and they hoped she would soon obtain relief. He also hoped Mifflin had obtained relief for his eyes.[16]

On May 29 Dalzell wrote again, indicating they had received both Mifflin's telegram and Carmen's saying Sarah's operation was a success but that it would be several days before they knew she was out of danger.[17] On June 4 Dalzell wrote again saying he was sorry that Mifflin had not received the benefits of treatment to get his sight back, but he had received the June 3 telegram saying Sarah was out of danger and that they had been fearful of the result of her operation. Then he made an interesting comment: "I would

Sarah Spohn's brother-in-law Robert Dalzell wrote Mifflin Kenedy on May 29, 1890, inquiring about Sarah's health and expressing hope that she was out of danger. Courtesy Brownsville Historical Association.

not be surprised at anything that Spohn would do."[18] In other words, he believed Spohn would go to any lengths to save Sarah or his other patients.

On June 13, Spohn wrote Mifflin to say they had received his kind letter that evening. He assured his father-in-law that Sarah was doing nicely, even better than could have been expected under the circumstances. She had sat up supported by pillows for the first time. Her wound had healed except for a glass tube inserted to drain the pus, and he thought that that measure could be discontinued before too long. Spohn wrote that she had lost a lot of weight and was very thin, but with nourishment she should be fine. He expressed his appreciation for the kindness of the family and all their friends.[19]

Evidently this incident with Sarah and her being cared for in a women's medical facility in Philadelphia further motivated Spohn to turn his interest to a specific branch of medicine. The University of Pennsylvania, located in Philadelphia, had established a medical school there in 1765.[20] By 1885 the university had added a nursing training school, where Spohn saw the importance of having good administrators to manage the hospital and wards. (He later turned to Catholic nuns to administer the hospital he founded in Corpus Christi.) Two years before Spohn took Sarah to Philadelphia, the Gynecean Hospital for the medical and surgical treatment of diseases of women had opened in that city.[21] Spohn knew where the best care for Sarah was, and he took her there without hesitation. Three years later he was elected to the Board of Census for the Medico-Chirurgical College in Philadelphia.[22]

Upon his return to Corpus Christi, Spohn devoted much of his time to women's medical problems. In a paper he presented in Waco, Texas, in 1893, he laid out his philosophy of treating women, again emphasizing the need to act decisively. In these days of numerous medical advances the general practitioner could no longer totally depend on specialists. In emergency cases of caesarean hysterectomy, acute septic peritonitis, or ectopic pregnancy, the patients could not wait. He explained his method of surgical treatment in such cases, hoping his approach would be helpful to his fellow physicians. He first suggested that the room be well ventilated and aseptic, with any bedding having been boiled before use. He described how to clean the patient, especially the vagina and the uterus, the diet necessary before surgery, and the cleaning of the instruments and preparation of the thread, which he did himself and placed in glass tubes filled with an aseptic solution. Horsehair was his favorite ligature. He turned to Gemrig & Son of Philadelphia and Geo. Tiemann & Co. of New York to make a knife and needle holder of his own design. He talked extensively about cleaning the wound with boric acid and using proper dressings. He discussed the importance of the cleanliness of his assistants and an operating apron he designed, as well as the care of his patients. Spohn left nothing to chance. He then described several surgical cases in which he had been assisted by Drs. Heaney, Westervelt, and Hamilton of Corpus Christi and students T. S. Burke and Jno. Westervelt.[23]

In his presentation Spohn described nine cases he had dealt with, including one case that was the "first operation for this condition ever performed in the United States," according to a Dr. Robert P. Harris of Philadelphia.[24] Seven of the other eight cases involved females ranging in age from six to forty-three. All of the cases were extremely difficult and Spohn had preserved specimens from the patients and brought them to Waco for display. Below are brief descriptions of the patients and their conditions.

Adela G. was six years old and apparently in good health. She had a large tumor in her abdomen on the right side. Spohn removed the tumor but was disturbed by the protrusion of the intestines. He wrote Dr. Robert P. Harris of Philadelphia asking him to review the case and said he thought the growth might be a carcinoma or cancer. That information, if confirmed, would be devastating to the family.

M. C. was eighteen and single. Her family noticed she was getting large and her menses had ceased, causing alarm in the family. Spohn put her under chloroform and conducted a transrectal examination. Several days later he removed an ovarian tumor and found the left ovary was also enlarged (about the size of a lemon), so he removed both ovaries.

Mattie L., age twenty-six, had no signs of a specific disease but was very weak and emaciated. She had been in constant pain for three years and sometimes required morphia for relief. Spohn operated, finding extensive adhesions, and removed both ovaries. She made a quick recovery.

Mrs. B was thirty-one and the mother of one child. She had been an invalid for ten years after being thrown from a carriage. Due to the pain she had been experiencing, her family agreed to let Spohn operate. He removed both ovaries and her uterus, and she was liberated from the pain that had followed her like a shadow.

Mrs. D was thirty-eight and had had one child eighteen years before. She was very weak and anemic and had been an invalid since the birth of her child. She could not sit up or walk. Spohn was afraid she might die before he could operate, as she had to be brought three hundred miles by railroad on a bed. Her right ovary was about the size of a large orange, and the tube was firmly bound to surrounding parts by adhesions. The left ovary was the same and there was severe hemorrhaging during surgery, but she recovered.

He reported one case in which opening the abdominal cavity became necessary because the patient was very weak from shock and loss of blood. Mr. H., age thirty-eight, had attempted to draw a Winchester rifle from a carriage and caught it by the wrong end. It discharged, and the ball entered him over the region of the liver and came out three inches to the right of the spine. Spohn operated, but the patient complained of severe pain. The doctor had to carry him six miles in an ambulance (carriage) and fifteen by rail car to get him to Corpus Christi. He operated on him again and found a brass buckle of his suspender that had been carried in by the bullet. The patient made a recovery without complications.

Spohn was not always successful. Mrs. M was age thirty-four with four children. When Spohn saw her, she had a temperature of 105 and was vomiting a greenish-black fluid. She had miscarried three weeks before and the physician in attendance thought the case hopeless but suggested that the family consult with Spohn. He determined she was suffering from severe septic peritonitis and advised operating, which he did, and found the ovaries ruptured, with an abscess on each one. She passed away, and Spohn said she was one of those unfortunate cases where delay in treatment and lack of proper treatment led to her death. He urged that women had to have their uteruses thoroughly cleaned out and treated after miscarriages. Once again he took his treatment a step further and instructed Gemrig & Son of Philadelphia to produce an instrument that he designed to place his solution into the uterus for complete cleaning.[25]

Spohn was ahead of his time. It took the triumph of bacteriology in the 1880s to begin to convince physicians that germs were responsible for puerperal fever. Still, misguided doctors took hygienic shortcuts to save time and did not provide sterile environments. In 1900 about 90 percent of births were home births in germ-infested bedrooms.[26]

In the case of Mrs. G, a forty-two-year-old, Spohn again found himself in an emergency situation. She was very short and stout and had nine children. She suffered from malacosteon, a condition in which the bones soften, and her spine was bent as a result. Spohn had delivered her last two children under extremely difficult conditions. She was so bent over that her curvature was only two and one-half inches from her pubic arch. Spohn had told her after the previous delivery that she should not give birth again. On November 20, 1891, he was called to see her again and to his surprise found her in full-term labor. She had been in labor for three days and he realized it was impossible for her to give birth to her child. He opened the abdomen in a very complicated procedure but by working fast was able to deliver the well-developed living child and remove her uterus without complications. Spohn was relieved that the child was healthy because he had worried about the pressure on the child's head. He saw the mother a year later and she was still making her living grinding corn for tortillas. When he saw her on the street she was carrying a sack of corn on her head and did not look like she had undergone an operation for coelo-hysterectomy, to use his term (abdominal hysterectomy).[27] As the case of this patient suggests, another thing that distinguished Spohn from some other physicians was that he treated all people no matter what their economic situation. Regretfully, many patients went unrecorded and his medical records were presumed lost in 1919 when a hurricane destroyed the Spohn Sanitarium.

Spohn firmly believed in the importance of sharing new ideas and best practices to improve the medical services physicians provided to their patients. Although medical meetings were disruptive to his practice and

Dr. Arthur Spohn found himself too heavy to try the new "wheel," or bicycle, for exercise in 1894 but said he thought it was safe for outdoor exercise. *Corpus Christi Caller-Times.*

he had to travel long distances to attend, Spohn nevertheless attended them to learn from his fellow physicians' papers and to debate the issues of the day. Most of these discussions were scholarly, but occasionally they assumed a lighter tone.

On January 10, 1894, Spohn attended a meeting of the Central Texas Medical Association. Spohn's fame had spread throughout Texas, and his arrival was well anticipated. In the January 4 *Waco Evening News* it had been announced that "Dr. A. E. Spohn, the distinguished Corpus Christi surgeon, will visit Waco next week."[28] During the meeting Spohn entered into an interesting discussion on the merits of bicycle exercise. Dr. H. C. Black of Waco discussed the evil effects of bicycling on pulmonary, cardiac, and pelvic structures. He thought excessive use was very injurious to the health. He made the point that only the legs were enhanced and the rest of the body was forced into an unhealthy stooping posture. The other physicians assailed his opinion; they thought bicycling could be beneficial. Spohn, perhaps tongue in cheek, said he regretted that he was too old and too large to ride a "wheel" for exercise. He did say he thought it was generally safe for those who needed outdoor exercise.[29]

Chapter 14

Challenging Times

1895–1899

The last years of the nineteenth century were filled with loss, tragedy, conflict, and challenges for Arthur and Sarah. Important events had occurred in the family leading up to this time. Spohn's Canadian relatives in Texas had undergone many changes. In 1882 Spohn had lost his brother-in-law, Alexander Hamilton, as well as Alexander's son, Alexander, who had been attending medical school. Another brother, Jacob Van Wagner Spohn, who was a barrister in Canada, and his wife, Mary, came to Encinal, Texas, to ranch and be near his brother Henry, who was two years older than Jacob. They lived there until Jacob's death in 1893, when Mary returned to Ontario.[1]

Spohn's nephew Henry J. Hamilton (Harry) was Alexander and Catherine's son. Harry had completed his medical training at the University of Louisville in 1890 and returned to Texas to join his Uncle Arthur in establishing the Bay View Infirmary, where he served as an intern. He stayed for only about six months; when he found that Uncle Arthur collected all the money, he decided to leave. Spohn advised him to go to Mexico so that he could earn the money he needed. Harry took his advice and went to Guerrero, Mexico. Dr. Charles Winslow had been there twenty years earlier, when Spohn had been in Guerrero serving in the US Army. Harry became an American citizen and was appointed American consul at Guerrero. That job paid him $100 per month. He became a member of the board of health there and made forty to fifty visits daily. He made enough money in Guerrero to go to Philadelphia for postgraduate courses.[2] In 1892 he was back in Texas, where his life took some unexpected turns.

The 1892 election of Grover Cleveland as president of the United States ended the sheep boom in Texas because the new president lifted the embargo on sheep from Mexico, decimating the market for American sheep. Harry was obligated to travel first to the Spohn Ranch to help his mother sell her sheep. While he was there, the Spohn siblings (Arthur, Henry, and Catherine) decided to switch from sheep to cattle and went into partnership with Webb Sullivan of San Patricio County.[3]

Spohn telegraphed Harry that Sullivan had pneumonia and asked him to go to Corpus with a buckboard and a cowboy, round up a herd of cattle, and take the livestock to the ranch. Harry later reported that he had found the cattle herd, recovered all the cattle after they stampeded, and finally got to the ranch with fifteen more than he started with. They didn't teach any of those skills in medical school.[4]

While Harry was at the ranch, the commissioners court in neighboring La Salle County asked him to be their county health officer because their present health officer was causing a significant problem: he was diagnosing Anglos as having roseola and Mexicans as having smallpox. Harry accepted the position and went to the county seat, Cotulla, taking two gunmen with him as guards because Cotulla was known as a dangerous place. When he arrived there, he placed the county health officer in his home under guard because he had attended smallpox victims and later attended his sister, who caught the disease and died. The people in the town were furious with Harry and wrote the state health officer that Harry had the doctor locked up, which was against the law. The state officer, who happened to be a friend of Harry, wrote back that if Harry thought it was necessary to confine the doctor, then that was the way it was going to be. Since the county was considered lawless, a company of Texas Rangers was placed under Harry's authority. It took Harry about forty days to clean up the town, but he profited from doing so, since both the state and the county paid him.[5]

Harry then went to San Diego, in Duval County, but Spohn sent him a telegram asking that he go take care of a relative. This time Harry's cousin and Spohn's nephew, Angus Peter "Dumpy" Spohn, was in trouble. Angus had worked for Uncle Henry on the ranch and then in the town of Encinal. In 1887 he had been appointed mounted inspector for the customs service and assigned to Carrizo in Zapata County along the Texas-Mexico border.

Spohn told Harry that Dumpy had been shot, at or near Zapata, Texas, on April 24. Harry grabbed the instrument case he had bought in Mexico and boarded a train at once. After he got off the train, he rode fifty miles by horseback to reach his cousin.

During the trip Harry heard that Dumpy was dead. He abandoned his heavy operating case and only took his pocket case. Harry found his cousin about twenty-three miles south of Zapata, and to his amazement he was alive. A Mexican doctor had applied sulfate of iron to stop the external bleeding, but Angus was still bleeding internally. He was shot through the pelvis on the left side and the bullet had exited on his right side four inches above the anus. Harry sent to Mexico for an anal speculum and found where the bullet had passed through the gut. He was then able to wash out the wound. Harry rested that night, but about midnight Dumpy had very severe bleeding that Harry could not control. He sent a courier to Laredo to telegraph for Spohn to come and help. In the meantime Harry operated with a lantern for illumination, but Dumpy ended up kicking it over, so Harry had

Dr. Henry J. Hamilton was Arthur Spohn's nephew, and he served in the Marine Hospital Service, later known as the Public Health Service. He was on the front lines battling disease in South Texas and Laredo. The Marine Hospital Service inspected and sanitized ships and examined sailors for signs of infectious disease. They also inspected trains and guarded the borders to prevent the spread of contagious illnesses. Courtesy of Randolph Slaughter Jr.

to use a hand light. He managed to find the artery and tie it off, meanwhile keeping the circulation to his legs going with hot water bottles. Spohn had arrived by April 27, and they immediately performed an operation and were able to put in a drainage tube that provided some relief. Spohn was quoted in the newspaper as saying it was nearly impossible for a person to be shot in this way without almost immediate death.[6]

Harry then moved to Laredo to establish his own medical practice. In 1898 he was appointed surgeon in charge of the US Public Health Service at Laredo. Harry's brother, Arthur Claud Hamilton, opened his law practice in Laredo in 1894.[7] Spohn's family was thus well established in the Laredo area and along the border. Angus (Dumpy) recovered from his wound and in 1897, as noted earlier, was appointed county judge of Zapata County, where he became known as the "King of Zapata."[8]

This photograph of guests at a house party at the home of Sarah and Arthur Spohn was taken in 1885. Standing in back, left to right, are Sam Rankin, Royal Givens, Atlee McCampbell, Tom Southgate, Miss Hamm, and Robert Kleberg. Second row: Dr. A. E. Spohn with wife, Sarah, behind him, Miss Maude White, unknown woman, Mr. Lackey, and Mrs. Lackey. Courtesy of *Corpus Christi Caller-Times*, Corpus Christi Public Libraries. Enhanced by Phojoe Photo.

Meanwhile, since 1885 Sarah had experienced several losses: her brother James; her mother, Petra; and her brother Tom, the "man about town" in Brownsville, who was ambushed and killed.[9] After Tom's death, Sarah's only Kenedy relatives were her brother John, his wife Marie Stella, and the wife and son of her deceased brother James (Corina Kenedy and George Kenedy). However, she still had many relatives from Petra's side and also her newly adopted sister, Carmen Morell, with whom she seemed to be close at the time.

Carmen was accepted as Mifflin's daughter not only by Sarah but also by Corpus Christi society. She was prominent enough that the *Corpus Christi Caller* reported on August 19, 1892, that Miss C. Morell Kenedy was confined to her room with an illness.[10] On September 2 it was reported that her many friends would be delighted to learn she had almost completely recovered.[11] She was well enough by October 28 to have the newspaper describe her exquisite black gabardine dress that she wore at the Columbian Ball. Perhaps she special ordered the dress from Wolff & Marx in San Antonio.[12]

Sarah and Arthur also entertained in Mifflin Kenedy's famous mansion that he'd built for Petra, with the paintings, statuary, books, and items they had collected on their European and Mediterranean trips. In February 1891, Arthur and Sarah hosted a pre-Lenten entertainment at the mansion, in honor of Sarah's sister-in-law Marie Stella. The newspaper reported that guests could spend hours looking in the spacious rooms filled with Venetian glass, lace, bejeweled objects, and handsomely carved oak chairs and frames. The reporter commented that Sarah had inherited her taste in art from her father, who had one of the finest art collections in Texas. The entertainment throughout the evening was by good friends and family. Sarah and Marie Stella performed a duet. The group persuaded Robert Kleberg to sing "In the Days of Old, When Knights Were Bold," reminding everyone why he was always in demand. Mrs. Henry Redmond arranged a game of book title charades for everyone's delight. Dr. Redmond entered the room dressed in a long black coat buttoned to his throat, a dotted veil over his face, and an old paper in each hand. The guests were told that he represented three books. After much gaiety, Mrs. G. R. Scott won the prize by guessing the books were *Man in Black*, *The Veiled Doctor*, and *Pages from an Old Volume of Life*.[13]

During this period, Spohn was away from home a great deal of the time. His passion was medicine, so when he was not traveling long distances to see patients, he was reading, writing for medical journals, and traveling to meetings. Not unlike physicians today, his time was not his own and many times not Sarah's either. This led to a lonely life for Sarah. They had no children, so she turned to friends to keep her company.

Spohn continued to be on call during this time, for Sarah's family as well as the King and Kleberg families, and he also maintained his regular practice. As already noted, he delivered five of Robert and Alice King Kleberg's children. John and Marie Stella Kenedy's little girl, named for her aunt Sarah Spohn and called Sarita (little Sarah), became ill in the middle of November 1894. Mifflin, who always attended to every detail, was very worried about his only granddaughter and sent a telegram to John at La Parra wanting to know if Dr. Spohn had arrived.[14] Two days prior, John had telegraphed Spohn asking how to treat Sarita, who evidently had chickenpox. He prescribed a warm bath with a tablespoon of baking soda or borax to a gallon of water. He also suggested sterilizing baking flour and

Mifflin Kenedy died suddenly without a will, and his death had many repercussions throughout his complex family. The *San Antonio Express* reported, "He was a man of deed, not words, and the loss is irreparable."

placing it on the eruptions. With chickenpox the sores are first clear, then yellow, and then dry up. He also suggested using red curtains to filter the light to protect her eyes.[15]

Also that month the *Brownsville Daily Herald* noted that "Dr. Spohn made a shipment of his famous rattlesnake medicine last week to India, the party having seen Dr. Spohn's article on the subject in the London *Lancet*. Spohn apparently felt pleased to have received an order from such a great distance. The medicine appeared to work very effectively, stockmen said, who had used it when bitten."[16] Spohn described his snakebite treatment in an article, "Rabies and Anti-Rabic Inoculations," based on a paper he presented at the Twenty-First Annual Session of the Texas Medical Association in San Antonio, April 23–26, 1889 (see the text of his paper in appendix 1). He related that his friend Professor Croft of Toronto University had inspired him to develop the treatment by demonstrating that iodine is a chemical antidote for the poison of the rattlesnake.[17]

Evidently the use of iodine for snakebite was known in other parts of the world. In the *Queensland Agricultural Journal*, Dr. E. F. Brown, who practiced in Lake City, Florida, related a case in which a boy plowing the fields was bitten by a ground rattler. Dr. Brown did not see him until three or four hours later, when it was too late to treat the outward wound, so he put ten drops of iodine tincture into ten teaspoons of water and gave him a teaspoon every five minutes. He then lengthened it to every half hour. The next morning the patient was once again plowing the fields, with no ill effects.[18] Spohn had his own remedy and always excised the wound to relieve the patient's mind. He then used equal parts tincture of iodine, aqua ammonia, glycerine, and tincture of belladonna to wash the wound and take internally. He said it was a "popular remedy in my section of the State; is kept in almost every house, and, I am told gives excellent results."[19]

In March, Mifflin Kenedy died suddenly. When a man with the stature of Mifflin Kenedy dies, the impact is felt in many areas, but with the complex Kenedy family tree his death was particularly disruptive. Mifflin was known for his attention to every detail. He was famous for micromanaging not only his affairs but also those of everyone around him. Mifflin died without a will, which was not in keeping with his personality. He had allowed Petra to die without a will because he did not have the cash to settle with her heirs and did not want to sell land to pay them. There has always been a question of whether Mifflin did not have a will or that the will disappeared. Regardless, he officially died intestate.

Mifflin died on March 14, 1895, with the newspapers reporting his death the next day. According to one article, "His death cast a gloom over the city with deep regret on every hand," especially as his death was sudden and unexpected. He was at his office the night before his death, visiting pleasantly with friends, and he had retired in good health. In the morning he had his coffee in his room as usual and about half past seven he complained of not feeling well. Drs. Heaney and Spohn were called immediately, with Dr. Heaney arriving first. Mifflin told him he was suffocating and felt bad. He began to sink fast and died at fifteen minutes to eight, having been sick only about thirty minutes.[20]

Spohn sent for John at La Parra, seventy-five miles away. Rosa Putegnat was visiting at the time, and she and John reached Corpus Christi at about ten at night after a twelve-hour drive. Mifflin was seventy-six years old. He was survived by his son John Gregory Kenedy, daughter Sarah ("Mrs. Dr. Spohn"), adopted daughter Miss Carmen Morell Kenedy, and four stepdaughters: Mrs. Robert Dalzell, Mrs. Putegnat, Mrs. Starck, and Mrs. Rodriguez. He also had a brother, Capt. E. J. Kenedy, of Brownsville, and a sister, Josephine, in Pennsylvania.[21]

Newspapers carried notices of his death across the state. The *San Antonio Express* article called him "one of the commercial pioneers of the State.

Corina Ballí Treviño married James Kenedy and after his death raised their son, George Kenedy (pictured with his mother), in Laredo and was a benefactor of the Catholic Church. George was one of Mifflin Kenedy's heirs. Courtesy of McAllen Ranch Archives and Mary Margaret McAllen.

A great believer in the advantages of increased transportation facilities, it is due to him, first, that the Lower Rio Grande country was put in touch with the rest of the world by means of steamers, and second, that the San Antonio & Aransas Pass Railway now travels eight hundred miles of Texas territory, the people of twenty-one counties thereby being directly benefited. ... He was a man of deeds, not words, and the loss is irreparable."[22]

Mifflin's death was difficult not just in terms of emotions. It also disrupted the family's cohesiveness and had serious consequences for Sarah. The settling of the estate eventually caused great friction between Carmen, the adopted daughter, and the blood relatives. She was now a full heir entitled to one-fourth of Mifflin's estate. The blood relatives were Sarah Kenedy Spohn, John Kenedy, and James Kenedy's son George, who was eleven years old. John immediately took charge of all the business affairs and began to try to sort out the estate, and once again there was the issue of not dividing up the Kenedy Pasture Company holdings. Mifflin had placed the La Parra ranch and its holdings into the company, and John did not want Carmen to have one-fourth interest in it. George's mother, Corina Kenedy, also had to be dealt with, and John thought it best to appoint a guardian for George, someone to handle his business affairs until he came of age. He turned to their family friend and lawyer, Robert Kleberg, to be George's guardian.[23]

John Kenedy took charge of settling his father's estate and handling his business affairs. Mifflin Kenedy's heirs were Carmen (Morell) Kenedy, Sarah Kenedy Spohn, John Kenedy, and James Kenedy's son, George.

John had to make immediate arrangements to care for Corina and George and wrote a detailed letter to her on May 22, 1895, suggesting that she move to Corpus Christi temporarily so there would be no question of jurisdiction. He wanted her in Corpus by early June and thought the guardianship hearing would be in early July. He wrote that he was renting her a small cottage on the beach. She was to bring bedding and linens with her and he would take care of getting furniture. Stella was to take care of any of her needs, as Sarah might be away for treatment. He also told her that Carmen and her sisters were living in San Antonio until the partition of the estate was completed.[24] On the same day John wrote to Corina he also sent a letter to the Houston Bros. law firm in San Antonio telling them Sarah might be traveling north in about two weeks and could come through San Antonio and give them her power of attorney.[25]

Sarah Spohn was a prominent member of Corpus Christi society, but she developed health problems after Mifflin's death and Dr. Spohn took her to Canada for treatment. Kenedy Family Collection, A1995-036.xxx, South Texas Archives, James C. Jernigan Library, Texas A&M University–Kingsville.

John divided up Kenedy real estate across Texas into fourths and did likewise with the businesses Mifflin had owned: the Juanita Mining Company in Colorado, Caller Printing Company in Nueces County, San Antonio & Aransas Pass Town Site Company, San Antonio Land & Improvement Company, Alamo Fire Insurance Company, Kenedy Pasture Company, and promissory notes.[26] Each of the four heirs received items valued at about $233,196, an amount today equal to about $6,657,142. The big problem was the homestead on the bluff. Carmen had been living there since her formal adoption, and her sisters often occupied the cottage behind the house. Sarah had hoped to inherit the house, but Carmen was determined to keep it. Initially each of the four heirs had one-fourth interest.

There was a more pressing problem for Sarah and her family, however. It is not known when Sarah Kenedy Spohn developed her addiction problem, but it certainly manifested itself after Mifflin's death and may have been present earlier. It was not unusual for women of the day to take the "vapors," which was a form of opium. These products were sold in pharmacies without prescriptions and were advertised as "non-addictive substitutes" for morphine. One producer was Bayer, selling Bayer's Heroin. Another branded product was Coca Wine. The product manufactured by Angelo Mariani was so popular that Pope Leo XIII used to carry a bottle of it with him, and he awarded Mariani with a Vatican gold medal. "Vapor-oil" was advertised to help asthma. C. F. Boehringer and Soehne in Germany were proud to be the biggest producer in the world of products containing quinine and cocaine. Vapor-oil, which was 10 percent alcohol with three grains of opium per ounce, was considered good for asthma and other spasmatic conditions. Cocaine drops were used for toothaches. Paregoric, for cough and colic among children age five days to adulthood, was produced as a more dilute opium in an alcohol base.[27]

Sarah's problem may have involved a number of different drugs, but it had evidently progressed to the point where morphine was involved, as indicated in a telegram Carmen sent to Sarah's treatment specialist in October 1895.[28] Shortly after Mifflin's death in March 1895, Spohn decided to take action to help Sarah. For help he turned to his relatives in Canada.

Spohn's Canadian family was also talented and accomplished. His nephew, Dr. Herbert Spohn Griffin, had received his medical degree at Toronto University, where he also served on the faculty. He did postgraduate work at Bellevue Hospital and the University College of Physicians and Surgeons in New York. He also studied in London, Edinburgh, Paris, and Vienna. He was a surgeon and one of the founders of the Canadian Medical Association. He practiced in Hamilton, Ontario, and that is probably where he met Dr. Stephen Lett.[29]

Dr. Lett was the first addiction specialist in Canada. He was superintendent of the Homewood Retreat in Guelph, Ontario, and Sarah entered it for treatment, probably referred by Griffin. Lett had been educated at Upper Canada College and was a member of the College of Physicians and Surgeons. He had worked at the Malden Asylum, Toronto Asylum, and Hamilton Asylum before going to Homewood.[30] Homewood was the first private addiction asylum in Canada, and it was founded by John Woodburn Langmuir, who saw the need for a private asylum for paying patients. The facility provided a quiet community and assured anonymity to guests. It was easily reached on the Grand Trunk railway line. It was luxurious for an asylum, having nineteen acres of wooded land and housing for twenty-five men and twenty-five women. The rooms were large. It had a drawing room, conservatory, billiard room, amusement hall, and chapel. The fee was from ten to twelve dollars a week, or patients could pay as much as twenty dollars a week for the best suite. The patients were affluent and urban—senior civil servants, politicians, clergy members, lawyers, merchants, and physicians. In the nineteenth century many professionals and housewives had difficulties with drugs, and Homewood patients suffered from many addictions.[31]

The problem of drug addiction among physicians affected even the famous surgeon Dr. William Halsted, whom Spohn had encountered eleven years before in New York, when Halsted was completing his medical training. Morphine and opium use was widespread, and then along came cocaine, which was considered a marvelous substitute for them. In April 1884, Sigmund Freud wrote the Merck Company of Darmstadt, Germany, to inquire about purchasing a gram of their newly available cocaine alkaloid. He had been reading a great deal about the unique properties of the drug, which was said to enable German soldiers to fight like supermen without sleep. Abstinence from food was possible for days without feeling hunger, and users reported a mild euphoria and general sense of well-being. The substance, long used by South American Indians in religious rituals, had recently been extracted from the coca leaf by Merck chemists and made available for sale.[32]

In 1884 dentists were using general anesthesia for major dental surgery. However, they then began to use cocaine injected along regional nerves before surgery as a safer method than general anesthesia. Dr. Halsted was elated with the news of this new approach, and he and his assistants performed more than one thousand minor surgeries under cocaine local anesthesia.[33] The students and teachers enjoyed the drug so much that they began to use cocaine snuff and injections, neglecting their duties. Dr. Halsted himself became addicted, went away for treatment, and was given morphine, which left him with a double-barreled addiction. As a surgeon he was extraordinary, becoming chief of surgery at Johns Hopkins, but as an addict he was a mess. The *New York Times* referred to him as the drug addict who gave America modern surgery. As an addict he missed work, disappeared for long stretches, and bowed out of operations at the last minute. His article on cocaine anesthesia was gibberish, yet he continued to function and "pioneered treatments for breast cancer, hernias and gall-stones."[34]

Dr. Lett was a proponent of the disease concept of drug abuse rather than believing that patients could abandon their addiction if only they wished to. Dr. Levinstein, a leading physician at the time, supported a method of abrupt and total withdrawal, making the experience close to inhumane torture. Dr. Lett's treatment consisted of a gradual withdrawal, with decreasing amounts of the drug being given in fractions. When the point was reached where only one grain was consumed in twenty-four hours he felt that they were cured. This usually took three to four weeks. He also used tonics, bromides, and cannabis indica to help the patients during this time. Today we recognize this last drug as one of the forms of marijuana.[35]

Sarah did well at Homewood, considering all that happened soon after she arrived. On June 19, John had wired Spohn in Guelph to say that Carmen was offering to accept a payment of $36,000 for the mansion and grounds, or $9,000 from each heir, in exchange for her share of the ranch. John thought they should take the deal and let her have the house, but he did hope he could take the family portraits hanging in the mansion. He wanted to be wired quickly on what to do.[36]

On June 20 John wrote Sarah a letter, with the salutation being "Sally," which was unusual. He described the difficulty of finishing the estate partition on June 19. Mr. Houston, their lawyer in San Antonio, had received a communication from Carmen advising that there were parties who were going to buy the house for $20,000 and that he should offer double if they wanted the house. The appraisers had fixed the value at $20,000, so Carmen's offer upset the whole idea the Kenedy heirs had had in mind, which was that Sarah was to have the house. So that was the reason for John's urgent telegram to Canada.[37]

Carmen wired back, asking when she would have possession of the house. John advised Sarah that he and Robert Kleberg thought it best to buy out Carmen's interest in the ranch property, so they needed to take the deal. John did not think sentiment played any part in Carmen's decision. It was made for selfish reasons, in their view. Carmen also contacted him about selling him the cottage for $8,000, saying that she had another buyer for it. This time John called her hand and refused.[38]

It must have been a blow to Sarah to lose the home that her father had built for her mother. Not only that, but she was also going to lose all of the furnishings they had picked out and ordered from around the world to make it one of the finest houses in Texas.

Carmen was not through yet. The next bizarre incident occurred on October 7, 1895, when John received a letter from Dr. Stephen Lett, informing John that he had received a telegram from Miss Carmen Kenedy, who said that the American consul in Canada was authorized to prosecute him before the law for having intercepted her correspondence to her sister, Mrs. A. E. Spohn. She wrote that she was not guilty of furnishing morphine to Mrs. A. E. Spohn and for that false accusation she would make him pay. Dr. Lett wrote that he must have been misrepresented to Miss Kenedy, and he did not know what action the US consul would take. Should he regard it as a foolish piece of nonsense or what? He would look to John and Dr. Spohn for protection and indemnification.[39]

The family had wondered who had been helping supply Sarah with narcotics, and it appears they had accused Carmen and asked the superintendent (Dr. Lett) to hold her letters to prevent Carmen having any contact with Sarah. Both John and Spohn felt it would be good for Sarah to be away from Corpus Christi after her recovery, so Spohn proposed a trip to Paris for her.[40]

In the meantime Arthur had taken Sarah to Toronto to stay with his brother-in-law, Rev. W. S. Griffin, while he handled the cattle business for John. Reverend Griffin had married Arthur's sister, Mary Margaret, who died at twenty-four in 1856. Reverend Griffin was a Methodist minister and head of the Methodist Church in Upper Canada, serving as superintendent three different times.[41] Arthur knew Sarah would be safe with him. He was also urging her to go to Europe. In a letter to John, Arthur said Sarah was doing well and he thought she could make the trip. He also thought that $2,000 would be enough money for the trip and asked John to wire it to him.[42]

John wrote to Sarah on September 18 after returning from seeing her in Canada. He wrote that he had talked to a Mr. Mallory about her business, as she had asked, and he urged her to take the trip to Europe with Arthur. He had talked with many friends about her taking the trip—Mrs. King, Mrs. Kleberg, Mr. and Mrs. Hirsch, Mr. Mallory, Houston Bros., and all members of her family—and all agreed she should take the trip. He added a postscript: "The Dr. [Spohn] seems down hearted and I think his heart was set on taking you off and I think he did this more for your good than for the pleasure there might be in a trip for himself." He said that she should remember that Arthur had his troubles also.[43]

Sarah consented to go on the trip and wrote to John from New York on board ship on October 12 before it sailed. She told him she had signed

Arthur took Sarah to Europe, Mexico, and Colorado after her recovery in 1895 and after urgings from family and friends. Kenedy Family Collection, A1995-045.0480, South Texas Archives, James C. Jernigan Library, Texas A&M University–Kingsville.

all the paperwork that was needed and Arthur had gone to mail it. She still was not enthusiastic about the trip, but she would not dwell on it. She wanted him to know how much she appreciated everything he had done for her and that she would send a letter from Havre before they left for Paris.[44]

Arthur and Sarah returned home from Paris to find that his visit to the American consular officer in Canada before they sailed to France had been successful, because nothing had resulted from Carmen's threats.[45] Carmen, in a gesture of goodwill toward Sarah and in an effort to repair the damage to their friendship, made a gift to her after she returned home on February 13, 1896. The deed transferring the house to Carmen stated that, "in consideration of the . . . love and affection which I have and bear towards my sister Sarah Kenedy Spohn . . . I give [her] the described oil paintings: *Madame Maintenon, La Madonna de Raphael, A Mythological Picture, The Pope, The Boma, The Greek, The Cook*, and *Austria*, a German Picture, Statuary, *Napoleon* and *The Three Graces*, all belonging to the Kenedy Homestead." This was some of the artwork that Mifflin had bought for Petra and their new home.[46] In March, Carmen held the traditional requiem to mark Mifflin's death. The booklet that was prepared for the memorial was dedicated to the "Sweet Memory of Capt. M. Kenedy and to my friends who stood by me in my bereavement by his daughter Carmen Morell Kenedy."[47]

By June things had evidently turned ugly again, and Arthur had taken action against Carmen. John received a letter from Carmen on June 3, 1897, saying, "Your men appeared in my home and made me believe that Corina was influencing you," meaning that Dr. Spohn had signed an affidavit against her. A Mr. Harriston had told her Dr. Spohn was not her friend, confirming her father's fear that Dr. Spohn was not her friend, which made her sad. She was sure he would influence Sarah.[48]

Arthur decided that travel and taking Sarah out of Corpus Christi would be best. They were in Saltillo, Mexico, on July 9, 1897, when Arthur wrote to John Kenedy saying that they were looking forward to having him and Stella join them there. The weather was perfect and they were sleeping under blankets at night. He and Robert Kleberg had gone bear hunting in the mountains and did not see a bear but saw hundreds of wild pigs. He told John the fruit would all be in season in about two weeks and that there were children everywhere. He suggested John and Stella bring some good clothes because the people were very hospitable and showed them a lot of attention.[49]

By October, Sarah was writing to John and Stella from the Albany Hotel in Denver, Colorado. She and Arthur were off on their long-expected trip to California and had made it as far as Denver. She was surprised that it was such a lovely city, with elegant public buildings and residences. They had seen a good deal of the city before a snowstorm hit, but it was now clearing. They were supposed to leave for Salt Lake City, but the trains had been delayed. They hoped to leave the next day. Major Atwood and Nettie (Henrietta "Nettie" King) had called when they arrived and wanted them to stay at their place for a while, but they thought it best not to inconvenience them. The Spohns stayed instead at the Albany, an elegant hotel that featured the Colonial Room for fine dining. The Atwoods had been exceedingly attentive and Nettie wanted to be kindly remembered to everyone. Sarah noted that she had an engagement with Nettie so she had to close. She sounded well in the letter and closed by saying, "With much love for yourselves, Rosa, Lena, and a kiss for the children."[50]

Chapter 15

A New Century

1900–1905

E arly in 1905, Spohn operated on a woman with a 328-pound tumor, and she survived. After 113 years Spohn still holds the world record for the largest tumor ever removed successfully. Spohn reported on this operation at a meeting of the Texas Medical Association in Houston on April 28, 1905. He said he had been called to see Mrs. G., age forty-three, a mother of seven children. She had been suffering from an ovarian tumor for several years, and it had been tapped several times. When he walked into the room he was surprised to see a mass about the size of a barrel. He had to look over the mass to see the small head of the woman attached to it. Mrs. G. was emaciated and could take food only by spoonfuls and usually could not retain it. The tumor stretched from her chin to midway between her knees and feet. When she lay on her side in a three-quarter bed, the tumor had to be supported by two chairs, and the only way to move her was to move the tumor. Spohn had seen a professor in Philadelphia remove a large tumor, but the patient had died on the table. Spohn had previously removed a 166-pound tumor, but after a few hours that patient also died.[1]

Spohn decided to try to reduce the tumor over a week to avoid a collapse that had caused the other patients' deaths. He also sent for his trusted Canadian physician relatives to help him during this difficult procedure—his brother Dr. Henry Spohn and nephew Dr. H. J. Hamilton. While reducing the tumor over the week, Spohn first drained off about

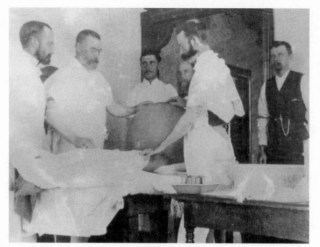

Dr. Arthur Spohn, along with his brother Dr. Henry Spohn and nephew Dr. Henry Hamilton, operated on a woman with a 328-pound tumor. After 113 years Spohn still holds the Guinness World Record for the largest tumor ever removed successfully. *Corpus Christi Caller-Times.*

thirty gallons of a gelatinous fluid. Then he opened the abdomen and found scar tissue from the previous tapping, making it very difficult to work. He found a tumor on the left ovary and opened it, removing six gallons of fluid, and then he was able to remove the forty-pound sac, but his troubles were not over. There were other fluids and tissues that had to be removed during the procedure. He found he could not close the abdominal walls because there was so much serum and blood escaping, so he had to leave the wound open and packed with gauze to facilitate the drainage. It took two months of care before he could close the abdomen. He had used chloroform for anesthesia, and the case was a success, with the patient making a good recovery.[2]

It took a confident and competent surgeon to even attempt what Spohn did. As was his usual demeanor, he refused to walk away from a difficult case and was determined to take the extra care needed to cure a patient. Mrs. G. and her family may or may not have known that her life was in the hands of one of the most competent surgeons in the United States.

In a paper published in 1901 in the *Texas State Medical Journal*, Spohn had taken on the importance of addressing uterine diseases. "It is surprising how much trouble a small tumor in the uterine wall will sometimes give, even before it is possible to detect them," he wrote.[3] The patients he reported on ranged from eighteen years of age to fifty. Some were married and some single. Some had as many as eight children and some had none. All of them had suffered for several years from pain, and some had constant hemorrhaging. In most cases, nothing had been done. Spohn operated and relieved their conditions so they could resume a normal life. Again, Spohn pleaded for action to be taken to treat women's health problems.[4]

Spohn had become interested in women's health issues in Philadelphia when Sarah was so ill, and he had begun concentrating his practice on treating women. In his article on fibroid tumors of the uterus, he cited twenty-one cases of women who came to him with various problems. Normally they presented with painful and sometimes continuous hemorrhaging. Their tumors ranged from very small to filling the uterus; one tumor was the size of a child's head. Some of these tumors were so large they impeded elimination and caused a variety of other severe problems. Spohn described the procedures he used in each case and noted that all of the women found welcome relief.

Spohn revealed to the medical reader that a fibromyoma of the uterus, when found beneath the mucous membrane (now called the endometrium), is called sub-mucous. When the tumor is buried in the wall of the uterus it is interstitial, and when located under the serous or peritoneal covering it is sub-serous. Spohn explained the surgical technique used in each case (the text of his article is in appendix 1).

Spohn described the removal of a sub-mucous tumor (Case 1):

> A young lady of 18 consulted me for pain in the uterine region, with almost continual hemorrhage. I found the os (entrance) open with a growth about the size of a walnut in the cervical canal (leading from the opening into the main chamber where fetal growth takes place). In passing a sound around the tumor a pedicle was detected attached to the anterior wall front of the uterus, just inside of the inner os. The cervix was dilated under chloroform, tension made on the growth and the pedicle excised with curved scissors, removing a small portion of the inner uterine wall where the pedicle was attached. The part was slightly packed with gauze. Recovery.[5]

He also described the removal of an interstitial tumor (Case 2):

> A lady, age 36, mother of five children. Consulted me for uterine, endometritis, etc., (an infection) caused by deep bilateral laceration of the cervix. After curetting[,] the neck of the uterus remained quite large, and while operating to close the laceration, I found a fibroma in the posterior [back side] lip about the size of a pigeon's egg, which after incision was easily turned out. Recovery.

He also describes the removal of a sub-serous tumor (Case 4):

> Age 42, mother of two children, had suffered several years with pain and hemorrhage. A large tumor filled the uterine cavity. A sound could be passed around the mass anteriorly. After dilating the cervical canal under chloroform, an incision was made through the mucous membrane, which was separated from the tumor as much as possible, and the growth extracted with forceps, separating it from surrounding parts with the end of a vectis during the operation. There was not much hemorrhage. The cavity was packed with gauze. She made a rapid recovery and has since been quite well.

These cases are interesting but not as unusual as his description of his surgical approach through the abdominal wall. His technique was to leave clamped any bleeding vessels inside the patient, covering all with gauze dressings, and then two days later removing the clamps and closing the wound to avoid infection problems associated with sutures inside, which is essentially a typical war injury treatment. This open wound approach to healing is as old as medical history as, after all, no sutures were used for millennia as far as is known, other than what plant needles offered to hold the skin together. Wounds were cauterized with fire or chemical, covered with wildlife of some type to discourage infection, and left to heal beneath the crust and then separating the crust for new skin to grow over from the edges. As always, Spohn advocated operating to cure his patients and helping them live a normal, pain-free life.

Spohn's description of his preferred method for hysterectomy certainly reflects his approach to avoiding the Achilles heel of surgery, that is, infection. The sutures of his day were derived from natural products such as silk and animal product, referred to as gut threads. He does not mention wire. Sterilization of these products using various antiseptic soaks was imperfect. The skin and vaginal tract cannot be totally sterilized even today. The masterful human body still must eradicate pervasive bacteria in order to heal. Over millennia the natural protective process of healing has evolved without surgeons to close many layers with fine, sterile synthetic sutures. Even today, reinforced by periodic experiences during "primitive" conditions of wartime, the basic principle of removing foreign objects (those that are not natural parts of the body) and leaving a wound open to naturally contract upon itself, with natural processes working to close the wound and then remodel each layer of tissue until the wounded area is functional again, still works and is a basic part of the surgeons' training. Spohn found a way to control hemorrhage without the infectious sutures.

However, Spohn's ability to close an abdominal wound, enclosing the intestinal contents while excluding the vaginal remnant to allow natural drainage and avoiding the use of sutures (a foreign material) during the healing process, was certainly a technical feat. He knew bacterial contamination would occur and so took advantage of natural processes to help prevent infection. This description further supports this man's genius. He did not just cut out growths and close up and pray for recovery; he understood that surgical technique could be the main source of failure.

In an article on skin grafting he published in 1901, he cited a frontier accident. A young man of twenty was on horseback and carried his pistol in a holster around his waist. The holster rested partly on the saddle, and the pistol accidentally discharged near his thigh, with the bullet going through the saddle and into the back of the horse. His thigh was injured by the burn and concussion of the shot, leaving an area of five to nine inches completely destroyed. There was no sensation in the area, and eventually the whole piece of injured flesh dropped off. He was injured on December 17, 1900, and the first grafts were inserted on January 20, 1901. Spohn utilized twenty-three small grafts donated from the arm of the man's brother. He used an unusual dressing for the grafts: a perforated plate of gelatin film, the same material photographers used. He perforated the film with darning needles about every one-fourth inch and then sterilized it. He placed the film over the wound and covered it with gauze and held it in place with a pressure bandage. The perforated film allowed the gauze covering to absorb all discharges, and because the film was transparent the grafts could be examined without disturbing them. By March 1 Spohn had applied new grafts between the old ones that had not grown much. He observed that the new grafts grew much faster than the first ones, leading him to suggest the skin grafts should not be inserted until new skin formed at the edges of the wound.[6]

In 1905 Spohn wrote an article entitled "Typhoid Perforation of the Bowel with Obstruction—A Plea for Exploratory Abdominal Incisions." Spohn believed that perforation and obstruction of the bowel was a common complication of typhoid fever and was almost always fatal. In two cases he expressed sorrow that he had not realized soon enough that operating could have saved the patients' lives, and he wanted to share this knowledge.

One of his patients was a trained nurse who had contracted typhoid fever. He appeared to be doing well by the fifteenth day and at four that evening Spohn visited him again. The first thing the young man said to him was, "Doctor, I am a dead man. . . . I have had a sudden pain in my abdomen. . . . It is tense and rigid, is distending. . . . I have perforation of the bowel." He died before morning and Spohn reflected that he had that man's life in his hands, and if he had known then what he did now he would have operated and perhaps saved his life.[7]

In another case the patient lived twenty miles from Corpus Christi, and when Spohn arrived the patient was seriously ill. Spohn instructed the family to look for the symptoms of perforation, telling them how dangerous it was. He went to depart, but before he had reached his carriage in the yard they called him back because the young man had had a severe hemorrhage. He died later that night. If Spohn had operated, he might have saved his life. Cases such as this weighed heavily on Spohn's conscience, taking their toll both mentally and physically. He learned from his experiences and shared them in the article. However, in the case of a sixteen-year-old girl in Alice, Texas, he was successful. He had to drive twenty miles at night and reached the patient at about 11:00 p.m. She had suffered typhoid for about four weeks. When he arrived she was critical. She had a quick pulse, and her abdomen was very distended. She had not been able to retain anything due to vomiting for several days. Her pain was being controlled with hypodermic injections of morphia. Spohn did not think she would live till morning. He decided to operate and explained the procedure in detail. She survived and Spohn felt that it would not be too long before typhoid fever would be treated as a surgical disease.[8]

Spohn was keen on the idea of physicians having associations to oversee the proper practice of medicine, share experiences, and promote good medical service. Twenty-five years prior, in 1876, he had helped organize the first Nueces County Board of Medical Examiners. In the same year he helped facilitate the formation of the Medical Association for Western Texas. The formation of this group was precipitated by the yellow fever threat. Because only a few doctors lived in Nueces County, they sought members from throughout the western part of Texas. Spohn served as corresponding secretary, and the president was Dr. T. H. Nott, from Goliad, who went on to be president of the Texas Medical Association. Spohn's brother-in-law, Dr. Alexander Hamilton, was the treasurer. The Medical Association for Western Texas meeting was in Dr. Hamilton's home. In 1903 the *American Medical*

Association Journal announced that Dr. Arthur E. Spohn was councilor for the Sixth District of the Texas Medical Association. The district consisted of several counties. The officers were Dr. Arthur E. Spohn, president; Dr. Alfred G. Heaney, vice president; Dr. Henry Redmond, secretary; and Dr. J. D. Hooker, of Alice, treasurer. Other members were Dr. Henry Burke, Corpus Christi; Dr. W. T. Harris, of Mathis; and Dr. Walter F. McMullen, of Rockport. Interestingly, when Arthur proposed raising the two-dollar annual dues to three dollars, many of the members threatened to quit. So the dues remained at the two-dollar level.[9]

Spohn maintained an intellectual curiosity about all science, not just medical science. In 1901 he completed the requirements to enroll as a member of the American Association for the Advancement of Science. This group was an international society dedicated to advancing science around the world. One of the specific goals of the association was to unite many affiliated groups under one banner to share information and to spearhead programs. The Texas Academy of Science was one of the affiliated groups.[10]

On the first day of 1905 Spohn was elected to active membership in the Association of Military Surgeons as an acting assistant surgeon in the Public Health and Marine Hospital Service. The association was chartered by Congress in 1903 and represented federal government and international health professionals. It promoted the advancement of health care and was dedicated to all aspects of medical care provided by entities of the federal government. The Marine Hospital Service had been in operation since 1798, but in 1902 it had adopted a new name, the Public Health and Marine Hospital Service, while continuing to administer domestic and foreign quarantines.[11]

In 1908 Spohn and sixty-five other Texas physicians attended the sixth annual meeting of the International Association of Tuberculosis in Washington, DC.[12] The American branch of the association had been struggling to raise enough money to host an international meeting. They decided to ask Theodore Roosevelt, president of the United States, to accept the presidency of the International Congress meeting to be held in September. On May 5, 1908, they received a letter from President Roosevelt accepting the presidency. The president stated, "We lost 200,000 people a year to the disease in the United States and over 1,000,000 worldwide." He thought it very important that "we joined together in the brotherhood of man and unite against our common foe."[13] The president's influence was apparent when the US Congress appropriated $40,000 so that the association could use the new National Museum for the meeting. The still incomplete building was perfect for the meeting because it had plenty of floor space for exhibits and meetings. The congress was held from September 28 to October 12. In advance of the meeting the governors of the states formed committees and produced posters, circulars, and written material to distribute, all urging physicians and health providers to attend. The meeting was to present the newest and most approved methods of treating tuberculosis around the world. The American branch of the association prepared a book ahead of time to be distributed, *The Campaign against Tuberculosis in the United States*, listing the facilities such as hospitals, camps, sanitariums, and clinics fighting the disease in the United States. On September 28 delegates presented a review of the fight against tuberculosis being waged by the association. These delegates were from twenty-eight different countries, including Russia, Japan, Mexico, Britain, Canada, France, Germany, and Italy, to name a few. There were five thousand delegates present to attend seminars and receive the latest information available from around the world.[14]

In 1903 Spohn traveled to the Mediterranean region to investigate and give health advice on maintaining sanitary conditions.[15] Spohn was respected both in the United States and internationally. The Texas governor had called on him in 1882 to help stem the yellow fever epidemic that swept the Rio Grande border region. In 1904 it appeared Spohn was again involved in Texas and Mexico negotiations about another epidemic but this time in an unofficial capacity.

In 1903 Mexico suffered a severe yellow fever epidemic, and when infected people crossed the border the disease spread in Texas as well. In February 1904, George R. Tabor, the Texas state health officer, asked Dr. E. Liceaga, president of the Superior Board of Health in Mexico, to institute quarantine regulations to protect citizens against the spread of the disease. Dr. Liceaga refused and Tabor issued a quarantine order for people crossing the border and entering Texas. As the crisis developed, negotiations were established between Liceaga and Tabor. Tabor wanted to station inspectors in the major Mexican cities and areas where yellow fever existed. They would be US public health inspectors and would issue certificates to anyone wanting to enter the United States. The certificates stated that the individuals had not been in any area where yellow fever existed for the previous five days. Without these certificates they would not be permitted into the United States. Tabor also offered the same opportunity for Mexican inspectors in the United States, saying they would be treated with respect in every way. Also, all local passenger trains coming to the United States from Mexico would be disinfected at Saltillo. All freight cars would be disinfected and tagged as disinfected or they would not be permitted to enter. This quarantine was met with great criticism in Mexico.[16]

On May 11, 1904, the *Brownsville Daily Herald* reported that Dr. and Mrs. A. E. Spohn were staying at the Reforma Hotel in Mexico City with his family and party. The article identified him as the United States Marine Hospital surgeon in charge of Corpus Christi. Spohn told the reporter that he was there on a pleasure trip and was not there in an official capacity. He did say he was "merely in the way of [making] friendly suggestions to the United States Marine Hospital Service." Spohn said that he understood there had been a long telegram from Surgeon General Walter Wyman to Dr. E. Liceaga. Evidently the two agencies came to agreement and Mexico allowed the inspectors to be stationed in Mexico. The newspaper credited the resolution to Dr. Liceaga's tact.[17]

While in Mexico Sarah became ill and had to be hospitalized at Mercy Hospital in Laredo, Texas. She remained in Laredo to recuperate, staying with her sister-in-law Corina Kenedy. Sarah and Arthur left Laredo on May 24 to return home. At the same time John and Stella Kenedy and Arthur's brother, Dr. Philip Howard Spohn from Canada, left Corpus Christi for La Parra. It is possible that they were all in Mexico together and part of Spohn's party.[18]

Spohn's Canadian cousin Dr. Fred Bowman was taking postgraduate courses at Johns Hopkins Medical School in 1907 and was studying under Dr. William Welch, the famous professor of pathology. Canadian professors there were William Osler, William Thayer, and Thomas Futcher. Dr. Lewellys Barker, another Canadian, succeeded Dr. Osler as physician in chief at Johns Hopkins. Dr. Barker had been asked by the US government to "recommend someone for a position as bacteriologist in the Bureau of Science in Manila," and he offered the post to Fred Bowman, who accepted and served there four and a half years. While he was there he worked with patients having such illnesses as malaria, leprosy, typhoid, cholera, and yaws, which is a bacterial infection affecting the skin and bones. Malaria was the greatest worry, and in some areas 80 percent of the malaria patients died.[19]

Midway through the first decade of the century, the Mexican government took over the main railroad in the country. At the same time a charter was granted for the St. Louis, Brownsville and Mexico Railway.[20] This railroad was the partial fulfillment of a dream for Henrietta King and Robert Kleberg, who had been wanting to secure not only a railroad but a town as well. They got their wish. The incorporators of the railroad sounded like the Who's Who of South Texas landowners. The incorporators were Robert J. Kleberg Sr., A. E. Spohn, Robert Driscoll Sr., Uriah Lott, Richard King II, John G. Kenedy, James B. Wells, Francisco Yturria, Thomas Carson, Robert Driscoll Jr., E. H. Caldwell, George F. Evans, Caesar Kleberg, John B. Armstrong, and John J. Welder. These large landowners knew the value of having the railroad cross their properties. The capitalization was $1 million. Henrietta King's wishes were realized on July 4, 1904, when the train rolled into the new town of Kingsville. Mrs. King stood in a wagon and watched as flags waved, cannons sounded, and the band played.[21] As for Spohn, he served as chief surgeon for the railroad and as one of the directors. The railroad began at Sinton, crossed the line of the San Antonio and Aransas Pass Railroad, and continued through San Patricio, Nueces, Hidalgo, and Cameron Counties to the Rio Grande near Brownsville, with a branch to Starr County.[22] These railroads helped tame the Wild Horse Desert as towns sprang up and flourished across the countryside.

Sarah and Arthur experienced the perks and prosperity of the railroad in their community. For example, in 1903 Corpus Christi Normal conducted a six-week summer program. Professor Menger of Corpus Christi and Professor Garrison of Floresville conducted the classes. In addition to the regular normal school curriculum there were courses on the US Constitution taught by the Honorable R. W. Stayton, and Spohn lectured on physiology and health. The attendance had grown from 60 to 104 students over the prior two years. People came from twenty-six counties to enjoy the lectures.[23]

Spohn had supported the development of the railroads and was interested in the deep harbor project. Thus, on March 2, 1905, Arthur and Sarah entered the banking business. They received notice that they and Clark Pease, Mr. Cohn, George S. Evans, and Henry G. Heaney had received approval of their application for a charter for the City National Bank of Corpus Christi. This bank succeeded the Pease Private Bank.[24]

The year 1901 was an exciting time for Corpus Christi. The year before, George Blucher had ordered the first automobile seen in Corpus Christi.

Dr. Arthur Spohn bought a red Cadillac with a steering wheel in 1901, and many people in town thought he had wasted his money. *Corpus Christi-Caller Times.*

Blucher went to the Pan-American Exposition in Buffalo, New York, and met Ransom Olds, who took him for a ride in one of his automobiles. In October 1901 the car arrived in a crate. It had a tiller instead of a steering wheel and got forty miles to a gallon of gas. Gas cost twenty cents a gallon (the equivalent of about $5.00 today). The motor was under the backseat and the automobile cost $650. It could travel twenty miles an hour. Blucher took his children to school the next day with his girls riding and the boys walking.

The race was on. In a few months Dr. Alfred Heaney bought an automobile, too. He put it to good use. He was called to see Sam Anderson, the ranch foreman at the Coleman-Fulton Pasture Company. His horse had fallen on him and he was knocked unconscious. The ranch was about thirty miles from Corpus Christi, near Rockport. In order to reach Anderson, Dr. Heaney drove his new Oldsmobile to the reef road at North Beach, changed to a special bicycle to cross the San Antonio and Aransas Pass Railroad trestle, and then obtained a horse and buggy. Dr. Heaney also tried to pick up Father Claude Jaillet and take him for a ride in his new automobile. Father Jaillet would have no part of it and refused association with what he called a devilish contraption.[25]

Spohn and Dr. Heaney were fierce competitors, so as soon as Dr.
Heaney bought his automobile, Spohn ordered one too. Spohn selected a
red Cadillac with a steering wheel. A family picture shows Spohn sitting
in his new car in front of his home at 423 N. Broadway. In the backseat
is Sarah's niece, Sunie Putegnat, of Brownsville. Many people thought
Spohn had wasted his money because you could walk anywhere in town.
The dairyman, Peter McBride, told the story that he was on his way to
town in a mule cart when he saw Dr. Arthur Spohn coming in his automobile. He said his mules were so scared that even though he was trying
to hold them back, he could not stop them. A collision was avoided when
Spohn was able to stop his automobile so they could get by.[26]

Chapter 16

A Hospital at Last

1905

Spohn entered the twentieth century full of vitality and at the peak of his medical career. He was fifty-five years old, had traveled the world, and was well respected in medical circles in Texas and the United States. Now at home in Corpus Christi he began an earnest pursuit to establish a hospital to serve Corpus Christi and the surrounding area. There were many poor and needy people who had no place to be treated. In the past Spohn had operated on kitchen tables by lamplight or sunlight with only well water for washing and only rudimentary equipment. It was high time Corpus Christi had a real hospital, and he was determined to make his dream of such a facility come true.

He had been fortunate that two very kind young women, Concha Rodriguez and Charlita Verin, had been operating a little hospital out of their home. They took care of patients Spohn sent them. Father Jaillet often went there and left money to pay for what the patients needed. He helped them with both their physical and spiritual needs. He was a great comfort to the women in their work of taking care of the sick.[1] A Mrs. Culpepper also offered her home as a place where Spohn's patients could go.[2] With the growth and development of Corpus Christi, it was time for something better. During the first few years of the new century this project consumed much of Spohn's time.

It is not surprising that when Spohn and others in the Corpus Christi community began the drive for a hospital to provide first-class medical

Mother Madeleine
Chollet in San Antonio
negotiated with Alice
Kleberg to arrange for
the building of the
new Spohn Sanitarium
in 1905. Courtesy of
Sisters of Charity of
the Incarnate Word
Archives, San Antonio,
Texas.

The Most Reverend Peter Verdaguer
of the vicariate of Brownsville, Texas,
helped to facilitate the plan for the
Sisters of Charity of the Incarnate Word
in San Antonio to run the new Spohn
Sanitarium. Courtesy of Incarnate Word
Archives, San Antonio, Texas.

care it was Alice Kleberg who led the effort. The King and Kleberg families owed Spohn a great deal. In the late 1890s and early 1900s Alice had begun to raise money for a patient care facility. Alice made it clear from the beginning that the hospital would be named in honor of Dr. Spohn because of his accomplishments in medicine and his service to the people of Corpus Christi. There were two major aspects of the project to be considered. First, money had to be raised and a plan developed. Second, someone had to manage the hospital, bear the ongoing expenses, and take on the day-to-day staffing of it.

While Alice was working on the funding, Spohn approached his long-time friends, the Sisters of the Incarnate Word and Blessed Sacrament, about managing the hospital, but they declined the offer because their apostolic work was limited to teaching.[3] Upon the advice of Bishop Peter Verdaguer, Spohn turned to the Sisters of Charity of the Incarnate Word in San Antonio.[4] The bishop offered reasons why he thought they would be the best group to manage the hospital in Corpus Christi. This congregation had a large number of sisters to carry on the work, it had the means to support itself and the new hospital, and when the hospital became successful, the sisters would put the money to good use by helping the poor and orphans, which was what they had done in San Antonio.

Bishop Verdaguer approached Mother Madeleine Chollet about operating the hospital.[5] After receiving the bishop's inquiry, Sister M. Gabriel in San Antonio replied that the order operated several hospitals. In one, the building was given over to the management of the sisters, and they bore the expenses of the hospital except for construction. In the other hospitals the owners paid the sisters for their services and bore the management expenses. After negotiations an agreement was reached, and Mother Madeleine and the Sisters of Charity of the Incarnate Word accepted the responsibility of both owning and managing the Corpus Christi facility.

In the meantime, Alice, Robert, and Henrietta were having difficulties raising money. The biggest problem they faced was religious prejudice. Bishop Verdaguer wrote to Mother Madeleine and described how Mrs. Kleberg's friends had turned against her because she was going to give the hospital to the Catholics.[6] Alice and her family were staunch Presbyterians and Spohn was Episcopalian, but both knew that they needed the services of the Catholic women religious if the hospital was going to succeed. Years later, Alice, recalling her experience in raising money for the first Spohn

Hospital, wrote a strong editorial against what she viewed as religious bigotry:

> I had ups and downs, many of them, in our work sixteen years ago. Some even refused to help then because the hospital was to be run by Catholic sisters. To them I made answer, "Keep your money." I, for one, do not want a single penny contributed to the hospital without the right spirit behind it. I am a Presbyterian, but many of my dearest friends are Catholics. They do not love me less because I am Protestant. Should I love them less because they are Catholics? Our paths are all leading upward. I have given one contribution to the hospital and I expect to add others. Now that we understand each other, we shall press on to the mark. Again, I thank our earnest helpers and urge others to fall in line for the good cause.[7]

Sister Gabriel presented a plan for the new hospital on July 8, 1903. It was for a brick building that would face south, and the kitchen and sisters' apartments would be separate from the hospital proper.[8] Alice wrote to the bishop on July 23 that she had raised $4,000 so far but did not feel she could raise more than about $5,000 or $6,000 total. She asked him to get her an estimate for a wooden building. She did not want to pay for plans for something they could not afford. No one could have foreseen the loss that would occur later due to that decision. A hurricane in 1919 reduced the entire hospital to rubble. The only structure left standing nearby was made of brick.[9]

Alice also sent the bishop a circular she was using in her fundraising efforts. The circular said Corpus Christi was a healthy and ideal location for the facility, that John G. Kenedy had donated a beautiful spot on the bluff, and that the Sisters of Charity had agreed to manage the hospital at their own expense. The facility would be known as Spohn Hospital and would be open to all first-class physicians and their patients. She listed the donors: S. G. Ragland, $25; Mrs. H. M. King, $1,000; Robert J. Kleberg, $500; M. D. Monserrate, $5; J. J. Welder, $100; D. Sullivan, $100; G. R. Scott, $100; and Mildred Seaton, $10. James F. Scott donated the lumber for the east gallery of the hospital, and Joseph Hirsch agreed to raise the money to pay for the labor on the gallery.[10]

Alice wrote to Sister Gabriel on August 28, 1903, offering to pay for the furnishings and provide the lots. The limit of her potential donors list had been reached, except for Dr. and Mrs. Spohn, who might raise their dona-tion to $5,500, possibly $100 or $200 more.[11] On January 7 Alice returned Sister Gabriel's plans to her. She had decided to take matters into her own hands. She had her husband Robert draw a rough sketch of their own proposal for the hospital. It showed the location, oriented the building to catch the sunlight and prevailing breeze, would have sliding doors where practical, and would feature steam heating (with the furnace situated outside) and electric lighting. She also wanted an elevator and stairs. She said she had only been able to raise $6,000 and disliked waiting any longer. She wanted an estimate on this frame building her husband Robert had drawn.[12]

Bishop Peter Verdaguer was a powerful force along the border. In 1894 he had invited the Sisters of Mercy to establish a hospital in Laredo, and they also built their motherhouse there. He encouraged the building of numerous new churches, and new ones were indeed built, in Laredo, Mercedes, Raymondville, and Harlingen. He was dedicated to the service of his flock and welcomed the opportunity to support a much-needed hospital in Corpus Christi.[13]

An agreement was reached to build the frame building, not on the donated land on the bluff but at North Beach. The deed for the land listed the owners as R. J. Kleberg, Olivia B. Hirsch, George M. Kenedy, John G. Kenedy, and Sarah J. Spohn, "joined by her husband A. E. Spohn."[14] These owners allowed Dr. Spohn to transfer the deed of ownership for the North Beach property as he saw fit, and he offered it to Bishop Verdaguer. The bishop then invited the Reverend Mother Madeleine to have her order accept ownership of it for the new sanitarium.[15] The bishop wrote to Mother Madeleine on October 19, 1904, that Robert Kleberg was ready to transfer the deed for the hospital and wanted to know to whom the deed should be made out. It did not matter to the bishop; all he desired was that there be a hospital in Corpus Christi and that it would be managed by her order. Bishop Verdaguer added the following interesting information—that Mrs. John Kenedy had placed her daughter Sarita with her order for her education, and he was glad of that. He hoped that Sarita, instead of her family having to pay very high rent for a house in San Antonio, as they had the previous winter, would take room and board with the sisters.[16] Sarita became good friends with Elena Seuss while at school in San Antonio. The school picture of them in their uniforms shows two beautiful young women. Sarita introduced Elena to her brother John Gregory Kenedy Jr., and they later married.

Sarita Kenedy (*right*)
and Elena Seuss (*left*)
were classmates in
San Antonio and later
sisters-in-law, after Elena
married Sarita's brother,
John Kenedy Jr. Kenedy
Family Collection,
A1995-045.0294, South
Texas Archives, James
C. Jernigan Library,
Texas A&M University–
Kingsville.

As construction on the hospital neared an end, Alice wrote Mother Madeleine to update her on the progress. Alice told her they had good physicians in place and the promise of fine nurses, and "I feel that we have every reason to thank the good Lord for his wonderful kindness to the children of men."[17] Alice wrote again on July 9, saying, "I have worked hard to make my part a success & with you & the Drs. lie the hope of success for many will come partly convalescent to enjoy the sea breeze in a well received hospital—already Dr. Spohn has a request from Mexico for a room."[18]

Dan Reid of Corpus Christi built the hospital. The total cost was $13,013.92. Alice Kleberg had raised $8,886.50. The sisters assumed the ownership and the debt of $4,127.42.[19] The hospital was ready for a grand opening.

Sisters Cleophas Hurst, Conrad Urnau, Regina O'Byrne, and Austin Kyne arrived on July 16, 1905, to begin operating the hospital. Sister Cleophas, born in Ireland, was up to the challenge because she had opened St. Anthony's Sanitarium in Amarillo just four years earlier. She thought that working in Corpus Christi would be much easier because they did not have howling winds, dust, and tumbleweeds blowing across the land. Two years after arriving in Corpus Christi she became the superior at Spohn Hospital. Sister Conrad Urnau, born in Germany, had previously been at St. Joseph's Hospital Infirmary in Fort Worth and at

Mother Cleophas Hurst was the first administrator of Spohn Sanitarium in Corpus Christi, Texas, in 1905. Courtesy of the Sisters of Charity of the Incarnate Word Archives, San Antonio, Texas.

Sister Regina O'Byrne (shown here with her sister, Sister Virginia) shared the job of caring for the patients and being responsible for housekeeping and laundry. Courtesy of Sisters of Charity of the Incarnate Word Archives, San Antonio, Texas.

Sister Conrad Urnau was in charge of preparing meals and tending the garden at the new Spohn Sanitarium. Courtesy of the Sisters of Charity of the Incarnate Word Archives, San Antonio, Texas.

Baptist St. Anthony's Hospital and Sanitarium in Amarillo. Sister Austin Kyne, born in Ireland, had served at St. Joseph's Hospital Infirmary in Fort Worth and at Christus Santa Rosa in San Antonio, where she received her graduate nursing degree in 1904. Sister Regina O'Byrne, born in Ireland, had served at the IW Hospital and Josephine Heitkamp Hospital in St. Louis, Missouri.[20]

The sisters divided up the management responsibilities. Sister Conrad was in charge of meal preparation and tending the kitchen garden they used to reduce food costs. Sister Austin and Sister Regina took care of the patients and were responsible for housekeeping and laundry. Sister Cleophas took care of patient admissions and hospital finances.[21]

An instruction sheet from 1887 lists the regulations the nurses were expected to follow. They should sweep and mop the floors daily, dust the patients' furniture and windowsills, and maintain an even temperature in the ward by bringing in a scuttle of coal for the day. Each nurse's notes were important in aiding the physicians' work, so "your pens should be carefully made." They would report at 7:00 a.m. and leave at 8:00 p.m. except on the Sabbath, when they would be off from noon to 2:00 p.m. Graduate nurses in good standing with the director of nurses would be given an evening off each week for courting purposes or "two evenings a week if you go regularly to church." Each nurse was to lay aside from each payday a goodly sum of her earnings for her benefits during her declining years so that she would not become a burden: "For example, if you earn $30 a month you should set aside $15. Any nurse who smokes, uses liquor in any form, gets her hair done at a beauty shop, or frequents dance halls will give the director of nurses good reason to suspect her worth, intentions, and integrity." The nurse who performed her labors and served her patients and doctors faithfully and without fault for a period of five years would be given an increase by the hospital administration of five cents a day, providing she had no outstanding hospital debts.[22]

Bishop Verdaguer blessed the new sanitarium on July 26, 1905. Spohn gave the dedicatory address for the hospital that he had helped establish and that was named in his honor (see appendix 4 for the text of Spohn's address). Spohn dedicated the hospital to providing better care for the sick and unfortunate, offering all that science and invention could produce, and utilizing that knowledge for the relief of the sick and suffering. The physicians there would work together and devise better means to combat

Dr. A. E. Spohn hosted the Texas Medical Association in 1908 in Corpus Christi, Texas. Kenedy Family Collection, A1995-045.1237, South Texas Archives, James C. Jernigan Library, Texas A&M University–Kingsville.

Dr. Alfred Heaney, Arthur Spohn's colleague and good friend, admitted the first patient to the Spohn Sanitarium in 1905. Courtesy of Murphy Givens.

The Spohn Sanitarium opened on July 26, 1905, after a blessing by Bishop Verdaguer and proud remarks by Dr. Arthur Spohn. *Corpus Christi Caller-Times.*

Spohn Hospital was a great success. Located one hundred yards from the bay, it grew quickly, gaining an annex and, in 1911, a separate chapel. *Corpus Christi Caller-Times.*

disease. The women religious would bring tender care to assuage pain and distress. This was altogether a grand institution, bearing Spohn's name, with all physicians having equal rights and privileges.[23]

As the chaplain of the hospital, Monsignor Claude Jaillet celebrated the first mass. His French background made him a close friend and advisor to the sisters at the new sanitarium. It was situated about one hundred yards from the bay and was quiet and private. Dr. Alfred Heaney admitted the first patient.[24] The hospital was soon treating many more patients, and, just one year after the hospital opened, an annex with more rooms was added. In 1911 a separate chapel was built.[25]

Spohn Hospital was a great success. The hospital was beautiful, peaceful, and delivered excellent care under the sisters' management. The care the physicians provided was the other critical element. Spohn's treatment of a ranching family is an excellent example of the dedication that he and the hospital staff displayed to save a life. Lena Henrichson Crafford told the story of her family's life-saving experience with Spohn. With the Henrichson family, Dr. Spohn knew that they did not call him unless it was a grave situation, and he never spared his horses or lost any time in getting to the Henrichson ranch. One time when Mayme Henrichson was a little girl, she became delirious with a high fever. Dr. Spohn got to her in time to relieve her condition and have her removed to his hospital to treat her for typhoid fever. Her mother stayed at the hospital with her to aid in her treatment. Her father made the trip to Corpus Christi and back to the ranch three or four times each week to bring the mother clean clothes and to check on his daughter. One day, late in the evening before sundown and after he had made a trip to Corpus Christi, George Henrichson drove his team and two-seated buggy up to the hitching post. As he got out of the buggy and walked to the long trough that held feed corn, he saw Comley, his youngest son, lying in the end of the trough. At first he thought that Comley was asleep, but as he felt him he knew that Comley was probably unconscious, for his face and arms were burning to the father's touch.

George carried him to the house and got a wet cloth to bathe his face, while the older boy in the house harnessed a fresh team to the buggy for a return trip to Corpus Christi. The father held Comley while the son drove. It was rather late when they reached the hospital, but it was before Dr. Spohn had made his last visit to the patients for the night. Dr. Spohn was talking to one of the nurses, one who had just returned from a dance and was still dressed in her blue silk dress when the Henrichson group entered. At a glance the doctor took in the situation and diagnosed the case. The doctor turned to the nurse and said, "Here, Sally, take this boy to the bay and cool him off!"

Sally gasped, "Doctor, couldn't you let me change my dress first?" Dr. Spohn returned, "No, Sally, there is no time to lose; go now! I'll buy you another dress!" So Sally ran with the boy in her arms for the Corpus Christi Bay and waded in until she was far enough out that she could hold him on her knees. In this half-squatting position in the water, she bathed his face. After a few minutes Comley opened his eyes and, looking at her and the water, began to struggle. "Oh, it's all right. I won't let you fall!" Then as if to chide him, she said, "Look at my pretty dress, though, look how it is ruined! Now what are we going to do?" She could see that he was conscious, so she turned and carried him back to the hospital, where the attendants had readied a bed in the same room with his sister. Now the mother could watch them both.[26]

Chapter 17

City of the Bluff and Seas

1906–1908

S pohn was sixty-one years old and finally had his new hospital, thanks
to his friends and supporters. He was loved by his family and community and was at the peak of his profession. One of his patients wrote
a poem about him after his death that expressed how the ordinary
person felt about him and how revered he was by the people he treated. It
appeared in the *Corpus Christi Caller* in 1919.[1] This is the first stanza (see
appendix 2 for the full poem):

> His sort of man! Oh! What can we say
> When we think of what he's gone and done without pay!
> His sort of man! Just the kind that we want
> Oh how his memory will everywhere haunt
> The homes of this town, when the records we want
> That show us the full measures—his sort of man!

Spohn traveled many miles in his practice. His fame had spread all over
South Texas and Mexico. He was even called to Matamoros, Mexico, to
treat one of the most prominent citizens there, Don Bonifacio de Guinea,
a well-known merchant. The *Brownsville Herald* reported on March 15,
1906, that Guinea was critically ill at his home. On April 4 the newspaper reported that Dr. Spohn had been called to see him. Guinea died on
April 28, after suffering from stomach cancer for two years and growing

gradually worse. Spohn had tried to help, but Guinea's trouble was too far advanced.[2]

The following patient accounts offer a glimpse into the diverse and demanding practice Spohn handled on a daily basis. On January 15, 1906, Ernest R. Petzel, twenty-four years old, was hunting with his friend, Mart Howell, on the Santa Petronila ranch.[3] They were thus about twenty-two miles west of Corpus Christi when Mart's double-barrel shotgun accidentally discharged, both loads entering Ernest's body and mutilating it. He was brought to Spohn's new hospital at once, and for a while it looked like he might recover, but he took a turn for the worse and gangrene set in. He died seven days later, on January 22.[4] This young man's case shows the relationship that Spohn had built up with many of the families in the area. Ernest's grandmother, Marie Berg Petzel, had been a nurse for Dr. Spohn and Dr. Heaney and had helped with most of the childbirths in town. Sometimes the babies did not wait for the doctors to arrive, so she delivered them herself.[5]

In October 1907, Spohn received a call from the Palo Alto ranch concerning Robert Driscoll.[6] Robert was an earnest Catholic, and Spohn knew him through the Kenedy family. Robert had been assisting in gathering cattle when he was suddenly taken ill and had to be removed from his horse. For a while he was prostrate and semiconscious, so it was decided to send for Spohn. Instead Spohn had him brought by train to the new Spohn Sanitarium so he could have the best of care. His illness was probably due to the jolting he had received while riding horseback during the roundup. He recovered quickly.[7]

Robstown was the site of another accident in 1908, when a railway official named W. W. Woolridge made the mistake of trying to board a moving train. His foot slipped and he was thrown to the ground. He was taken to the Spohn Sanitarium for treatment of a painful sprain to his right ankle. The injury was serious enough that he had to stay for three weeks before he could return home.[8]

Spohn's relationship with the Kings and Klebergs was once again solidified in September 1908. Spohn was in Boulder, Colorado, with Sarah when he received a telegram saying that Henrietta King had become seriously ill and asking him if he would come quickly. That was no easy task, because Spohn had to travel one thousand miles to reach her. It meant numerous changes of trains and connections, but he did it and the newspaper reported on September 10 that Mrs. King was recovering.[9]

On April 17, 1908, Spohn had a "case that was looked upon as one of the most remarkable in the history of the medical profession." Eunice Masters of Corpus Christi was bitten by an insect near her right temple and tetanus developed.[10] Tetanus is a serious bacterial disease that affects the nervous system and leads to painful muscle contractions, especially around the jaw and neck. It causes difficulty in breathing and threatens life, often proving fatal. The common name for it is "lockjaw." There is no cure for tetanus, and it is treated by managing the complications from the toxins.[11] Miss Masters was critical for several days. Spohn was called and remained at her bedside almost continually "combating the ravages of the deadly germ."[12] Without his constant vigilance and knowledge she would certainly have died. Instead she was able to resume her studies and was graduated from high school that year, with her life ahead of her. Spohn often spent hours with his patients regardless of the toll it took on him.

He continued serving his community and kept his national and international interests as well. He continued his memberships in the US Association of Military Surgeons, American Association for the Advancement of Science, the second Pan-American Congress, and the International Association of Tuberculosis.[13] Despite his interest in medicine being practiced around the world, his real interest had always been to promote progressive medical care in rural Texas. In 1908, he succeeded in bringing the annual meeting of the Texas Medical Association to Corpus Christi. It was a personal triumph and one of the highlights of his career.

It was hard to understand how isolated and difficult it had been for Spohn to practice medicine in a community that for many years had no hospital or staff. However, he was fortunate to have been surrounded by talented physicians who cared about the delivery of care and good practices. He also had dedicated citizens and religious sisters who generously provided nursing expertise in their homes and at the convent.

The distances they had to travel to participate in professional associations, medical seminars, and demonstrations handicapped these physicians. Transportation was limited at best. Often travel was by hot, dusty trains or by boat. It could take days to complete a professional trip, and on one occasion the Texas Medical Association members recognized Spohn for having traveled the farthest to attend their meeting in Waco.[14] The meetings were held primarily in cities where larger medical societies had a presence and that the majority of Texas physicians could reach easily.

In 1908, despite the distance everyone had to travel, Spohn enticed the Texas Medical Association to hold their annual meeting in Corpus Christi. The area was experiencing bumper cotton crops, and newfangled inventions were changing the social climate. Edison's new "kinescope," the forerunner of motion pictures, was making an appearance. Some "snorting and evil-smelling" machines called automobiles had invaded the streets. Electric lights were becoming common, and telephones were growing in popularity. Money was easier to come by. A street carnival had even come to town, and the first hamburgers were being served. The shooting galleries were offering fat turkeys as prizes, and visitors were coming in from the distant ranches and cotton plantations. Some of the big ranches were being broken up to allow for cotton production, truck farming was increasing, and Herefords were replacing longhorns.[15]

Against this background and with enthusiastic support from the community and Sarah, Spohn was to welcome the Texas Medical Association annual meeting attendees to Corpus Christi in May 1908. It was the first time in the forty-two-year history of the TMA annual meeting that the gathering was held south of San Antonio. Preparations in Corpus Christi proceeded at a fever pitch. A meeting was held at the end of January 1908 to plan the big event. They were expecting about fifteen hundred people. The population of Corpus Christi was only about five thousand.

The medical association was one of the largest associations in the state, and the annual convention was usually well attended. The goal of the convention committee was to impress guests so much that they would want to come to the convention each year. To reach that goal, the doctors first set about finding the cleanest city in the state. When Corpus Christi was selected, they wanted the streets paved with a new coat of shell and the boulevard that ran from South Bluff to the Alta Vista Hotel to be as smooth as glass for automobiles. The committee also proposed that poles be erected along the way and strung with lights.[16] The question of rooms and meals would be one of the biggest problems they faced, so they requested the people of Corpus Christi to let them know who would have rooms to let and the rates they would charge.

The steering committee appointed committees to work on arrangements. Spohn was chair of the Services and Entertainment Committee, made up of T. J. Turpin, G. R. Scott, E. H. Caldwell, George Clarke, W. G. Blake, and A. D. Evans. Dr. H. G. Heaney chaired the Transportation Committee, made up of Joe Hirsch, Roy Miller, Captain Crouch, George Grim, and C. W. Gibson. Dr. C. P. Yeager chaired the Registration Committee, with E. Cubage Badge working with him. Dr. John Evans chaired the Exhibit Committee, and Dr. G. W. Gregory, Perry Lovenskiold, and T. A. Anderson served with him.[17]

The chairperson of the Executive Committee of Women was Mrs. A. E. Spohn, with Mrs. Henry Redmond, Mrs. T. J. Turpin, Mrs. W. Carruth, Mrs. C. P. Yeager, and Mrs. H. G. Heaney serving with her. Dr. W. Carruth chaired the Hotel Committee with J. W. Ennis, J. F. Williams, J. J. Copley, Mrs. Wm. Horne, and E. A. Borne. Roy Miller chaired the Bureau of Information with Tom Southgate, and Miss Hallie Robertson served with him. Boyd Brooks handled the ushers. E. T. Merriman chaired the Press Committee, with J. W. Yates and Mrs. Maude Hardwicke assisting.[18] The committee lists read like the Who's Who of Corpus Christi, and the people on those lists had their work cut out for them.

By April, Spohn was busy overseeing work on terracing the bluff in front of his home. Men were also working on a triangular plaza at the corner of Williams and Mesquite.[19] Sarah and the committee women were exceedingly busy with many elaborate events planned for the enjoyment of the wives and daughters of the doctors. On Tuesday, May 12, they would be hosting an informal reception at Arthur and Sarah's home. The ladies were going to enjoy that because it had been described as the "finest house in Texas" when Mifflin built it. Sarah and Arthur had been able to occupy it after Carmen's death and had worked to have everything ready for the reception. On Wednesday, May 13, the visiting ladies would be taken for a drive around the city. They would leave at nine o'clock in the morning from the Seaside Hotel, visit the Alta Vista Hotel, ride out the shell road, and see all the principal points of the city. On Thursday, May 14, they would start their activities with a luncheon at the Seaside Pavilion. Following that they would have time to prepare for the ball that would be held at the same venue on Thursday evening. The committee was also planning other entertainments throughout the convention. One of the events would be a fish fry at Epworth by the Sea. Dr. Redmond reported that since everyone realized the TMA was one of the most important conventions ever held in the city, people had been cooperating in raising money to offset the entertainment expenses.[20]

Mayor Dan Reid decided that it would be good to finally improve one of Corpus Christi's major assets. From the time that the very first settlers

The Texas Medical Association convened in Corpus Christi on May 12–14, 1908. It was the first time the association had held an annual meeting south of San Antonio, Texas. The climax of the social events for ladies was the elaborate course dinner given at the Seaside Pavilion. It featured a band, beautiful floral decorations, and dainty menu cards. Courtesy of Anita Eisenhauer.

had pitched their tents on the waterfront, the high bluff overlooking the sea had been a beautiful spot. As the town developed, there was mainly commercial development on the lower level and, at first, elaborate homes were built on the bluff to take advantage of the magnificent view. Mansions belonging to the Kenedys, Kings, and Rabbs were built there. Mayor Reid moved to beautify the area and connect the lower and upper parts of the city with two levels of beautiful terraces, pedestrian walkways, and roads on either end of the terraces. The preliminary cost for the project was $2,400. The mayor was waiting to see how much extra expense there would be. He was hopeful the property owners along the bluff would pick up their pro rata share of the additional expenses. The mayor and many citizens thought this building project would make Corpus Christi the most beautiful city in the country.[21]

On May 8, four days before the visitors would arrive, Mrs. Turpin put out an appeal in the newspaper. There was still a need for vehicles to drive the ladies and guests around Corpus Christi. She listed the following as already donating their services: E. L. Beynon, Pitts Livery Co., Horace Johnson, E. R. Oliver, Claude Fowler, Jose Castinida [sic], John Jordt, O. C. Lovenskiold, Filipe Castinida [sic], C. D. Craig, Sam A. Bagnall,

S. T. Casas, Dr. A. E. Spohn, J. J. Copley, Dr. Harry Heaney, and
J. C. Baldwin. Mrs. Turpin said she wanted to make provisions for all
their guests and listed her phone number and residence so people could
contact her.[22]

Transportation into Corpus Christi was a problem. However, with
Spohn's railroad connections through the Kenedys and Kings, they received excellent cooperation from the railroads. In the resolutions at the
end of the meeting the association thanked Mr. Lupton of San Antonio,
general passenger agent of the San Antonio and Aransas Pass Railroad,
and William Doharty, traffic manager of the St. Louis, Brownsville and
Mexico Railway, for the careful arrangements of rates, trains, and sleepers
they provided.[23]

The opening ceremonies were held at the Ladies Pavilion, which was
decorated with impressive displays of ferns and palms. The Marine Band
played the "Grand Old Flag," and Pres. C. E. Cantrell of the Texas Medical Association asked the delegates and presidents to come to the stage.
He then called the meeting to order, and Rev. H. E. Springall led them
in prayer. State senator John G. Willacy gave a welcome on behalf of the
mayor and praised the importance of the family physician. He congratu-
lated them for forming an association and said that "an association of men,
honorable men and men of character and intellect like you, have the right
to be heard by the government of this land."[24] Then it was Dr. Spohn's turn
to address the assembly on behalf of the Nueces County Medical Society.

Spohn kept his remarks brief but welcoming. He thanked the society
for letting him welcome them and said they represented an organized
army that "wherever disease, pestilence or danger existed, they were found,
devoting their lives, scientific investigation and discoveries without remuneration to the prevention of that disease, relief of suffering and prolong-
ing human life. . . . The great problem throughout the world at the present
day is the prevention of disease and improvement in sanitary conditions
that the inhabitants may be healthy, prosperous and happy and life made
worth living." He then spoke directly to the delegates and their families,
saying, "We realize the fact that many of you have traveled long distances
and been put to considerable inconvenience, but you have reached the spot
which seems to have been specially designed by nature as a suitable place
for the habitation of man; a place almost free from disease, all that the
sanitarian could desire; in a land of sunshine, the perpetual home of the
beautiful flowers."[25] Their coming was one of the most important events

that had occurred in his section of the state. He concluded by saying he hoped their stay would produce a lingering desire to return.[26]

Dr. Cantrell gave a ten-year overview of the association, pointing out that in 1898 it had had 300 members and in 1908 it had 3,117 members. He mentioned the accomplishment in getting a State Medical Board appointed that would review and certify doctors with appropriate and uniform criteria to practice in the state of Texas. In the recent session of the legislature the association was able to get a bill enacted; the Pure Food Law made it next to impossible for people to be deceived as to the ingredients of medicine containing alcohol and opiates of any kind. The group was also able to obtain one of the best anatomical laws in the United States, making it possible for anatomical education to exist without criminal penalty. He then put in a plea for a Department of Public Health and Vital Statistics and cited the many things such an entity could do to assure good sanitation and safety for the citizens as well as to compile vital statistics on illnesses.[27]

On the local level the delegates passed a resolution in support of Corpus Christi seeking a deep harbor port.[28] They moved to establish an organization of all the city and county health officers and boards of health to better coordinate their activities. They also passed a resolution to be presented to the next state legislature to request an appropriation of not less than $100,000 for the construction, establishment, and maintenance of a sanitarium for the care and treatment of tuberculosis patients in the state. The resolution also included a requirement that all patients must be bona fide residents of the state for a period of three years. They received a ruling by the Texas state attorney general that the Texas State Medical Board could not conduct business without at least six members present.[29]

Sarah and all the women who worked with her had done a superb job entertaining their guests. They did such a good job that Joe Hirsch presented a resolution to the delegates requesting that they come back next year since so many people had expressed their desire to do so over the past few days. However, the delegates voted to go to Galveston for their next meeting.[30] A letter written to the association by a correspondent was published in the next *Texas Medical Association Journal* recalling the delightful nature of the hospitality they experienced during their annual meeting (see the end of appendix 1 for the text of the letter).

Chapter 18

Dr. Arthur Edward Spohn's Legacy

1908–1913

I n a 1967 issue, the *Medical Record and Annals* featured Dr. Arthur Spohn
on the cover, fifty-four years after his death. The editorial on his life
began with this statement: "HE WAS THE MAN FOR THE JOB."

His life had spanned an amazing period of discovery and innovation, one that had featured startling scientific and medical breakthroughs.
Spohn and his contemporaries learned these new things and ideas and introduced them to a geographic region that was still a frontier.[1]

By the time Spohn died, he had been practicing medicine in Texas for
forty-five years. When he first came to Texas in 1868 as a twenty-three-
year-old junior surgeon, he brought with him an excellent education, considerable talent, and a strong professional ethic passed down by his family.
This was a man who gave his life in service and dedication to the benefit of
his profession and humanity, a man who from the early days of his practice
invented new ways of improving the delivery of medical care, a man who
achieved many "firsts" during his career. He read, experimented, and was
never afraid of change, and he exchanged his ideas with others across Texas,
the United States, and Europe. Spohn was a physician who believed pas-
sionately in taking decisive action rather than allowing a patient to die. He
openly criticized the benign neglect practiced by timid or ignorant physicians who sympathetically stood by and did nothing or used antiquated
techniques.

Spohn had a driving quest for knowledge despite the remote environment in which he worked—Corpus Christi, a small port in South Texas. For most of his life the small city had no hospital and no medical or nurse training, but it did have storms that unpredictably and repeatedly destroyed homes, businesses, lives, and eventually even hospitals. For Spohn to attend a professional conference meant days of travel by train or boat. When a patient called, he might travel up to fifty miles in a horse and buggy on barely visible roads, during inclement weather. He often made such journeys at night, bringing with him only what he could carry in his medical bag. He operated on kitchen tables by lamplight or sunlight. Many times he had to invent methods and create supplies to be used when he had none. He refused to use his lack of resources as an excuse to stand idly by while patients suffered. He observed, assessed, and then acted, and that was his message over and over again to other physicians.

From the 1870s to the early 1900s Spohn persevered to bring the principle of antisepsis to surgery, to quarantine people with infectious illnesses, and to vigorously decontaminate to prevent the spread of such illnesses in Texas. Traveling to New York and Pennsylvania, he acquired new skills and knowledge that he shared with colleagues. He wrote many articles describing valuable experiences from his practice.

Arthur Edward Spohn died at 11:45 P.M. on Tuesday, May 5, 1913, after a paralyzing stroke. His death was not unexpected because his condition had become critical on Friday, and by Saturday the family knew his death was near.[2] Two and a half years earlier, in November 1910, his nephew, Dr. Henry Hamilton of Laredo, had received a telegram telling him that his Uncle Arthur had suffered a stroke. Henry immediately left to attend to his uncle. When he returned home on November 13, he reported to the newspaper that his uncle had been cranking his automobile when the stroke occurred. The stroke had affected his right arm and the right side of his face, but his tongue had been only slightly affected. Henry also told the newspaper that when he left Spohn, the esteemed physician had improved greatly and was doing well.[3] However, Spohn continued to have trouble, and his health deteriorated.

A year later, on November 21, 1911, Spohn began writing his will and started off with this statement: "I feel that I am very ill but my mind is clear. All my personal and real estate wherever situated I leave to my dear wife, Sarah Josephine Spohn." His witnesses were Henry Redmond and

Zara L. Moses.[4] In the will, Spohn listed some accounts with outstanding balances and indicated that G. R. Scott knew about them. He also included in the text of his will the combination to his safe.[5]

The *Brownsville Herald Times* reported that Spohn had retired from his practice early but was still sought after in delicate cases and by other physicians. He continued to answer calls of distress and suffering when he was physically able to do so.[6] He was active almost to the day of his death.[7]

Arthur Spohn made another important decision in the final weeks of his life. On February 5, 1913, three months before his death, Spohn was baptized into the Catholic Church. His sponsor was Irene Putegnat, Sarah's niece and the daughter of Rosa Putegnat.[8] Spohn had lived in a Catholic family since 1876. In those thirty-seven years, he had supported the activities of his mother-in-law, Petra, and his wife, Sarah. When he had needed someone to administer the new hospital and care for his patients, he had turned to the Sisters of Charity of the Incarnate Word in San Antonio. The Sisters of the Incarnate Word and Blessed Sacrament in Corpus Christi had befriended him from the beginning of his practice and had offered him their services for his sick and dying patients and for nursing others back to health. Father Jaillet had befriended the Kenedy family, buried James and Petra, and was now serving as the chaplain in Spohn's hospital. No doubt this priest continued to counsel Spohn in the wisdom of his conversion.

On May 6, when the newspaper reported Spohn's death, telegraph and word of mouth spread sadness throughout the region. Through the years Spohn had touched thousands of lives. A large number of people came to the mansion on the bluff to pay their respects. Many floral tributes arrived from numerous places throughout the state. The next morning, on May 7, funeral services were held. Mayor Roy Miller issued a proclamation in honor of Arthur Spohn and notified the community that the flag would be placed at half-staff at city hall and that city offices would be closed from 10:00 a.m. till noon. Many businesses and public schools were also closed for that period. The first part of the funeral service was held that morning at the Spohn home on North Broadway, and the second service was at St. Patrick's Catholic Church, with the Reverend John Schiedt officiating.[9]

Reverend Schiedt was the priest who had baptized Spohn into the Catholic faith.

The obituary printed in the *Texas State Journal of Medicine* is very revealing of what his fellow physicians thought of him and his abilities:

Dr. Arthur Spohn and Sarah Kenedy Spohn's grave at Rose Hill Cemetery in Corpus Christi, Texas, after her death on May 16, 1918. Kenedy Family Collection, A1995-045.0235, South Texas Archives, James C. Jernigan Library, Texas A&M University–Kingsville.

Dr. Spohn was widely known for his charitable acts. Innumerable stories are told of his great compassion for the needy and poor. A biographer summed up his characteristics in the following language:

"Among the able physicians of Texas there is not a more popular general practitioner or a man more learned or skillful in his profession than Dr. A. E. Spohn. That he has deserved the good fortune that has attended his efforts is indisputable, for he is not only honest, reliable and intelligent, but he has ever been sympathetic yet cheerful in the sick room and possesses the happy faculty of winning the confidences and liking of his patients, which has added greatly to their restoration to health."[10]

In San Antonio, the noted physician Dr. Adolph Herff recognized Arthur Spohn as one of the foremost men of his period and often said, "With Spohn, you are safe."[11] In Brownsville the newspaper carried a long tribute to him, praising him for giving valuable advice to the younger members of the medical profession and assisting in acute surgical operations during which particular skill and experience were needed. Most of all they spoke of his care for the less fortunate. Further paying tribute to Spohn, the article noted, "If on his grave wreaths be placed for each of God's unfortunate creatures to whom he rendered aid without prospect of remuneration, it will form a monument that will touch far heavenward as an utter ration of his charity and fatherly ministrations, and when the flowers begin to wither they will be likened unto the heads which now stand bowed in sadness at his departure."[12] Of all the tributes that were written perhaps the truest was from the *Corpus Christi Caller*. The people of that town knew him best, and their words described the man they knew and loved:

> Dr. Spohn was more than a surgeon, for his charities were large, his sympathies broad, his record as a citizen without blemish. Frequently, at great sacrifice to himself, he relieved suffering without thought of any reward more substantial than gratitude. He was not a man to make much of his own deeds. He was even harsh, at times, when modesty prompted him to ease the message of thanksgiving. In his attitude toward nice distinctions and small affairs of life, Dr. Spohn was consistently disinterested. His hours were full, his work exacting. He kept himself abreast of the world, thought deeply, endeavored to serve even the humblest patient in the most efficient and substantial way.
>
> Corpus Christi does well to mourn Dr. Spohn. During the whole of its history, the City has produced no bigger man, and his influence will be felt in years to come, and not only here, but abroad in all the ramifications of surgery and medicine.[13]

That last observation rings true, as will be seen. Spohn's finest legacies are his medical accomplishments and the hospital he created, which has served and is continuing to serve thousands of people from all walks of life throughout South Texas. Spohn would surely be astounded at how his small hospital on North Beach has evolved into a very large health service.

CHRISTUS Spohn Health System is the premier provider of health services throughout the Coastal Bend and South Texas. It has six acute care hospital campuses, a chest pain center, a cancer center, and an accredited stroke program, as well as six family health centers. In Corpus Christi CHRISTUS Spohn has a critical care center, heart program, stroke program, and cancer centers. It also has a 150-bed hospital offering full services for women. Spohn would have been especially proud of this facility because of his interest in women's care and his advocacy of operating on women to save their lives. The health system also has a full 341-bed teaching facility to train professionals to take care of the full spectrum of medical needs. In addition to these facilities there are hospitals located in Alice, Beeville, and Kingsville and family medical clinics located in Freer, George West, and Portland and on Padre Island.[14] Spohn spent many hours traveling long and arduous roads to reach these communities and provide medical aid to them. Now they have help around the corner.

Spohn traveled the world exploring the delivery of health care and how to prevent disease. Today the CHRISTUS Spohn Health System, the result of a merger with CHRISTUS Health, is an international Catholic, faith-based, not-for-profit health system providing services in more than seventy cities across Texas, Arkansas, Iowa, Louisiana, New Mexico, Georgia, Mexico, and Chile. The facilities operated by CHRISTUS include 60 hospitals and 175 clinics, and CHRISTUS Health employs about thirty-five thousand associates and nearly fourteen thousand physicians.[15]

When Spohn died, it was said that he was "skillful, intelligent, sympathetic, and deserved the good fortune that attended his efforts."[16] As the *Medical Record and Annals* reported, "Dr. Spohn was one of that favored group of Nineteenth Century physicians who helped establish in Texas the more elegant traditions of medical practice."[17] Texas and the world were blessed by his efforts, and today there are people still reaping the benefits and legacy he left to all of them.

No night was too dark, no way was too long, no poor so lowly
that when a call for help came Doctor Spohn did not answer, "I come."

Epilogue

D r. Spohn and Sarah had no children or heirs, but they each had members of their families living in Texas. Many members of Spohn's family had followed him and his brother in moving from Canada to Texas. All of them became an integral part of Spohn's Texas legacy. Family members had a strong dedication to each other as they pursued their careers, and each became in some way a vital part of the community, as described below:

1. Arthur's older brother, Henry, was the first to come to Texas, arriving in 1867 to work as a physician with the US Army at Fort McIntosh. When he established a medical practice in Laredo, he was the only Anglo doctor in town. He then opened a drugstore, bought ranch land in several counties, and established the town of Encinal. He was remembered as a perfect gentleman of the old school, gentle and kind. His life was filled with good deeds and charity. Henry died July 11, 1909, in Laredo.[1]

2. Angus Peter Spohn, son of Arthur's brother Peter, listed his immigration date as 1872. He had been a barrister in Canada.[2] In Texas he initially worked at his Uncle Henry's ranch and in Encinal until he was appointed a mounted inspector in the customs service in Zapata County. He later became a famous judge and politician known as the "King of Zapata."[3]

3. Spohn's sister, Catherine, and her husband, Alexander Hamilton, who had been Spohn's preceptor, came to Texas in 1875. He practiced medicine with Spohn in Corpus Christi, served as an officer with the Marine Hospital Service, and, along with his wife, Henry, and Arthur, owned ranch land around Laredo.[4]

4. Catherine and Alexander Hamilton had three sons. Alexander Jr. died young, while he was attending medical school. The other two, Henry (Harry) J. and Arthur Claud, were outstanding citizens of Laredo. Arthur

Claud Hamilton was an influential and powerful member of the legal profession; he graduated from the University of Texas in 1892 and received his law degree in 1894. He married Henrietta Greer of Beaumont, had an active law practice in Laredo, and served as district attorney for the Forty-Ninth District from 1896 to 1902. The next year he became assistant US attorney.[5] Harry practiced with Spohn, went to medical school, then traveled to Mexico before establishing his practice in Laredo. Harry followed in his father's and uncle's footsteps in pursuing public health and established a large practice and excellent reputation as a physician and surgeon in Laredo. He also had the good fortune to marry Lamar Benavides, daughter of the wealthy and influential Cristobal Benavides.[6] He made a name for himself across the state. In 1898 he was appointed surgeon in charge of the US Public Health Service in Laredo.

5. Jacob Van Wagner Spohn, one of Arthur's older brothers, came with his wife Mary in 1886 and lived near Encinal on a ranch. Jacob had graduated from Victoria College in Canada and had been a barrister and notary public before moving to Texas. He served as a judge in Encinal and as a director of the National Association of Woolen Manufacturers.[7]

6. Last to make the move to Texas was Arthur's nephew Douglas, son of his brother Philip Howard, in 1910. He practiced with Arthur at the new Spohn Sanitarium. When World War I broke out, he volunteered with the Royal Army Medical Corps and he and his wife Maude went to England. She worked with the British Red Cross while they were there. They came back to practice in Corpus Christi but returned to Canada after the hurricane of 1919.[8]

Dr. Douglas Spohn was sent to Texas in 1910 by his father, Philip, to help out his uncle Arthur. After serving in WWI with the British army, he and his wife, Maude, returned to Corpus Christi to practice medicine. They left after the hurricane of 1919 to return to Canada.

The Spohn family remained influential in Canada. When Arthur and Sarah traveled to Canada along with their niece, Sarita, to his nephew's wedding, the prime minister of Canada was there to give the wedding toast. The family also had outstanding physicians who continued to treat Canadians through the years.

In addition to his own family, Spohn had married into the extraordinary Kenedy clan when he married Sarah Kenedy. Her family became his family, too. He treated them medically, participated in their business investments, shared their tragedies and triumphs, and took care of Sarah. They are also part of his story and legacy.

Spohn married Sarah in 1876. She was well educated, spoke French along with her native Spanish and English, painted, and was an accomplished pianist. She was also an heiress to one of the largest fortunes in Texas. Her mother, Petra Vela, had been a devout Catholic, and passed this faith on to all her children.

Sarah had lost most of her siblings by the time of Arthur's death: her brother Willie, as a young man; James, just as he became a new father; and Tom, when he was assassinated. Her Vidal siblings from Petra's first alliance had all stayed close to the family, but they too were dying. Rosa

"Grey Fox" in Corpus Christi Bay.

When twenty-four-year-old George Mifflin Kenedy came to visit Arthur and Sarah Spohn in February 1908, he sailed into Corpus Christi Bay in the most expensive private vessel ever to dock in Corpus Christi. The *Grey Fox* carried a crew of eight men and cost $47,000, today equivalent to approximately $1.2 million. Courtesy of Anita Eisenhauer.

Putegnat died in 1904; Luisa Dalzell in 1907, although Spohn had journeyed to her side to try to help save her; and Luisa's husband, Robert Dalzell, and Concepcion Rodriguez in 1910. That left Sarah with Maria Vicenta Starck and other Vidal nieces and nephews. On the Kenedy side there was John Kenedy and his family and George Kenedy (James's son).

George Kenedy came to visit his family in February 1908, when he was twenty-four years old and had come into his inheritance. He was enjoying his money; he came sailing into Corpus Christi Bay in the most expensive and largest private boat ever to come to Corpus Christi. It had cost $47,000, which would be approximately $1.2 million today. With a crew of eight on the *Grey Fox*, George had sailed from New York in his new yacht, covering thousands of miles along the Atlantic and Gulf coasts. As for his personal life, George married first Sofia Rivadulle and later Beatrice Samano. He died in 1920 of tuberculosis, having no children, and was buried in the Kenedy family plot in Brownsville, Texas.[9]

Through the years Sarah had been an integral part of Corpus Christi society. She had entertained on many occasions and had helped put on an elaborate event for the Texas Medical Association. She traveled the world with Spohn, collecting many valuable paintings and furnishings for their home. The one thing missing was a child. They had lost one pregnancy and had no others. Childlessness provided a certain form of loneliness and disappointment when people around them were enjoying their children.

Sarah had a great deal to do with the success of the drive to see Spohn's hospital built. She worked with Alice Kleberg, Henrietta King, and others to raise the money to build the hospital. Sarah was a determined woman, and through the King/Kleberg and Kenedy connections her efforts were successful.

Sarah was getting ready for a party in her home on the evening of May 16, 1918, when she collapsed and died from a heart attack. She was sixty years old.[10] She had previously erected a marker at Rose Hill Cemetery in Corpus Christi in honor of her husband after his death in 1913. She was laid to rest beside him.[11] Sarah left her entire estate to her brother John, including what Spohn had left her. Sarah's estate was valued at $380,389, which today would be approximately $4,388,375.[12]

John Kenedy had been very close to Sarah and taken care of her. He had married Marie Stella Turcotte in New Orleans in 1884, and they had two surviving children: John Gregory Kenedy Jr. (Johnny) and Sarah Josephine Kenedy (Sarita). Their son Johnny married Elena Seuss of Saltillo, Mexico,

John and Marie Stella Kenedy with their young children, John
Kenedy Jr. and Sarah "Sarita" Kenedy. Kenedy Family Collection,
A1995-045.0296, South Texas Archives, James C. Jernigan
Library, Texas A&M University–Kingsville.

John Kenedy Jr. had no heirs, and
his half of the Kenedy fortune
was left to his wife, Elena Seuss
Kenedy. After her death, the
estate was left to the John G.
Kenedy Jr. Charitable Trust.

Sarita Kenedy married Arthur East, who was from a prominent ranching family, and they had no children.

This is possibly Elena Seuss Kenedy, photographed in a Paris studio on her honeymoon with John G. Kenedy Jr. Kenedy Family Collection, A1995-045.0095, South Texas Archives, James C. Jernigan Library, Texas A&M University–Kingsville.

and they lived at La Parra, near his parents. They had no children.[13] Johnny had sustained a severe case of mumps in his youth and also suffered from brucellosis, commonly known as undulant fever. These diseases' residual effects can be arthritis, depression, chronic fatigue, high fever, and infertility.[14]

Sarita married Arthur East and they also lived at La Parra. They had no children. Sarita became pregnant early in their marriage but had a miscarriage. She never conceived again. She had a prolapsed womb and like her brother had suffered from brucellosis, probably contracted by consuming unpasteurized or raw dairy products.[15]

Johnny and Sarita's mother, Marie Stella, first suggested that if there were no surviving children the estate should be left to the Catholic Church; she especially wanted to recognize the Oblate fathers and their efforts to help ranches across the Wild Horse Desert.[16] When John and Marie Stella Kenedy died, they left everything to Johnny and Sarita. The Kenedy Ranch was divided between the two children. Johnny inherited

Sarita Kenedy willed La Parra to the Missionary Oblates of Mary Immaculate, stipulating that the building be used for a religious purpose. The Oblates converted the grand ranch house into Lebh Shomea (Hebrew for "a listening heart") House of Prayer in 1973. It has remained a religious retreat ever since. Sarita willed the rest of her estate to the John G. and Marie Stella Kenedy Memorial Foundation in honor of her parents.

the northern half with the exception of the La Parra division. He died on November 26, 1948, and is buried in the Kenedy Cemetery at La Parra next to his parents.[17]

Sarita inherited the southern half of the Kenedy Ranch and the La Parra division. She died of cancer in New York City at the age of seventy-one on November 11, 1961. She is buried next to her husband, Arthur East, at La Parra.[18] Her will left her half of the ranch to the John G. and Marie Stella Kenedy Memorial Foundation in honor of her parents. Because of her close association with Brother Leo, a Trappist monk, and a last-minute change to her will, the will was challenged by the Catholic Church, her cousins the Turcottes and the Easts, and the descendants of Petra and Luis Vidal. The lawsuit lasted for almost twenty years, but the claims of the foundation were ultimately upheld in the courts. Between September 27, 1960, and July 31, 2015, the foundation has awarded grants totaling more than $300 million to charitable community groups across Texas.[19]

Sarita willed the ranch house to the Missionary Oblates of Mary Immaculate, on the condition that the building would be used for a religious purpose. The Oblates made the home at La Parra into Lebh Shomea House of Prayer in 1973. It has remained a religious retreat house ever since.[20]

Elena Kenedy, Johnny's wife, was the last surviving member of the family, dying March 1, 1984.[21] She too was buried at La Parra next to her husband. She followed Sarita's decision and left her northern half of the ranch to the John G. Kenedy Jr. Charitable Trust.

Both Sarita and Elena were recognized by the Vatican for their contributions to the Catholic Church and were awarded the Equestrian Order of the Holy Sepulchre of Jerusalem, the highest papal honor awarded to a woman.[22] Petra's strong faith and the faith of her family members would stay strong through the generations. The wealth they accumulated was given to support the Catholic Church and the poor and needy. That work is still a viable effort in Texas today.[23] In 2004, a *Texas Monthly* article valued the assets of the John G. and Marie Stella Kenedy Memorial Foundation and John G. Kenedy Jr. Charitable Trust together at between $500 million and $1 billion, with 80 percent going to the Catholic Diocese of Corpus Christi, the CHRISTUS Spohn Health System, and various Catholic charities.[24]

Dr. A. E. Spohn was an integral part of the Kenedy family that had created this extraordinary foundation and trust, but his greatest legacy will always be his work in medicine. He was indeed "the man for the job."

Appendix 1

Medical Journal Articles by Dr. Spohn

"Fracture of the Clavicle"

Medical and Surgical Reporter 67 (1887): 796

The chest, viewed from any side, has the appearance of an irregular cone: the diameters increasing from above downwards to a plane corresponding with the centre of the sternum. Upon this cone the upper extremities, as it were[,] hang, through the medium of the scapula and clavicle; which being bound together by ligaments, rest on the chest like a collar, held in position by the various muscles; the only fixed point being the sterno-clavicular articulation. Fixed at this point, the clavicle on each side serves as a brace to hold the shoulder-joint in position; and, when fractured, the anterior support of that joint is lost, which allows it to droop and be carried downwards[,] forwards and towards the chest; because the scapula rests on a surface pressing diagonally downwards and forwards, while the broken clavicle, which before held the joint in position, now allows the joint to fall in towards the chest, the ends of the bones generally overlapping. Pressure against the shoulder-joint backwards will carry the scapula back over the same surface upwards and backwards, when the broken bone may easily be replaced; but, from its peculiar position, it is almost impossible to retain it in such a position as to prevent more or less deformity, and at the same time to cause the patient much inconvenience.

The device I have lately adopted is to adjust a splint which shall replace the broken clavicle and restore the lost support to the shoulder-joint. This splint I have called the subclavicular or anterior chest-splint. It is simply a piece of wood or sole leather made to fit the anterior surface of the chest just below the clavicular bones, two inches wide, and long enough to reach the outer side of each arm.. This splint should be well padded and covered with strong muslin. Two pads are now made to place under each end of the splint, to fit into what I have chosen to call the lateral triangular space of the chest. Viewing the articulated skeleton from the front, the arms hang-ing down, there is on each side a tri-angular space, bounded above by the clavicle, acromion and coracoid pro-cesses; externally, the head and upper third of the humerus; internally by a line drawn from the centre of the clavicle to the junction of the upper and middle thirds of the humerus. Crossing this space, which, in cases of fracture, draws the joint forwards, downwards, and towards the chest, we have the pectoralis minor muscle.

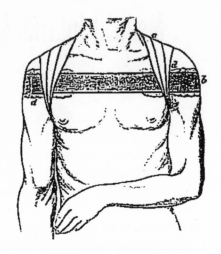

This space does not show well on the body, but can be distinctly out-lined by a little pressure. Firm pressure, directed backwards over a pad in this space, while the arm is in a sling, will thoroughly fix the shoulder-joint and carry it upwards, outwards, and backwards, thus meeting every indi-cation in treating fracture of the clavicle; because the scapula rests upon a surface directed downwards, forwards, and outwards, which course it takes when the anterior support (clavicle) is removed; while firm backward pres-sure will reverse things and force the scapula over the same surface upwards, backwards, and towards the spine, which must raise the shoulder-joint and increase the space between the acromion process and clavicular notch of the sternum; so that, were the clavicle entirely removed, the shoulder would remain in proper position as long as this support is kept up.

When fractured, the clavicle is practically removed, even worse, and distorted. The subclavicular or anterior chest-splint replaces the broken clavicle; also presses the pad into the triangular space above described, giving the required support.

This pad should be thicker in the middle than at either end, so that it will press well against the outer end of the clavicle, coracoid and acromion processes, and sink in, as it were, between the upper part of the arm and side of the chest[,] thus forcing the shoulder-joint outwards. The pad should now

be firmly stitched to the splint and a figure-of-eight bandage applied, first putting a little cotton or, better, a small pad under each arm; place the arm in a sling, when the dressing is complete.

In order to appreciate this dressing, see [figure not shown], showing the relation of the figure-of-eight bandage to the scapula. The surface on which the scapula rests is directed upwards and backwards; consequently this bandage carries that bone upwards and backwards, elevating the shoulder-joint; while the anterior splint, thus held in position resting on an inclined plane, supports the front of the shoulder and restores as it were, the broken clavicle, while the patient is put to very little inconvenience: he can walk about or lie down with perfect safety. The dressings must be thoroughly stitched together.

I have during the past few months, treated several cases in this manner, and with better success than I ever saw by other appliances; sometimes simply placing the splint under a tight-fitting vest, with the arm in a sling, and the vest sewn or pinned to the splint.

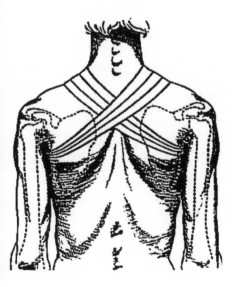

"Rabies and Anti-Rabic Inoculations"

Transactions of the Texas Medical Association, Twenty-First
Annual Session, San Antonio, April 23–26, 1889

Member Kings County Medical Society, New York; Texas State, and West Texas Medical Associations; Acting Surgeon United States Marine Hospital Service; Health Officer City of Corpus Christi, Texas.

In the paper I am about to read before this Association, I do not pretend to submit anything original. Not having had the opportunity of putting in practice the preventive inoculation of M. Pasteur, but having had the pleasure of studying that method as practiced up to the present time, in the Institute in Paris, and being impressed with the great work of that great man, I have considered it my duty, as a physician, to present you our State Medical Association the subject of anti-rabid inoculation; giving an account of the method as practiced by M. Pasteur. . . . I will state, that the result of my investigations has been drawn largely from the Pasteur Institute, and others of a similar kind, now in operation, in various parts of the world; also from the general literature on that question.

The subject of rabies has been lately extensively considered throughout the whole world; surgeons have dealt with it cautiously, some denying the existence of such a disease, while others pass it with a few casual remarks, under the head of animal poisons.

Up to the researches of M. Pasteur, in his laboratory in Paris, the description of this affection uniformly accepted, was given by Mr. Youatt: an affection essentially due to the inoculation of the human body by the saliva of a rabid animal, followed by characteristic symptoms, always terminating in death.

It is [due] to the experiments made by M. Pasteur, that we are enabled to investigate one of the most dreaded diseases known to mankind. It is true that, in order to demonstrate the result of same, many animals have perished; yet what difference if hundreds of dogs, rabbits, etc., have perished, provided we have been able to discover the cause of rabies, which means to protect humanity from this terrible scourge?

The disease is generally described as having three stages: melancholy, irritation, and paralysis.

Each stage has its peculiar symptoms. A person is bitten by a rabid animal; before the period of incubation, of from 16 to 199 days, has passed, if the patient is very nervous, we are liable to have emotional symptoms, or spurious rabies, where the symptoms will simulate all accounts of Hydrophobia he ever read or heard of. I have known them to have attacks of intense melancholy, commencing within a few hours of the injury. I believe many persons die from spurious rabies; and while in no way depending upon a specific virus, if continued, will run into melancholy, irritation, and death. It is in such cases, and they are far the most frequent, where properly directed treatment will have a beneficial effect; while for true rabies there is, at present, no known remedy, our only hope being in prevention.

This period of incubation, or latent period, lasts from 16 to 199 days, an average of 48.73, which corresponds with the period given by Mr. Youatt, of from 42 to 49 days. During this latent period, the wound generally heals; the person returns to his ordinary avocation, still is not free from suffering, often becoming extremely nervous, restless, and excitable—living in constant dread of the approaching results. It is this state of uncertainty which makes rabies such a terrible affection. On many occasions I have been consulted by persons months, and even years, after they had been bitten by supposed rabid animals, telling me that their lives were completely useless; living in constant dread of the horrible results. One man who was under my observation, had been bitten by a wolf. For about a year and a half he suffered intensely; was not able to attend to business, and died of paralysis. I have no doubt that this man died from the result of the injury—rabies.

After this period of latency, comes the first stage of rabies.

I will here describe the disease in the dog, which in some points resembles that in man. The following symptoms have been lucidly described by Mr. Youatt and Prof. Virchow. 1st. Stage of sullenness and melancholy. 2nd. Furious stage of irritation. 3rd. Paralysis or collapse. In the first stage the dog becomes changed, restless, loses his appetite or may have a depraved appetite with fever and thirst. He does not fear water as generally supposed and it is well to bear this fact in mind. The wound may inflame; he acts as if in pain; he will pick up and try to eat unpalative articles; he may have excessive sexual excitement; he has difficulty in drinking on account of spasmodic contraction of the muscles of deglutition. His affection for his master is changed, at times not recognizing him; he has muscular tremblings—an evidence of weakness. This stage may last from one to three or four days, when he passes into the stage of excitement, with great restlessness and irritability; leaves his home, runs from place to place biting at everything coming in his way. If chased and excited, still more all the symptoms of madness are increased such as panting and foaming at the mouth; with his tongue hanging out. He is, as it were in a state of mania; angry and furious. His voice changes, howling as if in distress. His tongue, fauces and nose will be swollen, with great difficulty in swallowing. He is impulsive[,] moves from place to place impatiently[.] This stage may last from three to four days, when the third stage of paralysis and general prostration comes on; dying in collapse, with all its attending symptoms; or in a paroxysm of convulsions in from five to eight days.

Other animals are capable of taking the disease and communicating it to man. On several occasions epidemics of rabies have existed among the deer in the English parks. These deer run in herds and are very numerous. The greatest losses were in 1795–1798, 1872, 1880, 1886 and 1887. The disease was not known until investigated by A. C. Cope and Prof. Horsley, at the Royal Veterinary Institute, where they had them under observation. By inoculating rabbits with the cerebellum of deer, which had died with the disease, they succeeded in producing rabies.

Richmond Park contains 2300 acres, with 1200 deer. In this park alone between June and September, they lost 264 animals with rabies. It is quite possible that the great mortality often seen among the deer of southern Texas is due to the same cause for, in this country, rabies is a common affection among the wolves. Dogs inoculated from the Richmond Park deer became furious and died with characteristic symptoms of rabies. At the same time there was an epidemic of rabies among the dogs of London and vicinity. The deer transmitted the disease by biting each other. One animal with the disease was shut up with a well one. The rabid one became furious [and] ran at its companion, biting its ears and nose. The bitten animal was isolated, and in eighteen days presented characteristic symptoms of the rage. It was for a long time supposed that herbivorous animals, on account of having no upper incisive teeth, could not transmit the rage; but experience proves that they do transmit the disease by biting.

In man many symptoms are similar to those in animals. The following case was the first M. Pasteur lost, after commencing anti-rabic inoculations, which illustrates forcibly the ordinary symptoms: On the 9th of November 1885, Louise Pelletier, ten years of age, was brought to the institute for treatment. She had been bitten, thirty-seven days before by a large mountain dog. Besides a deep wound in her armpit, she was almost scalped. "Why did you not bring this child very much sooner?" said M. Pasteur, with a great deal of anxiety, to the parents of the child. While waiting for Dr. Grancher to make the first inoculations, M. Pasteur said:

"We are commencing a desperate case. The explosion of the rabies is on the eve of being produced. It is too late for the preventive treatment to have the least effect. Should I not, in the interest of science refuse to treat this child, brought so late, under such exceptional conditions?" The problem was doubtful. The bad results predicted by M. Pasteur led him to think he was risking his many months of labor, and was liable to throw doubt into the minds of those he was so long convincing, and discourage others from coming to the laboratory. Yes, this was all true; but, besides these hypothetic considerations, he had there, in that little waiting room, a father and mother, full of anguish, anxious for their little girl. "Even if I had but one chance in ten thousand to save this child, I will risk it all." Humane sentiments overcame all scientific objections. The treatment had been completed [in] several days. She had been taken to the apartments of her parents, who were beginning to hope for her recovery, when the first symptoms of hydrophobia commenced. She refused all drink; the contractions of her throat opposed the passage of any liquid; spasms of choking would keep her from articulating; she would become angry and irritable, then sob pitifully, when the paroxysm left her. The morning of the second of December a period of calm commenced, which was prolonged about eight hours. It seemed as if a war was going on in her system between the effects of the inoculations and the rage. They recommenced a series of inoculations every two hours, but the invasion was too complete[;] rabies was the stronger. That night she was taken with hallucinations; she said she felt as if water was running over her whole body; at certain moments she did not recognize her father, then suddenly noticing her mistake, she would make all kinds of excuses and caress him. She would call M. Pasteur, take his hands and say, "Please stay near my bed, I'll be so afraid if you leave me." The words, which were brokenly spoken, seemed to come with a great deal of pain from her throat. Death was already fixed in her countenance; her large black eyes would look at you anxiously, and on the third of December little Louise Pelletier died. As predicted by M. Pasteur he was severely criticized, not only in Paris, but the whole world; yet that great good man, nothing daunted by this unfortunate case, continued his scientific investigation and today there stands in the city of Paris a monument to his success in scientific investigations—one of the grandest structures in the world, built by the grateful recipients of his beneficence and an admiring public—the Pasteur Institute of France, inaugurated November 14, 1888, with the remarkable subscription of 2,586,680 frs.,—an institute devoted to the prevention of the rage, where rich and poor, from all parts of the world, are treated and cared for, free of charge.

Post Mortem Appearances

After passing through such terrible agony one would expect to find results which would naturally follow; great excitement, delirium and convulsions, produced by central nervous irritation; and it is here where we must look for pathological conditions. There is congestion of the brain, cerebellum and spinal cord. The most congestion is in the cerebellum; there is no effusion of lymph, or evidence of inflammation. There is turgescence of the peripheral veins of the brain, a red coloring of the cortical substance; ramollisment of the white substance, cerebro medullary, of certain pairs (Meynert); tumefaction of the calciform papilla of the tongue; injection of the pharyngeal region; pulmonary engorgement, with bloody effusion on the posterior border of the lung; albumin in the urine; conditions which would naturally follow rabic convulsions.

Treatment

I will first consider the treatment immediately after the injury, during the period of incubation or latency, and after the invasion of the rage has set in, and terminate with the preventive and anti-rabic inoculations; rather reversing the order in which they are really carried out.

After a person is bitten by a supposed rabid animal, the first thing should be to cauterize the part deeply with a red hot iron; but, while heating the same, there are a few details it will be well to carry out: First, tie a ligature above the part, i.e., if an extremity, sufficiently tight to arrest the venous circulation only, and thus facilitate hemorrhage. The wound may be washed with some antiseptic solution. If no iron is at hand or fire convenient, the part should be cauterized with any cautery (Mr. Youatt recommends nitrate of silver) and then excised. The period of incubation being very long, the virus no doubt may lie dormant in the wound a long time; in fact, one of the most common and constant symptoms of the first invasion of the disease in man is pain in the bitten part, with neuralgic pains running from same. I prefer the hot iron, because it destroys the tissues in the immediate vicinity, and coagulates the fluids for some distance, preventing absorption. Then, as soon as the effect of the burn shows its extent, excise the part freely, cutting as wide as possible of the wound. When the part cannot be excised we must be content with the cautery. I use in other poisoned wounds a mixture of equal parts of tinc, iodine, aqua ammonia glycerine and tinc of belladonna, especially in snake bites, to wash the wound and take internally. It has become a popular remedy in my section of the State; is kept in almost every house, and, I am told, gives excellent results. It might be useful in bites of rabid animals. The antidote was suggested to me by my friend, the late Prof. Croft, of Toronto University, one of our most eminent chemists, who demonstrated the fact that iodine is a chemical antidote for the poison of the rattlesnake. In all poisoned wounds I invariably excise the part, the removal of which is a great relief to the patient's mind—an important point in the successful management of such cases. In my details, while preparing to treat the wound, I forgot the dog, or animal, inflicting the injury. What should be done with him? Catch him, if possible; in fact, he must be caught, not killed. It is one of the greatest mistakes to kill a supposed mad dog, especially if he has bitten any other animal. In the first place, the injury is already done. The poor animal may have bitten his master, but he is suffering from a dreadful mania, if mad, and not responsible. The main object, though, is this: if the animal has rabies, he will certainly die, and within a short time. Should he be destroyed—then all hope of ever knowing whether he was mad or not is lost. If he does not die, then he was not mad, and your patient is safe. What a relief to his mind, the value of which cannot be estimated. Treat the animal kindly; don't annoy or irritate him; keep a record of anything unusual in his actions. If he dies, never allow the patient to know it; and send his head, also a copy of his symptoms, to some person prepared to make the necessary experimental inoculations. Now we have only to await results; and during this latent period we must amuse and divert our patient's mind from the injury; never mention or allow him to read anything about hydrophobia, acting as if he had only a simple wound. Everything must be done to keep the patient in good health, without showing undue interest. An occasional Turkish bath, and plenty of exercise will be necessary. He must rest well. Should the disease make its appearance, all is lost; still it is well to keep him as quiet as possible. I think the comp. liq. of hydrate of chloral one of the best preparations for this purpose, with stimulating anodyne applications to the spine. Frequent Turkish baths should be given with antipyrin or pilocarpine to assist diaphoresis. Should the paroxysm become severe, hypodermic injections of morphine with atropia, or inhalations of chloroform, according to circumstances; but our main object at the present time, and the one most interesting, is the prevention of the disease, or anti-rabic inoculations.

In order that you may fully appreciate this comparatively recent method, I will carry you, as it were, through the Institute, show the source of and method of preparing the virus, the inoculations and results.

This institution, devoted to the prevention of the rage in persons who have been recently bitten by supposed rabid animals, is situated in the Rue d'Ulm, where, up to the present time, about 6,000 persons, from all parts of the world, bitten by supposed rabid animals, have been gratuitously treated by this remarkable man and his assistants. It is built after the style of Louis XIII., and on the front is the following inscription: "Public Subscription, 1888." The hours for treatment are from 10 to 11:30 a.m., and from 9 to 10:30 p.m. This laboratory is a part of the normal school of Paris and from the large amount of money at the disposal of this institution, they are enabled to conduct their experiments in the most perfect and extensive manner. At the kind invitation of M. Pasteur, I was permitted to have access to, and study the process carried on in the department devoted to the rage. For in this institution they also study and investigate all diseases peculiar to the human species, and the scientific means to combat them,—diph., feb. typh., tuberculosis, etc.

I made the remark on the steamer, when on my way with Mr. Chamberlain to consult M. Pasteur[,] that a man must have nerve and determination, who could inoculate a human being with virus from animals which had died from hydrophobia and on reaching the institution, heard my remarks confirmed, when M. Pasteur told me that he trembled when he thought of the method, after having experimented successfully with rabbits, etc. M. Pasteur is a gentleman about 55 years of age, not tall, stoutly built, erect and of remarkable appearance. Just such a man one would suppose could deal with life and death. Calm, courteous, and decisive; speaks extremely slow, as if every word were studied and weighed, and might be taken as conclusive on the subject in question. When questioning a patient who had presented himself rather late for treatment, one can see in his countenance a look of painful, suffering pity for the unfortunate. I don't think I ever saw him smile, and the same thing may be said of his assistants; indeed, the subject of their researches is so grave, that when one enters the institution, it is with awe and astonishment. From the child in its mother's arms to the old man, all races and stations of mankind, may be seen answering to their names, as they step forward to receive the preventive inoculation. In the yard adjoining the institute, may be seen iron cages made expressly for mad dogs, cages for rabbits, guinea pigs, birds, etc, etc. Here they keep the animals for experiments, and they are in all stages of this dreadful malady. Some have just been inoculated, and still feel stupid from the anesthetic; for in order to perpetuate the rabic virus for inoculations, two rabbits are inoculated every day, and three every third day,—others are running around in the cages, as if in perfect health in the period of latency, or incubation, four to six days; others are in the first stage of rabies; other[s], furious[,] some dying, some dead.

You will notice [a] period of latency or incubation four to six days, while when describing rabies in the first part of this paper, I gave a period of latency of 48.73 days. Why this difference? We are now dealing with a fixed virus, which will destroy an animal producing rabies in its most terrible form in the short space of ten to eleven days with very little variation—traveling, as it were, by lightning express, while ordinary rabies goes by stage. Which should win? The fixed virus, provided the other has not had too long a start. Whence comes this fixed virus? It is the result of years of labor and scientific investigation; not the creation of the imagination. After M. Pasteur had finished his experiments, on charbon, fermentation, measles in pork, chicken cholera, etc., he turned his attention to hydrophobia. He first experimented with the saliva, but found it contained foreign microbes. He then selected the portion of the body showing greatest evidence of the disease, and found that the brain and spinal cord gave better results, producing uniform effects. The principal problem was, to isolate, if possible, the microbe, and discover the means to prevent this terrible disease. Did there exist a means to prevent the rage in dogs, as they had prevented chicken cholera and charbon, by inoculation? A dog had died of rabies. M. Pasteur inoculated a rabbit by trephining, injecting a small portion of the cerebellum of the rabid dog, rubbed up with a little sterilized beef tea, beneath the dura mater of the rabbit. After an incubation of fifteen days, the rabbit died of the rage. He then inoculated other rabbits from the cerebellum of this dead rabbit, continuing these experiments through twenty-five successive rabbits, and found that the period of incubation became shorter up to the ninetieth passage, after which the period of incubation became fixed producing first symptoms in from four to six days, and death in ten to eleven; while the ordinary rabid virus produces first symptoms by trephining, in fifteen days, in bites forty-eight days; hence, the stronger virus transmitted through rabbits is called fixed virus and is used for the preventive inoculations in man.

Was it possible to modify this virus? M. Pasteur subjected this virus to dessication [*sic*], cutting sections from the spinal cord and hanging them in bottles, in the bottoms of which were pieces of hydrated potash. The bottles were corked with sterilized wool and placed in a dark room, with a temperature of 20° to 25° cent. After fourteen days desiccation, he ground the virus in sterilized beef tea, and injected it into dogs, under the skin, continuing the inoculations daily for thirteen days, using virus of one day's less dessication each day[,] the last injection being of virus of but one day's dessication.

Dogs subjected to this series of progressive inoculations, became refractory to the rage, and resisted inoculations of strong virus, also bites of rabid animals. Was it possible to prevent the disease after having been bitten, by this same method, which he had repeated so successfully? These experiments in the etiology and prophylaxis of the rage, so important and precious as a scientific investigation, to M. Pasteur still seemed insufficient. What he wished was some method applicable to the human species bitten by rabid animals; and "although I have succeeded so well with dogs," said M. Pasteur, "I fear my hand will tremble when the day comes to inoculate man." An accident happened in Alsace, during these observations. On the 4th of July, 1885, Joseph Meslier, nine years of age, was bitten by a rabid dog. He was going to school, when the dog jumped upon him. He did not run, but covered his face with his arms; the dog bit him, threw him down and continued to bite him, until a mason saw them, and drove the dog away with a bar of iron. The dog was afterwards shot. He was furious, frothing at the mouth, and had bits of straw and wood in his stomach, which rendered it probable he was mad. The wounds, fourteen in number, were cauterized by Dr. Webber, who advised Mr. Meslier to take his little son to Paris, where he might find some person who could give him good counsel, "and that one lives in the Rue d' Ulm," said the doctor, "and his name is M. Pasteur." They arrived at the laboratory on the morning of July 6. M. Pasteur was very much troubled at the misfortune of these poor people, and in anguish at the idea of practicing his inoculations on this child. He sent for M. Velpeau and Dr. Grancher, Professor in the Faculty of Medicine, his student and friend, and presented the situation face to face. They examined the child's wounds and agreed with M. Pasteur, to make a trial in this child, almost condemned, of the method which had certainly succeeded with dogs, and commenced their inoculations, injecting a solution of the dessicated [*sic*] cord under the skin just above the hips. As the inoculations continued and the virus used became more and more virulent M. Pasteur became painfully uneasy, passing anxious days, and nights without sleep. Quick transitions of grand experiments, and terrible prostration, came from all this glory. Little Meslier returned home on the 27th of July, perfectly well, and has kept up a regular correspondence with M. Pasteur since.

On the 26th of October, M. Pasteur made a verbal communication of his experience and of the result of his method, after five years of labor, to the French Academy of Sciences, which society made a favorable report. The case of little Meslier created a profound sensation throughout the entire world—the first successful case of anti-rabic inoculations. An official commission was sent from England, composed of the most learned and celebrated men, with a young and experienced physiologist, Professor Horsley, for reporter. They arrived in Paris very incredulous. After a profound investigation, the committee returned to England, and repeated the experiments of M. Pasteur. They were over one year making their investigations, and reported that Pasteur had discovered a preventive method against the rabies, compared to vaccination against the small-pox. M. Charcot said, with reference to Pasteur's method, "Yes, the inventor of anti-rabic vaccination can to-day, more than ever, walk with his head erect, and pursue his glorious task, without allowing himself to be turned for one instant by those clamoring against him, or by the insidious murmurs of incredulity." These words, from so great a man, had the effect of quieting all opposition to the Pasteur method during the year 1888.

The report by Hygiene and Health, for the Department of the Seine, for the year 1887 by Dr. Dujardin Beaumetz, which is taken from the documents of the Prefecture of Police,—that part which concerns the persons inoculated at the Pasteur Institute shows that in 1887 there were 306 persons bitten and inoculated, of which only three died, a mortality of 1.02 per cent. On the other hand, there were seven deaths in the same report, out of forty-four cases of persons bitten by rabid animals, who were not inoculated. In this group, the mortality reached 15.90 per cent. Figures given by M. Leblanc, and which M. Pasteur and Bronordel accepted as representing the average mortality before inoculation was practiced.

The report of M. Beaumetz contains another interesting conclusion: that rabies is a disease we cannot combat through administrative sanitary measures. It is not spontaneous, is always transmitted, by inoculation, from one animal to another, and of all animals, the dog is the most susceptible. The Registrar general of Great Britain, in his report for 1888, says that the mortality in that kingdom is very much diminished since the advent of the Pasteur method.

Notwithstanding some of our journals are severely criticizing the institute of Pasteur and his method, notwithstanding they have prophesied the downfall of that institution[,] it still lives and prospers, not only in Paris, but in various parts of the world. For instance, seven in Russia, five in Italy, one in Vienna, one in Constantinople, one in Barcelona, one in Bucharest, one in Rio Janeiro, one in Buenos Ayres, one in Havana, and being organized in San Antonio, Texas. The institute in Paris is in correspondence with the above named institutions, the directors of which studied the method in the institute in Paris, and are now practicing same with satisfactory results.

"Communications: Gunshot Wound of the Abdomen"
Medical and Surgical Reporter 63 (November 15, 1890): 20

In time of peace gunshot wounds of the abdomen are comparatively rare, especially those inflicted by large missles [*sic*], which are seldom seen except on the frontier, where the old-fashioned Colt six-shooter is to be found. It was with one of these 45-caliber old timers that the following wound was made.

At 10 o'clock on the morning of June 25, 1889, Adrian Bocanegra, a healthy young man twenty years old, was playing with a pistol, which was accidentally discharged while the barrel rested against his abdomen. The nature of such an injury may easily be imagined; the ball entered about two inches to the left of and a little above the navel, passed through the abdominal cavity and lodged under the skin about one inch to the left of the spine near the tenth dorsal vertebra. The man fell backwards and then got up and walked across the street. In about half an hour he commenced vomiting blood. There was no hemorrhage from the wound, externally. I did not see him until almost 12 o'clock. He was then lying on his back pallid, with very feeble and frequent pulse, evidently suffering from profuse internal hemorrhage. Air passed occasionally from the abdominal wound, and there was a crackling emphysematous sound, showing that gas had escaped into the loose tissues. There was neither ingested matter nor blood escaping from the wound. I gave half a grain of morphia hypodermically, and made arrangements to open the abdominal cavity immediately.

Dr. Jones, of this city, and Dr. Cock, of San Marcos, assisted in the operation. I sterilized about 10 gallons of water by boiling, and to a part of this I added ten per cent of carbolic acid, for the hands and instruments; to the remainder five per cent of boric acid, for flooding the abdominal cavity. I washed the surface of the abdomen with a ten per cent solution of carbolic acid[,] shaved off all its hair, and dusted with powdered boric acid. It was two o'clock when Dr Jones commenced administering the chloroform. I made an incision through the linea alba, from the navel to about two inches above the pubes, arresting all hemorrhage with hot water, and ligatures where necessary. The peritoneal cavity contained clots of blood, and ingested matter; gas also escaped from the intestines. The hemorrhage, which had been very profuse, had evidently ceased, but recommenced when I began to examine the intestines, one point bleeding very freely—where the ball had passed through the transverse mesocolon very near the bowel, and cut off quite a large vessel, which I ligated. While examining the intestines I kept the cavity well flooded with the boric acid solution, at a temperature of from 100° to 112°. I found four wounds in the intestines, one in the transverse portion of the duodenum, and three in the small intestines, eight openings in all; besides these the mesentery was cut in several places, and contained between the folds several large clots of blood, which I pressed out, ligating the bleeding points when necessary. After persistently flooding the cavity and searching for bleeding points, the water was still very bloody, so much so that I feared there was some bleeding point that I had not detected. I now enlarged the opening by [cutting?] the incision about two inches above the navel, and again carefully examined for hemorrhage. Upon passing my hand into the cavity of the pelvis, I found it filled with clotted blood, which I removed by flooding the cavity and gently paddling with my hand.

I next turned my attention to closing the openings in the intestines, using ordinary sewing needles, and a fine ligature known as "West India Islands grass line," which I described in the *Medical and Surgical Reporter*, August 10, 1887, page 270—a line I believe made from raw silk—composed of three separate threads twisted together, which I separated, using one of the fine threads for ligatures, as they are very strong and durable. The first wound closed was the one from which there was so much hemorrhage, in the transverse mesocolon. The ball had passed very near the bowel, which was contused for some distance and I believe would eventually have given way. I treated the wounded part[,] as an opening existed, closed the opening in the mesentery—inserting reinforcing stitches near the intestine, and also stitched the bowel on each side, keeping well outside of the contused portion, which was pressed into the canal. I used the Lembert suture, which I think gives better satisfaction than any other in such cases. The openings in the intestines were large and ragged[,] one being almost completely severed. I did not pare the edges of the wound, for I think it a mistake to do this, because it takes time, may produce hemorrhage, and removes the ragged surface, which naturally falls together, interfacing, as it were, and assists in keeping the opening well closed. I inserted the stitches lengthwise of the bowel, a procedure which may shorten the intestine, but does not decrease in caliber, which I consider an important point in closing intestinal wounds. The intestines being held by the mesenteries, like an open fan, have a tendency to drop together, and if shortened by resection or the closure of a wound, there is little or no strain on the stitches, while the caliber of the bowel is not diminished. On the other hand, if the stitches are inserted crosswise of the intestine, not only will the caliber be diminished, but there will also be a strain on the part. Shortening the intestine by doubling it over has a tendency to strengthen it. I placed the stitches about one-fifth of an inch apart, sometimes closer, inserting extra stitches when the parts did not appear to be effectively closed. All the stitches of a given opening were inserted before any were tied. After closing all the wounds—that is nine of the intestines, and three in mesenteries—I flooded the cavity very freely by pouring the water in from a pitcher, and then raising the side of the table to let it run out, continuing until the water came out clear, at the same time examining carefully for clots or ingested matter. I then wiped the cavity out very carefully with soft sponges, passing them deep into the pelvis, until all fluids had been removed, then closed the abdominal incision, using the grass line, full strength, placed one inch apart, including the peritoneum; between these and to close any gaping points, I inserted specially prepared horsehair sutures, which I find excellent for fine work. The horsehair is prepared by being washed with soap and water, soaked for forty-eight hours in a ten per cent solution of carbolic acid, and then placed in a glass tube filled with a fifty per cent solution of boro-glyceride, and securely corked. The hair thus prepared is very elastic and quite strong.

I did not insert a drainage-tube, and do not think they are necessary, when the abdominal toilet is nicely perfected and there is no hemorrhage. I covered the abdominal incision with boric acid, then a narrow strip of borated cotton, passing a few strips of rubber adhesive plaster across, to give additional support, dusted boric acid very freely over the whole surface, and covered all with pad of borated cotton, which, with a light bandage, completed the dressing.

The opening where the ball entered was very much torn and powder burnt, and I simply covered it with boric acid and borated cotton. I did not remove the bullet, not wishing to make any more openings into the cavity, last removed it several days after.

I was two and a half hours from the commencement of the operation in the completion of the dressing. My patient rallied well and made a very quick recovery, without any complications. The following is selected from the notes taken daily at the bedside:

Morphia was used to procure rest of the bowel; the urine was drawn with a catheter; mucilaginous drinks and beef peptonoids were administered, and by the third day a little milk with a little coffee and the next day some chicken broth. The sixth day an enema of glycerine and milk, of each two ounces brought about an action of the bowels containing considerable fecal matter.

On July 4 I dressed the abdominal wound for the first time. I found the dressings dry[,] just a little soiled along the line of the incision. The wound was completely healed. I removed all the stitches and washed the abdomen with a five per cent solution of carbolic acid, using sterilized water, applied a few strips of adhesive plaster dusted with boric acid, and replaced the pad of borated cotton and the bandage. The patient's pulse was 72, his respiration was 20, his temperature 99 1/2° and he was feeling quite comfortable.

July 9 I removed the bullet from his back, which was not causing any inconvenience, the slight incision soon healing. Of course, while I now considered my patient quite well, I kept him under observation, allowing but little exercise and a very restricted diet. It is now three months since the operation and he enjoys his usual health and is able to do a hard day's work.

I have given a very full report of the above case because it is one of great importance, not only from its gravity, but because it may assist my professional brethren of the rural districts in coming to a conclusion as to what course to pursue in cases of gunshot wounds of the abdomen and their proper management. That they need not allow the unfortunate sufferer to die, because there is no specialist at hand, I have always believed; and I maintain that one man can do just as much as another, if he only thinks so; that surgery, after all, is only a question of anatomy and good judgment. When I made my first abdominal section I had to ride fifty miles on horseback, give chloroform, and operate alone for obstruction of the bowels—and the operation was successful.

In looking back over the above case, I see no change I would make, the treatment being the same that I follow in all cases of abdominal section; and my success has been all I could have desired. There are a few details I consider of great importance, viz.: a well-ventilated room kept at a temperature of from 98° to 100° F., during all capital operations; plenty of sterilized water, and the utmost cleanliness in operator and assistants. I always take a bath and change my clothing just before all serious operations and require the same, if possible, of all assistants—at least their hands must be thoroughly disinfected, using a strong solution of carbolic acid. In dressing all wounds I use a large quantity of boric acid, enough to absorb any moisture. In abdominal sections I scarcely ever examine the wound before the fifth day, and do not change the dressings until the ninth or tenth day, when I remove the stitches. I adopt the same course in amputations.

I would not rely on the hydrogen-gas test, because a bullet may pass in close proximity to the intestine, cutting partly through it, which will be followed by perforation and certain death. No surgeon would, in my opinion, be justified in treating a penetrating wound of the abdomen, who did not immediately make an exploratory incision, in order to arrest hemorrhage, repair any injury to the intestines and cleanse the cavity. On October 1, 1890, I chanced to be traveling on the car from Corpus Christi to San Diego, Texas. At one point we stopped to take on wood, and I left the car for a little walk along the track and found a man lying on the ground, supposed to be dying. Upon examination, I found he had been shot—the ball passing through the abdominal cavity, entering about three inches to the left of and a little below the navel, passing out a little to the right of the spine. I had not time to operate where he was, so I put him in the baggage car, and at the next station opened the cavity. There was nothing to indicate that the intestines were injured. It was now eight hours since he was shot, there was no emphysematous sound, no air or blood escaping from the wound; the only thing showing severe injury was his weak and quick pulse and collapsed condition. There was considerable blood in the cavity, the ball having penetrated the descending colon and cut a small artery in the mesentery. The blood in the cavity was evidently from this artery, which I ligated at once. The wound in the intestine was large and very peculiar, the mucous coat being turned out, completely stopping up the openings. I closed the opening—using Lembert's sutures—washed out the cavity, stitched it up and used the ordinary dressing after laparotomy, and left the man with his friend giving instructions, which I suppose were not followed.

On the fifth day after, he sent to ask me if he could have something to eat. I was told he felt well, and had little or no fever and so I allowed him a very little liquid food. I have since heard that he died, and that he had paralysis of the lower extremities. I have no doubt but that the ball injured the cord and probably fractured one of the vertebra. The fact is I had no one to assist me except ordinary passengers, and one of them fainted just as I opened the abdominal cavity so that I had no time to examine as to the course of the ball. Even under the circumstances, had the ball not injured the cord I am satisfied this man would have recovered. He had no surgical attendance, but lay in a little Mexican hut.

This case simply illustrates the fact that we may often save lives by acting promptly and fearlessly. I frequently see notices in our State papers saying: "Shot through the bowels; died a few hours after"; and I find invariably that no attempt was made to save the unfortunate, or at least to give him a chance for life. I live in a rural district myself, or rather in a little country town, so that I know how one feels to stand by and see the life of a fellow-man slowly ebbing away; and if this report will stimulate my fellow-practitioners of the rural districts to do their duty under all circumstances, I am more than repaid for my trouble in making it.

"Skin Grafting"

Transactions of the Texas State Medical Association 33 (1901): 245–4

During the past three months I have had under observation an interesting case of skin grafting. A young man, age 20, in good health, was accidentally injured by the discharge of a pistol. He was on horseback, the pistol carried in a holster, fastened to a belt around his waist. The holster rested partly on the saddle, near his thigh, when the pistol discharged. The bullet passed through the saddle, into the back of the horse. His thigh, midway between hip and knee, outer side, was injured by burn and concussion, a surface five by nine inches, completely destroyed, no sensation, appearing very much like an over-burned brand on an animal. In a few days a line of demarcation formed, and in course of time the whole piece dropped out, the entire thickness of the skin, leaving well defined edges. I used ordinary antiseptic dressings, expecting to skin graft as soon as granulations were well formed. The part looked very healthy, no inflammation in or around it. The granulations were condensed by using weak solutions of bluestone, which I find beneficial in similar cases. The accident occurred on the 17th of December, 1900, and the first grafts, twenty-three, were inserted on the 20th of January, 1901. The part was thoroughly disinfected, using a solution of carbolic acid then peroxide of hydrogen, one part to three of water, carefully removing any discharges clinging to the surface with a small piece of cotton. The grafts were cut from his brother's arm, with small curved scissors, each graft being as small as possible, the object being to cause as little bleeding as possible. After placing the grafts in position, the part was covered with a perforated plate of gelatin film, same used by photographers. The film is perforated with an ordinary darning needle, about every one-fourth of an inch. The opposite side will be rough. After being sterilized it is placed in position with the smooth surface next to the grafts, and covered with a few layers of gauze held in position by a small pad of cotton and roller firm enough to keep up gentle elastic pressure, and allowed to remain two or three days. The perforated film permits absorption of all discharges by the gauze covering, and being transparent, the grafts can be examined at any [time] without disturbing them. A normal salt solution, with a little carbolic acid, is excellent to cleanse the part when necessary which may be done quite well without removing the film. On the fifth day the film was removed, surface cleansed, and the grafts seen like little white specks where placed. Of the twenty-three inserted, twenty-three remain. When a transparent covering is no longer necessary, the film may be replaced by thin perforated rubber, which was used in this case, the perforations increasing in size as the grafts grow. This treatment was continued up to March 1st, the grafts remaining in place, some surrounded by red rings about one-fourth of an inch in diameter, but making little or no growth. I applied new grafts between the others, on two occasions, in all thirty-seven, all remaining, as it were, dormant. I could not understand this condition. Had frequently skin grafted, for old ulcers, burns, etc., successfully. This continued until new skin commenced forming at the edges of the injured part, when the grafts commenced growing, and in a few days the whole surface was covered with new skin. In this case the grafts inserted one month after the first grafts covered as large a space in one week as the first did in six weeks; indeed the grafts did not seem to grow until new skin began to form at the edges of the wound, which would suggest that skin grafts should not be inserted until new skin begins to form at the edges of the part affected.

"Elastic Rubber-Ring Tourniquet: Haemorrhage (Surgical, Prevention of)"

Richmond and Louisville Medical Journal 22 (1876): 425–30

I noticed an article in the American edition of the "London Lancet" for August, 1876, on "An Improved Appliance for Bloodless Operations," which purports to be an improvement made by Mr. H. L. Browne, Surgeon to the West Broomwich Hospital.

As the subject of elastic-ring tourniquets has been attracting my attention for the past six years, during which time I have made many experiments with the same, I can not, in justice to myself, allow said article to pass unnoticed, as it seems to me impossible that the use of said tourniquet, which has been on exhibition in many of the principal cities of America, been shown and explained in several prominent hospitals and before several medical societies should not have reached Mr. H. L. Browne; however, should the use of the elastic rings have been conceived by Mr. Browne independently and without knowledge of their use in America I can not, of course, take any exception to said article.

The rings used by myself and shown to the Profession consist of a set of nine, six of which were precisely similar to those described in the "Lancet," with three smaller rings for the thumb and fingers, which completes the set as made by Geo. Tiemann & Co., of New York, the following being an extract from a letter from that firm, dated June 17, 1876: "Regarding your new idea of rolling rubber rings for Esmarch's operation, we think the idea is capital. It must be a remarkably quick process and so simple." Again they write me: "New York June 29, 1876. We just now finished a number of your new tourniquet rings. The idea strikes us as really excellent."

In a communication of October 15, 1875, they write: "You must publish them—the sooner the better—before others may catch the idea."

My elastic-ring tourniquet was exhibited at Charity Hospital, New Orleans, La., to Drs. Choppin, Schuppert, and Smythe, October, 1875; at the Boyle County (Ky.) Medical Society, September 1875; at the city of Hamilton, Canada, in August and at the January (1875) meeting of the

Southwestern Texas Medical Association, of which I have the honor to be
Vice-President, thus placing the general knowledge and use of the instrument pretty well before the Profession.

The following is an article forwarded for publication in the "New York
Medical Record," February, 1876, but as it was not published, I suppose it
must have been miscarried or lost:

A New Elastic Rubber-Ring Tourniquet—As so many new surgical instruments are now brought before the attention of the Profession, it almost
seems necessary for me to offer some apology for introducing a new tourniquet for bloodless operation, also for general use where such instruments
are indicated. This instrument I have called the "elastic rubber-ring tourniquet." The necessity for such an instrument was brought to my notice
when residing in the city of New Mexico [sic; probably in Mier, Mexico,
where he was stationed at the time], while attempting to remove a needle
from the thumb of a young lady, April, 1870. Having made several unsuccessful attempts, on account of haemorrhage, I wound an ordinary elastic
band around the end of the thumb, and rolled it back beyond the site of
the needle, noticing that the thumb was completely bloodless, presenting
a waxy appearance, which enabled me to remove the needle without difficulty or loss of blood.

The idea of an elastic ring tourniquet for bloodless operations did not
then enter my mind, nor indeed until I noticed the favorable reports of
the instruments devised by Professor Esmarch, and in using his instruments for the removal of a thorn from the knee of a young man October
7th, 1874. I thought a simpler method might be adopted by using solid
and hollow rubber rings of assorted sizes to fit every limb, and requested
Messrs. George Tiemann & Co., of New York, to have a set made for me,
which really surpassed my expectations, easily adjusted and perfectly controlling the circulation. The rings described in the "Lancet" are precisely
similar to the first set I had made (the small[est] of which is the fingers
and wrist) were perfect; but in applying the rings to the thigh, I found the
solid rings would not roll well, especially in cases of considerable obesity,
and by the advice of my partner, Dr. T. Somerville Burke, I had the larger
rings made hollow, which, I believe, is a decided advantage, making them
roll with greater facility, also preventing the hairs from rolling around the
ring, which is to be avoided, as it is the cause of much pain.

In applying the rings, one side may be raised to pass painful or diseased parts, or the ring may be stretched and thus placed above the meat
of the part injured or diseased, thereby avoiding the entrance into the

circulation of septic fluids[,] an objection which has been made against the use of the elastic bandage.

The simplicity of this instrument will, I believe, at once recommend its general use, whether for bloodless operations or as a simple tourniquet. I find that very little elastic pressure is necessary to control the circulation even in the stoutest subjects, and by using a very weak ring over the arm outside of the ordinary clothing, I have rendered the whole limb perfectly pulseless, a fact that would make such an instrument invaluable on the battle-field, where numerous lives are sacrificed by the inability of most persons in applying the ordinary instrument now in use.

In using the tourniquet, that part of the instrument lying over the main artery should be raised before closing the wound, so that in case there is any haemorrhage the vessel may be ligated or twisted. The rings for the arm and forearm should fit the wrist firmly; those for the thigh and leg, the ankle.

The great advantage I claim for this instrument is its simplicity and facility of application, forcing the blood out of the limb gradually in its direct channel without injuring the tissues, which must necessarily occur in using the bandage, which is rolled around the limb, leaving, as it must, blood between the different turns of the roller, producing on many occasions ecchymosis from injury done to the minute capillaries.

I have applied the instrument many times upon my own arm, rendering it perfectly blanched and bloodless, and have never felt the least inconvenience after using the strongest rings.

There are many cases for which I might recommend this instrument, but believe it will suggest its own use whenever necessary to prevent loss of blood, or the entrance into the circulation of any poisonous matter which may be brought in contact with the extremities, as dissection wounds, bites of animals, reptiles, etc. by stretching a firm ring and placing it above the poisoned part.

To say more, would simply be a repetition of what has already been published regarding the advantages derived from the use of the admirable instrument devised by Prof. Esmarch, of which I consider my rings an improvement, trusting they may be of some service to the Profession, and those who may be so unfortunate as to require their use.

The above, I trust, will satisfactorily explain the origin and use of the "Elastic Rubber-Ring Tourniquet" first used by myself in 1870, and manufactured by George Tiemann & Co., of New York, June 1876; not that I wish to claim priority over Esmarch in the use of the elastic tourniquet, but to show that the "Elastic Rubber-Ring Tourniquet" was used by myself, and brought before the notice of the Profession in America at least two years previous to the publication in the "Lancet," describing an instrument precisely similar to those manufactured for me by Tiemann.

Cases in which I have used the instrument successfully:

Case I.—A young lady consulted me March 16, 1875, for contraction of one of her fingers, caused by a whitlow. The finger was perfectly useless, being drawn down into the palm of the hand. I rolled a ring over the hand as far as the wrist, rendering it perfectly bloodless, made a V-shaped incision, and divided all the adhesions drawing the finger down. There was *not a drop* of blood lost, enabling me to complete my dissections without injuring the tendons. I straightened the finger without difficulty, applied a palma[r] splint, and in a few weeks she recovered perfect use of her finger, and at the present time the deformity is scarcely perceptible.

Case II.—On the 16th of October, 1875, a young man came into my office suffering severely from the effects of a splinter deeply embedded in the palm of his hand. Several unsuccessful attempts had been made to remove it, but the haemorrhage obscured a thorough examination of the parts involved. I have no doubt but the elastic bandage would have answered equally well in this case, but having one of my rings with me, I rolled it over the hand and removed the splinter without difficulty or the loss of blood. After removing the ring a little haemorrhage occurred, but not sufficient to require attention. I have since used them many times on similar occasions, with good success; also in amputation of fingers, etc.

Case III.—On the 4th of July, while firing the midday centennial salute, Mr. Stanley Welch, Deputy Collector U.S. Customs, District of Corpus Christi, had his right hand and half of the forearm blown away by the accidental discharge of a cannon. He lost considerable blood, which was difficult to control until I placed one of my rings over the arm near the shoulder, when the haemorrhage immediately ceased. The forearm was amputated near the elbow, and although the instrument was not rolled up, but applied as an ordinary tourniquet, there was no haemorrhage during the operation. He made a quick recovery.

I may here state to show how little *elastic pressure* is necessary to control the circulation, that after Mr. Welch's arm was dressed, there was considerable oozing from, I think, a small vessel we omitted to ligate. One of the surgeons in attendance wished to reopen the stump, but by my advice a weak ring was placed around the arm above the stump. It controlled the haemorrhage but made too much pressure, becoming painful. It was replaced by a very weak elastic band, which I had found very useful in similar cases, answering equally well; also beneficial in keeping the parts in apposition, moulding as it were one upon the other, an improvement on the ordinary mode of dressing.

It seems impossible to estimate the elastic force necessary to control the circulation; and in my experience, which extends over several years, I find very weak rings are quite sufficient for any operation, nor do I consider the plug, as shown in the "Lancet," of any use whatever; on the contrary, the vessel is apt to slip to one side or the other, and rest in a notch between the plug and ring; a small rubber pad might be used over deep-seated vessels, but I think the rings alone are sufficient.

This instrument is manufactured by Messrs. Geo. Tiemann & Co., No 67 Chatham street, New York.

—Arthur E Spohn, Corpus Christi, Texas

"Notes on Current Medical Literature"

Reviews and Book Notices, Medical and Surgical Reporter 48
(February 10, 1883): 6

As far back as 1870 Dr. Arthur E. Spohn of Corpus Christi, Texas, used elastic rubber ring tourniquets, and at various times since has brought their advantages to the notice of the profession through different medical journals. The advantage he has derived from them are so obvious that his experience and methods should be studied by those who would employ this effective and painless means to control hemorrhage. Reprints may be had by applying to him as above.

"Treatment of Rupture of the Perineum"

Medical and Surgical Reporter 58 (January–June 1888)

This morning (October 21, 1887) I removed the stitches from the perineum of a patient upon whom I operated for ruptured perineum nine days ago, and found the result perfect. While the case is fresh in my mind, I have considered a short article on this operation not out of place. This subject has been so freely discussed in the journals lately that I almost hesitate in adding to the discussion the conclusions from my limited experience. The fact that I have succeeded in securing admirable results by what I believe to be a new method of treatment, is the only apology I have to offer for this short article.

In the case in question the laceration was recent; the patient having been confined on the 9th of October of her first child. She was 30 years old, and her perineum was so rigid that I could not prevent a slight rupture. In regard to the case of the perineum, I have lately come to think the obstetrician should carefully watch the progress of the second stage of labor, exposing the parts to view. I have long since abandoned the practice of supporting the perineum, but I believe it is absolutely necessary to control the head of the child, and to direct the progress of labor so as to prevent a rupture of the parts. This can be done most successfully by bringing the occiput or chin as the case may be, well forward under the pubic arch, and by holding the child's head back by well directed pressure until the perineum is slowly and successfully passed. If a perineum can be saved, I think this will do it. As an adjunct to the method, I invariably pour warm olive oil or Vaseline into the vagina, between the pains, when the head is pressing against the perineum.

After the third stage of labor is completed, a careful examination should be made by thoroughly cleaning away all blood with a warm water antiseptic solution. For this purpose I prefer boric acid. If, then, any rupture be detected, no matter how small it may be, it should be stitched up immediately; for in this, as in any other wound, the sooner the parts are nicely adjusted the better.

The following is the method I am now using, and I am pleased to say with perfect results. In a recent rupture, with the parts so much swollen that if the thighs are pressed together the perineum bulges forward, the deeper parts are firmly pressed together and the ruptured portion is really in good position to heal. This would, no doubt, often take place did not a clot of blood now and then sweep through, having irritating discharges in contact with the torn surfaces. But, bearing in mind that this is very likely to happen, I treat these ruptures just as I would any other wound, by first irrigating the part with some antiseptic lotion; then, as soon as all bleeding has ceased, I stitch it up very carefully so that there is no gaping between the stitches and no point exposed to the discharges which must necessarily pass through the outlet of the vagina. I never insert deep sutures, and do not consider them necessary in cases of recent rupture. After washing out the vagina with a syringe, using hot water and boracic acid, I pass a pledget of raw cotton tied to a string into the vagina, carrying it well above the ruptured part. I use raw cotton because it will not absorb the blood or allow it to pass. I now irrigate the wound with the hot boracic acid solution until all hemorrhage ceases, and then adjust the mucous membrane nicely and stitch it carefully with silk thread, using an ordinary sewing needle. I next smear a little Vaseline over the part, remove the cotton and wash out the vagina. This completes the operation, and the patient is afterward treated as if no rupture has taken place. I remove the stitches on the eighth or ninth day. In conclusion I may state that I always bathe the genitals of a lying-in woman, and wash out the vagina once or twice daily with a boracic acid solution and dust the parts with powdered boracic acid whenever any lesion has taken place.

"Treatment of Carbuncle"

Texas Courier-Record of Medicine 8 (March 1891): 184–85

Several years ago I was called to see a patient, living fifty miles away in the country—a very frequent occurrence in Southwestern Texas, where pastures contain from ten to five hundred thousand acres in one enclosure. I met on the road a man suffering fearfully with carbuncles. He had, then, one on his face, one on his wrist and one on the back of his neck. I don't think I ever saw any person suffer as he did. The only medicine I had with me which I thought could give relief was a saturated solution of chloral hydrate in water and glycerine. Of this I poured one teaspoonful over bread poultices, and applied them to the carbuncles, expecting as soon as the man was relieved of pain to make the ordinary incisions. To my surprise he was soon relieved of pain, and the next morning the carbuncles looked so much better that I concluded to continue the treatment, without making incision. I did not see this man again for about two months, when he came into my office for a prescription of the medicine I used, saying, that he had had no trouble after I left; that his carbuncles had diminished in size without sloughing, and that they soon got well. The carbuncle on his back was fully three inches in diameter. He has had several carbuncles since, using the same treatment successfully, I have not seen him recently; but I am told that he is falling off in weight. I did not examine his urine at the time, but think he is probably suffering with diabetes. I have now under treatment four cases of carbuncle. It is strange that nearly all of the cases of carbuncle I have seen in this climate occur during February, March and April. This fact has impressed me with the idea that they are due to some climate condition. Two of my patients have carbuncle on the back, one on the side of the neck. I am treating these cases with a ten per cent solution of chloral hydrate in glycerine and water, applied constantly by means of absorbant [sic] cotton. The patients are doing well and having little or no pain. Internally I give sulphide of calcium. I have a patient who had carbuncle in April, 1887, and again in September, accompanied by numerous boils. He has diabetes, his urine containing six grains of sugar to the ounce. He now has caries of the ilium on the right side. I removed the carious part twice, but the bone would not take on healthy action. I am now irrigating the diseased surface with a ten per cent solution of phosphoric acid. The patient seems to be improving; and there is very little discharge from the two sinuses leading down to the bone, one of which passes in the direction of the sacro-iliac articulation.

While speaking of this patient, I wish to mention an artesian well in this city, the water of which is very beneficial in cases of diabetes. The well is about 400 feet deep; flows about five feet above the surface of the ground in a small stream; and its capacity is about 60,000 gallons daily. This water contains principally chloride of sodium and sulphate of sodium, strongly impregnated with sulphuretted hydrogen gas. It sparkles in a glass like champagne. It is laxative, in doses of an ordinary glassful; in larger quantities it is a brisk cathartic, causing little or no inconvenience. The water belongs to the city and is free to all. It will not bear transportation under the present methods of bottling.

I was very much pleased when I read the lecture on the treatment of carbuncles by Prof. Verneuil of Paris, in the *Reporter* of February 11, 1888. I have used carbolic acid, but not as a spray. I think the treatment by chloral is quite as successful and more easily carried out. The principal merit in the two methods is the avoidance of the old crucial incision, which I find still recommended in my latest works on surgery. I never make incision into a carbuncle; they are useless and painful, and expose a fresh surface to the virus. It is impossible to open every cell, as it were; and I consider the crucial incision to be a relic of surgical barbarism. There may be cases, with an accumulation of pus, requiring an incision; but they are very rare. A man came into my office some months ago, and asked me to look at the back of his neck. He was a railroad magnate, and of course, very anxious to get well. He had been told he was getting a carbuncle, and that a crucial incision was necessary. I don't know about the carbuncle, but I do know he had the incision. The skin on a man's back is—as near as I can estimate it—about a quarter of an inch thick; in this case I think it was about three quarters of an inch; the length of each incision was two inches, and when I looked at them I thought, if I had my choice between such an incision and a two-inch carbuncle, I would take the carbuncle. Whether the man ever got the edges of that incision together or not is questionable; but I fancy he carries a crucial brand, which in Texas is considered quite an ornament.

"Multicystic Ovarian Tumor Weighing 328 Pounds"

American Journal of Clinical Medicine 13 (April 1906), also read at a meeting of the State Medical Association of Texas, Houston, April 28, 1905, and printed in Transactions of the Texas State Medical Association (Austin), February 1906

This case is not important, except for the enormous size of the tumor. Mrs. G., age 43, the mother of seven children, had been suffering for several years with an ovarian tumor. During this time she had been tapped frequently. When called to see her, imagine my surprise on entering her room to find on the bed an immense mass as large as a barrel. I could not see the woman, but looking over the mass could just see her head attached to it like an appendix. The tumor came almost up to her chin, and extended to midway between her knees and feet. When she lay on her side on a three-quarter bed it had to be supported on two chairs. She could not reach her navel with her hands by one and one-half feet and was so emaciated that without her tumor companion would hardly make a shadow. She could only take nourishment by the spoonful, and seldom retained it. When they wished to move her they rolled the tumor, and she went with it. I had seen Professor Goodell, of Philadelphia, remove a very large tumor, the patient dying on the table. I removed one myself weighing 166 pounds, the patient dying in a few hours. I had little to expect from this case. In the other cases the tumors had not been reduced before operation, death being caused by collapse. I decided to reduce this tumor for one week, and with a small trocar succeeded in removing thirty gallons of a gelatinous fluid. On opening the abdomen I found many adhesions at points where she had been tapped. The tumor was of the left ovary, multicystic. I opened one cyst of large size, removing over six gallons. The thickened sac, removed with difficulty on account of adhesions, weighed 40 pounds, giving the tumor, as near as I could estimate[,] a total weight of 328 pounds. In closing the incision I had great difficulty getting the abdominal walls in satisfactory shape. There was so much serum and blood escaping that I was compelled to open a part of the incision and insert large pieces of gauze for drainage, treating the abdomen partly open. It took two months to close the abdomen. The patient made a good recovery. I was assisted by Drs. H. Spohn and H. J. Hamilton, of Laredo; anesthetic used, chloroform.

"Country Practice in Texas: Medicated Bougies"
Medical and Surgical Reporter 57 (August 20, 1887): 8

Some time ago I was treating a case of enlarged prostate and wished to introduce cocaine directly to the irritable membranous portion of the urethra, and keep it there. I tried the porte-caustique and bougies, made of coca [*sic*] butter, etc. At last I thought of the ordinary tallow candle; selected a tube of proper size and length [and] pulled a wick through it made of several threads of silk twist. I then melted in a test tube, oil of theobroma, medicated to suit the case, pouring it into the tube, so as to have the medicated portion just where I wanted it. The tube is then held a few moments in ice water until the oil hardens. Now rub gently through the fingers and the oil next [to] the tube softens. When the candle is drawn out, again insert it in ice water and it immediately hardens, and you have a medicated bougie, manufactured in less time than I can describe it, at a nominal cost. I always prepare them at the bed-side, and have used them in all cases of gonorrhoea, stricture, diseased prostate; in fact, whenever I wish to keep the diseased surfaces apart, or introduce remedial agents into cavities, sinuses, etc.

Grass Line for Ligatures

In two cases of ovariotomy I recently performed, I was at a loss what to use to ligate the pedicle. On other occasions I had used silk, but the only samples I could now procure were the iron-dyed, and so brittle, I could not safely rely on them. I chanced to examine some fine grass lines, i.e., fish lines, very fine, yet exceedingly strong, which I used in ligating the pedicle. In the last case I removed both ovaries, using the grass line ligature. My patient made an excellent recovery, the highest temperature being 99 3/4°, and was quite well in twelve days. I don't know what the grass fish line is made from, but it is certainly the best material for ligatures I ever saw. I enclose herewith a specimen, and would like very much to know how it is made.

[Note:] The tackle dealers state that this line is known as West India Islands grass line.—Editors of the *Reporter*.

"Turpentine in Affections of the Throat and Lungs"

*Medical and Surgical Reporter 61 (October 19, 1889): 16, also printed
in the Hickman (Kentucky) Courier, December 27, 1889*

I have been using pure oil of turpentine in affections of the throat and lungs for some time, and find better, and more satisfactory results, than from any other remedy I ever tried. I use the ordinary hand atomizer, and throw spray of the liquid into the throat every few minutes, or at longer intervals, according to the gravity of the case. The bulb of the instrument should be compressed as the act of inspiration commences, so as to insure application of the remedy to the whole surface, which can be done in cases of children very successfully. It is surprising how a diphtheritic membrane will melt away under an almost constant spray of pure oil of turpentine. I now use the turpentine spray whenever a child complains of sore throat of any kind.

In cases of tuberculosis of the lungs, bronchitis, and the later stages of pneumonia, I have found the turpentine inhalation very beneficial. I use an atomizer, or paper funnel, from which the turpentine may be inhaled at will. I hang around the bed, and in the room flannel cloths saturated with oil of turpentine, in all cases of catarrhal bronchitis—in fact, in all affections of the air passages; and my patients invariably express themselves as being very much relieved.

"Recent Cases of Coeliotomy"

*Daniel's Texas Medical Journal (Austin), 8, no. 8 (February 1893),
and read at a joint session of the Austin District Medical Society
and Central Texas Medical Society in Waco*

I have selected this subject for your consideration this evening, being rather, a report of my experience in abdominal surgery at the Bay View Sanitarium in Corpus Christi, Texas, during the past few months.

It is impossible to estimate the recent advancement, or possibilities of excellence, which may be attained in this branch of surgery, in the near future. Such has been the success, that diseased conditions heretofore considered incurable, are now being treated rationally and successfully, thereby materially reducing the number of invalid women in our communities. We might naturally ask, why such brilliant results have been reached. Is it because we treat our patients differently, or any change of technique in our methods? I think not; but that we appreciate pathological conditions more fully, and realize the fact that a lesion, or diseased condition, wherever found should be remedied, the part restored to its normal state, or removed as a useless and disturbing portion of the economy [*sic*; anatomy?].

In these days of advancement, the general practitioner can no longer relegate all his unfortunate cases to the care of a specialist; he is compelled to be prepared to meet certain emergencies, be it a case of Caesarean hysterectomy, acute septic peritonitis or ectopic pregnancy. Rare as they are, they do occasionally occur, and it has been my fortune, and misfortune, to have seen several such cases recently; and if occurring in the practice of one located in a small town surrounded by a thinly populated district, they must certainly be much more frequent in large cities. [Here Spohn read a poem he wrote concerning a tubal pregnancy. See appendix 2 for the text of the poem.]

Before giving a report of special cases, I will give a resume [résumé] of my method of making an abdominal section. Not that it differs much from that of other surgeons, still here are certain steps I think peculiar to myself; or rather, I have selected what I have chosen to term a rational method,— no reason without a cause, no cause without a reason,—and if you consider my method or treatment worthy of imitation, I shall consider myself more than paid for the trouble in preparing this report.

Having decided it is necessary to open the abdominal cavity, a certain technical preparation of the patient, instruments, assistants and operator is of the greatest importance.

I will presume the operator has selected a well ventilated room in a healthy locality, with good hygienic surroundings; and I think small, private hospitals, outside of crowded cities, much preferable for this work, and will be attended with much better results, where the surgeons are equally skillful, than in densely populated centres. "The safeguard of every community no matter how situated, is to see to it that it has, and encourages some man by its support to devote himself sufficiently to such study and investigation as will enable him to rise equal to an emergency of this order, with good hope of success."

In preparing a patient for coeliotomy, the most rigid cleanliness must be observed. The room should be aseptic; all bedding, in fact, clothing coming in contact with the patient, should be previously boiled. It is not sufficient to bathe with an antiseptic solution the day of the operation. A daily bath should be given several days before, using green soap over and around the site of the operation, after which the parts are dusted with boric acid. The vagina should also be irrigated daily with a five per cent boric acid, or one to three thousand corrosive sublimate solution. All water used should be sterilized by boiling. If there is much secretion coming from the uterus, its cavity should be wiped out carefully with dry aseptic cotton, then cleansed with peroxide of hydrogen, 15 vol. solution, one part to three of water, the vagina wiped dry and dusted with boric acid. If the parts are to be shaved, it should be done at one of the dressings, ostensibly for the purpose of cleansing, and not when under the influence of an anaesthetic. During this preparation, a light, nutritious diet should be given, bowels regulated, and the morning of the operation a dose of salts given, to insure free action of the bowels, and only a little tea or water allowed. The instruments should be carefully selected, to meet any emergency arising, avoiding a useless display, boiled in water containing a little bicarbonate of soda, and placed in a tray of boiling water. I keep my thread, catgut and horsehair, also silkworm gut ligatures, in straight glass tubes, about two feet long, which always keeps them straight, avoiding delay by twisting and coiling up. The tubes may be filled with some aseptic solution to suit the surgeon. I prefer horsehair to all other ligatures for outside work, and closing incisions, and prepare it myself, as follows: Select long black hair, wash it thoroughly in sterilized water, using green soap. It is then placed in a ten per cent solution of carbolic acid, or one to two thousand corrosive sublimate solution, for forty-eight hours. Wash again in sterilized water, and place it in a glass tube containing boro-glyceride, fifty per cent. One end of the tube may be sealed, the other closed with a cork. Prepared in this way, the horsehair is strong, quite elastic, and will keep any length of time. I use a strong, round pointed, double edge knife, with aluminum handle, a needle and holder, which carries several sizes of thread, being quite useful for quick work. The knife was made by Gemrig & Son, of Philadelphia; the needle by Geo. Tiemann & Co., of New York, from designs I furnished them. I have long since abandoned the use of sponges, using instead aseptic gauze, and when the gauze is to be inserted into the abdominal cavity, the edges should be folded and stitched, or made into pads. All water should be filtered, boiled, and kept in large jars or pitchers, well covered with aseptic cotton; some hot, others cold. And the gauze can be conveniently kept in one of these jars, a good plan being always to use the same number of pieces of gauze, a record of which, together with all instruments used, should be kept. A large fountain syringe should hang convenient to the operating table, with a large metal tube, for washing the abdominal cavity. The tube I use is my own design, made by Gemrig & Son, consisting of a large tube with round conical end, an opening on either side one inch from the end, a slot passing from the opposite sides entirely around the end, allowing the water to flow, not only from the two openings, but also in a broad stream from the sides and end of the tube. All ligatures should be sterilized. Those left within the cavity may be of specially prepared catgut; still, when I use a ligature I wish one with good staying qualities, consequently I prefer silk, and have never known them to give trouble in any of my operations, having in one case of gunshot wound of the abdomen inserted seventy-two stitches, besides several ligature[s], where there were nine openings in the intestines, my patient making a quick and uncomplicated recovery [see above, "Communications: Gunshot Wound of the Abdomen"].

A drainage tube should be used when there have been many adhesions; there is hemorrhage, or an escape of foreign matter into the cavity; but drainage tubes should be avoided as much as possible. I always leave a temporary drainage tube, passing into the sac of Douglas, until ready to close the abdominal incision, to be sure there is no hemorrhage. In closing the incision I use silk and horse hair, with cat-gut to approximate the muscles or tendon, as buried sutures; the horse hair and silk alternating, and remove the silk first; the horse hair does not irritate, and may be left until the union is quite firm. The line of incision is wiped very dry, then covered with boric acid, using it freely, about one-fourth of an inch thick, extending one inch on either side of the incision. A piece of borated cotton, about two inches wide, is next laid over the incision, extending one inch above and below. This makes a dry absorbent, aseptic dressing; which need not be disturbed until ready to remove the stitches, on the 7th, 8th, or 9th day. The next step is to apply the adhesive strips, which I consider quite important, the object being to fix, as it were, and give support to the line of incision. I use strips of good rubber plaster two inches wide, and long enough to extend about four or six inches on either side of the incision, thus fixing and supporting the central line, allowing motion of the abdominal walls on either side. I again dust the surface of the abdomen freely with boric acid, cover the borated, or recently baked cotton, and apply a well-fitting flannel bandage quite firmly. I have never seen failure of union by primary adhesion, under above method, and have never been compelled to change the dressing until ready to remove the stitches. It is in my opinion an ideal dressing. I have never used iodoform, and consider anything useless and dangerous, that will mask an offensive odor by one still more offensive.

Returning to the operator and his assistants, I have only to state that the utmost cleanliness should be observed; in fact a surgeon should not be present in clothing worn during general practice; and at my infirmary I furnish my assistants aseptic linen aprons. The hands should be carefully cleansed, using a brush and green soap, with sterilized water, then a one to one thousand solution of corrosive sublimate, followed by a saturated solution of oxalic acid, wiped dry and washed in alcohol. The vicinity of the incision may be treated in the same manner. During the operation sterilized water is used only. An exceedingly nice operating apron is made as follows: enough of what is known as butcher's linen to reach from the ankles over the shoulder and fall back behind reaching to the waist; corresponding to the neck cut an opening, also extending down the back. A band or narrow collar is fitted to the neck portion, which with the slit down the back is made to button. Tapes are fastened on either side; also a portion dropping over the shoulder, which are tied. Such an apron costs but about 75 cents.

The after treatment is quite simple. I allow the lips to be moistened with water, and sometimes give a little crushed ice, or an occasional teaspoonful of cool water or tea, during the first day, increasing the quantity a little the second day if the stomach is not irritable. The afternoon of the second day I give 1-10th of a grain of calomel, with bicarbonate of soda, every hour, until one-half to one grain has been taken, followed next morning by teaspoonful doses of salts in a little water, every two hours until the bowels act freely. When there is much trouble with flatus I insert a long glass drainage tube into the rectum, and through this tube wash out the bowel. Opiates should be avoided if possible, but since most cases are old sufferers when operation is attempted, accustomed to the use of morphine, it is advisable in such to continue the opiate for a time.

This report includes nine cases of coeliotomy for various causes; two ovarian abscess[es]; one caesarean hysterectomy, a malacosteon; one ovarian tumor; one salpingitis with prolapsed adherent ovaries; one fibroid tumor, multinodular, requiring coelo hysterectomy; one fibroid tumor in a girl six years of age; one acute septic-peritonitis; one gunshot wound of the liver. I was assisted in the operations by Drs. Heaney, Westervelt and Hamilton, of Corpus Christi, and my students, T. S. Burke and Jno. Westervelt.

Case 1. Mattie L., age 26, married, no children, no miscarriages, no evidence of specific disease, very weak and emaciated. This young woman had been a constant sufferer for three years, previous to the operation. Severe dysmenorrhoea, with almost constant pain over seat of ovaries. I attended her from time to time, being compelled to give morphia for relief. Her temperature ranged from 101° to 103° F., with fever, night sweats and chilly sensations at irregular intervals. The uterus was fixed, left ovary very much enlarged and painful, right very painful and enlarged. I made a coeliotomy on the 1st of November, 1891, and found the parts as I had anticipated. The adhesions were very extensive, and I removed both ovaries and tubes, with difficulty. She made a quick, uncomplicated recovery. Highest temperature, 99 1/2° F. Specimen No. 1 contains her ovaries and tubes. The left ovary is very much enlarged, covered with a mass of adhesions. There is a cyst in the tube containing pus, and under the ovary a quite a large abscess. The right ovary is also enlarged, and the tube is very large, containing pus. I had to tear these ovaries and tubes from behind the broad ligaments, with the greatest difficulty, as may be readily seen from the extensive adhesions. No drainage.

Case 2. Caesarean hysterectomy in a malacosteon. This case is of unusual importance, being the "first operation for this condition ever performed in the United States." (Dr. Robert P. Harris Phila.) Mrs. G., age 42, very short and stout, the mother of nine children. About four and six years ago I attended this woman in childbirth,—both deliveries difficult, instrumental; the last extremely difficult. I then told her she could never give birth to a child again. She is a malacosteon, and from her peculiar position working, kneeling with the body bent forward (a tortillera), her spinal column had curved forward, in the lower dorsal and lumbar regions, until the apex of the curvature was but two and one-half inches from and a little above the pubic arch. On the 10th of November, 1891, I was again called to see her, and was very much surprised to find her again in labor, at full term. She had been in labor three days. Upon examination, I found it impossible for her to give birth to her child, and decided to open the abdomen, and finish by removing the uterus and appendages. The membranes had ruptured. I irrigated the vagina, and as far into the uterus as possible, with sterilized water; also a bichloride solution, 1 to 4000. The surface of the abdomen was also carefully cleansed. She presented quite a peculiar appearance, the head of the child resting above the brim of the pelvis, with the uterus standing prominently out, like a large conical elongated body. I made an incision through the navel, extending well down in the pubes. Upon entering the abdominal cavity, I enlarged the incision sufficiently to allow the fundus of the uterus to protrude a little, which was caught with strong vulsellum and held while I cut directly into it, having a rubber tube ready to tighten around the organ as I drew it out. I next passed two fingers of each hand into the incision in the uterus, and as I drew it out tore it open, and before the uterus was delivered, or as soon as torn sufficiently open, the child was forced out by contractions. The rubber tube was tightened as the uterus came through the abdominal incision and a long piece of aseptic gauze wound around the uterus to prevent the escape of any of its contents into the abdominal cavity. I made the incision directly into the center of the placental attachment. There was very little hemorrhage. It is surprising how easily the uterus can be torn, and you will see, in specimen No. 2, how extensively I tore it open. I was but two minutes delivering uterus and contents,—a well-developed, living child.

The next step was to secure the pedicle, which was quite difficult, on account of the great thickness of the abdominal wall. I passed four long, steel knitting needles through the pedicle just above the constricting rubber tube; above these I placed a strong ligature, to diminish the size of the pedicle, and support the needles. The rubber tube, being quite small was passed twice around the pedicle, and tied. I cut the uterus away near the ligature above the needles and applied actual cautery to the end of the pedicle, using a small copper soldering iron. The pedicle was composed of the round ligaments, tubes, broad ligaments, and a portion of the neck of the uterus. The appendages were removed with the uterus. I had carefully avoided the bladder, by keeping a sound in that viscus while removing the uterus. The abdominal cavity was washed out with sterilized water, no drainage tube was used, and the abdominal incision closed with silk, the stitches near the pedicle passing through it just below the constricting tube of rubber. The incision was dressed with boric acid, and pads of borated cotton placed under the knitting needles. The pedicle came away on the tenth day, leaving a continuous opening between the vagina and abdominal incision, which gradually closed by granulation, and in thirty days she was quite well.

This woman had no pain after the operation, did not know for fifteen days how her child had been delivered, rested well, and had no more trouble than after an ordinary labor. Her child was healthy and strong. I feared, at first, it was injured from pressure against the apex of the curvature, which had made a deep indentation into the child's head, as if pressed in by a hard substance as large as an orange. She did not nurse her child, for some cause, having very little milk, the same condition existing with previous children. It is nearly a year since the operation. Mother and child are quite well, and she still makes her living grinding tortillas. I met her on the street a few days ago, carrying a sack of corn on her head, when she stated she was well and strong, looking very little like a malacosteon who had undergone an operation for coelo-hysterectomy.

Case 3. M. C., single, age 18. In September, 1891, her family noticed she was getting large; her menses had ceased for several months. I examined her and found quite an enlargement in the abdominal cavity and had some difficulty in determining the cause of her trouble. I made a careful examination while under chloroform, and through the rectum could easily outline the uterus. On the 6th of April, 1891, I made a coeliotomy, removing a large multilocular ovarian tumor, right side. The left ovary was enlarged; size of a lemon with commencing cystic degeneration. I removed it also. She made a good recovery. The only interest in this case is the pathological specimen No. 3, commencing cystic degeneration of an ovary, in which may be seen numerous small cysts. Since reporting this case I have been consulted by this girl for an abscess near line of incision, which I opened, and found a sinus, which believing it was caused by a ligature, I tried to remove. I passed a probe made of doubled horse hair into the sinus, turning it occasionally; at the end of a few hours the probe was withdrawn with the ligature caught in one of the loops. This little mishap gives me an opportunity of describing a simple yet most effective method for removing ligatures from sinuses. To make this probe I use about 30 [a]septic horse hairs, 12 inches in length. They are doubled and the free ends clamped with a shot; a thread is tied to each end and so fastened as to keep the hair straight; the hair is now wet with aseptic glue by boiling, twisted a little and dried. When passed into a sinus the glue becomes moist, liberating the hair thus placing in the vicinity of the ligature 30 loops which when withdrawn will have the ligature caught in one of them.

Case 4. Mrs. B., age 31; mother of one child, born August 1891. This lady has been an invalid for 10 years. Her trouble began after being thrown from a carriage, producing retroversion of the uterus; followed by pain in the left ovarian region, with severe dysmenorrhoea, and great difficulty and pain in having an action from bowels. In 1890, she had influenza, which very much aggravated her ovarian trouble. She first consulted me in March, 1892. I found the ovaries prolapsed and extremely sensitive. She did not complain of pain in adjacent parts, but whenever I touched the region of ovaries, it caused severe paroxysms of pain, so great, that I was compelled to inject morphia. She had gone the usual rounds seeking relief, and I tried without success, almost everything recommended for such conditions, with rest; and finally considered her case one requiring, at least, an exploratory incision. Upon opening the cavity I found just what I had anticipated, a retroverted uterus; prolapsed and adherent ovaries both of which I removed. She made a quick recovery, and has been free from pain since, being completely liberated from the distress which followed her as a shadow. . . .

Case 5. Adela G., age 6 years; well nourished and apparently in good health. This little girl was sent to me by the Laureles Pasture Company. I found quite a large tumor in the abdomen, right side, which I supposed, at first, was a lipoma, probably in the abdominal walls. In attempting to remove the growth, I found it dipped down into the pelvis cavity, and was attached by a pedicle to the right broad ligament, near the uterus, or the uterus itself. The pedicle was ligated and tumor cut away. She made an excellent recovery and is now apparently quite well. Operation was performed September 10th, 1892. The incision was quite extensive and I was very much troubled by protrusion of the intestines. I wrote to Dr. Robt. P. Harris, of Philadelphia about this case, and he thinks the chances are that the growth is a carcinoma. Specimen No. 5 is the tumor, the nature of which I have not yet determined. [The rest of the cases have not been included here.]

Anonymous Letter to the Texas Medical Association

Texas State Journal of Medicine 4, no. 2 (June 1908): 48

I promised to write you a letter on the sidelights of the Corpus Christi meeting. As you said, the real biography of a meeting is not contained in the minutes any more than one's personal history in an epitaph.

My first Impression of Corpus was an awakening, as the sleeper crossed the long trestle that bridges Nueces Bay. The waves were rolling, now and then the sharp back fin of a fish would cut the water and the gulls were circling about. We seemed to be crossing a deep sea, but they told us that the line of posts to be seen marked a wagon road, the water being very shallow. The depot is in a large sandy plaza. When we arrived Tuesday morning the Corpus papers announced that seventy-five doctors were already on the ground. The newspapers of Corpus—the *Sun*, the *Herald*, and the *Caller*—all gave careful reports of the convention. The *Caller* published pictures of the President and Secretary and the complete program. On Tuesday five hundred people arrived. The Secretary said that four hundred and twenty-five members registered and there were four hundred and twenty-five to four hundred and seventy-five doctors present, these with about two hundred and fifty visiting ladies made the total number of visitors, between seven to eight hundred. The crowds were everywhere on trains, at hotels and at the meetings were larger than any one had expected. Perhaps the crowds were due to the large number of pamphlets describing the advantages of Corpus Christi that were sent out by the local doctors, the Commercial Club, and the elaborate illustrated description of the place published in the State journal.

The city had made elaborate preparations for our coming. The profession and citizens had expended a large sum. The carriages and automobiles at the station were decorated with plaques resembling the State button, banners fluttered on the streets, the postcard stands had special convention postcards and folders containing views of physicians' residences, hospitals, etc. The pavilion in which the larger meetings were held presented one of the most artistic pieces of decoration I ever saw. The Interior had been freshly painted white [and] along the walls was a six-foot frieze of palms and ferns. The same decorations were elaborately arranged over and about the stage. Between each window on each pillar and over the stage were large plaques bearing the design of the State button. That button, by the way, has few, if any, competitions for artistic beauty and simplicity of design. There were thirty or forty of these plaques, some of them very large and painted in oil; one of these I noticed over the Seaside Hotel entrance.

The badges issued were among the happiest thoughts of the meeting. At the top was a metallic frame containing a card bearing the wearer's name, below this was a printed red ribbon[,] and a pendant completed the badge, stating whether the wearer was a member, delegate or guest.

When the convention opened the white caps were rolling under the pavilion on the shore, the marine band was playing, the salt sea breeze blowing, the sun shining and every one had a feeling of well being. High winds and waves made it difficult at times to hear well in the pavilion. The morning *Caller* had placed in the seats copies of the convention poem which was published that morning in the papers. . . .

About one hundred and fifty visiting ladies left the seaside in autos and carriages for the complimentary drive at 10 a.m. Wednesday. Mrs. J. J. Turpin led the drive in the first machine. They visited the Spohn Sanitarium, where punch was served; then drove over the sand and shell roads of the city, and finally reached the Alta Vista Hotel. This is the most commodious and quiet hotel on the beach, two miles from the city. The local reception committee received the visitors on the first and second floors, where punch was served and everyone introduced.

The reception at Mrs. A. E. Spohn's residence was a beautiful and elaborate affair. She received with Mrs. G. R. Scott and the wives of local physicians. This home is one of the most beautiful and spacious in Texas, filled with American and foreign art, statuary and bric-a-brac. It was beautifully decorated with flowers, an orchestra furnished music and delightful refreshments were served. About one hundred and twenty-five visiting ladies called.

I suppose the minutes will give a good account of the real work accomplished. Everything moved smoothly except the Memorial Exercises. A large audience gathered, but not a member of the committee was present to conduct the service, nor had they made any arrangements to have them held in their absence. The peculiar nature of the exercises made the neglect particularly regrettable.

There was an alumni smoker given by the alumni of the State University at 9 P M. on Wednesday at Mr. Sam Rankin's residence. A jolly time is reported.

The fish fry at Epworth-by-the-Sea attracted eight hundred and one thousand people. The San Antonio Aransas Pass train carried us out. Chairs and tables had been arranged in the pavilion and on the grounds. A delicious fish supper was served—no one ever tasted fresher or better cooked fish. The linen and flowers and Mexican band all gave it a tone [quite] unusual for a picnic or barbecue. We had some interesting speeches afterward from Mr. Joe Hirsch, President of the Commercial Club; Dr. Cantrell, Dr. Meyer of New Orleans, Dr. Saunders, Dr. Jeff Davis, Dr. Marvin Graves and Dr. Chase. Dr. Jno. O. McReynolds was toastmaster. The outing closed by singing "Auld Lang Syne." A dance given at the Alta Vista after the fish fry was enjoyed by about one hundred and fifty at which a dainty supper was served.

The climax of the social feature for ladies was the elaborate course dinner given at the Seaside Pavilion. This pavilion is a beautiful three-story structure built over the bay. On the dancing floor of the second story, tables for one hundred and forty-two ladies were arranged in a U-shape. A band, beautiful floral decorations, and dainty menu cards added to the occasion. Mrs. Henry Redmond, wife of the President of the Nueces Medical Society, presided as toastmaster. Toasts, music, a brisk sea breeze and the noise of the waves, together with some very good eating, enlivened a large part of the afternoon.

The principal trains north were delayed until midnight of the last day and a closing ball at the Seaside Pavilion was given. A terrible rain kept the less enthusiastic members from attending, but those present had a delightful time.

The sea bathing was enjoyed morning, noon and night by large crowds. The beach is almost ideal, and bathing arrangements perfect. Special rates were on to Rockport and Brownsville, and many stayed over a day or two for the side trips and fishing. Very few had boat rides on account of prevailing high winds.

As I look back upon it, the meeting seems like a pleasant dream—undoubtedly the most delightful social session ever held by the Association, and good from a scientific standpoint.

Poetry by and about Dr. Spohn

Dr. Spohn presented a treatise to the Texas Medical Association about the senseless and unfortunately all too common loss of a young woman with a ruptured tubal pregnancy, easily remedied by a simple operation. The following poem, written in 1893, provides a glimpse into his passion, as well as some frustration with his colleagues.

> There is no case more tests the skill
> The steady nerve, and power of will,
> Than where from causes now unknown,
> A living ovum has been thrown
> Into the tube, is fixed and grows,
> And by increasing slow, so slow
> That tube no longer can contain
> Its living contents, bursts, in twain is rent,
> The life blood flows from unclosed vent,
> The mother sinks, her eyes grow dim,
> All hope seems lost. Hold! See, Come in
> A noble mind, the bravest heart
> A steady hand well trained in art;
> He ope's the wall, a string is laid
> Around the tube, her life is saved.
> There is no time so sure we stand,
> Holding a fellow life in hand,
> Decision, acting well our part,
> Steady of nerve and brave at heart.

Doing no more than should be done
To our own selves, were we the one.

This poem was read at the Texas Medical Association meeting that Spohn worked so hard to host in Corpus Christi:

Did you feel the gentle zephyrs
While you still were on your way,
Greeting you with welcome kisses
As you neared our lovely bay?
They were echoes from the wavelets,
Wafted o'er the balmy breeze;
You were nearing, Corpus Christi,
City of the bluff and seas.
Did you hear the lingering murmur
And the low and distant roar?
Twas the welcome of the ocean
Dashing 'gainst the pebbly shore.
Do we always have those breezes?
Do they never cease to blow?
Yes, they're constant, always with us,
Fan our cheeks to ruddy glow.
In this time of health and beauty,
In this land of tropic sun,
Gentle breezes ever fan us
Till our race of life is run.
And when called to leave our station,
We are ready for that hour—
Lived a life of early pleasures,
Die as dies the natural flower.

The *Corpus Christi Caller* printed this poem by an unknown author on May 17, 1919:

His Sort of Man

His sort of man! Oh! What can we say
When we think of what he's gone and done without pay!
His sort of man! Just the kind that we want
Oh how his memory will everywhere haunt

The homes of this town, when the records we want
That show us the full measures—his sort of man!

All fits and all honors that folks seek to bring—
How small now they seem in the light of the thing
That he's brought to the people who live here, who feel
Has been the good services he has given, manifold
Are the deeds of his life in true service of gold!

His sort of man! Yes, tis rare, that's the truth!
With the touch of the sun in his nature of youth
With breadth in his mind, with belief in the cross,
The manners of a Prince, words never at loss,
Such a brightener of places made dark, but for men
That stand as he stood—for a clean heart again!

How faint grow the hours that love would confer
On his kind of man! How our eyes feel the blur
Of the tears of great gladness when such natures arise
To make our earth seem, where they dwell like the skies
Of some special heaven of beauty, most bright
Bent over to keep it, and us going right!

His sort of man! Ah, we say it today
With honor and pride and in sorrow's own way!
For Corpus well known what a treasure it is—
A noble, broad nature, as manly as his,
All Texas knows, too—and surgery and skill
The worth of his straight forward, dominant will.

Yes, love him and honor him—tell of his worth
And all he has wrought for his corner of earth!
While we—well we love him, for what he has done
To bring to dark agony sweet gift of sun,
And hope out of desperate ache and despair
For men like Arthur Spohn in this world are rare!

Spaun/Spohn, Vela and Vidal, and Kenedy Family Trees

Kenedy Family Tree

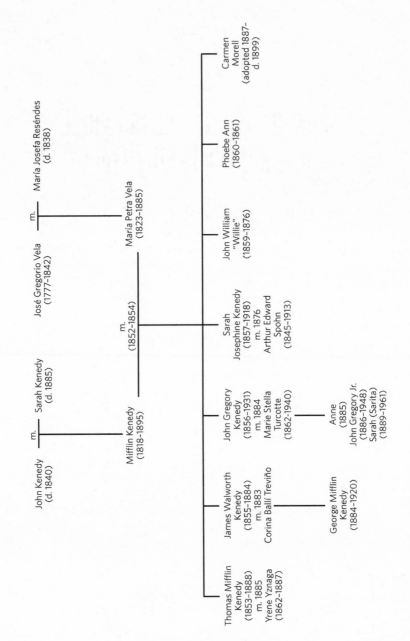

Courtesy of Father Francis Kelly Nemeck, OMI.

Spaun/Spohn Family Tree

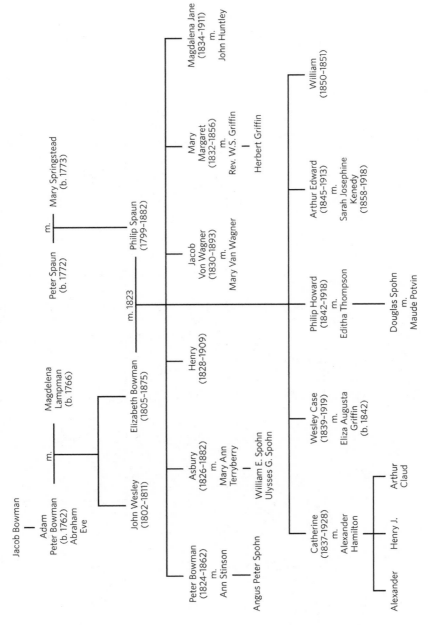

From Peter Spaun's Bible. Courtesy of Paul T. Harris.

Vela and Vidal Family Tree

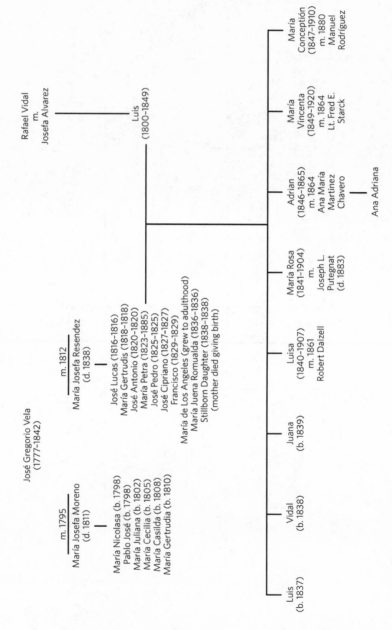

José Gregorio Vela
(1777–1842)

m. 1795
María Josefa Moreno
(d. 1811)

María Nicolasa (b. 1798)
Pablo José (b. 1798)
María Juliana (b. 1802)
María Cecilia (b. 1805)
María Casilda (b. 1808)
María Gertrudia (b. 1810)

m. 1812
María Josefa Resendez
(d. 1838)

José Lucas (1816–1816)
María Gertrudis (1818–1818)
José Antonio (1820–1820)
María Petra (1823–1885)
José Pedro (1825–1825)
José Cipriano (1827–1827)
Francisco (1829–1829)
María de Los Angeles (grew to adulthood)
María Juena Romualda (1836–1836)
Stillborn Daughter (1838–1838)
(mother died giving birth)

Rafael Vidal
m.
Josefa Alvarez

Luis
(1800–1849)

Luis
(b. 1837)

Vidal
(b. 1838)

Juana
(b. 1839)

Luisa
(1840–1907)
m. 1861
Robert Dalzell

María Rosa
(1841–1904)
m.
Joseph L.
Putegnat
(d. 1883)

Adrian
(1846–1865)
m. 1864
Ana María
Martínez
Chavero

Ana Adriana

María
Vincenta
(1849–1920)
m. 1864
Lt. Fred E.
Starck

María
Conceptión
(1847–1910)
m. 1880
Manuel
Rodríguez

Courtesy of Father Francis Kelly Nemeck, OMI.

Spohn Sanitarium Dedicatory Address

Dr. Arthur Spohn delivered these remarks at the opening of the Spohn Sanitarium in Corpus Christi on July 26, 1905:

> Ladies and Gentlemen: We are living in an age of advancement. Nations and municipalities and people are vying with each other in the erection and maintenance of institutions for the reception, care, and better treatment of the sick and unfortunate.

> When the erection of the beautiful hospital in our city, now almost completed, was organized and instituted, Corpus Christi ascended many rounds in her advancement to among the progressive cities of our times.

> We no longer look with fear and dread at the idea of entering a hospital. Here all that science and invention can produce, all that study and research can unfold, is utilized for the relief of the sick and suffering, to bring an unendurable condition to one of health, to make life worth living.

> Here the physicians can meet in closer communion and by their deliberations devise better means to combat disease. Here you will find the sisters of mercy with their gentle, tender care, soothing the throbbing brow, and assuaging the pangs of pain and distress.

> What a grand institution we are about to inaugurate in our city—one built by the people and in which we are all interested. Although bearing my name, an unexpected honor which I greatly appreciate, it will not be under my supervision, but that of the Sisters of Charity where all physicians will have equal rights and privileges, the object being to maintain and perpetuate an institution equal to any of its kind throughout our country.

Notes

Chapter 1. The Spohn Family, from Canada to the United States

1. "Crawford Long (1815–1878)," *New Georgia Encyclopedia*, original entry by M. Leslie Madden, May 14, 2004, last updated by NGE staff August 5, 2015, http://www.georgiaencyclopedia.org/articles/science-medicine/crawford-long-1815-1878. The authors gratefully acknowledge the input of Courtney Townsend, MD, FACS, president of the American College of Surgeons and editor in chief of the *Sabiston Textbook for Surgery: The Biological Basis of Modern Surgical Practice*.

2. *Ancaster's Heritage: A History of Ancaster Township*, vol. 1 (Ancaster, Ont.: Ancaster Township Historical Society, 1973), 1.

3. Information submitted to the Ottawa Loyalist of the United Empire Loyalists, inscribed on the United Loyalist statue in Hamilton, Ont., Canada, provided by Paul T. Harris, descendant of Peter Bowman and Elizabeth Bowman Spohn, Ottawa, Ont., to authors, June 30, 2011.

4. Adolphus Egerton Ryerson was born into a prominent loyalist family in what is now southwestern Ontario. He was an important figure in the development of Methodism and the promotion of religious freedom in nineteenth-century Canada. Claude W. Doucet, "Egerton Ryerson, 1803–1882," Ryerson University Library and Archives, June 2002, https://library.ryerson.ca/asc/archives/ryerson-history/ryerson-bio/.

5. "1763: The French and Indian War Ends," *This Day in History*, History Channel, accessed February 22, 2017, http://www.history.com/this-day-in-history/the-french-and-indian-war-ends.

6. Elizabeth Bowman Spohn, letter to Dr. Egerton Ryerson, dated July 23, 1863. Ryerson incorporated Elizabeth's letter into an article he wrote that was published as "Elizabeth Bowman Spohn" in the *Christian Guardian* in February 1875. Paul T. Harris submitted Elizabeth Spohn's letter and Ryerson's comments for publication in the *Loyalist Gazette*, and they appeared in the Fall 1997 issue on page 25.

7. First Nations people are descendants of the original inhabitants of what is now Canada. Many people who were misnamed "Indians" now prefer to be called First Nations. They identify themselves by the nation to which they belong, for example, Mohawk, Cree, Oneida, and so on. "First Nations People in Canada," Indigenous and Northern Affairs Canada, accessed December 22, 2016, https://www.aadnc-aandc.gc.ca/eng/1303134042666/1303134337338.

8. Barbara E. Chipman, B.A. Hons., family historian, details on history of Canadian Loyalists, provided to author(s) October 17, 2012. See also Charles Miner, *History of Wyoming: In a Series of Letters from Charles Miner to William Penn Miner* (Philadelphia: J. Crissy, 1845); and James Edward Brady, "Wyoming: A Study of John Franklin and the Connecticut Settlement into Pennsylvania" (PhD diss., Syracuse University, 1973), provided by Barbara Chipman, B.A. Hons., also available at http://surface.syr.edu/hst_etd/468.

9. Chipman details on Canadian Loyalists; Miner, *History of Wyoming*; Brady, "Wyoming."

10. Paul T. Harris, information submitted to authors, June 30, 2011. The family story was that the British were billeted in the Lampman home in New York and while there wrote the song "Yankee Doodle Dandy" to ridicule the ragtag patriot army.

11. "The Harris Family of Worcestershire, England," provided by Paul T. Harris, a descendant living in Ottawa, Ontario, to author(s), June 30, 2011.

12. *Ancaster's Heritage*, 1:13–15.

13. *Ancaster's Heritage*, 1:29.

14. Copy of Peter Spaun's family Bible, furnished by descendant Paul T. Harris to the authors, June 30, 2011.

15. Paul T. Harris, descendant of Peter Bowman and Elizabeth Bowman Spohn, information submitted to authors, June 30, 2011.

16. Copy of Peter Spaun's family Bible.

17. Information provided by family historian Barbara E. Chipman, B.A. Hons.

18. Rev. Egerton Ryerson, obituary notes on Elizabeth Spohn, written in 1875 and printed in the Hamilton, Ont., newspaper, provided by descendant Paul Harris to author(s), June 6, 2011.

19. Information provided by family historian Barbara E. Chipman, B.A. Hons.

20. Information provided by family historian Beth Dubeau.

21. Ibid.

22. Information provided by family historian Beth Dubeau.

23. *Ancaster's Heritage: A History of Ancaster Township*, vol. 2 (Ancaster, Ont.: Ancaster Township Historical Society, 1998), 95.

24. Information provided to authors by family historian Beth Dubeau.

25. Ibid.

26. Today Raymond Wilson owns the property across the street from the Spohn homestead. The land he farms originally belonged to the Spohn family. One of the barns he still uses was built by Spohn's brother, Philip Howard Spohn.

27. "Scarlet Fever," Mayo Clinic, March 13, 2014, http://www.mayoclinic.org/diseases-conditions/scarlet-fever/basics/definition/con-20030976.

28. John C. Waller, *Health and Wellness in 19th-Century America* (Santa Barbara, Calif.: Greenwood, ABC-CLIO, 2014), 118.

29. Information provided by family historian Barbara E. Chipman, B.A. Hons.

30. Waller, *Health and Wellness*, 118.

31. Ibid.

32. Mrs. Stanley C. Tolan, "Christian Warner, a Methodist Pioneer," presentation at the Ontario Historical Society, Niagara Falls, Ont., September 1941, http://images .ourontario.ca/Partners/NOTL/NOTL002486711pf_0001.pdf.

33. *Ancaster's Heritage*, 1:191.

34. Ibid.

35. Ibid.

36. Ibid., 1:59.

37. Ibid.

38. Information provided by family historian Barbara E. Chipman, B.A. Hons.

39. Virgil N. Lott and Mercurio Martinez, *The Kingdom of Zapata* (San Antonio: Naylor, 1953), 62.

40. "The Terryberrys: Two Centuries of Family History in Hamilton," *Hamilton (Ontario) Spectator*, December 27, 2005, https://www.thespec.com/news-story/2239038 -digging-up-your-roots/.

41. Information provided by family historian Barbara E. Chipman, B.A. Hons.

42. Henry Spohn obituary, *Laredo Weekly Times*, July 11, 1909.

43. Peter Van Wagner Spohn, CA0N009F FOND CA0N000(F4486), Fonds F4486– Van Wagner–Hamilton Fond, Archives of Ontario, Toronto, Ont., Canada.

44. Information provided by family historian Barbara E. Chipman, B.A. Hons.

45. Ryerson, obituary notes on Elizabeth Spohn.

46. Marriage license of Catherine Spohn and Dr. Alexander Hamilton, Ontario, Canada, Marriage Licenses, 1801–1926, Ancestry Library Edition, Ancestry.com.

47. Copy of Peter Spaun's family Bible.

48. Beth Dubeau, Spohn family historian and descendant, Waterloo, Ont., telephone interview by author(s), August 6, 2010; Fieldcote Museum records, Ancaster, Ont.; John Hoff, *Historical Atlas of Simcoe County Ontario* (Toronto: H. Belden & Co., 1881).

49. Information provided to authors by family historian Beth Dubeau.

50. Marriage license of Catherine Spohn and Dr. Alexander Hamilton, Ontario, Canada.

51. Andrew F. Hunter, *A History of Simcoe County* (Barrie, Ont.: County Council, 1909), 10.

52. Su Murdock, Brad Rudachyk, and K. H. Schick, *Beautiful Barrie—The City and Its People: An Illustrated History of Barrie, Ontario* (Barrie, Ont.: DBS Heritage Consulting and Communications, 2005), 59.

53. Lori Podoisly, acting university archivist, McGill University Archives, email to the author(s). September 20, 2013.

54. Richard L. Cruess, JD, "Brief History of Medicine at McGill," 1–5, McGill University Faculty of Medicine, www.mcgill.ca/medicine/about/glance/history.

55. Michael Bliss, *William Osler: A Life in Medicine* (New York: Oxford University Press, 1999), 59–60.

56. Ibid., 60.

Chapter 2. From the University of Michigan to Postwar New York City

1. Biography of Arthur Spohn in Joseph Howard Raymond, MA, MD, *History of the Long Island College Hospital and Its Graduates Together with the Hoagland Laboratory and the Polhemus Memorial Clinic* (Brooklyn, N.Y.: Association of the Alumni, 1899), 129.

2. "The Medical School: Admission and Curriculums," in *The University of Michigan, an Encyclopedic Survey*, ed. Wilfred B. Shaw (Ann Arbor: University of Michigan Press, 1941), accessed September 2, 2017, https://quod.lib.umich.edu/u/umsurvey/AAS33 02.0002.001/1:4.2.1.1?rgn=div4;view=fulltext.

3. "A Wounded Nation," *Freedom: A History of US*, webisode 7, segment 1, PBS, accessed July 31, 2014, http://www.pbs.org/wnet/historyofus/web07/segment1_p.html.

4. "History of the University of Michigan Medical School," University of Michigan, 2011, 792, http://um2017.org/2017_Website/Histories_of_UM_School_of_Medicine .html.

5. Ibid., 793.

6. Ibid., 785.

7. Ibid.

8. "Memoir: Corydon La Ford," Faculty History Project, University of Michigan, 814, http://um2017.org/faculty-history/faculty/corydon-la-ford/memoir.

9. Ibid.

10. "History of the University of Michigan Department of Anatomy," http://um 2017.org/2017_Website/History_of_Anatomy.html.

11. "Memoir: Corydon La Ford," 809. See also David Oshinsky, *Bellevue: Three Centuries of Medicine and Mayhem at America's Most Storied Hospital* (New York: Doubleday, 2016), 66–67.

12. Frederick G. Novy, "Medical School" (1942), *University of Michigan, an Encyclopedic Survey: Bicentennial Edition*, accessed January 27, 2018, http://hdl.handle.net /2027/spo.13950886.0003.040.

13. "Memoir: Corydon La Ford," 786–87.

14. Ibid., 799.

15. James F. O'Gorman, review of *New York 1880: Architecture and Urbanism in the Gilded Age*, by Robert A. M. Stern, Thomas Mellins, and David Fishman (New York: Monacelli Press, 1999), *New York Times Book Review*, December 19, 1999, http://www .nytimes.com/books/first/s/stern-1880.html.

16. *Report of the Council of Hygiene and Public Health of the Citizens' Association of New York upon the Sanitary Condition of the City* (New York: Appleton & Co., 1865), 502. See also Oshinsky, *Bellevue*, 106–7.

17. *Report of the Council of Hygiene and Public Health*, 502.

18. Oshinsky, *Bellevue*, 104.

19. "Cholera in 1866," *NYCdata*, Baruch College, http://www.baruch.cuny.edu/ nycdata/disasters/cholera-1866.html.

20. Ibid.

21. Ibid. See also Oshinsky, *Bellevue*, 109.

22. *Report of the Council of Hygiene and Public Health*, 502.

23. "Bellevue Hospital," Wikipedia, https://en.wikipedia.org/wiki/NYC_Health_%2B_Hospitals/Bellevue.

24. "Founding of America's First College Hospital," in Raymond, *History of the Long Island College Hospital and Its Graduates*, 11.

25. Henry Spohn obituary, *Laredo Weekly Times*, July 11, 1909.

26. Bobby A. Wintermute, *Public Health and the U.S. Military: A History of the Army Medical Department, 1818-1917* (New York: Routledge, 2010), 32.

27. John C. Waller, *Health and Wellness in 19th-Century America* (Santa Barbara, Calif.: Greenwood, ABC-CLIO, 2014), 210–11.

28. Quoted in ibid., 207.

29. Oshinsky, *Bellevue*, 95.

30. Ibid., 125.

31. Ibid., 112.

32. Ibid., 113–14. See also Emily Abel, "Patient Dumping in New York City, 1877–1917," *American Journal of Public Health* 101, no. 5 (2011): 789–95.

33. Oshinsky, *Bellevue*, 126. See also Raymond, *History of the Long Island College Hospital and Its Graduates*, 13.

34. Raymond, *History of the Long Island College Hospital and Its Graduates*, 13.

35. Ibid., 16.

36. Ibid., 15.

37. Dr. Alfred Jay Bollet, MD, *Plagues and Poxes: The Impact of Human History on Epidemic Disease* (New York: Demos Medical Publishing, 2004), 6. See also Oshinsky, *Bellevue*, 145.

Chapter 3. The Spohns to Lawless Texas

1. Tom Lea, *The King Ranch* (1957; Boston: Little, Brown, 1980), 25.

2. Loyd M. Uglow, *Standing in the Gap: Army Outposts, Picket Stations, and the Pacification of the Texas Frontier, 1866–1886* (Fort Worth: Texas Christian University Press, 1952), 76.

3. Joseph B. Wilkinson, *Laredo and the Rio Grande Frontier* (Austin: Jenkins, 1975), 311.

4. Mark Odintz, "Buffalo Soldiers," *Handbook of Texas Online*, accessed April 12, 2017, http://www.tshaonline.org/handbook/online/articles/qlb01.

5. Wilkinson, *Laredo and the Rio Grande Frontier*, 230.

6. Ibid.

7. Ibid., 313.

8. Mary Margaret Amberson, James A. McAllen, and Margaret H. McAllen, *I Would Rather Sleep in Texas: A History of the Lower Rio Grande Valley and the People of the Santa Anita Land Grant* (Austin: Texas State Historical Association, 2003), 309. "Brache" probably means a breach or break, as in a levee.

9. Jane Clements Monday and Frances Brannen Vick, *Petra's Legacy: The South Texas Ranching Empire of Petra Vela and Mifflin Kenedy* (College Station: Texas A&M University Press, 2007), 178.

10. Ibid., 179.

11. Ibid., 178.

12. Paul H. Carlson, "Shafter, William Rufus," *Handbook of Texas Online*, accessed April 12, 2017, http://www.tshaonline.org/handbook/online/articles/fsh02. See also William E. Gorham, "Buffalo Soldiers: The Formation of the Twenty-Fourth Infantry Regiment, October 1866–1871" (thesis, US Army Command and General Staff College, Fort Leavenworth, 1993).

13. John C. Waller, *Health and Wellness in 19th-Century America* (Santa Barbara, Calif.: Greenwood, ABC-Clio, 2014), 120.

14. Ibid., 99–100.

15. Henry Spohn obituary, *Laredo Weekly Times*, July 11, 1909.

16. Monday and Vick, *Petra's Legacy*, 27, 29

17. Ibid., 37.

18. Ibid., 15–16.

19. Ibid., 20.

20. Ibid., 19.

21. Ibid., 22.

22. Ibid., 19.

23. Amberson, McAllen, and McAllen, *I Would Rather Sleep in Texas*, 219; Monday and Vick, *Petra's Legacy*, 25.

24. Marriage certificate of Mifflin Kenedy and Petra Vela de Vidal, Jonathan Day Folder, Corpus Christi District Court Records, Corpus Christi warehouse.

25. Monday and Vick, *Petra's Legacy*: Tom, 44; James, 58; John, 62; Sarah, 64; William, 66; Phebe Ann, 84.

26. Monday and Vick, *Petra's Legacy*, 38, 52.

27. Ibid., 58.

28. Ibid.

29. Ibid., 90.

30. John Mason Hart, "Stillman, Charles," *Handbook of Texas Online*, accessed April 12, 2017, http://www.tshaonline.org/handbook/online/articles/fst57.

31. Amberson, McAllen, and McAllen, *I Would Rather Sleep in Texas*, 192.

32. Monday and Vick, *Petra's Legacy*, 94, 96–97, 120–21.

33. Milo Kearney, *More Studies in Brownsville History* (Brownsville, Tex.: Pan American University at Brownsville, 1989), 193.

34. Monday and Vick, *Petra's Legacy*, 104.

35. Ibid., 104–5.

36. Jerry Thompson, "Mutiny and Desertion on the Rio Grande: The Strange Saga of Captain Adrian J. Vidal," *Military History of Texas and the Southwest* 12, no. 3 (1975): 161–64.

37. "The Mexican Adventure," account of the murder of Jeff Barthelow by Adrian Vidal, reported in an 1891 issue of a Laredo newspaper, copied by Elizabeth Winn, June 8, 1997. See also *Houston Tri-Weekly Telegraph*, November 12, 1863, quoting the *Brownsville–Fort Brown Flag*, October 30, 1863; Lea, *King Ranch*, 204–5; Jerry Thompson, *Cortina: Defending the Mexican Name in Texas* (College Station: Texas

A&M University Press, 2007), 112–13, 276n59; "Juan Cortina," *New Perspectives on the West*, PBS, http://www.pbs.org/weta/thewest/people/a_c/cortina.htm.

38. Thompson, "Mutiny and Desertion on the Rio Grande," 156–57.

39. Ibid., 113.

40. Lea, *King Ranch*, 217–18.

41. Newspaper clipping from Kingsbury Papers 1858–72, Vol. 1–2R72, Briscoe Center for American History, University of Texas at Austin.

42. Monday and Vick, *Petra's Legacy*, 138–39, 143–44.

Chapter 4. Spohn in Texas

1. War Department Notice, Surgeon General's Office, Washington, DC, issued May 24, 1865, Fifth Military District (FS3): "Notice[:] Dr. A. E. Spohn's contract signed May 10, 1868 at New York City for duty at the 5th Military District has been approved by the Surgeon General with the compensation at the rate of $100 per month. Signed Dr. A. E. Spohn Acting Assistant Surgeon USA," in Kenedy Ranch Archives, Sarita, Tex. Numerous publications on Spohn's life state that he came to Texas in 1868 and served in the army until 1869. One reference has him listed as serving from 1868 to 1871; see "Medicine & Public Health in Galveston, Texas: Diseases and Disasters in the Oleander City, 1861–1900," National Library of Medicine, History of Medicine Division, Bethesda, Md.

2. *Handbook of Texas Online*, "Spohn, Arthur Edward," accessed January 21, 2018, http://www.tshaonline.org/handbook/online/articles/fsp15; Biography of Arthur Spohn in Joseph Howard Raymond MA, MD, *History of the Long Island College Hospital and Its Graduates Together with the Hoagland Laboratory and the Polhemus Memorial Clinic* (Brooklyn, N.Y.: Association of the Alumni, 1899); A. A. Surgeon Arthur Edward Spohn, Association of Military Surgeons of the United States: Personal Record of Members—1905, Scudder-Stark Collection, Container MSC 142, Box 6, Association of Military Surgeons, National Library of Medicine, History of Medicine Division, Bethesda, Md.

3. Jacy Teston and Mason Meek, "Yellow Fever in Galveston, Texas," *East Texas History*, accessed January 21, 2018, http://easttexashistory.org/items/show/251.

4. Ibid.

5. "Calhoun County, Texas: Epidemic News," Texas Genealogy Trails, genealogytrails.com/tex/gulfcoast/calhoun/epidemics.html.

6. Ibid.

7. Peggy Hildreth, "Howard Associations," *Handbook of Texas Online*, accessed March 25, 2017, http://www.tshaonline.org/handbook/online/articles/vwh01.

8. *The Advertiser* (Corpus Christi), extra ed., Wed., August 14, 1867, Corpus Christi Yellow Fever File, La Retama Public Library, Corpus Christi, Tex. See also "Calhoun County, Texas: Epidemic News," Texas Genealogy Trails, genealogytrails.com/tex/gulfcoast/calhoun/epidemics.html.

9. Ibid.

10. Bruce Cheeseman, "The King–Spohn Family Friendship: A Productive Partner-

ship Embodying Heritage, Hope & Leadership," speech presented to Spohn Health System executives at a corporate retreat in Santa Fe, N.Mex., copy provided to Jane Monday, March 2000.

11. Loyd M. Uglow, *Standing in the Gap: Army Outposts, Picket Stations, and the Pacification of the Texas Frontier, 1866–1886* (Fort Worth: Texas Christian University Press, 1952), 11.

12. Ibid., 68.

13. Ibid., 80.

14. Ibid., 14.

15. John A. Adams Jr., *Conflict and Commerce on the Rio Grande: Laredo, 1755–1955* (College Station: Texas A&M University Press, 2008), 97.

16. Uglow, *Standing in the Gap*, 14.

17. Ibid., 74.

18. Homero Vera, telephone interview by Jane Monday, March 6, 2016. Robert Uribe, a descendant of Don Treviño, related the family history: "This is a story about a person buying land on the north side of the Rio Grande in 1828 and building a ranch house on the property for the protection against the Indians and also to be used as a storage room. The room grew into a full-sized fort and from there the rancho named San Ygnacio became a town by the same name." The rancho was built with eighteen-inch-thick walls, and the floor was of dirt. The room had no windows and only one entrance. The door was two inches thick and made of solid mesquite, and it was held together with wooden dowels and wedges. The roof was flat with a lookout perch. They also built two turrets on either side of the door, with an opening facing the door so they could retreat into the room if under attack. For storing their valuables they built a compartment on the east wall covered by a stone. Outside they built a hundred-foot fence and gate so the livestock could be brought into the compound for protection during raids. In 1859, nine years before Spohn's arrival, Don Blas María Uribe decided to move his family to the ranch permanently, and a walled fort was built next to the existing structure. The new structure had thick walls and loopholes for firing muskets from inside the compound. At the same time the fort was a built, a sundial was placed above the portals of the gate. Don Blas María Uribe remembered the story of two thirteen-year-old boys, one named José Villarreal, who were captured by the Native Americans and taken north into Texas. After ten days they managed to escape, and at first they traveled north by following the North Star, to fool their captors. Then they turned south and reached a small town north of Laredo, where they were nursed back to health. They then returned to Revilla. José never forgot the importance of the stars and asked Don Blas María if he could make a sundial and place it at the entrance. He constructed and set it during the equinox, with the arrow pointing to the North Star. It has functioned for many years. Roberto D. Uribe, *San Ignacio: A Tribute to Bob and Joe Uribe*, chap. 2, http://www.incdef.com/san%20ignacio/chapter2.asp. See also Dick D. Heller Jr. "San Ygnacio, Texas," *Handbook of Texas Online*, http:www.tshaonline.org/handbook/online/articles/HLS15.

19. Uribe, *San Ignacio*, http://www.incdef.com/san%20ignacio/Ignacio.asp, 1–13.

20. Quoted in J. B. Wilkinson, *Laredo and the Rio Grande Frontier* (Austin: Jenkins, 1975), 324.

21. Ibid., 233.

22. Ibid., 236–37.

23. George N. Putegnat, interview by Rosita Putegnat, January 31, 1956, copy of transcript provided to Jane Monday.

24. Col. P. M. Ashburn, Colonel Medical Corps, US Army, *A History of the United States Medical Department* (Cambridge: Riverside Press, 1929), 89.

25. Ibid.

26. Jennings quoted in court-martial records for Hamilton C. Peterson (PP-954), RG 153, Entry 15A, Court-Martial Case Files, 1809–1894, 7E3, 14/28/1, Box 2630, Item REP0006C, National Archives and Records Administration, General Services Administration, Washington, DC.

27. Court-martial records for Hamilton C. Peterson (PP-954).

28. Quoted in ibid.

29. Ibid.

30. Ibid.

31. Ibid. Texas Ranger N. A. Jennings described a fiesta and the game of monte in Nuevo Laredo in 1869. He wrote that in a big adobe building a game of monte was being played. On a long table down the middle of the main room were stacks of Mexican silver dollars. There were also half-dollars and quarters. About five thousand silver dollars were placed out, and the bank was good for any amount up to $50,000. There were numerous dealers around the table, with men as many as four deep around them. Monte is a Spanish gambling game and the national card game in Mexico. It usually is played with several players and a dealer. The dealer lays out two cards and the players bet on the cards for a match. The dealer then turns up a card to place on each card on the table and pays the players one for one for a match or, if there is no match, takes the money for himself. N. A. Jennings, *A Texas Ranger* (New York: Charles Scribners Sons, 1899), 17–19, paraphrased from a Texas Ranger Hall of Fame ebook, http://www.tex asranger.org/E-Books/A%20Texas%20Ranger%20(Jennings).pdf.

32. N. A. Jennings, *A Texas Ranger*, edited by Ben Procter (Chicago: Lakeside Press, R. R. Donnelley & Sons, 1992), 39–40.

33. Scott M. Grayson, "Henry Redmond" (2012), 1–4, http://www.crutchwilliams .com/TEXAS/HenryRedmond.html.

34. David Parsons Holton and Frances Holton, "Winslow Memorial: Family Records of the Winslows and Their Descendants in America, with the English Ancestry as Far as Known," 1877, https://archive.org/details/winslowmemorialf001holt.

35. Quoted in Jennings, *Texas Ranger*, edited by Procter, 26–31.

36. Court-martial records for Hamilton C. Peterson.

Chapter 5. Mier, Mexico

1. Antonio Ma. Guerra, *Mier in History: A Translation of "Mier en la historia,"* trans. José María Escobar and Edna Garza Brown (Edinburg, Tex.: New Santander Press, 1989), 4–5, 19–21.

2. Ibid.

3. Property Division, Surgeon General's Office, Washington, DC, to Arthur E. Spohn, Acting Assistant Surgeon, April 6, 1870.

4. Arthur E. Spohn, Acting Assistant Surgeon at Mier, Mexico, Communication to Property Division, Surgeon General's Office, Washington, DC, December 30, 1871.

5. Charles Mayer, Commercial Agent for Mier, Mexico, to William Hunter, Washington, DC, nominating Dr. A. E. Spohn as vice-commercial agent, March 5, 1872, Dispatches from United States Consuls in Mier, 1870–78, National Archives Microfilm Publications, microcopy no. 297, 1963, National Archives and Records Administration, General Services Administration, Washington, DC.

6. Dr. Henry (Harry) Hamilton (nephew of Arthur Spohn), Laredo, Tex., to Gretchen Spohn (Hamilton's cousin and a niece of Arthur Spohn), Canada, August 24, 1942, provided by the family to the author(s).

7. Arthur E. Spohn, "Elastic Rubber-Ring Tourniquet," *Richmond and Louisville Medical Journal* (Richmond, Va.), 22 (November 1876): 425–30.

8. "Biography of Arthur Edward Spohn," in *The Corpus Christi Chronicles* (Corpus Christi: Nueces County Historical Society and Corpus Christi Chamber of Commerce, 1992), 13.

9. Guerra, *Mier in History*, 49.

10. Mayer, Commercial Agent for Mier, Mexico, to Hunter, Washington, DC, nominating Dr. Spohn, March 5, 1872.

11. Guerra, *Mier in History*, 48.

12. Ibid., 49.

13. Thomas Gilgan, US Commercial Agent, Nuevo Laredo, dispatch of April 1872, Dispatches from United States Consuls in Mier, 1870–78.

14. John A. Adams Jr., *Conflict and Commerce on the Rio Grande, Laredo, 1755–1955* (College Station: Texas A&M University Press, 2008), 99.

15. Paul Garner, *Porfirio Diaz: Profiles in Power* (London: Routledge, 2001).

16. Charles Mayer, Commercial Agent for Mier, Mexico, to William Hunter, Washington, DC, including Dr. A. E. Spohn's oath of allegiance, March 31, 1872, Dispatches from United States Consuls in Mier, 1870–78.

17. Charles Mayer, Commercial Agent, to Charles Hunter, Washington, DC, May 31, 1872, Dispatches from United States Consuls in Mier, Mexico, 1870–78.

18. Ibid.; Yearly report of collected fees for January 1–December 31, 1872, including fees collected by Agent Arthur E. Spohn, in Report to Hon. William Hunter, 2nd Assistant Secretary of State, Washington, DC, stamped "received" by the Department of the Secretary of State, Dispatches from United States Consuls in Mier, Mexico, 1870–78.

19. Garner, *Porfirio Diaz*, 55–58.

20. Ibid., 37.

21. Ibid., 24.

22. Charles Mayer, Commercial Agent to William Hunter, Washington, DC, February 9, 1873, Dispatches from United States Consuls in Mier, Mexico, 1870–78.

23. Jane Clements Monday and Frances Brannen Vick, *Petra's Legacy: The South Texas Ranching Empire of Petra Vela and Mifflin Kenedy* (College Station: Texas A&M University Press, 2007), 195–97.

24. Mary Margaret Amberson, James A. McAllen, and Margaret H. McAllen, *I Would Rather Sleep in Texas: A History of the Lower Rio Grande Valley and the People of the Santa Anita Land Grant* (Austin: Texas State Historical Association, 2003), 328.

25. Monday and Vick, *Petra's Legacy*, 198.

Chapter 6. Corpus Christi, the City by the Sea

1. *Nueces Valley*, February 1, 1873, accessed in Microfilm #5, Corpus Christi Public Library, Corpus Christi, Tex. See also Bruce Cheeseman, "The King–Spohn Family Friendship: A Productive Partnership Embodying Heritage, Hope & Leadership," speech presented to Spohn Health System executives at a corporate retreat in Santa Fe, N.Mex., copy provided to Jane Monday, March 2000.

2. *Nueces Valley*, February 15, 1873.

3. *Nueces Valley*, February 22, 1873.

4. [Reuben] Holbein to Mifflin Kenedy, February 28, 1873, GGII 002045-04579. (All sources cited with a "GGII" notation are from the George Getchow Documents, copied from the vault at the Big House at La Parra, given to the King Ranch Archives, and produced in Litigation, Cause No. C-291-93-D, Manuel de Llano [et al.] v. the John G. and Marie Stella Kenedy Memorial Foundation [et al.], District Court, Hidalgo County, Tex., 206th Judicial District).

5. *Nueces Valley*, March 22, 1873.

6. "Smallpox," Centers for Disease Control and Prevention, https://www.cdc.gov/smallpox/index.html.

7. Ibid.

8. John C. Waller, *Health and Wellness in 19th-Century America* (Santa Barbara, Calif.: Greenwood, ABC-CLIO, 2014), 13. See also David Oshinsky, *Bellevue: Three Centuries of Medicine and Mayhem at America's Most Storied Hospital* (New York: Doubleday, 2016), 24.

9. Sir William Osler and Thomas M. Rae, *The Principles and Practice of Medicine*, 9th ed. (New York: D. Appleton and Company, 1921), 102–3.

10. Waller, *Health and Wellness*, 13.

11. Ibid., 14–15.

12. Oshinsky, *Bellevue*, 102.

13. Ibid., 103.

14. Waller, *Health and Wellness*, 21.

15. Oshinsky, *Bellevue*, Insert A, page 7, caption with photo of Hamilton.

16. Waller, *Health and Wellness*, 19.

17. Maurice Hood, MD, *Early Texas Physicians, 1830–1915* (Austin: State House Press, 1999), 4.

18. Ibid., 5.

19. *Nueces Valley*, July 26, 1873.

20. The Meuly Building was constructed in 1852 of "shellcrete," made of a concreted mix of burned oyster shells. The rooms had fourteen-foot ceilings and nine-foot doorways. The front was distinctively decorated with iron grillwork from New Orleans. It had a colorful history illustrating the "Wild West" element existing in Texas at the time.

In 1866, a mob that was determined to lynch a man tried to fix a rope on the upper porch, but Mrs. Meuly would not allow a man to be hanged from her gallery. The target of the mob was considered a drunk and disreputable man, Jim Garner, accused of shooting a respected storekeeper, Emanuel Scheuer, through the heart, as well as two other men. A mob had formed, then found Garner and put a rope around his neck. When they could not use the Meuly Building, they found a mesquite having a limb that was high enough to pull a man up off his toes. The men grabbed the end of the rope after it was thrown over the mesquite and pulled tight on the rope until Garner strangled to death. Garner's father came and took his body away and reported that he had gotten a good rope from the hanging. The lack of tall trees for hanging was considered a problem for lynch mobs. Murphy Givens, "Corpus Christi History," *Corpus Christi Caller-Times*, June 13, 2001, http://www.caller2.com/2001/June/13/today/murphygi/2689.html.

21. "Medical History of Corpus Christi," compiled by the Nueces County Medical Society Auxiliary, District VI, in *The Corpus Christi Chronicles* (Corpus Christi: Nueces County Historical Society and Corpus Christi Chamber of Commerce, 1992), 4.

22. Ibid.

23. "Biography," compiled by the Nueces County Medical Society Auxiliary, Corpus Christi, District VI, printed in the *Gazette*, January 5, 1876, and reprinted in *Corpus Christi Chronicles*.

24. *Nueces Valley*, July 4, 1874, 2 (cols. 1–2).

25. Sister Mary Xavier (Holworthy), *A Century of Sacrifice: The History of the Cathedral Parish, Corpus Christi, Texas, 1853–1953* (1953; Corpus Christi, Tex., 1965).

26. Arthur Spohn to Amelia Meuly, ca. 1874, Folder 3.15, Box 3, Meuly-Daimwood Family Papers, Mary and Jeff Bell Library, Texas A&M University–Corpus Christi (hereafter, TAMU-CC).

27. 1880 Nueces County Census, Meuly-Daimwood Family Papers, TAMU-CC.

28. *Nueces Valley*, July 12, 1873.

29. Jane Clements Monday and Frances Brannen Vick, *Petra's Legacy: The South Texas Ranching Empire of Petra Vela and Mifflin Kenedy* (College Station: Texas A&M University Press, 2007), 168–69, 204.

30. *Corpus Christi Caller*, June 22, 1873, accessed in Corpus Christi Public Library, Corpus Christi, Tex.

31. William Kelly to Captain Kenedy, September 18, 1873, unbound copies of King, Kenedy & Co. Correspondence, 1873 #0539, transcribed by Lillian Embree, Corpus Christi Museum, Corpus Christi, Tex.

32. Dr. Arthur Spohn, "Tumors," *Richmond and Louisville Medical Journal* (Louisville, Ky.), 1875, IC Series 1, IC Volume 14, IC page 865, ID Number 11408651820, University of Texas Southwestern, Dallas, Tex.

33. Ibid.

34. *Brownsville Daily Herald*, vol. XV, no. 232 [April 1, 1907], article on the Combe family; Compilation on Charles B. Combe, Asst. Surgeon Military Records, 1860 Census.

35. Spohn, "Tumors," *Richmond and Louisville Medical Journal*, 1875.

36. William Kelly to Captain Kenedy, September 18, 1873, GGII 006457-006471; William Kelly to Joseph Cooper, October 13, 1873, King, Kenedy & Co. Correspondence, 1873 #0539, Corpus Christi Museum.

37. William Kelly to Mifflin Kenedy, October 8, 1873, King, Kenedy & Co. Correspondence, 1873, #0539, Corpus Christi Museum.

38. William Kelly to [Reuben] Holbein, November 19, 1873, King, Kenedy & Co. Correspondence, 1873, #0539, Corpus Christi Museum.

39. Richard King to Mifflin Kenedy, July 12, 1874, GGII 002096-000349.

40. "Texas Medical Board History," Texas Medical Board, www.tmb.state.tx.us/page/medical-board-history.

41. Sister Jeanne Francis Miner, "The Early Development of Education in Corpus Christi, Texas, 1846–1909" (master's thesis, Catholic University of America, 1950), 56.

42. Ibid.

43. "Friedrich von Esmarch: German Surgeon," *Encyclopaedia Britannica*, https://www.britannica.com/biography/Friedrich-von-Esmarch; *Richmond and Louisville Medical Journal* 22 (November 1876).

44. "Acute Compartment Syndrome: Background, Anatomy, Pathophysiology," *Medscape*, last updated January 17, 2017, emedicine.medscape.com/article/307668-overview.

45. George Tiemann & Company, https://www.georgetiemann.com.

46. "History of the Medical Society," prepared by the Nueces County Medical Society Auxiliary, in *Corpus Christi Chronicles*.

47. Murphy Givens, "Old Houses of the Past," *Corpus Christi History Caller-Times*, [n.d., ca. 2001], 2.

48. Tiemann & Co. letters quoted in *Richmond and Louisville Medical Journal* 22 (November 1876).

49. Rev. Egerton Ryerson, obituary notes on Elizabeth Spaun, written in 1875 and printed in the Hamilton, Ont., newspaper, and reminiscences of the American Revolution and early settlers of Canada, provided by descendant Paul Harris to author(s), June 6, 2011.

50. Ibid.

51. Elizabeth Spaun will, filed January 31, 1871, and executed on her death (January 24, 1875) in Wentworth County, Ontario, provided by family descendant Harry Spohn of Hamilton, Ontario.

52. *Richmond and Louisville Medical Journal* 22 (November 1876).

53. *New Orleans Medical and Surgical Journal* 47 (July 1895).

54. Ibid.

55. Julia Girouard, review of *Luisiana*, by Paul E. Hoffman, *Louisiana History* 35, no. 3 (1994): 378–80.

56. Walter Prescott Webb, *The Texas Rangers: A Century of Frontier Defense* (Austin: University of Texas Press, 1980), 167.

57. Quoted in Tom Lea, *The King Ranch* (1957; Boston: Little, Brown, 1980), 280.

58. Chuck Parsons and Marianne Hall Little, *Captain L. H. McNelly, Texas Ranger: The Life and Times of a Fighting Man* (Austin: State House Press, 2001), 199–200.

59. Monday and Vick, *Petra's Legacy*, 232.

Chapter 7. A Pivotal Year

1. Dr. Henry (Harry) Hamilton (nephew of Arthur Spohn), Laredo, Tex., to Gretchen Spohn (Hamilton's cousin and a niece of Arthur Spohn), Canada, August 24, 1942, provided by the family to the author(s).

2. Ibid.

3. *Corpus Christi Daily Gazette*, January 4, 1876, accessed in Corpus Christi Public Library, Corpus Christi, Tex.

4. *Corpus Christi Daily Gazette*, January 13, 1876, 4 (col. 1).

5. *Corpus Christi Daily Gazette*, February 3, 1876.

6. *Corpus Christi Daily Gazette*, February 11, 1876.

7. *Corpus Christi Daily Gazette*, June 15, 1876, 3 (col. 2).

8. "Public Health in Texas, 1828–1870," 258–60, Transcripts Relating to the Medical History of Texas, vol. 28, Joint Project of the Texas Medical Association and the University of Texas Library Archives, 1923–53.

9. Old Bayview Cemetery records, researched by Rev. Michael A. Howell with transcription by Geraldine D. McGloin of the Nueces County Historical Commission, Corpus Christi Public Library, Corpus Christi, Tex.

10. *Corpus Christi Daily Gazette*, February 12, 1876.

11. *Corpus Christi Daily Gazette*, March 15, 1877.

12. *Corpus Christi Daily Gazette*, March 23, 1877.

13. Information provided by descendant and family historian Barbara E. Chipman, B.A. Hons.

14. *Corpus Christi Caller*, March 2, 1876, accessed in Corpus Christi Library, Corpus Christi, Tex.

15. *Corpus Christi Caller*, May 24, 1876.

16. Arthur Spohn, "Elastic Rubber-Ring Tourniquet," *Richmond and Louisville Medical Journal* (Richmond, Va.), 22 (November 1876).

17. Ibid.

18. "Memory of Eleven Pioneers Honored in Catholic Diamond of City Gardens," *Corpus Christi Caller-Times*, October 8, 1936.

19. Lt. W. H. Chatfield, *The Twin Cities of the Border, Brownsville, Texas, and Matamoros, Mexico, and the Country of the Lower Rio Grande*, Centennial Oration by the Hon. William Neal (New Orleans: E. P. Brandad, 1893), 14. See also Robert B. Vezzetti, ed., *Tidbits: A Collection from the Brownsville Historical Association and the Stillman House Museum* (n.p., n.d.), 17.

20. Jane Clements Monday and Frances Brannen Vick, *Petra's Legacy: The South Texas Ranching Empire of Petra Vela and Mifflin Kenedy* (College Station: Texas A&M University Press, 2007), 169–70.

21. 1870 Census, Duval County, Tex., August 1, 1870, Mifflin Kenedy, line 2, series M593, roll: 1600, page: 198.

22. Patrick J. O'Connell, *The Kenedy Family at Spring Hill College* (Mobile, Ala.: privately printed, 1986–87), 16.

23. "We Have an Inspiring Heritage," Ursuline Academy, New Orleans, https://www.uanola.org/page/about/ursuline-heritage. Founded in 1727 and the oldest con-

tinuously operating school for girls and the oldest Catholic school in the United States, Ursuline was founded to promote the moral, spiritual, intellectual, and social growth of each student.

24. Information from Ursuline Convent archival records provided by Mary Lee Berner Harris, curator, Ursuline Convent Collection, Archives, and Museum, New Orleans.

25. Ibid.

26. Ibid.

27. Ibid.

28. Ibid.

29. Information provided by Homero S. Vera, director of the Kenedy Ranch Museum in Sarita, Texas.

30. Information from Ursuline Convent archival records provided by Mary Lee Berner Harris, curator, Ursuline Convent Collection, Archives, and Museum, New Orleans.

31. Quoted in *Corpus Christi Caller*, July 5, 1876.

32. Metairie Cemetery Association, New Orleans, La., records #16–50. John William "Willie" Kenedy was born April 22, 1859. He was a quiet, studious, sensitive boy. He appeared to have had many of Mifflin's characteristics. Willie was a high-ranking student at Spring Hill College. A year before his death, on January 1, 1875, he wrote his father a letter expressing how sorry he was about the damage the destructive storm had done to the ranch at the end of 1874. He wrote that his love for Mifflin could not be expressed in words. He also wrote how well his father had discharged his duties toward all his children and how he had worked night and day for them. He wrote that he would repay him for his efforts with his mercies and wished him a long and happy life. Then he wrote that he would meet him face to face in heaven, where all his troubles would cease. It is easy to see why this death was so hard on both Petra and Mifflin but particularly Mifflin. This was the child most like him and one he probably hoped would come home and be a comfort as they grew old. Willie Kenedy to Mifflin Kenedy, January 1, 1875, GGII 002444-002507.

33. Information from Ursuline Convent archival records provided by Mary Lee Berner Harris, curator, Ursuline Convent Collection, Archives, and Museum, New Orleans.

34. Sarah Kenedy and Arthur Spohn, Certificate of Marriage, November 22, 1876, Appendix D, Corpus Christi Cathedral Marriage Records, Catholic Diocese of Corpus Christi, Tex.

35. John Kenedy, deposition, Exhibit 5, GGII 013737-013750.

36. Frank Wagner, "Doddridge, Perry," *Handbook of Texas Online*, http://www.tsha online.org/handbook/online/articles/fd042. See also Murphy Givens, "Orphan from Alabama Built the Town's First Bank," *Corpus Christi Caller-Times*, http://www.caller .com/opinion/Columnists/murphy-givens/orphan-from-alabama-built-the-towns-first -bank. Perry Doddridge was essentially an orphan whose parents died when he was seven. He began working for Richard King and Mifflin Kenedy on their riverboat line at age fourteen. He was promoted to shipping agent at Mier, Mexico, which gave him something in common with Spohn. He became deputy director of customs at Roma and then formed his own business. He moved to Corpus Christi on June 12, 1862, and married Rachel Fulleton, the sixteen-year-old daughter of Capt. Samuel Fulleton.

Unfortunately they lost their four-year-old son in September 1867 in the yellow fever epidemic. Doddridge promoted the building of railroads and enlarging the port. He also served as mayor of Corpus Christi and as president of the school board. He was very close to Mifflin Kenedy and Richard King throughout the years and served as one of Richard King's executors.

37. *Corpus Christi Caller*, November 26, 1876.

Chapter 8. In New York

1. Richard H. Kessin, PhD, and Kenneth A. Forde, MD, "How Antiseptic Surgery Arrived in America," *P&S: The College of Physicians and Surgeons of Columbia University* 28, no. 2 (Spring–Summer 2008), www.cumc.columbia.edu/psjournal/archive/spring...2008/surgery_in_america.html.

2. Ibid.

3. "Historical Events in 1876," *On This Day*, www.onthisday.com/events/date/1876.

4. Celeste Brewer, archives assistant, New York University Archives, email to author, January 15, 2015.

5. Course description from the 1877–78 University of the City of New York *Bulletin* provided in ibid.

6. *Bellevue Hospital Medical College Annual Circular, 1876–7; Annual Catalogue, 1875–76*, 12, https://archives.med.nyu.edu/islandora/object/nyumed%3A1256.

7. "The Grand Central Hotel: Murders, Suicides, Scandals, and Disasters in New York's Most Famous Forgotten Inn," *Keith York City*, January 21, 2013, https://keith yorkcity.wordpress.com/2013/01/31/the-grand-central-hotel-murders-suicides-scan dals-and-disasters-in-new-yorks-most-famous-forgotten-inn. Another grand hotel in New York was the Manhattan Beach Hotel, located on Coney Island. It opened for business on July 4, 1877. The description of the hotel gives an insight into what these grand hotels were like. The hotel faced the beach and had deep verandas and 250 lavish rooms. The hotel was set back and surrounded by wide green lawns and elaborate flowerbeds, and Pinkerton detectives patrolled the grounds for security. The hotel took pride in a large dining room and lavish dinners that cost at least $3.50, which was half the wages an ordinary New Yorker would earn in a week. Some of the items featured were baked bluefish for forty-five cents, roast lamb with vegetables for sixty cents, and a dessert of meringue glacé for thirty cents. Dress was formal, and evening entertainment included music and fireworks. Sarah and Arthur Spohn had traveled in Europe and experienced lavish surroundings, but the United States had grand hotels as well. Lisa M. Santoro, "The Upper-Class Brooklyn Resorts of the Victorian Era," *Curbed New York*, June 27, 2013, http://ny.curbed.com/2013/6/27/10226192/the-upper-class-brooklyn-resorts-of-the-victorian-era.

8. "What Happened in 1877," *On This Day*, https://www.onthisday.com/date/1877.

9. "The Colorful History of America's Dog Show," Westminster Kennel Club, http://www.westminsterkennelclub.org/about-sensation/history/.

10. "Tenements," *History.com*, www.history.com/topics/tenements.

11. "The Panic of 1873: U.S. Grant, Warrior," *American Experience*, PBS-WGBH, www.pbs.org/wgbh/americanexperience/features/general/grant/panicof1873.

12. David Blanke, "Panic of 1873," National History Education Clearinghouse, Teaching History.org, http://teachinghistory.org/history-content/beyond-the-textbook/24579.

13. Joseph Adamczyk, "Great Railroad Strike of 1877," *Encyclopaedia Britannica*, https://www.britannica.com/topic/Great-Railroad-Strike-of-1877.

14. Joseph Howard Raymond, MA, MD, *History of the Long Island College Hospital and Its Graduates Together with the Hoagland Laboratory and the Polhemus Memorial Clinic* (Brooklyn, N.Y.: Association of the Alumni, 1899).

15. William Thompson Lusk obituary, "Record of Graduates of Yale University Deceased during the Academic Year ending in June, 1897," *Proceedings of the Connecticut Medical Society, 1899*, 343–49, https://archive.org/stream/39002011129435.med.yale.edu/39002011129435.med.yale.edu_djvu.txt.

16. Ira M. Rutkow, MD, *The History of Surgery in the United States, 1775–1900: Textbooks, Monographs, and Treaties* (San Francisco: Norman Publishing, 1988), 340–41, https://books.google.com.

17. S. W. Gross and A. H. Gross, eds., *Autobiography of Samuel D. Gross, M.D.*, 2 vols. (Philadelphia: George Barrie, 1887), 2:161, quoted in Nirav J. Mehta, MD, Rajal N. Mehta, MD, and Ljaz A. Khan, MD, "Austin Flint: Clinician, Teacher, and Visionary," *Texas Heart Institute Journal* 27, no. 4 (2000): 386–89, https://www.ncbi.nlm.nih.gov/pmc/articles/PMC101108/.

18. J. M. Da Costa, MD, LLD, "Biographical Sketch of Dr. Austin Flint," *Transactions of the College of Physicians Philadelphia*, 3rd ser., vol. 9 (n.d.): cdlxvi–vii, https://archive.org/stream/101488816.nlm.nih.gov/101488816#page/n0/mode/2up.

19. Clark Bell, ed., *Medico-Legal Journal* 24, no. 1 (1906): 81–91.

20. David Oshinsky, *Bellevue: Three Centuries of Medicine and Mayhem at America's Most Storied Hospital* (New York: Doubleday, 2016), 151; "William Stewart Halsted: Surgical Pioneer," *Endocrine Today*, Healio, February 2010, https://www.healio.com/endocrinology/news/print/endocrine-today/%7Ba9c025da-1d33-43a9-b7f6-7664abee1a9c%7D/william-stewart-halsted-surgical-pioneer.

21. John Cameron, MD, host, "William Stewart Halsted: The Birth of American Surgery," Johns Hopkins Medicine: Pathology, http://pathology.jhu.edu/department/about/history/celebratehistory.cfm.

22. Gerald Imber, MD, *Genius on the Edge: The Bizarre Double Life of Dr. William Stewart Halsted* (New York: Kaplan, 2010), 349, reviewed by F. David Winter Jr., in *Baylor University Medical Center Proceedings* 25, no. 1 (2012), https://www.ncbi.nlm.nih.gov/pmc/articles/PMC3246868/.

23. Imber, *Genius on the Edge*, 25 (quote); Dr. Michael Echols and Dr. Doug Arbittier, "Frank Hastings Hamilton, M.D.," *American Civil War Medicine and Surgical Antiques*, http://www.medicalantiques.com/civilwar/Medical_Authors_Faculty/Hamilton_Frank_Hastings.htm.

24. *Eighteenth Annual Announcement of the Bellevue Hospital Medical College, Sessions of 1878–1879*, with the Annual Catalogue for 1877–1878, *Pathological Anatomy and Histology*, 9, https://archives.med.nyu.edu/islandora/object/nyumed%3A1233/datastream/OBJ/view.

25. Robert B. Vezzetti, ed., *Tidbits: A Collection from the Brownsville Historical Association and the Stillman House Museum* (n.p., n.d.), 113; John Mason Hart, *Handbook*

of Texas Online, "Stillman, James," accessed January 22, 2018, http://www.tshaonline. org/handbook/online/articles/fstbp. William Rockefeller Jr., like Mifflin Kenedy and Richard King, had made his money on his own without help from his parents. His father, William Rockefeller Sr., had been a con artist. Senior had once bragged, "I cheat my boys every chance I get. I want to make 'em sharp." William Rockefeller Sr. married Eliza Davison, they had six children, and he remained married to her all his life. However, when William Jr. was a teenager, William Sr. abandoned his family. While he had been married to Eliza he had sired two daughters by his mistress and housekeeper, Nancy Brown. After leaving both families, he assumed the name Dr. William Levingston and married Nancy Brown in Canada, making him a bigamist. Dan Bryan, "The Dissipated Life of William A. Rockefeller," *American History USA*, April 12, 2012, www.americanhistoryusa.com/strange-life-of-william-rockefeller/. The quote is from James Corbett, "Meet William Rockefeller, Snake Oil Salesman," *The Corbett Report*, June 22, 2011, https://www.corbettreport.com/meet-william-rocke feller-snake-oil-salesman/.

26. "Fashions for June 1877," *Two Nerdy History Girls*, twonerdyhistorygirls.blog spot.com/2014/06/fashions-for-june-1877.html.

27. "Brief History of the Cornwall Grail Center," Grail Retreat Center, www.the grailatcornwall.org/about/history-of-the-cornwall-grail-center.

Chapter 9. The Wild West

1. Deed conveyance from Henry Spohn to Dr. A. E. Spohn, April 30, 1876, for one-third interest in ranch near Laredo, Texas, for $4,755, Kenedy Ranch Archives, Sarita, Tex. (hereafter, Kenedy Archives).

2. Inflation Calculator, DollarTimes, www.dollartimes.com/calculators/inflation.htm.

3. Henry Spohn obituary, *Laredo Weekly Times*, July 11, 1909.

4. Paul H. Carlson, *"Sheep Ranching," Handbook of Texas Online*, accessed June 30, 2017, http://www.tshaonline.org/handbook/online/articles/aus01.

5. Ibid.

6. Angus Spohn entry, Hamilton, Ontario, City Directory 1875–76; 1900 Census, Justice Precinct 1, Zapata, Tex., Angus Spohn, roll: 1681, page: 1B, Enumeration District: 0124; FHL microfilm 1241681, via Ancestry.com.

7. Angus Spohn, Laredo, Tex., to Dr. Alexander Hamilton, Corpus Christi, Tex., February 14, 1877, Kenedy Archives.

8. Art Leatherwood, "Fort Ewell," *Handbook of Texas Online*, accessed March 29, 2017, http://www.tshaonline.org/handbook/online/articles/qcf03.

9. Angus Spohn at the rancho to Dr. Alexander Hamilton, Corpus Christi, Tex., March 12, 1877, Kenedy Archives.

10. Angus Spohn at Buena Vista Rancho to Dr. Alexander Hamilton, Corpus Christi, Tex., October 19, 1877, Kenedy Archives.

11. Henry Spohn at the rancho to Dr. Alexander Hamilton, December 5, 1877, Kenedy Archives.

12. "Biography of Ridge Paschal," Access Genealogy, last updated July 29, 2012, www.accessgenealogy.com/native/biography-of-ridge-paschal/htm.

13. Henry Spohn at the rancho to Hamilton, December 5, 1877.

14. Keith Guthrie, "Borden, Sidney Gail," *Handbook of Texas Online*, accessed April 24, 2017, http://www.tshaonline.org/handbook/online/articles/fboae.

15. Henry Spohn to Alexander Hamilton, January 16, 1878, Kenedy Archives.

16. Dr. Henry (Harry) Hamilton to Gretchen Spohn, August 24, 1942, provided by the family to the author(s).

17. "Raid of 1878," La Salle County Genealogy, http://www.historicdistrict.com/genealogy/lasalle/raid.asp.

18. Ibid.

19. Dr. Henry Spohn, deposition before Joseph Fitzsimmons, US Circuit Court for the Eastern District of Texas, Corpus Christi, Tex., May 25, 1878.

20. Ibid.

21. John G. Johnson, "Mexican and Indian Raid of 1878," *Handbook of Texas Online*, accessed June 30, 2017, http://www.tshaonline.org/handbook/online/articles/btmrv.

22. John Leffler, "Encinal, TX," *Handbook of Texas Online*, accessed March 29, 2017, http://www.tshaonline.org/handbook/online/articles/hle20.

23. Ibid.

24. Virgil Lott and Mercurio Martinez, *The Kingdom of Zapata* (San Antonio: Naylor, 1953), 62–77.

25. Ibid.

26. Ibid.

27. Ibid.

28. Dr. Henry (Harry) Hamilton to Gretchen Spohn, August 24, 1942, provided by the family to the author(s).

29. Marriage certificate of P. H. Spohn and E. S. Thompson, July 24, 1878. Details provided by descendant and family historian Beth Dubeau.

30. Information provided by descendant and family historian Barbara E. Chipman, B.A. Hons.

31. Henry Spohn at the rancho to Dr. Alexander Hamilton in Corpus Christi, August 28, 1878, Kenedy Archives.

32. See Jane Clements Monday and Frances Brannen Vick, *Petra's Legacy: The South Texas Ranching Empire of Petra Vela and Mifflin Kenedy* (College Station: Texas A&M University Press, 2007), 254–63, for the full story.

33. State of Texas, District Court, County of Nueces, by Pat McDonough, Clerk District Court, November 4, 1878.

34. "Two Centuries of Health Promotion," Images from the History of the Public Health Service, https://www.nlm.nih.gov/exhibition/phs-history/intro.html; "U.S. Public Health Service: Marine Hospital Service (MHS) 1798," Social Welfare History Project, Virginia Commonwealth University, http://socialwelfare.library.vcu.edu/programs/health-nutrition/u-s-public-heath-service/.

35. Ibid.

36. Robert Rutherford, "History of Quarantine in the State of Texas from 1878–1888," *American Public Health Association Report* 14 (1888–89): 125–33, from a presentation at the Sixteenth Annual Meeting of the American Public Health Association, Milwaukee, Wisc., November 20, 1888, https://www.ncbi.nlm.nih.gov/pmc/articles/PMC2266126/.

37. Ibid.

38. Jno. H. Pope, "Annual Report by Sanitary Inspector," Corpus Christi, Tex., August 2, 1879, in *Annual Report of the National Board of Health, 1879–1885* (Washington, DC: US Government Printing Office, 1881), 24.

39. Ibid.

40. Ibid.

41. 1880 Census, June 1880, Corpus Christi, Nueces County, GGII 006797. In that same census, Sarah's parents' family ranch, Los Laureles, was recorded as having 168 people in residence. Their son Tom was twenty-six and listed as a ranchero, and son John was twenty-three and listed as a sheep raiser. The inhabitants of the ranch included vaqueros, housekeepers, overseers, and five servants. The ranch contained 172,000 fenced acres, and more than twenty families of Mexican origin, with forty children, lived there. Petra and Mifflin employed W. A. Walls, a white male twenty-eight years old and a widower from Canada, to educate the ranch children. 1800 Census, University of Texas–Pan American, Edinburg, Texas, Cameron Co. Hidalgo Co., Starr Co., Webb Co., Zapata Co., T0009, 1294, 1311, 1327, 1332, 1334, GGII 006798.

42. *Semi-Weekly Ledger* (Corpus Christi, Tex.), July 25, 1880.

43. *Semi-Weekly Ledger*, September 22, 1880.

44. *Semi-Weekly Ledger*, November 21, 1880.

45. *Semi-Weekly Ledger*, December 5, 1880.

46. *Semi-Weekly Ledger*, January 2, 1881, GGII 020002.

47. Bruce Cheeseman, *Perfectly Exhausted with Pleasure: The 1881 King-Kenedy Excursion Train to Laredo* (Austin: Book Club Texas, 1992), 27. See also Bill Walraven, *Corpus Christi: The History of a Texas Seaport*, sponsored by Nueces County Historical Society and Corpus Christi Chamber of Commerce (Woodland Hills, Calif.: Windsor Publications, 1982), 62.

48. *Semi-Weekly Ledger*, April 6, 1881.

49. Ibid. Dr. DeRyee had established his store in 1865 and treated many citizens during the yellow fever epidemic in 1867. He had lost his only child in the epidemic. He was an outstanding chemist and had a lifelong interest in mineralogy. He filled his store with natural curiosities and was widely regarded as one of the most learned persons in the city. Frank Wagner, "DeRyee, William," *Handbook of Texas Online*, accessed March 29, 2017, http://www.tshaonline.org/handbook/online/articles/fde44.

50. Old Bayview Cemetery records, researched by Rev. Michael A. Howell with transcription by Geraldine D. McGloin, of the Nueces County Historical Commission, Corpus Christi Public Library, Corpus Christi, Tex.; *Semi-Weekly Ledger*, April 20, 1881.

51. Old Bayview Cemetery records, Corpus Christi Public Library.

52. Cheeseman, *Perfectly Exhausted with Pleasure*, 27.

53. Ibid.

54. Quoted in ibid.

55. Cheeseman, *Perfectly Exhausted with Pleasure*, 27.

56. Information provided by descendant and family historian Barbara E. Chipman, B.A. Hons.

Chapter 10. Medical and Family Drama

1. Quoted in "The Yellow Fever Scourge: An Increase of the Disease at Brownsville Quarantine Precautions," *New York Times*, August 23, 1882, via ProQuest.

2. John B. Hamilton, Surgeon-General, U.S. Marine-Hospital, Commercial Relations, Treasury Department, Washington, DC, Directive to All Marine Surgeons, August 11, 1882, from Minutes of the Thirty-Second Session of the Texas Medical Association, 1900, in Minutes, *Texas State Journal of Medicine*, p. 105, Archives of the Texas Medical Association, Knowledge Center, Austin, Tex.

3. "Yellow Fever: A Circular from Surgeon-General Hamilton—The Disease in the South," *New York Times*, August 12, 1882.

4. Ibid., August 13, 1882.

5. Arthur Spohn, "The Marine Hospital Service in Texas and Yellow Fever Epidemics," *Transactions of the Texas State Medical Association* (Austin, Tex.), 32 (1900): 105–7.

6. Ibid.

7. Ibid.

8. Ibid.

9. Ibid.

10. "A Public Service Defended," *New York Times*, October 2, 1882.

11. Ibid., October 3, 1882.

12. John McKiernan-González, *Fevered Measures: Public Health and Race at the Texas-Mexico Border, 1848–1942* (Durham: Duke University Press, 2012), 42–46.

13. Ibid., 40.

14. *Galveston Daily News*, July [n.d.] 1882.

15. Jane Clements Monday and Frances Brannen Vick, *Petra's Legacy: The South Texas Ranching Empire of Petra Vela and Mifflin Kenedy* (College Station: Texas A&M University Press, 2007), 280–81.

16. Ibid.

17. *Galveston Daily News*, July [n.d.] 1882.

18. Monday and Vick, *Petra's Legacy*, 178.

19. Mr. Mann, Mann and Mann, Attorneys at Law, Laredo, Tex., to Dr. H. J. Hamilton, August 18, 1945, provided by family descendant Randolph Slaughter, grandson of Dr. Henry J. Hamilton.

20. Mifflin Kenedy to Yturria, January 14, 1883, GGII 019634-019698.

21. *Daily Cosmopolitan* (Brownsville, Tex.), April 6, April 7, April 9, 1884, James C. Jernigan Library, Texas A&M at Kingsville.

22. Mifflin Kenedy to John Kenedy, September 4, 1884, GGII 0020092.

23. Mifflin Kenedy, telegram to John Kenedy, August 1, 1884, GGII 0020157.

24. *Corpus Christi Caller*, August 12, 1883, accessed at Corpus Christi Public Library.

25. *Corpus Christi Caller*, April 20, 1884.

26. *Corpus Christi Caller*, March 9, 1884.

27. *Corpus Christi Caller*, January 7, 1884.

28. *Times Democrat*, January 31, 1884, reprinted from *Brownsville Reporter*, February 9, 1884, accessed at Corpus Christi Public Library.

29. Father Francis Kelly Nemeck, email to Jane Clements Monday, December 18, 2005.

30. *Corpus Christi Caller*, March 18, 1883.

31. Mifflin Kenedy to Mr. Scott, October 6, [1884], GGII 0020202-3.

32. Mary Margaret McAllen Amberson, James A. McAllen, and Margaret H. McAllen, *I Would Rather Sleep in Texas: A History of the Lower Rio Grande Valley and the People of the Santa Anita Land Grant* (Austin: Texas State Historical Association, 2003), 341.

33. Ibid.

34. Mifflin Kenedy to Anita Vidal, September 7, 1884, GGII 008336-38.

35. Ibid.

36. Old Bayview Cemetery Records, Corpus Christi Public Library.

37. "Arthur Claud Hamilton," in *Border Biographies*, ed. Stanley Green, 2nd ed. (Laredo, Tex.: Border Studies, 1992), 56.

38. Information provided by descendant Paul Harris.

39. Ibid.

40. Petra Vela Kenedy, Corpus Christi, Texas, to Salomé Ballí McAllen, April 26, 1883, McAllen Family Archives via Ella Howland Archives, Laredo, Tex.

41. Tom Lea, *The King Ranch* (1957; Boston: Little, Brown, 1980), 355.

42. Monday and Vick, *Petra's Legacy*, 302.

43. Ibid.

44. Mifflin Kenedy, telegram to Rosa Putegnat, August 10, 1884, GGII 002017 and GGII 0020174. He then sent instructions to get the very best conveyance and to come via the San Pedro Gate to La Parra and then to Santa Gertrudis. Captain King was then to send her to Collins (now Alice, Texas) to catch the train.

45. Monday and Vick, *Petra's Legacy*, 331.

46. *Village Record* (Chester County, Pa.), provided by Barbara J. Ruiz, researcher for Chester County Historical Society Archives, West Chester, Pa.

47. Saint Patrick's Church Interment Book, Corpus Christi Cathedral Archives, Catholic Diocese of Corpus Christi, Tex.

Chapter 11. Tragedy and Triumph

1. Jane Clements Monday and Frances Brannen Vick, *Petra's Legacy: The South Texas Ranching Empire of Petra Vela and Mifflin Kenedy* (College Station: Texas A&M University Press, 2007), 342.

2. Ibid., 353–54.

3. Mifflin Kenedy to Jo Kenedy Thompson, March 1885, GGII 021087-02046.

4. Ibid.

5. *San Antonio Express*, March 2, 2015.

6. Ibid. See also Missionary Oblates of Mary Immaculate Archives #479-84-85, Lebh Shomea House of Prayer, Sarita, Tex.

7. Mifflin Kenedy to Robert Dalzell, March 1885, GGII 020087-020246.

8. Monday and Vick, *Petra's Legacy*, 347.

9. Capt. William Kelly Letterbook, GGII 007956.

10. Cynthia E. Orozco, "Kenedy, Petra Vela de Vidal," *Handbook of Texas Online*, accessed March 31, 2017, http://www.tshaonline.org/handbook/online/articles/fkerl.

11. Tom Lea, *The King Ranch* (1957; Boston: Little, Brown, 1980), 366.

12. Quoted in ibid.

13. Ibid., 368.

14. Capt. William Kelly Letterbook, GGII 007956.

15. Edward Sanchon, "Surgeries at Charity Hospital, New Orleans," *Gaillard's Medical Journal* 44 (1887): 197.

16. Monday and Vick, *Petra's Legacy*, 348.

17. Ibid., 348–49.

18. Robert J. Kleberg to his parents, July 24, 1881, Kleberg Correspondence, Special Collections and Archives, Mary and Jeff Bell Library, Texas A&M University–Corpus Christi. See also Monday and Vick, *Petra's Legacy*, 277.

19. Robert J. Kleberg to Miss Alice G. King at Santa Gertrudis, Collins, Nueces County, May 13, 1884, Kleberg Correspondence, TAMU-CC. See also Jane Clements Monday and Frances Brannen Vick, *Letters to Alice: Birth of the Kleberg-King Ranch Dynasty* (College Station: Texas A&M University Press, 2012), 41.

20. Robert J. Kleberg to Miss Alice G. King at Santa Gertrudis, Collins, Nueces County, July 6, 1884, Kleberg Correspondence, TAMU-CC. See also Monday and Vick, *Letters to Alice*, 53.

21. Monday and Vick, *Letters to Alice*, 53.

22. Ibid., 93.

23. Ibid., 122.

24. Ibid., 129.

25. Robert J. Kleberg to Mrs. Robert J. Kleberg, Collins, Nueces Co., July 27, 1887, Kleberg Correspondence, TAMU-CC. See also Monday and Vick, *Letters to Alice*, 132.

26. Robert J. Kleberg to Mrs. Robert J. Kleberg, August 24, 1885, Collins, Nueces Co., Kleberg Correspondence, TAMU-CC. See also Monday and Vick, *Letters to Alice*, 135.

27. Monday and Vick, *Letters to Alice*, 136.

28. Ibid., 350–51.

29. Ibid.

30. *Semi-Weekly Ledger* (Corpus Christi, Tex.), December 18, 1886, accessed at Corpus Christi Public Library.

31. Carmen Morell's Autograph Book, GGII 012693-97.

32. Ibid.

33. *Semi-Weekly Ledger*, March 7, 1886.

34. *Semi-Weekly Ledger*, June 13, 1886.

35. Ibid.

36. Ibid.

37. "Henry J. Hamilton," Old Bayview Cemetery, http//www.cclibraries.com/local history/oldbayview/hamiltonabioinfo.htm.

38. *Corpus Christi Caller* (Corpus Christi, Tex.), October 10, 1886.

39. Patricia M. Gunning, *To Texas with Love: A History of the Sisters of the Incarnate Word and Blessed Sacrament* (Austin: Von Boeckmann-Jones, 1971).

40. Arthur E. Spohn, "Country Practice in Texas," *Medical and Surgical Reporter* (Philadelphia, Pa.), August 20, 1887, 57–58, American Periodicals Series Online, p. 269.

41. Arthur E. Spohn, "Treatment of Rupture of the Perineum," *Medical and Surgical Reporter* (Philadelphia, Pa.) 58 (February 11, 1888): 171.

Chapter 12. A Race to Paris and the Pasteur Institute

1. Murphy Givens, "Our Willie Is Saved," audio clip, KEDT Radio, December 14, 2001, Corpus Christi Public Library Digital Archives, Corpus Christi, Tex.

2. Murphy Givens, "Martha Rabb, Cattle Queen of Texas," *Corpus Christi Caller-Times*, April 9, 2008, http://www.caller.com/news/2008/apr.09/martha-rabb-cattle-queen -of-texas/?print=1.

3. "Pasteur Saved Him," *Fort Worth Daily Gazette*, vol. 13, no. 280, May 18, 1888, 4, https://texashistory.unt.edu/ark:/67531/metapth89616/m1/4/.

4. Ibid.

5. "Pasteur's Patient," cable from Herald Station, No. 49 Avenue L'Opera, Paris via Havre, *New York Herald*, April 2, 1888.

6. Arthur E. Spohn, "Rabies and Anti-Rabic Inoculations," presentation at the Twenty-First Annual Session of the Texas Medical Association, April 23–26, 1889, Austin, Tex. See also *Transactions of the Texas State Medical Association* 21 (1889): 144–59.

7. "Pasteur's Patient," *New York Herald*, April 2, 1888. See also "The Mad Wolf's Victim," *Omaha Daily Bee*, April 2, 1888.

8. Spohn, "Rabies and Anti-Rabic Inoculations."

9. Barbara Chipman, B.A. Hons., family historian, email to author(s), September 3, 2015.

10. "Louis Pasteur," Chemical Heritage Foundation Library, Museum, and Center for Scholars, Philadelphia, https://www.chemheritage.org/historical-profile/louis-pasteur.

11. "Emile Roux—Pasteur, Rabies and Diphtheria," *Awesome Stories*, https://www .awesomestories.com/asset/view/Emile-Roux-Pasteur-Rabies-and-Diphtheria.

12. "Louis Pasteur," Chemical Heritage Foundation.

13. Spohn, "Rabies and Anti-Rabic Inoculations."

14. "Pasteur Saved Him," *Fort Worth Daily Gazette*, May 18, 1888.

15. Arthur E. Spohn, "Cures for Hydrophobia," *Texas Courier-Record of Medicine* (Texas Medical Publishing Co., Dallas, Tex.), May 1888, 354.

16. Recalled by Barbara Chipman, B.A. Hons., and Beth Dubeau, family historians, in emails to Jane Monday, August 9, 2013.

17. "Pasteur's Patient," *New York Herald*, April 2, 1888.

18. "City of Laredo," *A Twentieth Century History of Southwest Texas*, vol. 2, chap. 27, 780, Ancestry.com, http://interactive.ancestry.com/27907/dvm-LocHist(011946-00398-1/713?backurl=http"//trees…

Chapter 13. Medical Passions

1. David Oshinsky, *Bellevue: Three Centuries of Medicine and Mayhem at America's Most Storied Hospital* (New York: Doubleday, 2016), 152–54. See also "The Death of President Garfield, 1881," Eyewitness to History.com, http://www.eyewitnesstohistory .com/gar.htm.

2. Arthur E. Spohn, "Communications: Gunshot Wound of the Abdomen," *Medical and Surgical Reporter* 63 (November 15, 1890): 20. For the text of the article, see appendix 1.

3. Ibid.

4. Ibid.

5. Ibid.

6. A. E. Spohn, "Turpentine in Affections of the Throat and Lungs," *Medical and Surgical Reporter* 61 (October 19, 1898): 16. For the text of the article, see appendix 1.

7. Ibid.

8. A. E. Spohn, "Treatment of Carbuncle," *Medical and Surgical Reporter* 64 (February 7, 1891): 6. For the text of the article, see appendix 1.

9. Ibid.

10. Keith Guthrie, "Fulton, George Ware, Sr.," *Handbook of Texas Online*, accessed April 1, 2017, http://www.tshaonline.org/handbook/online/articles/ffu08.

11. Biographical research on Price Staples, Old Bayview Cemetery records, researched by Rev. Michael A. Howell with transcription by Geraldine D. McGloin of the Nueces County Historical Commission, Corpus Christi Public Library, Corpus Christi, Tex., http://www.cclibraries.com/localhistory/oldbayview.

12. Wolff & Marx, San Antonio, to Captain M. Kenedy, Corpus Christi, April 19, 1890, Kenedy Collection, James C. Jernigan Library, Texas A&M University–Kingsville (hereafter, TAMU-K).

13. Wolff & Marx, San Antonio, to Capt. M. Kenedy, Corpus Christi, May 1, 1890, Kenedy Collection, TAMU-K.

14. Robert Kleberg, Kings Ranch, Collins, Nueces Co. Tex., to Capt. M. Kenedy, Corpus Christi, May 6, 1890, Kenedy Collection, TAMU-K.

15. Arthur E. Spohn, Phil., Pa., to Capt. M. Kenedy, Corpus Christi (undated but ca. June 1), 1890, Kenedy Collection, TAMU-K.

16. Robert Dalzell, Brownsville, Tex., to Capt. M. Kenedy, Corpus Christi, May 25, 1890, Kenedy Collection, TAMU-K. Mifflin relied on Dalzell more and more as a business partner. He had brought Dalzell into the steamboat business during the Mexican War and later gave him a one-eighth interest in King, Kenedy & Co. after he became family by marrying Petra's daughter Luisa. Jane Clements Monday and Frances Brannen Vick, *Petra's Legacy: The South Texas Ranching Empire of Petra Vela and Mifflin Kenedy* (College Station: Texas A&M University Press, 2007), 145.

17. Robert Dalzell, Brownsville, Tex., to Capt. M. Kenedy, Corpus Christi, May 29, 1890, Kenedy Collection, TAMU-K.

18. Robert Dalzell, Brownsville, Tex., to Capt. M. Kenedy, Corpus Christi, June 4, 1890, Kenedy Collection, TAMU-K.

19. Arthur E. Spohn, Phil., Pa., to Capt. M. Kenedy, Corpus Christi, June 13, 1890, Kenedy Collection, TAMU-K.

20. Frank N. Thorpe, "The University of Pennsylvania," *Harper's New Moon Magazine*, no. 542 (July 1895).

21. George W. Corner, *Two Centuries of Medicine* (Philadelphia: J. B. Lippincott, 1965), 250–52.

22. Ibid.; "Schools and Hospitals Absorbed by Penn Medicine," University of Pennsylvania Archives and Records Center, http://www.archives.upenn.edu/histy/features/medical/merged.html#1.

23. Arthur E. Spohn, "Recent Cases of Coeliotomy," paper presented in Waco at joint session of the Austin District Medical Society and Central Texas Medical Association, published in *Daniel's Texas Medical Journal* (Austin, Tex.), (February 1893), 8. See appendix 1.

24. Spohn, "Recent Cases of Coeliotomy," 8.

25. Ibid.

26. John C. Waller, *Health and Wellness in 19th Century America* (Santa Barbara, Calif.: Greenwood, ABC-CLIO, 2014), 77.

27. Spohn, "Recent Cases of Coeliotomy." The modern term for caesarean hysterectomy is abdominal hysterectomy.

28. *Waco Evening News* (Waco, Tex.), January 4, 1894.

29. "Doctors Assemble—Proceeding of the Session," *Waco Evening News*, January 9, 1894; "Medicos Adjourned," *Waco Evening News*, January 10, 1894.

Chapter 14. Challenging Times

1. Van Wagner, Peter Spohn (1818–1906), Fonds F4486, Van Wagner–Hamilton Fond-CA0N0000 9F 4486, Archives of Ontario, Toronto, www.archives.gov.on.ca/en/index.aspx.

2. Dr. Henry (Harry) Hamilton to Gretchen Spohn (his first cousin), Laredo, Tex., August 24, 1942, provided by the family to the author(s).

3. Ibid.

4. Ibid.

5. Ibid.

6. *Galveston Daily News* (Galveston, Tex.), May 2, 1892, via Ancestry.com.

7. "Arthur Claud Hamilton," in *Border Biographies*, ed. Stanley Green, 2nd ed. (Laredo, Tex.: Border Studies, 1992), 56.

8. Virgil N. Lott and Mercurio Martinez, *The Kingdom of Zapata* (San Antonio: Naylor, 1953), 62.

9. Jane Clements Monday and Frances Brannen Vick, *Petra's Legacy: The South Texas Ranching Empire of Petra Vela and Mifflin Kenedy* (College Station: Texas A&M

University Press, 2007), 337–41. After Tom Kenedy married Yrene Yznaga, daughter of a wealthy Brownsville businessman, on July 29, 1885, Mifflin gave them three lots in Brownsville. Tom engaged Mifflin's contractor to build a six-thousand-square-foot home with twenty-six rooms. In July 1887, Yrene, who was pregnant, fell on the stairs in the house, and both she and the unborn child died. The next year Tom was running against Sheriff Santiago Brito for his job and dating Elvira Maria Esparza, the estranged wife of the sheriff's deputy, Jose Esparza. Sheriff Brito urged Jose to get rid of his competition, and on Tom's thirty-fifth birthday, as he and Elvira were returning from Matamoros, Jose ambushed the couple and killed Tom. Jose escaped into Mexico, and Mifflin sent Petra's two grandsons, Frank and George Putegnat, to catch him. They found him tied to a tree by Mexican officers, and when the Putegnat brothers refused to kill him the officers said they could take him to Texas. Jose escaped from them and later was said to be living in Texas. Sheriff Brito was assassinated four years later, perhaps in retribution for Tom's death. It was never proved who did it, but everyone thought it was Mifflin Kenedy's *pistolero*, Herculano Berber.

10. *Corpus Christi Caller* (Corpus Christi, Tex.), August 19, 1892.

11. *Corpus Christi Caller*, September 2, 1892.

12. *Corpus Christi Caller*, October 28, 1892. According to the newspaper report, "The crowd arrived about 8:30 at the Ritter's Pavilion that was brilliantly lighted. The sponsor and her maids of honor welcomed the military boys in uniform. The young couples danced over a glassy floor to dreamy waltzes. The young ladies were lovely, the young men gallant and the music sweet and the event ended at 1:30 in the morning."

13. *Corpus Christi Caller*, February [n.d.] 1891.

14. M. Kenedy, telegram to John G. Kenedy at La Parra, November 19, 1894, GGII 019917.

15. Arthur Spohn, telegram to John G. Kenedy at La Parra, November 17, 1894, GGII 019915.

16. "Dr. Spohn's Snake Medicine Sent to India," *Daily Herald* (Brownsville, Tex.), November 22, 1894, via Portal to Texas History.

17. Arthur E. Spohn, "Rabies and Anti-Rabic Inoculations," presentation at the Twenty-First Annual Session of the Texas Medical Association, April 23–26, 1889, Austin, Tex. See also *Transactions of the Texas State Medical Association* 21 (1889): 144–59. Dr. Henry Holmes Croft, born in London and educated in England and Germany, was offered the chair of chemistry and experimental philosophy at King's College in Toronto in 1842, when he was only twenty-two. He had a considerable reputation in the field of toxicology, was skilled in detecting the presence of poisons, and was consulted in homicide cases. In 1880, after several family members had died, he retired to Texas to live on his son's farm.

18. Dr. E. F. Brown, "Tincture of Iodine an Antidote to the Bite of Venomous Serpents," in *The Homeopathic Recorder* (Philadelphia and Lancaster: Boenake & Tafel, 1892), 270, via Google Books.

19. "Dr. Spohn's Snake Medicine Sent to India," *Daily Herald* (Brownsville, Tex.), November 22, 1894.

20. *San Antonio Express* (San Antonio, Tex.), March 20, 1895, via Portal to Texas

History. Requiem mass booklet for Mifflin stated he died March 14, 1895 at 7:45 a.m. GGII 013223.

21. *Daily Herald* (Brownsville, Tex.), March 18, 1895, via Portal to Texas History.

22. *San Antonio Express*, March 20, 1895, via Portal to Texas History.

23. John G. Kenedy to Mr. A. W. Houston, San Antonio, Tex., April 17, 1895, GGII 012031.

24. John G. Kenedy to Mrs. C. B. Kenedy, Laredo, Tex., May 22, 1895, GGII 012054.

25. John G. Kenedy to Houston Bros., San Antonio, Tex., May 22, 1895, GGII 102046.

26. Partition made by all the heirs of M. Kenedy, deceased, San Antonio, Tex., June 1895, GGII 010175–GGDII 010214.

27. Paper on drug usage during the nineteenth century provided by family historian Barbara E. Chipman, B.A. Hons.

28. Dr. Stephen Lett, Homewood Retreat, Guelph, Ont., about Carmen Kenedy, to John G. Kenedy Esq., Corpus Christi, Tex., October 9, 1895, GGII 016143-44.

29. Dr. Herbert Spohn Griffin biography from Barbara Chipman, B.A. Hons., family historian.

30. Cheryl L. Krasnick, "The Aristocratic Vice: The Medical Treatment of Drug Addiction at the Homewood Retreat, 1883–1900," *Ontario History: The Quarterly Journal of the Ontario Historical Society*, December 1, 1983, accessed at Whitehern. Museum Archives, http//www.whitehern.ca/result.php?doc-id=Bos%2015-007.

31. Ibid.

32. Gerald Imber, *Genius on the Edge: The Bizarre Double Life of Dr. William Stewart Halsted* (New York: Kaplan Publishing, 2011), 47.

33. Ibid., 91.

34. Ibid., 281.

35. Krasnick, "Aristocratic Vice."

36. John G. Kenedy to Dr. A. E. Spohn, at Homewood Retreat in Guelph, Ont., June 19, 1895, GGII 012074.

37. John G. Kenedy to Sarah (Sally) at Homewood Retreat, Guelph, Ont., June 20, 1895, GGII 012082-90.

38. Ibid.

39. Dr. Stephen Lett, Medical Superintendent, Homewood, to John G. Kenedy Esq., Corpus Christi, Tex., October 9, 1895, GGII 016143-44.

40. Ibid.

41. Biography provided by Barbara Chipman, B.A., Hons., family historian.

42. A. E. Spohn, Rossin House, Toronto, Ont., to John Kenedy, September 28, 1895, GGII 016216.

43. John G. Kenedy to Sarah [Spohn], September 18, 1895, GGII 012174.

44. Sarah J. Spohn, New York, to John Kenedy, Corpus Christi, Tex., October 12, 1895, GGII 016138-40.

45. A. E. Spohn, New York City, to John Kenedy, Corpus Christi, Tex., October 9, 1895, GGII 016141.

46. Deed of Transfer from Carmen Morell Kenedy to her sister Sarah Kenedy, filed at the County of Nueces, February 13, 1896, GGII 012657.

47. Carmen Morell Kenedy, Requiem program for Capt. Mifflin Kenedy, "A Sweet Memory of Capt. M. Kenedy," GGII 013224.

48. Carmen Morell to John Kenedy, June 3, 1897, GGII 019885.

49. Arthur E. Spohn, Saltillo, Mexico, to John Kenedy, July 9, 1897, GGII 018720.

50. Sarah J. Spohn, Colorado Springs, Colo., to John and Stella Kenedy, October 27, 1897, GGII 018826.

Chapter 15. A New Century

1. Arthur Spohn, "Multicystic Ovarian Tumor Weighing 328 Pounds," read before the Section on Gynecology, State Medical Association of Texas, Houston, April 29, 1905, and published in *Transactions of the Texas State Medical Association* (Austin, Tex.), February 1906, 216.

2. Ibid.

3. A. E. Spohn, "Fibroid Tumors of the Uterus," *Transactions of the Texas State Medical Association* 33 (1901): 334–40.

4. Ibid.

5. Ibid. The excerpts that follow are also from Spohn's "Fibroid Tumors" article.

6. Arthur Spohn, "Skin Grafting," *Transactions of the Texas State Medical Association* 33 (1901): 245–46.

7. Arthur Spohn, "Typhoid Perforation of the Bowel with Obstruction—A Plea for Exploratory Abdominal Incisions," paper read at the Thirty-Eighth Annual Meeting of the State Medical Association of Texas, Fort Worth, Tex., April 24–26, 1906.

8. Ibid.

9. "Dr. Arthur Spohn and Spohn Hospital," in *The Corpus Christi Chronicles* (Corpus Christi: Nueces County Historical Society and Corpus Christi Chamber of Commerce, 1992), 70.

10. Ibid.

11. Arthur Spohn, Personal Record of Members, submitted to Association of Military Surgeons of the United States, 1905, Kenedy Archives.

12. "Transactions of the Sixth International Congress on Tuberculosis," Washington, DC, September 25–October 5, 1908, https://archive.org/stream/transactionsofsi05inte/transactionsofsi05inte_djvu.txt.

13. Terence Chorba, "A Master Medalist, a President, Tuberculosis, and a Congress: Contributions More Lasting than Bronze," *Emerging Infectious Diseases* 21, no. 3 (2015): 553–54, https://www.ncbi.nlm.nih.gov/pmc/articles/PMC4344294/.

14. "Transactions of the Sixth International Congress on Tuberculosis," Washington, DC, September 25–October 5, 1908.

15. G. R. Tabor, "1903 Epidemic of Yellow Fever in Texas and the Lesson to Be Learned from It," paper presented to the Medical Department of the University of Texas, Galveston, Tex., January 6, 1905, and published in *Bulletin of the University of Texas*, Medical Series no. 3, June 1905.

16. Ibid.

17. "Quarantine Question," *Brownsville Daily Herald*, May 11, 1904, via Portal to Texas History.

18. *Brownsville Daily Herald*, May 24, 1904, via Portal to Texas History.

19. *Dominion Medical Monthly & Ontario Medical Journal*, 28–29 (1907), in Roberts Research Library, University of Toronto, Ont., Canada; information provided by Barbara Chipman, B.A. Hons., family historian.

20. "St. Louis, Brownsville and Mexico Railway," *Brownsville Daily Herald*, June 10, 1903, via Portal to Texas History.

21. Jane Clements Monday and Frances Brannen Vick, *Letters to Alice: Birth of the Kleberg-King Ranch Dynasty* (College Station: Texas A&M University Press, 2012), 143.

22. Ibid.

23. *Brownsville Daily Herald*, June 10, 1903.

24. *Corpus Christi Caller* (Corpus Christi, Tex.), March 2, 1905.

25. Murphy Givens, "The Fast and the Furious . . . in the Early 1900's," *Corpus Christi Caller-Times*, February 16, 2001.

26. Ibid.

Chapter 16. A Hospital at Last

1. Sister Mary Xavier, IWBS, "Saddlebag Priest of the Nueces," January 6, 1948, manuscript in file "Corpus Christi, Dec. 1873–1875," Kasner Reference Library, Catholic Archives of Texas, Austin.

2. Annie Moore Schwien, "When Corpus Christi Was Young: Recollections of Annie Moore Schwien," interviews from November 8, 1938, to May 15, 1941, transcribed by Rosa Gonzales, Corpus Christi Public Library, Corpus Christi, Tex., accessed at Old Bayview Cemetery, http://www.cclibraries.com/localhistory/oldbayview/index.php/component/content/article/63-misc/638-annie-moore-schwien.

3. "Spohn Health System: A Story of Sacrifice and Success," 159, manuscript in Kasner Reference Library, Catholic Archives of Texas, Austin.

4. Sister Margaret Patrice Slattery, CCVI, *Promises to Keep: A History of the Sisters of Charity of the Incarnate Word*, vol. 1, *1869–1994* (San Antonio, 1995).

5. Ibid.

6. Sister Mary Helena Finck, "The Congregation of the Sisters of Charity of the Incarnate Word of San Antonio, Texas" (MA diss., Catholic Sisters College of the Catholic University of America, 1925), 144.

7. Quoted in Bruce Cheeseman, "The King–Spohn Family Friendship: A Productive Partnership Embodying Heritage, Hope & Leadership," speech presented to the Spohn Health System executives at a corporate retreat, Santa Fe, N.Mex., copy provided to Jane Monday, March 2000.

8. Sister Gabriel to Mrs. R. J. Kleberg, July 8, 1903, Sisters of Charity of the Incarnate Word Archives, San Antonio.

9. Mrs. R. J. Kleberg to Bishop Verdaguer, July 23, 1903, Sisters of Charity of the Incarnate Word Archives. See also Mary Jo O'Rear, *Storm over the Bay: The People of*

Corpus Christi and Their Port (College Station: Texas A&M University Press, 2009), 85.

10. Slattery, *Promises to Keep*.

11. Mrs. R. J. Kleberg to Sister Gabriel, August 28, 1903, courtesy Sisters of Charity of the Incarnate Word Archives.

12. Mrs. R. J. Kleberg to Sister Gabriel, January 7, 1904, courtesy Sisters of Charity of the Incarnate Word Archives.

13. Mary H. Ogilvie, "Verdaguer, Peter," *Handbook of Texas Online*, accessed April 13, 2017, http://www.tshaonline.org/handbook/online/articles/fve07.

14. Slattery, *Promises to Keep*.

15. Ibid.

16. Bishop Verdaguer to Mother Madeleine Chollet, October 19, 1904, courtesy of the Sisters of Charity of the Incarnate Word Archives.

17. Mrs. R. J. Kleberg to Mother Madeleine Chollet, May 31, 1905, courtesy of the Sisters of Charity of the Incarnate Word Archives.

18. Mrs. R. J. Kleberg to Mother Madeleine Chollet, July 9, 1905, courtesy of the Sisters of Charity of the Incarnate Word Archives.

19. Slattery, *Promises to Keep*; "Spohn Health System: A Story of Sacrifice and Success," 159.

20. Sisters Biographical Report, provided by Angelique Lane, director of archives/records management, Sisters of Charity of the Incarnate Word, San Antonio.

21. Ibid.

22. "A List of Rules for Nurses . . . from 1887," *Communicator*, St. John's Hospital, Malta, 1969, reprinted in *Scrubs*, last updated October 6, 2016, http://scrubsmag.com/a-list-of-rules-for-nurses-from-1887.

23. "History of Spohn Hospital," quoted from "Dr. Arthur Spohn, Dedication of Spohn Sanitarium," July 26, 1905, Sisters of Charity of the Incarnate Word Archives, San Antonio.

24. Ibid.

25. Slattery, *Promises to Keep*.

26. Lena Henrichson, *Pioneers on the Nueces* (San Antonio: Naylor, 1963), 99.

Chapter 17. City of the Bluff and Seas

1. *Corpus Christi Caller* (Corpus Christi, Tex.), May 17, 1919.

2. "Don Bonifacio Guinea," *Brownsville Daily Herald* (Brownsville, Tex.), March 15, 1906, 4, via Portal to Texas History.

3. Santa Petronila Ranch was the first Spanish settlement in Nueces County and was established by Capt. Blas María de la Garza Falcón in 1762. Clotilde P. García, "Santa Petronila Ranch," *Handbook of Texas Online*, accessed April 13, 2017, http://www.tshaonline.org/handbook/online/articles/aps08.

4. Ernest Petzel obituary, Record of Interments, Old Bayview Cemetery Association, Corpus Christi, http://www.cclibraries.com/localhistory/oldbayview/index.php/component/content/article/61-individual/595-ernest-petzel.

5. The Petzel family had a colorful history in the area. Ernest's great aunt, Josephine

Hill, was married to his father's brother, William. She was an avid Confederate. She helped her brother mold bullets during the Union siege. As they made the hard round balls they would say over each one, "Get a Yankee, get a Yankee." When Union troops blockaded that area, some soldiers gave Josephine and her brother some US banknotes. The siblings were so loyal to the Confederacy that they burned the notes. They said they would use Confederate money. Petzel Family Tree: Descendants of John Ernest Petzel, http://www.Yourdeservelt.com/petzel.htm.

6. Robert Driscoll had played a major role in developing Nueces County and the surrounding counties. He developed the Rabb Pasture into farmland, founded the towns of Bishop and Robstown, and also developed the town of Driscoll, which he named for the family. At the peak of his holdings he owned 125,000 acres in Duval, Jim Wells, and Nueces Counties. He was president of many corporations in Corpus Christi and San Antonio and was an incorporator of the St. Louis, Brownsville and Mexico Railway. His sister, Clara Driscoll, was credited with helping to save the Alamo and was a philanthropist in her own right. In 1953 she helped fund the Driscoll Foundation Children's Hospital in South Texas. Frank Wagner, "Driscoll, Robert, Jr.," *Handbook of Texas Online*, accessed July 10, 2017, http://www.tshaonline.org/handbook/online/articles/fdr05; Dorothy D. DeMoss, "Driscoll, Clara," *Handbook of Texas Online*, accessed July 10, 2017, http://www.tshaonline.org/handbook/online/articles/fdr04.

7. "Col. Robert Driscoll III," *Brownsville Daily Herald*, October 28, 1907, 4, via Portal to Texas History.

8. "W. W. Woolridge," *Brownsville Daily Herald*, September 10, 1908, 2, via Portal to Texas History.

9. Ibid.

10. *Corpus Christi Caller*, April 17, 1908.

11. "Tetanus: Diseases and Conditions," Mayo Clinic, http://www.mayoclinic.org/diseases-conditions/tetanus/basics/definition/con-20021956.

12. *Corpus Christi Caller*, April 17, 1908, via Portal to Texas History.

13. Mrs. George Plunkett Red, *The Medicine Man in Texas* (Houston: Standard Printing and Lithographing, 1930), 299, via http://digitalcommons.library.tmc.edu/ebooks/6/.

14. "Medicos Adjourned," *Waco Evening News*, January 10, 1894, via Chronicling America, Library of Congress.

15. *Corpus Christi Caller: Centennial Journey, Part I* (Corpus Christi: Caller-Times Publishing, 1983), 109.

16. "When Doctors Meet in Corpus," *Corpus Christi Caller*, January 24, 1908.

17. Ibid.

18. Ibid.

19. "Work on the Bluff," *Corpus Christi Caller*, April 24, 1908.

20. "The Doctors' Ladies," *Corpus Christi Caller*, April 17, 1908.

21. "Mayor Reid Takes Lead," *Corpus Christi Caller*, May 6, 1908. In fact, this project was the forerunner of the 1914 bond issue to complete the effort. Information provided by Anita Eisenhauer, Corpus Christi historian.

22. *Weekly Corpus Christi Caller*, May 8, 1908.

23. *Texas State Journal of Medicine* 4 (May 1908–April 1909): 46.

24. Ibid., 35; *Corpus Christi Caller,* May 15, 1908.

25. *Texas State Journal of Medicine* 4 (May 1908–April 1909): 35. See also appendix 2 for the poem Spohn composed for the event.

26. *Texas State Journal of Medicine* 4 (May 1908–April 1909): 35.

27. Ibid.

28. Ibid.

29. *Texas State Journal of Medicine* 4, no. 2 (June 1908): 26.

30. Ibid., 46.

Chapter 18. Dr. Arthur Edward Spohn's Legacy

1. *Medical Record and Annals* (Houston, Tex.), 60, no. 1 (January 1967): cover.

2. "Dr. A. E. Spohn after Brief Illness Died at Home Last Night," *Corpus Christi Daily Herald,* May 7, 1913.

3. "Dr. Spohn Paralyzed," *Laredo Times,* November 13, 1910, http://interactive.ances try.com/52471/News-TE-LA-TL1910-11-13007/62398200.

4. Henry Redmond was the small son of a Mr. Redmond in Carrizo, Texas, whom Spohn had met in 1869 and who later became Spohn's great friend and fellow practicing physician and witness to his will. Zara L. Moses lived with the Doddridge family in Corpus Christi and was one of Sarah's closest friends.

5. Information provided to Jane Monday by the Kenedy Archives.

6. *Brownsville Herald Times,* May 5, 1913.

7. Mrs. George Plunkett Red, *The Medicine Man in Texas* (Houston: Standard Printing & Lithographing, 1930), 299.

8. Corpus Christi Cathedral Sacramental Records, vol. 6, p. 116, #776, Catholic Diocese of Corpus Christi. Information provided by Geraldine McGloin to Jane Monday.

9. "To Conduct Funeral: Dr. A. E. Spohn This Morning O'Clock," *Corpus Christi Caller and Daily Herald,* May 2, 1913.

10. A. E. Spohn obituary in *Texas State Journal of Medicine* 9 (July 1913): 120, via https://books.google.com/books?id=SqJEAAAAYAAJ.

11. Quoted in ibid.

12. *Brownsville Herald Times,* May 6, 1913.

13. "Dr. A. E. Spohn," *Corpus Christi Caller and Daily Herald,* May 7, 1913.

14. Michele Mora-Trevino, executive director for marketing and community relations with CHRISTUS Spohn, email to Frances Vick, February 15, 2017.

15. Ibid. CHRISTUS Health is headquartered in Dallas and is among the ten largest Catholic health systems in the United States.

16. Mora-Trevino, email to Vick, February 15, 2017.

17. *Medical Record and Annals* (Houston, Tex.), 60, no. 1 (January 1967): cover.

Epilogue

1. *Laredo Times,* July 11, 1909, http://newspaperarchive.com/Laredo-times/1909-07-11/ page-8?tag=spohn=henry&rtserp=Tags/spohn,-henry.

2. "Angus P. Spohn" record in *Canada, City and Area Directories, 1819–1906* (online database), via Ancestry.com.

3. Virgil N. Lott and Mercurio Martinez, *The Kingdom of Zapata* (San Antonio: Naylor, 1953), 62–77.

4. Information on Alexander Hamilton and Henry J. Hamilton from Old Bayview Cemetery Records, Corpus Christi Public Libraries, Corpus Christi, Tex., http://www .cclibraries.com/localhistory/oldbayview/index.php/component/content/article/61-indi vidual/382-alexander-hamilton-.

5. Francis White Johnson, *A History of Texas and Texans* (Chicago: American Historical Society, 1914), 2:56.

6. Cristobal Benavides, descended from the founders of Laredo, was captain of a company in his brother's Benavides Regiment during the Civil War. In 1864, he defended Laredo against Union forces intent on destroying five thousand bales of cotton, and he later served under Col. John S. Ford in the Confederate expedition to drive Union forces from the lower Rio Grande valley. He and his brothers were among the last to surrender. He married Lamar Bee, daughter of Confederate general Hamilton P. Bee, and had six daughters and four sons. He had a large sheep and cattle ranching operation in addition to his mercantile business and by 1890 was one of the wealthiest men in Webb County. Jose Francisco Segovia, "Benavides, Cristobal," *Handbook of Texas Online*, accessed April 11, 2017, http://www.tshaonline.org/handbook/online/ articles/fbelr.

7. Information provided by Barbara Chipman, B.A. Hons., family historian.

8. Douglas and Maude had barely gotten settled in their home when, on September 14, 1919, a hurricane hit Corpus Christi with winds of 110 mph and sixteen-foot storm surges. Their son, Douglas Spohn, had a home on North Beach, and Douglas was ill. As the hurricane bore down on the city, Maude Spohn managed to move her sick husband and small daughter and baby to the Nueces Hotel. The wind was so fierce that no one could stand up, so men formed a human chain from the hotel door to cars so as to pull people to safety in the lobby. When the Spohns made it inside, the water was ankle deep; by midnight the lobby looked like a swimming pool. There were no lights, there was no food, and worst of all there was no fresh water, as the town was surrounded by salt water. Kay Bynum, "Dr. and Mrs. Douglas Spohn . . . Hurricane Lore," *Corpus Christi Caller Times*, March 22, 1954, via Ancestry.com.

On North Beach, Spohn Sanitarium, with twelve patients, fourteen sisters, the chaplain, eight employees and their relatives, and two families that had taken shelter, was being lashed by the wind and waves. The sisters moved most of the patients to the south wing because it was getting less wind. By 2:00 a.m. Sunday morning the storm was so strong that the surge of seawater had crossed the bay and flooded the land, making escape to the bluff impossible. Some of the sisters remained on duty with the patients and others went to the chapel with Monsignor Jaillet to say the rosary and prayers for the dying, and later he heard confessions. Shortly after four o'clock the north wing split open and the roof fell in. Sister Thais, Mr. Plum, who was paralyzed, and Mr. Hernandez, an employee of the Corpus Christi powerhouse, were swept away. Sister Aloysius was pinned under debris, and they had to cut part of her habit away to free her. Sister Thais's body was found five days later near Portland, five miles away. She was identified by her religious habit. "Spohn Health System: A Story of Sacrifice and Success," Kasner Reference Library, Catholic Archives of Texas, Austin. The storm sank more than ten major vessels and killed hundreds of people. It was one of the deadliest hurricanes in the twentieth century. Other information from Beth Dubeau, family descendant and historian, and from "Angus P. Spohn" record in *Canada, City and Area Directories, 1819–1906* (online database), Ancestry.com.

9. Jesse O. Wheeler, editor, *Brownsville Daily Herald*, April 11, 1918. See also Jane Clements Monday and Frances Brannen Vick, *Petra's Legacy: The South Texas Ranching Empire of Petra Vela and Mifflin Kenedy* (College Station: Texas A&M University Press, 2007), 351.

10. "Mrs. S. Spohn Passes Away," *Brownsville Herald*, May 17, 1918, http://newspaper archive.com/Brownsville-herald/1918-05+dr+Arthur=spohn&rtserp=tags/dr-arthur -spohn.

11. Contract between Otto Zirkel of San Antonio, Tex., and Sarah Kenedy, January 7, 1914, for a monument, Kenedy Archives.

12. Details on the estate of Mrs. Sarah J. Spohn, April 24, 1920, provided by the Kenedy Archives.

13. Monday and Vick, *Petra's Legacy*, 351.

14. Father Francis Kelly Nemeck, interview by Jane Monday, Lebh Shomea House of Prayer, Sarita, Tex., January 15, 2006.

15. Ibid.

16. Monday and Vick, *Petra's Legacy*, 352.

17. Ibid.

18. Ibid.

19. Information provided to Jane Monday by the Kenedy Archives.

20. Ibid. Lebh Shomea is a Hebrew phrase meaning "a listening heart."

21. Elena Kenedy death record, Mooseroots, accessed February 12, 2017, http:// death-records.mooseroots.com/d/n/Elena-Kenedy.

22. Monday and Vick, *Petra's Legacy*, 353, 356.

23. Arthur Spohn's will, November 21, 1911, Kenedy Archives.

24. Gary Cartwright, "Sarita's Secret," *Texas Monthly*, September 2004, http://www .texasmonthly.com/articles/saritas-secret/.

Bibliography

Unpublished Sources

Archival Collections

Archives of Ontario. Toronto, Ont., Canada.
> Fonds, F4486–Van Wagner–Hamilton Fond
> Fonds, 9F 4486–Van Wagner, Peter Spohn

Blackland Museum Archives. Taft, Tex.

Briscoe Center for American History, University of Texas at Austin.
> Kingsbury Papers. 1858–72. Vol. I-2R72.

Chester County Historical Society Archives. West Chester, Pa.

Congregation of the Sisters of Charity of the Incarnate Word Archives. San Antonio, Tex.

Corpus Christi Museum. Corpus Christi, Tex.
> King, Kenedy Co. Correspondence (unbound), 1873. Transcribed by Lillian Embree.
> William Kelly to Captain Kenedy, September 18, 1873.
> William Kelly to Mifflin Kenedy, October 8, 1873.
> William Kelly to Joseph Cooper, October 13, 1873.
> William Kelly to [Reuben] Holbein, November 19, 1873.

Fieldcote Museum Archives. Ancaster, Ont., Canada.

Getchow, GEORGE [GG]. Documents. Copied from the vault at the Big House at La Parra Ranch, given to the King Ranch Archives, and produced in Litigation, Cause No. C-291-93-D, Manuel de Llano, Blanca A. de LL. de Aguilar, Martha Dell de Olivera, Carmen de Llano, Fernando de Llano and Josephina de Llano v. The John G. and Marie Stella Kenedy Memorial Foundation, John G. Kenedy Jr. Charitable Trust, Exxon Corporation, Exxon Company U.S.A., Exxon Exploration Co. and Mobil Oil Company, in the District Court, Hidalgo County, Tex., 206th Judicial District.
> Box #2. GGII 000314–GGII 002044
> Box #3. GGII 002045–GGII 003479
> Box #5. GGII 006447–GGII 007834
> Box #6. GGII 007836–GGII 008854

Box #7. GGII 008855–GGII 010169
Box #8. GGII 010170, GGII 010963–GGII 011762
Box #9. GGII 011763–GGII 013268
Box #10. GGII 013269–GGII 014763
Box #11. GGII 014764–GGII 016131
Box #12. GGII 016132–GGII 018489
Box #13. GGII 018490–GGII 020572
Box #14. GGII 020573–GGII 022395
Box #22. LBOOK 1 Press Book [1882–85]
    LBOOK 2 Press Book [1885–87]
    LBOOK 3 Press Book [1887–88]
    LBOOK 4 Press Book [1888–90]
    LBOOK 5 Press Book [March–December 1890]
    LBOOK 6 Press Book [1890–91]
    LBOOK 8 Press Book [1891–93]
    LBOOK 9 Press Book [January–September 1894]
    LBOOK 10 Press Book [1894–95]
Kasner Reference Library, Catholic Archives of Texas. Austin, Tex.
    "Spohn Health System: A Story of Sacrifice and Success." Manuscript.
    Xavier, Sister Mary. "Saddlebag Priest of the Nueces." January 6, 1948. Manuscript in file "Corpus Christi, Dec. 1873–1875."
Kenedy Ranch Archives. Sarita, Tex.
    Deed conveyance from Dr. Henry Spohn to Dr. A. E. Spohn, April 30, 1876.
    Spohn, Arthur E. "Complete Report on Malta," written on February 18, 1899, on board Hamburg America Line vessel and sent to U.S. State Department by telegram from Hamburg.
    Spohn, Angus. Letter to Dr. Alexander Hamilton, February 14, 1877.
    ———. Letter to Dr. Alexander Hamilton, October 19, 1877.
    Spohn, Henry. Letter to Dr. Alexander Hamilton, December 5, 1877.
    ———. Letter to Alexander Hamilton, January 16, 1878.
    ———. Letter to Dr. Alexander Hamilton, August 28, 1878.
King Ranch Archives. Kingsville, Tex.
    Consulate of the United States of America, letter of introduction for Dr. Spohn and Dr. Padgett, April 8, 1899.
McAllen Family Archives [from Ella Howland Archives]. Laredo, Tex.
    Petra Vela Kenedy, letter to Salomé Ballí McAllen, April 26, 1883.
McGill University Archives. Montreal, Que., Canada.
Mier Archives. Mier, Mexico. Research in court records by Homero S. and Leticia M. Vera.
Missionary Oblates of Mary Immaculate Archives, Lebh Shomea House of Prayer. Sarita, Tex.
National Archives and Records Administration, General Services Administration. Washington, DC.

Court-martial records for Hamilton C. Peterson (PP-954): RG 153, Entry 15A, Court-Martial Case files, 1809–94, 7E3m 14/28/1, Box 2630, Item REP0006C.

Dispatches from United States Consuls in Mier, Mexico, 1870–78. National Archives Microfilm Publications Microcopy no. 297.

Charles Mayer, Commercial Agent for Mier, Mexico, to William Hunter, Washington, DC, nominating Dr. A. E. Spohn as Vice-Commercial Agent, March 5, 1872.

Charles Mayer, Commercial Agent for Mier, Mexico, to William Hunter, Washington, DC, including Dr. A. E. Spohn's oath of allegiance, March 31, 1872.

Charles Mayer, Commercial Agent, to William Hunter, Washington, DC, May 31, 1872.

Charles Mayer, Commercial Agent, to William Hunter, Washington, DC, February 9, 1873.

Thomas Gilgan, US Commercial Agent, Nuevo Laredo, dispatch of April 1872.

Yearly report of collected fees for January 1–December 31, 1872, including fees collected by Agent Arthur E. Spohn.

National Library of Medicine, History of Medicine Division. Bethesda, Md.

Association of Military Surgeons of the United States: Personal Record of Members—1905. Surgeon Arthur Edward Spohn. Scudder-Stark Collection, Container MSC 142, Box 6, Association of Military Surgeons.

"Medicine & Public Health in Galveston, Texas: Diseases and Disasters in the Oleander City, 1861–1900."

Roberts Research Library, University of Toronto, Ont., Canada.

Dominion Medical Monthly and Ontario Medical Journal. George Eliot, MD, Managing Editor. Vols. 28, 29.

Simcoe County Archives. 1871 Simco[e] County Census. Unit A. Minesing, Ont., Canada.

Sisters of Charity of the Incarnate Word Archives, San Antonio, Tex.

Sr. Gabriel to Mrs. R. J. Kleberg, July 8, 1903.

Mrs. R. J. Kleberg to Bishop Verdaguer, July 23, 1903.

Bishop Verdaguer to Mother Madeleine Chollett, September 13, 1903.

Mrs. R. J. Kleberg to Sr. Gabriel, November 16, 1903.

Mrs. R. J. Kleberg to Sr. Gabriel, January 7, 1904.

Bishop Verdaguer to Mother Madeleine Chollet, January 30, 1904.

Bishop Verdaguer to Mother Madeleine Chollet, February 8, 1904.

Bishop Verdaguer to Mother Madeleine Chollet, October 19, 1904.

Mrs. R. J. Kleberg to Mother Madeleine Chollet, May 31, 1905.

Mrs. R. J. Kleberg to Mother Madeleine Chollett, July 9, 1905.

Sisters Biographical Report.

Spohn, Dr. Arthur. "History of Spohn Hospital." In "Dedication of Spohn Sanitarium," July 26, 1905.

South Texas Archives, James C. Jernigan Library, Texas A&M University–Kingsville. Kingsville, Tex.
    Kenedy Collection.
        Robert Dalzell to Capt. M. Kenedy, May 25, May 29, June 4, 1890.
        Robert J. Kleberg to Capt. M. Kenedy, May 6, 1890.
        Arthur E. Spohn to Capt. M. Kenedy, June [1,] 1890.
        Arthur E. Spohn to Capt. M. Kenedy, June 13, 1890.
        Arthur E. Spohn, telegram to John G. Kenedy, November 17, 1894.
        Wolff & Marx to Captain M. Kenedy, April 19, 1890.
        Wolff & Marx to Captain M. Kenedy, May 1, 1890.
Special Collections and Archives, Mary and Jeff Bell Library, Texas A&M University– Corpus Christi.
    Kleberg Correspondence.
        Robert J. Kleberg to his parents, July 24, 1881.
        Robert J. Kleberg to Miss Alice G. King, May 13, 1884.
        Robert J. Kleberg to Miss Alice G. King, July 6, 1884.
        Robert J. Kleberg to Mrs. Robert J. Kleberg, August 24, 1885.
        Robert J. Kleberg to Mrs. Robert J. Kleberg, July 27, 1887.
    Meuly-Daimwood Family Papers. Collection 108.
        Census 1880. Nueces County, Tex.
        Arthur Spohn, letter to Amelia Meuly, ca. 1874.
        Surgeon General's Office: Property Division. War Department, Washington, DC. Communications to and from Acting Assistant Surgeon Arthur Spohn.
Texas Medical Association Archives. Austin, Tex.
    Dr. Arthur Spohn medical articles.
University of Pennsylvania Archives and Records Center. Philadelphia, Pa.
University of Texas Southwestern, Dallas, Tex.
Ursuline Convent Archives and Museum. New Orleans, La.
Witte Museum Archives. San Antonio, Tex.
York Pioneer and Historical Society Archives, John Marshall Archivist. Toronto, Ont., Canada.

Government and Church Documents

Association of Military Surgeons of the United States: Personal Record of Members —1905. Surgeon Arthur Edward Spohn. In Scudder-Stark Collection, Container MSC 142, Box 6, Association of Military Surgeons, National Library of Medicine, History of Medicine Division, Bethesda, Md.
Baptismal Records. Immaculate Conception Church, Brownsville, Tex.
Census 1870. Duval County, Tex.; August 1, 1870, Mifflin Kenedy, line 2, series M593, roll: 1600, p. 198.
Census 1900. Zapata County, Zapata, Tex.
Corpus Christi Cathedral Marriage Records, 1876. Appendix D. Catholic Diocese of Corpus Christi, Tex.

Corpus Christi Cathedral Sacramental Records. Vol. 6, p. 116, #776. Catholic Diocese of Corpus Christi, Tex.

Corpus Christi District Court. Records. Jonathan Day folder. Corpus Christi warehouse.

"Dr. Arthur Spohn and Spohn Hospital." In *The Corpus Christi Chronicles*, part of a series created for the 1492–1992 500th Anniversary of Columbus Landing in the New World. Corpus Christi: Nueces County Historical Society and Corpus Christi Chamber of Commerce, 1992.

Hamilton, John C. Surgeon General, U.S. Marine-Hospital, Commercial Relations, Treasury Department, Washington, D.C. Directive to All Marine Surgeons, August 11, 1882. From Minutes of the Thirty-Second Session of the Texas Medical Association, 1900, in Minutes, *Texas State Journal of Medicine*, p. 105. Archives of the Texas Medical Association, Knowledge Center, Austin, Tex.

Hamilton Ontario City Directory, 1875–76. Angus Spohn entry.

Marriage License of Catherine Spohn and Dr. Alexander Hamilton. Ontario, Canada, Marriages, 1801–1926, Ancestry Library Edition, Ancestry.com.

Metairie Cemetery Association, New Orleans, La. Records #16–50. Old Bayview Cemetery Records. Researched by Rev. Michael Howell and Geraldine McGloin. Corpus Christi Public Library, Corpus Christi, Tex.

Pope, Jno. H. "Annual Report by Sanitary Inspector." Corpus Christi, Tex., August 2, 1879. In *Annual Report of the National Board of Health, 1879–1885*. Washington, DC: US Government Printing Office, 1881.

Saint Patrick's Church Interment Book. Corpus Christi Cathedral Archives, Catholic Diocese of Corpus Christi, Tex.

Spohn, Elizabeth Bowman. Will No. 6620. Ancaster, Ont., September 1893. Synod of the Anglican Diocese of Niagara, County of Wentworth, Ont., Canada.

Spohn, Dr. Henry. Deposition before Joseph Fitzsimmons, US Circuit Court for the Eastern District of Texas, Corpus Christi, Tex, May 25, 1878.

US Citizenship Document for Arthur E. Spohn. Sworn before State of Texas, District Court, County of Nueces, by Pat McDonough, clerk of court, November 4, 1878.

US Department of State, #2152, issued in Washington, DC. January 19, 1899, signed by John Hay, Secretary of State. Instructs all embassies abroad to extend all courtesies and assistance to Dr. and Mrs. Spohn. Accessed in Kenedy Ranch Archives, Sarita, Tex.

Vermont 17th Regiment Records. War Department, Surgeon General's Office, Washington, DC, May 24, 1865, Fifth Military District. Vermont in the Civil War (database), www.vermontcivilwar.org/index.

War Department, Surgeon General's Office, Fifth Military District (FS3) Washington, DC, May 24, 1865. Dr. Arthur Spohn's induction papers.

Interviews, Family Documents, and Correspondence

Brewer, Celeste (archives assistant). New York University Archives. Personal communication.

Cheeseman, Bruce. Letter to Jane Monday, March, 2000.

Chipman, Barbara, B.A. Hons. Details on history of Canadian Loyalists, provided to author(s), October 17, 2012.

Dubeau, Beth. Spohn family historian and descendant, Waterloo, Ont., Canada. Telephone interview by author, August 6, 2010.

Edward, Mary Lou, and Keith Edward. Interview by authors, Ancaster, Ont., Canada, August 5, 2010.

"The Gore District Militia of 1821." Wentworth Historical Society essay, provided to author by Barbara Chipman, Spohn family historian, October 30, 2012.

Hamilton, Dr. Henry. Letter from Laredo, Tex., to Gretchen Spohn, in Canada, August 24, 1942. Provided by family descendants.

Harris, Paul (descendant of Peter Bowman and Elizabeth Bowman Spohn). Family documents, privately held.

    Information submitted to the Ottawa Loyalist of the United Empire Loyalist, inscribed on the United Loyalist statue in Hamilton, Ont., Canada. Provided to author(s), June 30, 2011.

    "The Harris Family of Worcestershire, England." Provided to author(s), June 30, 2011.

    Ryerson, Rev. Egerton. Obituary notes on Elizabeth Spohn, written in 1875 and printed in the Hamilton, Ont., newspaper. Provided to author(s) June 6, 2011.

    Spohn, Elizabeth Bowman. Letter to Dr. Egerton Ryerson, July 23, 1863, published as "Elizabeth Bowman Spohn" in the *Christian Guardian*, February 1875. Submitted by Paul T. Harris to the *Loyalist Gazette* and published in the Fall 1997 issue.

    Spaun, Peter. Family Bible. Copy provided to author(s), June 30, 2011.

Mann and Mann Attorneys at Law. Letter to Dr. H. J. Hamilton, August 18, 1945. Provided to the author by Randolph Slaughter Jr. (family descendant).

McClemont, Nellie G. Letter to Paul T. Harris, February 11, 1961, provided to the authors by Paul Harris.

Mora-Trevino, Michele (Executive director, CHRISTUS Spohn Marketing & Community Relations). Email to Frances Vick, February 2017.

Nemeck, Father Francis Kelly. Emails to Jane Clements Monday from Lebh Shomea House of Prayer, Sarita, Tex., December 18, 2005, January 15, 2006.

Podoisly, Lori (Acting university archivist, McGill University Archives). Email to the author(s), September 20, 2013.

Putegnat, George N. Interview by Rosita Putegnat, January 31, 1956. Transcript provided to author.

Reneghan, Patricia (Petra Vela descendant). Telephone interview by Jane Monday, July 2001.

Spohn, P. H., and E. S. Thompson Marriage Certificate of July 24, 1878. Provided by descendant Beth Dubeau.

Swisher, Rosa Maria. Interview by Jane Monday, May 30, 2006.

Vera, Homero S. Telephone interview by Jane Monday, March 6, 2016.

Wilson, Raymond. Interview by authors, Ancaster, Ont., Canada, August 5, 2010.

Miscellaneous Unpublished Material

Brady, James Edward. "Wyoming: A Study of John Franklin and the Connecticut Settlement into Pennsylvania." PhD diss., Syracuse University, 1973. Provided by Barbara E. Chipman, descendant and family historian; also available at http://surface.syr.edu/hst_etd/468.

Cheeseman, Bruce. "The King–Spohn Family Friendship: A Productive Partnership Embodying Heritage, Hope & Leadership." Speech presented to Spohn Health System executives, Santa Fe, N.Mex. Copy provided to Jane Monday, March 2000.

Finck, Sister Mary Helena. "The Congregation of the Sisters of Charity of the Incarnate Word of San Antonio, Texas: A Brief Account of Its Origin and Its Work." MA diss., Catholic University of America, Washington, DC, 1925.

Gorham, William E. "Buffalo Soldiers: The Formation of the Twenty-Fourth Infantry Regiment, October 1866–1871." Thesis, US Army Command and General Staff College, Fort Leavenworth, 1993.

Graf, Leroy P. "The Economic History of the Lower Rio Grande Valley, 1820–1875." PhD diss., Harvard University, 1942.

Miner, Sister Jeanne Francis. "The Early Development of Education in Corpus Christi, Texas, 1846–1909." Master's thesis, Catholic University of America, 1950.

"Public Health in Texas, 1828–1870." Transcripts Relating to the Medical History of Texas, vol. 28. Joint Project of the Texas Medical Association and the University of Texas Library Archives, 1923–53.

"Three Generations of Kenedys: A Mosaic." Provided to the author by Father Francis Kelly Nemeck.

Villarreal, Robert M. "The Mexican-American Vaqueros of the Kenedy Ranch: A Social History." Master's thesis, Texas A&I University at Kingsville, 1972.

Published Sources

Books

Adams, John A., Jr. *Conflict and Commerce on the Rio Grande, Laredo, 1755–1955.* College Station: Texas A&M University Press, 2008.

Amberson, Mary Margaret, James A. McAllen, and Margaret H. McAllen. *I Would Rather Sleep in Texas: A History of the Lower Rio Grande Valley and the People of the Santa Anita Land Grant.* Austin: Texas State Historical Association, 2003.

Ancaster's Heritage: A History of Ancaster Township. Vol. 1. Ancaster, Ont.: Ancaster Township Historical Society, 1973.

Ancaster's Heritage: A History of Ancaster Township. Vol. 2. Ancaster, Ont.: Ancaster Township Historical Society, 1998.

Ashburn, Col. P. M., Medical Corps, US Army. *A History of the United States Medical Department.* Cambridge: Riverside Press, 1929.

Armando, Alonzo C. *Tejano Legacy: Rancheros and Settlers in South Texas.* Albuquerque: University of New Mexico Press, 1998.

Bailey, Thomas Melville. *Dictionary of Hamilton Biography, Volume I.* Hamilton, Ont.: W. L. Griffin, 1982.

Bliss, Michael. *William Osler: A Life in Medicine.* New York: Oxford University Press, 1999.

Bollet, Dr. Alfred Jay, MD. *Plagues and Poxes: The Impact of Human History on Epidemic Disease.* New York: Demos Medical Publishing, 2004.

Boyko, John. *Blood and Daring: How Canada Fought the American Civil War and Forged a Nation.* Toronto: Random House of Canada, 2014.

Brown, Brig. Gen John S. *American Military History: Volume 1.* Washington, DC: US Army Center of Military History, 2004.

Campbell, Marjorie Freeman. *A Mountain and a City: The Story of Hamilton.* Toronto: McClelland and Stewart, 1966.

Chatfield, Lt. W. H. *The Twin Cities of the Border, Brownsville, Texas and Matamoros, Mexico, and the Country of the Lower Rio Grande.* New Orleans: E. P. Brandad, 1893.

Cheeseman, Bruce. *Perfectly Exhausted with Pleasure: The 1881 King-Kenedy Excursion Train to Laredo.* Austin: Book Club of Texas, 1992.

Corner, George W. *Two Centuries of Medicine.* Philadelphia: J. B. Lippincott, 1965.

Corpus Christi Caller: Centennial Journey, Part I. Corpus Christi: Caller-Times Publishing, 1983.

The Corpus Christi Chronicles. Corpus Christi: Nueces County Historical Society and Corpus Christi Chamber of Commerce, 1992.

Craig, G. M. *Dictionary of Canadian Biography, Vol. XI.* Toronto: University of Toronto Press, 1966.

De León, Arnoldo. *The Tejano Community, 1836–1900.* Dallas: Southern Methodist University Press, 1997.

Devereux, Chauncy. *Charles Stillman, 1810–1875.* New York: C. D. Stillman. 1956.

Dictionary of Hamilton Biography. Volume 1. Hamilton, Ont.: W. L. Griffin, 1982.

Ellis, Wesley. *Lone Star 47.* New York: Jove Publications and Berkley Publishing Group, 1986.

Freeman, Bill. *Hamilton: A People's History.* Toronto: James Lorimer, 2006.

Garner, Paul. *Porfirio Diaz: Profiles in Power.* London: Routledge, 2001.

Graham, Don. *The Kings of Texas: The 150 Year Saga of an American Ranching Empire.* Hoboken, N.J.: John Wiley & Sons, 2003.

Green, Stanley, ed. *Border Biographies.* 2nd ed. Laredo, Tex.: Border Studies 1992.

Guerra, Antonio Ma. *Mier in History: A Translation of "Mier en la historia."* Translated by José María Escobar and Edna Garza Brown. Edinburg, Tex.: New Santander Press, 1989.

Gunning, M. Patricia. *To Texas with Love: A History of the Sisters of the Incarnate Word and Blessed Sacrament.* Austin: Von Boeckmann-Jones, 1971.

Henrichson, Lena. *Pioneers on the Nueces.* San Antonio: Naylor, 1963.

Hoff, John. *Historical Atlas of Simcoe County Ontario.* Toronto: H. Belden & Co., 1881.

Hood, Maurice, MD. *Early Texas Physicians.* Austin: State House Press, 1999.

Hunter, Andrew F. *A History of Simcoe County.* Barrie, Ont.: County Council, 1909.

Imber, Gerald, MD. *Genius on the Edge: The Bizarre Double Life of Dr. William Stewart Halsted*. New York: Kaplan Publishing, 2011.

Jennings, N. A. *A Texas Ranger*. New York: Charles Scribner's Sons, 1899. Paraphrased from a Texas Ranger Hall of Fame ebook. http://www.texasranger.org/E-Books/A%20Texas%20Ranger%20(Jennings).pdf.

———. *A Texas Ranger*. Edited by Ben Procter. Chicago: Lakeside Press, R. R. Donnelley & Sons, 1992.

Johnson, Francis White. *A History of Texas and Texans*. Chicago: American Historical Society, 1914.

Johnston, C. M. *The Head of the Lake: A History of Wentworth County*. Hamilton, Ont.: Wentworth County Council, 1967.

Kearney, Milo. *More Studies in Brownsville History*. Brownsville, Tex.: Pan American University at Brownsville, 1989.

Lea, Tom. *The King Ranch*. 1957. Boston: Little, Brown, 1980.

Lott, Virgil N., and Mercurio Martinez. *The Kingdom of Zapata*. San Antonio: Naylor, 1953.

Mary Xavier (Holworthy), Sister. *A Century of Sacrifice: The History of the Cathedral Parish, Corpus Christi, Texas 1853–1953*. 1953. Corpus Christi, 1965.

Matthews, Matt M. *The U.S. Army on the Mexican Border: A Historical Perspective*. Fort Leavenworth, Kans.: Combat Studies Institute Press, 1959.

McKiernan-Gonzalez, John. *Fevered Measures: Public Health and Race at the Texas-Mexico Border, 1848–1942*. Durham: Duke University Press, 2012.

Middleton, Jesse Edgar. *The Municipality of Toronto*. Vol. 2. Toronto: Dominion Publishing, 1923.

Miner, Charles, and William Penn. *History of Wyoming*. Philadelphia: J. Crissy, 1845.

Monday, Jane Clements, and Frances Brannen Vick. *Letters to Alice: Birth of the Kleberg-King Ranch Dynasty*. College Station: Texas A&M University Press. 2012.

———. *Petra's Legacy: The South Texas Ranching Empire of Petra Vela and Mifflin Kenedy*. College Station: Texas A&M University Press, 2007.

Morris, William, ed. *The American Heritage Dictionary of the English Language*. Boston: Houghton Mifflin, 1980.

Murdock, Su, Brad Rudachyk, and K. H. Schick. *Beautiful Barrie—The City and Its People: An Illustrated History of Barrie, Ontario*. Barrie, Ont.: DBS Heritage Consulting and Communications, 2005.

O'Connell, Patrick J. *The Kenedy Family at Spring Hill College*. Mobile, Ala.: privately printed, 1986–87.

O'Rear, Mary Jo. *Storm over the Bay: The People of Corpus Christi and Their Port*. College Station: Texas A&M University Press, 2009.

Oshinsky, David. *Bellevue: Three Centuries of Medicine and Mayhem at America's Most Storied Hospital*. New York: Doubleday, 2016.

Osler, Sir William, and Thomas M. Rae. *The Principles and Practice of Medicine*. 9th ed. New York: D. Appleton, 1921.

Paredes, Américo. *With His Pistol in His Hand*. Austin: University of Texas Press, 1971.

Parsons, Chuck, and Marianne E. Hall Little. *Captain L. H. McNelly, Texas Ranger: The Life and Times of a Fighting Man*. Austin: State House Press. 2001.

Pouchelle, Marie-Christine. *The Body and Surgery in the Middle Ages*. New Brunswick, N.J.: Rutgers University Press, 1990.

Quinn, Jane. *Minorcans in Florida: Their History and Heritage*. St. Augustine, Fla.: Mission Press, 1975.

Raymond, Joseph Howard. *History of the Long Island College Hospital and Its Graduates Together with the Hoagland Laboratory and the Polhemus Memorial Clinic*. Brooklyn, N.Y.: Association of the Alumni, 1899.

Red, Mrs. George Plunkett. *The Medicine Man in Texas*. Houston: Standard Printing & Lithographing, 1930.

Report of the Council of Hygiene and Public Health of the Citizens' Association of New York upon the Sanitary Condition of the City. New York: Appleton, 1865.

Ridley, Jasper Howard. *The Freemasons: A History of the World's Most Powerful Secret Society*. New York: Arcade, 2001.

Robertson, J. Ross. *History of Freemasonry in Canada*. Barton Lodge, no. 10. Toronto: Rose Hunter, 1899.

Scott, Winfield. *Memoirs of Lieut-General Scott, LLD*. New York: Sheldon, 1864.

Slattery, Sister Margaret Patrice, CCVI. *Promises to Keep: A History of the Sisters of Charity of the Incarnate Word*. San Antonio, 1995.

Stambaugh, J. Lee, and Lillian J. *The Lower Rio Grande Valley of Texas*. San Antonio: Naylor, 1954.

Thompson, Jerry. *Cortina: Defending the Mexican Name in Texas*. College Station: Texas A&M University Press, 2007.

Uglow, Loyd M. *Standing in the Gap: Army Outposts, Picket Stations, and the Pacification of the Texas Frontier, 1866–1886*. Fort Worth: Texas Christian University Press, 1952.

Vance, Jonathan. *History of Canadian Culture*. Don Mills, Ont.: Oxford University Press, 2011.

Vezzetti, Robert B., ed. *Tidbits: A Collection from the Brownsville Historical Association and the Stillman House Museum*. N.p., n.d.

Waller, John C. *Health and Wellness in 19th-Century America*. Santa Barbara, Calif.: Greenwood, ABC-CLIO, 2014.

Walraven, Bill. *Corpus Christi: The History of a Texas Seaport*. Sponsored by the Nueces County Historical Society and Corpus Christi Chamber of Commerce. Woodland Hills, Calif.: Windsor Publications, 1982.

Webb, Walter Prescott. *The Texas Rangers: A Century of Frontier Defense*. Austin: University of Texas Press, 1980.

Wilkinson, Joseph B. *Laredo and the Rio Grande Frontier*. Austin: Jenkins, 1975.

Wintermute, Bobby A. *Public Health and the U.S. Military: A History of the Army Medical Department, 1818–1917*. New York: Routledge, 2011.

Journals and Magazines

Abel, Emily. "Patient Dumping in New York, 1877–1917." *American Public Health Journal* 101, no. 5 (2011): 789–95.

Chase, Ira Carleton, ed. "Transactions of Annual Meeting, Corpus Christi, Texas." *Texas State Journal of Medicine* 4 (May 1908–April 1909).

Girouard, Julia. Review of *Luisiana*, by Paul E. Hoffman. *Louisiana History* 35, no. 3 (1994): 378–80.

Hamilton, Henry. "Mosquitoes and Quarantine." *Texas State Journal of Medicine* 7 (May 1906–April 1907).

Hill, Lawrence F. "The Confederate Exodus to Latin America." *Southwestern Historical Quarterly* 39, no. 2 (October 1935).

Journal of the American Medical Association. "Arthur E. Spohn Obituary." 60 (1913): 1651.

Kelly, Dora Mae. "Early Hidalgo Transportation." *Daily Review*, Centennial Edition, December 7, 1952. Pan American University Library, Edinburg, Tex.

Kirk, Sister Martha Ann, CCVI. "Ashes Could Not Stop Her: Mother St. Pierre and Community-Building in Texas." *Texas Journal* 11 (Fall–Winter 1988).

Medical Record and Annals (Houston, Tex.) 60, no. 1 (January 1967). Cover features Dr. Arthur Spohn.

Nance, H. T. "Steamboating on the Rio Grande." *Successful Attitudes* (Brownsville Historical Association), Fall 1988.

New Orleans Medical & Surgical Journal 47 (July 1895).

Sanchon, Edward. "Surgeries at Charity Hospital, New Orleans." *Gaillard's Medical Journal* 44 (1887): 197.

Spohn, Arthur E. "Communications: Gunshot Wound of the Abdomen." *Medical and Surgical Reporter* 63 (November 15, 1890): 20.

———. "Country Practice in Texas–Medicated Bougies." *Medical and Surgical Reporter* 57 (August 20, 1887): 8.

———. "Cures for Hydrophobia." *Texas Courier-Record of Medicine* (Dallas, Tex.), May 1888.

———. "Elastic Rubber-Ring Tourniquet." *Richmond and Louisville Medical Journal* (Richmond, Va.), 22 (November 1876): 425–30.

———. "Fibroid Tumors of the Uterus." *Transactions of the Texas State Medical Association* (Austin, Tex.), 33 (1901).

———. "Fracture of the Clavicle." *Medical and Surgical Reporter* (Philadelphia, Pa.), 67 (December 1887): 796.

———. "The Marine Hospital Service in Texas and Yellow Fever." *Transactions of the Texas State Medical Association* (Austin, Tex.), 32 (1900).

———. "Multicystic Ovarian Tumor Weighing 328 Pounds." *American Journal of Clinical Medicine* 13 (April 1906). Also read at meeting of the State Medical Association of Texas, Houston, April 28, 1905, and printed in *Transactions of the Texas State Medical Association* (Austin, Tex.), February 1906.

———. "Rabies and Anti-Rabic Inoculations." Presentation at the Twenty-First Annual Session of the Texas Medical Association, April 23–26, 1889, Austin, Tex., and published in *Transactions of the Texas State Medical Association* 21 (1889): 144–59.

———. "Recent Cases of Coeliotomy." *Daniel's Texas Medical Journal* (Austin, Tex.), 8 (February 1893).

———. "Rubber Ring Tourniquet." *Medical Surgical Reporter* (Philadelphia, Pa.), 49 (August 18, 1883).

———. "Skin Grafting." *Transactions of the Texas State Medical Association* 33 (1901): 245–46.

———. "Treatment of Carbuncle." *Texas Courier-Record of Medicine* 8 (March 1891): 184–85.

———. "Treatment of Rupture of the Perineum," *Medical and Surgical Reporter* (Philadelphia, Pa.), 58 (February 11, 1888).

———. "Tumors." *Richmond and Louisville Medical Journal* (Louisville, Ky.), 1875.

———. "Turpentine in Affections of the Throat and Lungs." *Medical and Surgical Reporter* 61 (October 19, 1898): 16.

———. "Typhoid Perforation of the Bowel with Obstruction—A Plea for Exploratory Abdominal Incisions." Paper read at the Thirty-Eighth Annual Meeting of the State Medical Association of Texas, Fort Worth, Tex., April 24–26, 1906, and published in *Texas State Journal of Medicine* (Austin, Tex.), April 1906.

Tabor, G. R. "1903 Epidemic of Yellow Fever in Texas and the Lesson to Be Learned from It." Paper presented to the Medical Department of the University of Texas, Galveston, January 6, 1905, and published in *Bulletin of the University of Texas*, Medical Series no. 3, June 1905.

Thompson, Jerry. "Mutiny and Desertion on the Rio Grande: The Strange Saga of Captain Adrian J. Vidal." *Military History of Texas and the Southwest* 12, no. 3 (1975): 159–70.

Thorpe, Frank N. "The University of Pennsylvania." *Harper's New Monthly Magazine*, no. 542 (July 1895).

Vera, Homero S. "Don Esteban Cisneros and Dona Eulalia Tijerina de Cisneros." *El Mesteño* 4, no. 43 (2001).

———. "Gregorio Vela–Rancher." *El Mesteño* 6, no. 1 (Winter–Spring 2003): 58.

Newspapers

Ann Arbor Observer, Ann Arbor, Mich.
Advertiser, Corpus Christi, Tex.
Brantford Expositor, Brantford, Ont., Canada
Brownsville Cosmopolitan, Brownsville, Tex.
Brownsville Reporter, Brownsville, Tex.
Corpus Christi Caller and *Caller-Times*, Corpus Christi, Tex.
Corpus Christi Daily Gazette, Corpus Christi, Tex.
Daily Colonist, Barrie, Ont., Canada
Daily Cosmopolitan, Brownsville, Tex.
Daily Herald, Brownsville, Tex.
Evening Times, Washington, DC
Fort Worth Daily Gazette, Fort Worth, Tex.
Galveston Daily News, Galveston, Tex.
Hamilton Spectator, Hamilton, Ont., Canada

Hamilton Times, Hamilton, Ont., Canada
Hickman Courier, Hickman, Ky.
Houston Tri-Weekly Telegraph, Houston, Tex.
Laredo (Weekly) Times, Laredo, Tex.
New York Herald, New York, N.Y.
New York Times, New York, N.Y.
Nueces Valley, Corpus Christi, Tex.
Omaha Daily Bee, Omaha, Nebr.
San Antonio Express, San Antonio, Tex.
Semi-Weekly Ledger, Corpus Christi, Tex.
Toronto Star, Toronto, Ont., Canada
Village Record, Chester County, Pa.
Waco Evening News, Waco, Tex.

Digital Sources

"Acute Compartment Syndrome: Background, Anatomy, Pathophysiology." Medscape, http://emedicine.medscape.com/article/307668-overview.
Adamczyk, Joseph. "Great Railroad Strike of 1877." Encyclopaedia Britannica. https://www.britannica.com/topic/Great-Railroad-Strike-of-1877.
"Albany Hotel." *What Was There?* http://www.whatwasthere.com/browse.asp#/11/.
Alfred, Randy. "Lister Cuts Clean, Saves Lives, June 17, 1867." This Day in Tech, *Wired*. Accessed June 17, 2011. http://archive.wired.com/thisdayintech.
Bell, Clark, ed. *Medico-Legal Journal* 24, no. 1 (1906): 81–91. https://books.google.com/books?id=5wVYAAAAYAAJ.
"Bellevue Hospital." Wikipedia. https://en.wikipedia.org/wiki/NYC_Health_%2B_Hospitals/Bellevue.
Bellevue Hospital History. "Bellevue 275 Anniversary." NYC Health Hospitals. http://www.nychhc.org/bellevue/html/about.history.htm/.
Bellevue Hospital Medical College Annual Circular, 1876–7; Annual Catalogue 1875–76. NYU Medical Archives. https://archives.med.nyu.edu/islandora/object/nyumed%3A1256.
"Biography of Ridge Paschal." Access Genealogy. Last updated July 29, 2012. www.accessgenealogy.com/native/biography-of-ridge-paschal/htm.
Blanke, David. "Panic of 1873." National History Education Clearinghouse, Teaching History.org. http://teachinghistory.org/history-content/beyond-the-textbook/24579.
Brackemyre, Ted. "Immigrants, Cities, and Disease: Immigration and Health Concerns in Late Nineteenth Century America." U.S. History Scene. http://ushistoryscene.com/article/immigrants-cities-disease/.
"Brief History of the Cornwall Grail Center." Grail Retreat Center. www.thegrailatcornwall.org/about/history-of-the-cornwall-grail-center.
Brown, Dr. E. F. "Tincture of Iodine an Antidote to the Bite of Venomous Serpents." In *The Homoeopathic Recorder*. Philadelphia & Lancaster: Boenake & Tafel, 1892. https://books.google.com/books.

Brown, Ida C. "Michigan Men in the Civil War." Bentley Historical Library, University of Michigan. http://bentley.umich.edu/legacy-support/civilwar/introduction.php.

Bryan, Dan. "Dissipated Life of William A. Rockefeller." *American History USA*, April 12, 2012. www.americanhistoryusa.com/strange-life-of-william-rocker feller.

"Calhoun County, Texas: Epidemic News." Texas Genealogy Trails. genealogytrails. com/tex/gulfcoast/calhoun/epidemics.html.

Cameron, John, MD, host. "William Stewart Halsted: The Birth of American Surgery." Johns Hopkins Medicine: Pathology. http://pathology.jhu.edu/department/ about/history/celebratehistory.cfm.

Canada, City and Area Directories, 1819–1906 (online database). Ancestry.com.

Carlson, Paul H. "Shafter, William Rufus." *Handbook of Texas Online*. Accessed April 24, 2017. http://www.tshaonline.org/handbook/online/articles/fsh02.

Carroll, John. *Case and His Co[n]temporaries or The Canadian Itinerants' Memorial: Constituting a Biographical History of Methodism in Canada*. Toronto: Samuel Rose and Wesleyan Printing, 1867. https://archive.org/details/caseandhiscotem 00carrgoog.

Cartwright, Gary. "Sarita's Secret." *Texas Monthly*, September 2004. http://www.texas monthly.com/articles/saritas-secret/ accessed 2/12/2017.

"Cholera in 1866." *NYCdata*, Baruch College. http://www.baruch.cuny.edu/nycdata /disasters/cholera-1866.html.

Chorba, Terence. "A Master Medalist, a President, Tuberculosis, and a Congress: Contributions More Lasting Than Bronze." *Emerging Infectious Diseases* 21, no. 3 (2015): 553–54. https://www.ncbi.nlm.nih.gov/pmc/articles/PMC4344294/.

"City of Laredo." *A Twentieth Century History of Southwest Texas*, vol. 2, chap. 27. Ancestry.com. http://interactive.ancestry.com/27907/dvm-LocHist(011946-00398- 1/713?backurl=http"//trees…

"The Colorful History of America's Dog Show." Westminster Kennel Club. http:// www.westminsterkennelclub.org/about-sensation/history/.

"Commissioned Corps of the U.S. Public Health Service-History." US Department of Health and Human Services, last modified September 5, 2014. https://www .usphs.gov/aboutus/history.aspx."Crawford Long (1815–1878)." *New Georgia Encyclopedia*, original entry by M. Leslie Madden, May 14, 2004. Last updated by NGE staff August 5, 2015. http://www.georgiaencyclopedia.org/articles/science -medicine/crawford-long-1815-1878. Suggested by Courtney M. Townsend, MD, FACS.

Cruess, Richard L., MD. "Brief History of Medicine at McGill." McGill University Faculty of Medicine. www.mcgill.ca/medicine/about/glance/history.

Da Costa, J. M., MD, LLD. "Biographical Sketch of Dr. Austin Flint." *Transactions of the College of Physicians Philadelphia*, 3rd ser., 9 (n.d.): cdlxvi–vii. https://archive. org/stream/101488816.nlm.nih.gov/101488816#page/n0/mode/2up.

"The Death of President Garfield, 1881." Eyewitness to History.com. http://www.eye witnesstohistory.com/gar.htm.

DeMoss, Dorothy D. "Driscoll, Clara." *Handbook of Texas Online*. Accessed April 24, 2017. http://www.tshaonline.org/handbook/online/articles/fdr04.

Doucet, Claude W. "Egerton Ryerson, 1803–1882." Ryerson University Library and Archives, June 2002. https://library.ryerson.ca/asc/archives/ryerson-history/ryer son-bio/.

Echols, Dr. Michael, and Dr. Doug Arbittier. "Frank Hastings Hamilton, M.D." *American Civil War Medicine and Surgical Antiques*. http://www.medicalantiques.com/civilwar/Medical_Authors_Faculty/Hamilton_Frank_Hastings.htm.

Eighteenth Annual Announcement of the Bellevue Hospital Medical College, Sessions of 1878–1879, with the Annual Catalogue for 1877–1878, *Pathological Anatomy and Histology*, 9. https://archives.med.nyu.edu/islandora/object/nyumed%3A1233/datastream/OBJ/view.

"1864 Surgeon General's Report." *Vermont in the Civil War*, October 1, 1864. http://vermontcivilwar.org/state/64/surgeon.

"The 1867 St Patrick's Day Riot: No Peace in the Lower East Side." *Bowery Boys History*. http://www.boweryboyshistory.com/2014/03/the-1867-st-patricks-day-riot-no-peace.html.

"Emile Roux—Pasteur, Rabies and Diphtheria." *Awesome Stories*. https://www.awesome stories.com/asset/view/Emile-Roux-Pasteur-Rabies-and-Diphtheria.

"Fashions for June 1877." *Two Nerdy History Girls*. http://twonerdyhistorygirls.blog spot.com/2014/06/fashions-for-june-1877.html.

"First Nations People in Canada." Indigenous and Northern Affairs Canada. Accessed December 22, 2016. https://www.aadnc-aandc.gc.ca/eng/1303134042666/13031 34337338.

"Friedrich von Esmarch: German Surgeon." *Encyclopaedia Britannica*. https://www.bri tannica.com/biography/Friedrich-von-Esmarch.

García, Clotilde P. "Santa Petronila Ranch." *Handbook of Texas Online*. Accessed April 24, 2017. http://www.tshaonline.org/handbook/online/articles/aps08.

Givens, Murphy. "Corpus Christi History." *Corpus Christi Caller-Times*, June 13, 2001. http://www.caller2.com/2001/June/13/today/murphygi/2689.html.

———.. "The Fast and the Furious . . . in the Early 1900's." *Corpus Christi Caller-Times*, February 16, 2001. http://www.caller.com/news/2011/feb/16/thefast-and-the-early-1900s/?print=1.

———. "Martha Rabb, Cattle Queen of Texas." *Corpus Christi Caller-Times*, April 9, 2008. http://www.caller.com/news/2008/apr.09/martha-rabb-cattle-queen-of-texas/?print=1.

———."Old Houses of the Past," *Corpus Christi Caller-Times*. http://www.caller2 .com/2001.

———."Orphan from Alabama Built the Town's First Bank." *Corpus Christi Caller-Times*. http://www.caller.com/opinion/Columnists/murphy-givens/orphan-from-alabama-built-the-towns-first-bank.

———. "Our Willie Is Saved." Audio clip, KEDT Radio, December 14, 2001. Corpus Christi Public Library Digital Archives, Corpus Christi, Tex.

"Grand Central Hotel: Murders, Suicides, Scandals, and Disasters in New York's Most Famous Forgotten Inn." *Keith York City*, January 21, 2013. https://keithyorkcity. wordpress.com/2013/01/31/the-grand-central-hotel-murders-suicides-scandals-and-disasters-in-new-yorks-most-famous-forgotten-inn/.

Grayson, Scott. "Henry Redmond." 2012. http://www.crutchwilliams.com/TEXAS/
    HenryRedmond.html.

"Grey Cup." *Canadian Encyclopedia.* http://www.thecanadianencyclopedia.ca/en/
    article/grey-cup/.

Guthrie, Keith. "Fulton, George Ware, Sr." *Handbook of Texas Online.* Accessed April
    24, 2017. http://www.tshaonline.org/handbook/online/articles/btmrv.

———. "Borden, Sidney Gail." *Handbook of Texas Online.* Accessed April 24, 2017.
    http://www.tshaonline.org/handbook/online/articles/fboae.

Handbook of Texas Online. "Spohn, Arthur Edward." Accessed January 21, 2018. http://
    www.tshaonline.org/handbook/online/articles/fsp15.

Hart, John Mason. "Stillman, Charles." *Handbook of Texas Online.* Accessed January 22,
    2018. http://www.tshaonline.org/handbook/online/articles/fst57.

Heller, Dick D., Jr. "San Ygnacio, TX." *Handbook of Texas Online.* Accessed April 24,
    2017. http://www.tshaonline.org/handbook/online/articles/hls15.

"Henry J. Hamilton." Old Bayview Cemetery. http//www.cclibraries.com/localhistory/
    oldbayview/hamiltonabioinfo.htm.

Hildreth, Peggy. "Howard Associations." *Handbook of Texas Online.* Accessed April 24,
    2017. http://www.tshaonline.org/handbook/online/articles/vwh01.

"Historical Ancaster." Hamilton Public Library (Ontario). http://www.hpl.ca/
    articles/historical-ancaster.

"History of the University of Michigan Medical School." University of Michigan, 2011.
    http://um2017.org/2017_Website/Histories_of_UM_School_of_Medicine.html.

"Historical Events in 1876," *On This Day.* www.onthisday.com/events/date/1876.

Holton, David Parsons, and Frances Holton. "Winslow Memorial: Family Records of
    the Winslows and Their Descendants in America, with the English Ancestry as
    Far as Known." 1877. https://archive.org/details/winslowmemorialf001holt.

Hruban, Ralph, MD. "William Stewart Halsted." http://halstedthedocumentary.org/
    halsted.php.

Johnson, John G. "Mexican and Indian Raid of 1878." *Handbook of Texas Online.* Ac-
    cessed June 30, 2017. http://www.tshaonline.org/handbook/online/articles/ffu08.

"Joseph Brant: Mohawk Chief." *Encyclopaedia Britannica.* https://www.britannica.com
    /biography/Joseph-Brant.

"Juan Cortina." *New Perspectives on the West,* PBS. http://www.pbs.org/weta/thewest/
    people/a_c/cortina.htm.

Kessin, Richard H., PhD, and Kenneth A. Forde, MD. *P&S: The College of Physicians
    and Surgeons of Columbia University* 28, no. 2 (Spring–Summer 2008). www.cumc
    .columbia.edu/psjournal/archive/spring...2008/surgery_in_america.html.

Knights, Edwin M, Jr. "Bellevue Hospital." *History Magazine.* http://www.History-
    magazine.com/Bellevue.html.

Krasnick, Cheryl L. "The Aristocratic Vice: The Medical Treatment of Drug Addiction
    at the Homewood Retreat, 1883–1900." *Ontario History: The Quarterly Journal of
    the Ontario Historical Society,* December 1, 1983. Accessed at Whitehern Museum
    Archives, http//www.whitehern.ca/result.php?doc-id=Bos%2015-007.

Leatherwood, Art. "Fort Ewell." *Handbook of Texas Online.* Accessed April 24, 2017.
    http://www.tshaonline.org/handbook/online/articles/qcf03.

Leffler, John. "Encinal, TX." *Handbook of Texas Online*. Accessed April 24, 2017. http://www.tshaonline.org/handbook/online/articleh0.

"A List of Rules for Nurses . . . from 1887." *Communicator*, St. John's Hospital, Malta, 1969. Reprinted in *Scrubs*, last updated October 6, 2016. http://scrubsmag.com/a-list-of-rules-for-nurses-from-1887.

"Louis Pasteur." Chemical Heritage Foundation Library, Museum, and Center for Scholars, Philadelphia. https://www.chemheritage.org/historical-profile/louis-pasteur.

Lusk, William Thompson, obituary. "Record of Graduates of Yale University Deceased during the Academic Year ending in June, 1897." *Proceedings of the Connecticut Medical Society, 1899*, 343–49. https://archive.org/stream/39002011129435.med.yale.edu/39002011129435.med.yale.edu_djvu.txt.

Magic Lantern Exhibition. Musée McCord Museum, Montreal. https://www.pinterest.com/pin/260997740876122833.

Mallory, Sister Bernice, S.H.Sp. "Healy-Murphy, Margaret Mary." *Handbook of Texas Online*. Accessed April 24, 2017. http://www.tshaonline.org/handbook/online/articles/f47.

"The Medical School: Admission and Curriculums." In *The University of Michigan, an Encyclopedic Survey*, ed. Wilfred B. Shaw. Ann Arbor: University of Michigan Press, 1941. Accessed September 2, 2017. https://quod.lib.umich.edu/u/umsurvey/AAS3302.0002.001/1:4.2.1.1?rgn=div4;view=fulltext.

Mehta, Niray J., MD, Rajal N. Mehta, MD, and Ljaz A. Khan, M.D. "Austin Flint: Clinician, Teacher, and Visionary." *Texas Heart Institute Journal* 27, no. 4 (2000): 386–89. https://www.ncbi.nlm.nih.gov/pmc/articles/PMC101108/.

"Memoir: Corydon La Ford." Faculty History Project, University of Michigan. http://um2017.org/faculty-history/faculty/corydon-la-ford/memoir.

"900 Years of History—Sovereign Order of Malta." Order of Malta Official Site. http//www.orderofmalta.int/history.639/history-order-of-malta/?Lang=eng.

Novy, Frederick G. "Medical School" (1942). *University of Michigan, an Encyclopedic Survey: Bicentennial Edition*. Accessed January 27, 2018. http://hdl.handle.net/2027/spo.13950886.0003.040.

Nystrom, Justin A. "The Battle of Liberty Place." In *Encyclopedia of Louisiana*, edited by David Johnson, article published January 3, 2011. http://www.knowlouisiana.org/entry/the-battle-of-liberty-place.

Odintz, Mark. "Buffalo Soldiers." *Handbook of Texas Online*. Accessed April 24, 2017. http://www.tshaonline.org/handbook/online/articles/qlb01.

Ogilvie, Mary H. "Verdaguer, Peter." *Handbook of Texas Online*. Accessed April 24, 2017. http://www.tshaonline.org/handbook/online/article/fve07.

O'Gorman, James F. Review of *New York 1880: Architecture and Urbanism in the Gilded Age*, by Robert A. M. Stern, Thomas Mellins, and David Fishman (New York: Monacelli Press, 1999). *New York Times Book Review*, December 19, 1999. http://www.nytimes.com/books/first/s/stern-1880.html.

"Order of the Hospital of Saint John of Jerusalem." *Encyclopaedia Britannica*, 14th ed., 1966. Accessed at http://www.orderstjohn.org/osj/luke.htm.

Orozco, Cynthia E. "Kenedy, Petra Vela de Vidal." *Handbook of Texas Online*. Accessed April 24, 2017. http://www.tshaonline.org/handbook/online/articles/fkerl.

Padgett, Hazel, MD. "Maury County, Tennessee Biographies." *Genealogy Trails.*
    http://genealogytrails.com/tenn/maury/bioHazelPadgett.html.
"The Panic of 1873: U.S. Grant, Warrior." *American Experience*, PBS-WGBH. www
    .pbs.org/wgbh/americanexperience/features/general/grant/panicof1873.
"Pasteur Saved Him." *Fort Worth Daily Gazette*, vol. 13, no. 280, May 18, 1888, 4.
    https://texashistory.unt.edu/ark:/67531/metapth89616/m1/4/.
Petzel, Ernest, obituary. Record of Interments, Old Bayview Cemetery Association,
    Corpus Christi, Tex. http://www.cclibraries.com/localhistory/oldbayview/index
    .php/component/content/article/61-individual/595-ernest-petzel.
Petzel Family Tree. Descendants of John Ernest Petzel. http://www.Yourdeservelt
    .com/petzel.htm.
"Raid of 1878." La Salle County Genealogy. http://www.historicdistrict.com/
    genealogy/lasalle/raid.asp.
Rutherford, Robert. "History of Quarantine in the State of Texas from 1878–1888."
    American Public Health Association Report 14 (1888–89): 125–33, from a presen-
    tation at Sixteenth Annual Meeting of the American Public Health Association,
    Milwaukee, Wisc., November 20, 1888. https://www.ncbi.nlm.nih.gov/pmc/arti
    cles/PMC2266126/.
Rutkow, Ira M., MD. *The History of Surgery in the United States, 1775–1900: Textbooks,
    Monographs, and Treaties.* San Francisco: Norman Publishing, 1988. Accessed at
    https://books.google.com.
Sanchez, Juan O. "Vela, Isidro." *Handbook of Texas Online.* Accessed April 24, 2017.
    http://www.tshaonline.org/handbook/online/articles/fvepu.
Santoro, Lisa M. "The Upper-Class Brooklyn Resorts of the Victorian Era." *Curbed
    New York*, June 27, 2013. http://ny.curbed.com/2013/6/27/10226192/the-upper-
    class-brooklyn-resorts-of-the-victorian-era.
"Scarlet Fever." Mayo Clinic, March 13, 2014. http://www.mayoclinic.org/diseases-
    conditions/scarlet-fever/basics/definition/con-20030976.
Schwien, Annie Moore. "When Corpus Christi Was Young: Recollections of Annie
    Moore Schwien." Interviews from November 8, 1938 to May 15, 1941. Translated
    by Rosa Gonzales, Corpus Christi Public Library, Corpus Christi, Tex. Accessed
    at Old Bayview Cemetery, http://www.cclibraries.com/localhistory/oldbayview/
    index.php/component/content/article/63-misc/638-annie-moore-schwien.
Seaholm, Megan, and Chester R. Burns. "Texas Medical Association." *Handbook of
    Texas Online.* Accessed April 24, 2017. http://www.tshaonline.org/handbook/
    online/articles/sat05.
Segrest, Dr. Hiram Henderson (biographical information). "H H." Find a Grave.
    https://www.findagrave.com/cgi-bin/fg.cgi?page=gr&GRid=44579883.
"1763: The French and Indian War Ends." *This Day in History*, History Channel.
    Accessed February 22, 2017. http://www.history.com/this-day-in-history/the-
    french-and-indian-war-ends.
"Smallpox." Centers for Disease Control and Prevention. https://www.cdc.gov/
    smallpox/.

"Smallpox." History of Vaccines, College of Physicians of Philadelphia. https://www
.historyofvaccines.org/content/articles/history-smallpox.

Sonnichsen, C. L. "Sutton-Taylor Feud." *Handbook of Texas Online*. Accessed April 21,
2017. http://www.tshaonline.org/handbook/online/articles/jcs03.

Spohn, A. E., obituary. *Texas State Journal of Medicine* 9 (July 1913): 120. Accessed at
https://books.google.com/books?id=SqJEAAAAYAAJ.

"Spohn, Arthur E." *Handbook of Texas Online*. Accessed January 21, 2018. http://www
.tshaonline.org/handbook/online/articles/fsp15.

"Tammany Hall." George Washington University. https://www2.gwu.edu/~erpapers/
teachinger/glossary/tammany-hall.cfm.

"Tammany Hall." *History.com*. www.history.com/topics/tammany-hall.

"Tecumseh." *History.com*. http://www.history.com/topics/native-american-history/
tecumseh.

"Tenements." *History.com*. www.history.com/topics/tenements.

Teston, Jacy, and Mason Meek. "Yellow Fever in Galveston, Texas." *East Texas History*.
Accessed January 21, 2018, http://easttexashistory.org/items/show/251.

"Tetanus: Diseases and Conditions." Mayo Clinic. http://www.mayoclinic.org/dis
eases-conditions/tetanus/home/ovc-20200456.

"Texas Medical Board History." Texas Medical Board. www.tmb.state.tx.us/page/med
ical-board-history.

Tiemann Company, George. https:www.georgetiemann.com.

Tolan, Mrs. Stanley C. "Christian Warner, a Methodist Pioneer." Presentation at the
Ontario Historical Society, Niagara Falls, Ont., September 1941. http://images
.ourontario.ca/Partners/NOTL/NOTL002486711pf_0001.pdf.

"Transactions of the Sixth International Congress on Tuberculosis." Washington, DC,
September 25–October 5, 1908. https://archive.org/stream/transactionsofsi05inte/
transactionsofsi05inte_djvu.txt.

"Two Centuries of Health Promotion." Images from the History of the Public Health
Service. https://www.nlm.nih.gov/exhibition/phs-history/intro.html.

"We Have an Inspiring Heritage." Ursuline Academy, New Orleans. https://www.uanola
.org/page/about/ursuline-heritage.

"What Happened in 1877." *On This Day*. https://www.onthisday.com/date/1877.

"U.S. Public Health Service: Marine Hospital Service (MHS) 1798." Social Welfare
History Project, Virginia Commonwealth University. http://socialwelfare.library.
vcu.edu/programs/health-nutrition/u-s-public-heath-service/.

"U.S. Returns from Military Post 1806–1916: Post Returns, Ft. McIntosh, Laredo,
Texas" (Henry Spohn, September 1867–May 1869). Microfilm M617, roll 681,
National Archives. Accessed at Ancestry.com.

Uribe, Roberto D. *San Ignacio: A Tribute to Bob and Joe Uribe*. http://www.incdef.com/
san%20ignacio/ignacio.asp.

Wagner, Frank. "DeRyee, William." *Handbook of Texas Online*. Accessed April 24, 2017.
http://www.tshaonline.org/handbook/online/articles/fde44.

———. "Doddridge, Perry." *Handbook of Texas Online*. Accessed April 24, 2017. http://
www.tshaonline.org/handbook/online/articles/fd042.

————. "Driscoll, Robert, Jr." *Handbook of Texas Online*. Accessed April 24, 2017. http://www.tshaonline.org/handbook/online/articles/fdr05.

"William Stewart Halsted: Surgical Pioneer." *Endocrine Today*, Healio, February 2010. https://www.healio.com/endocrinology/news/print/endocrine-today/%7Ba9c025 da-1d33-43a9-b7f6-7664abee1a9c%7D/william-stewart-halsted-surgicalpioneer.

Winter, F. David, Jr. Review of *Genius on the Edge: The Bizarre Double Life of Dr. William Stewart Halsted* (New York: Kaplan, 2010). *Baylor University Medical Center Proceedings* 25, no. 1 (2012): 95–97. https://www.ncbi.nlm.nih.gov/pmc/articles/PMC3246868/.

"A Wounded Nation." *Freedom: A History of US*, webisode 7, segment 1, PBS. Accessed July 31, 2014. http://www.pbs.org/wnet/historyofus/web07/segment1_p.html.

"Yankee Doodle." Library of Congress. http://www.loc.gov/teachers/lyrical/Songs/yankee-doodle.html.

Index

Other Books in the Gulf Coast Books Series

Lighthouses of Texas
T. Lindsay Baker

Laguna Madre of Texas and Tamaulipas
John W. Tunnell and Frank W. Judd

Fishing Yesterday's Gulf Coast
Barney Farley

Designing the Bayous: The Control of Water in the Atchafalaya Basin, 1800–1995
Martin Reuss

Life on Matagorda Island
Wayne H. McAlister and Martha K. McAlister

Book of Texas Bays
Jim Blackburn

Plants of the Texas Coastal Bend
Roy L. Lehman and Tammy White

Galveston Bay
Sally E. Antrobus